Charting space

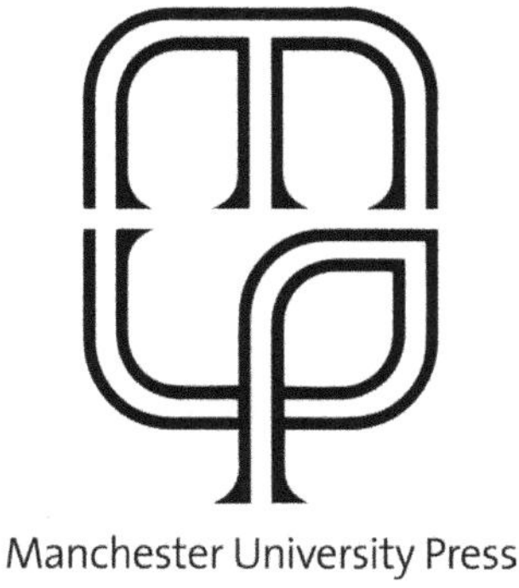

Manchester University Press

rethinking
art's histories

SERIES EDITORS
Amelia G. Jones, Marsha Meskimmon

Rethinking Art's Histories aims to open out art history from its most basic structures by foregrounding work that challenges the conventional periodisation and geographical subfields of traditional art history, and addressing a wide range of visual cultural forms from the early modern period to the present.

These books will acknowledge the impact of recent scholarship on our understanding of the complex temporalities and cartographies that have emerged through centuries of world-wide trade, political colonisation and the diasporic movement of people and ideas across national and continental borders.

To buy or to find out more about the books currently available in this series, please go to: https://manchesteruniversitypress.co.uk/series/rethinking-arts-histories/.

Charting space

The cartographies of conceptual art

Edited by

Elize Mazadiego

Manchester University Press

Published by Manchester University Press
Oxford Road, Manchester M13 9PL
www.manchesteruniversitypress.co.uk

British Library Cataloguing-in-Publication Data
A catalogue record for this book is available from the British Library

ISBN 978 1 5261 5995 3 hardback
ISBN 978 1 5261 9078 9 paperback

First published 2023
Paperback published 2025

EU authorised representative for GPSR:
Easy Access System Europe – Mustamäe tee 50, 10621 Tallinn, Estonia
gpsr.requests@easproject.com

Typeset by Newgen Publishing UK

Contents

List of figures   *page* vii
List of contributors   xi
Acknowledgements   xvi

Introduction: Maps, spatiality and conceptual art   1
Elize Mazadiego

Part I: Social cartographies

1 Borderline: Mapping out (social) spaces of representation in
   conceptual art   23
   Eve Kalyva

2 Adrian Piper: In and out of conceptual art   44
   Alexander Alberro

3 Remapping the public sphere: Conceptual art in 1970s London   56
   Jennifer Sarathy

Part II: Political geographies

4 Immaterial countercartographies: Approaches to the conceptual
   art of Gábor Attalai   77
   Katalin Cseh-Varga

5 Brian O'Doherty/Patrick Ireland: A modest proposal
   to decolonise Ireland   99
   Christa-Maria Lerm Hayes

6 The contemporary topographies of Anna Bella Geiger   116
   Dária Jaremtchuk

Part III: Sites and networks

7   Spatial play in Dennis Oppenheim's cartographic works   139
     Larisa Dryansky

8   Psychophysiology Research Institute, 1969–70: Envisioning
     an 'invisible museum'   158
     Reiko Tomii

9   Mapping a dialogue between some possible origins of IBMR
     and Art & Language   182
     Ann Stephen

Part IV: Itineraries

10   Itinerant cartographies: Nancy Holt's conceptualism   205
     Alena J. Williams

11   André Cadere's peripatetic art   224
     Inesa Brašiškė

12   *Delirium ambulatorium* – city walks as conceptual mapping:
     From Hélio Oiticica to Rasheed Araeen and Lee Wen   242
     Eva Bentcheva and María José Martínez Sanchez

     Index   264

Figures

0.1 Mieko Shiomi, *Spatial Poem #2* ('Invitation'), from *Spatial Poems*,
1965–75. Courtesy of the artist. © Mieko (Chieko) Shiomi.   4

0.2 Mieko Shiomi, *Spatial Poem #2* ('Fluxatlas'), from *Spatial Poems*,
1965–75. Courtesy of the artist and Watanuki Ltd. © Mieko
(Chieko) Shiomi.   5

1.1 Art & Language (Terry Atkinson and Michael Baldwin), *Map of
an Area of Dimensions 12″× 12″ Indicating 2,304 ¼″ Squares*, 1967.
Museum of Modern Art, New York. Gift of Donald Karshan.   26

1.2 Art & Language (Terry Atkinson and Michael Baldwin), *Map to
Not Indicate*, 1967. Tate, London.   29

1.3 Video stills from David Lamelas, *A Study of Relationships between
Inner and Outer Space*, 1969. LUX, London. Courtesy of the artist,
Sprüth Magers and Jan Mot.   31

1.4 Juan Carlos Romero, *4,000,000 m² de la ciudad de Buenos Aires*
(4,000,000 m² of the City of Buenos Aires), 1970. The archive of
Juan Carlos Romero. © Juan Carlos Romero.   36

2.1 Adrian Piper, *Catalysis IV*, 1970. Performance documentation.
Detail, photograph No. 1 of 5. Photo: Rosemary Mayer. Generali
Foundation, Vienna. Permanent Loan to the Museum der
Moderne Salzburg. © Adrian Piper Research Archive (APRA)
Foundation Berlin and Generali Foundation.   45

2.2 Adrian Piper, *Utah–Manhattan Transfer*, 1968. Timo Ohler.
Collection of the Adrian Piper Research Archive (APRA)
Foundation Berlin. © APRA Foundation Berlin.   48–9

2.3 Adrian Piper, *Untitled* ('The area described by the periphery
of this ad …')/*Area Relocation Series #2*, 1969. Photo: Timo
Ohler. Collection of the Adrian Piper Research Archive (APRA)
Foundation Berlin. © APRA Foundation Berlin.   51

2.4 Adrian Piper, *Hypothesis: Situation #6*, 1968. The Walker Art
Center, Minneapolis. T. B. Walker Acquisition Fund. © Adrian
Piper Research Archive (APRA) Foundation Berlin.   52

3.1 Felipe Ehrenberg, still from *La Poubelle; or, It's a Sort of Disease II*, timestamp 00:19, 1970. Photo: Tate. © Estate of Felipe Ehrenberg, London, 2018. 58

3.2 Stephen Willats, *The West London Social Resource Project*, public register board no. 2 at a local library, 1972. Courtesy of the artist. © Stephen Willats. 62

3.3 Stephen Willats, *The West London Social Resource Project*, Sheet 5, k, from the *West London Re-Modelling Book*, Project Area 2, 1972. Courtesy of the artist. © Stephen Willats. 63

3.4 Margaret Harrison, Kay Fido Hunt and Mary Kelly, *Women and Work: A Document on the Division of Labour in Industry 1973–75*, installation view at the South London Gallery, 1975. Photo: Ray Barrie. Courtesy of Mary Kelly. © Margaret Harrison, Mary Kelly and the Estate of Kay Fido Hunt. 66

3.5 Margaret Harrison, Kay Fido Hunt and Mary Kelly, map from the exhibition *Women and Work: A Document on the Division of Labour in Industry 1973–75*, 1975. South London Gallery. Photo: Ray Barrie. Courtesy of Mary Kelly. © Margaret Harrison, Mary Kelly and the Estate of Kay Fido Hunt. 67

4.1 Gábor Attalai, *Transfer of Japan, Continental Change I*, 1971. Klaus Groh-Collection, Forschungsstelle Osteuropa Archive, University of Bremen. Courtesy of Nóra Attalai. 78

4.2 Gábor Attalai, *Big Star Lake, Continental Change I*, 1971. Klaus Groh-Collection, Forschungsstelle Osteuropa Archive, University of Bremen. Courtesy of Nóra Attalai. 79

4.3 Gábor Attalai, *Negative Star* (from the *Negative Sculpture* series, *Star & Snow*), 1971. Vintage Gallery. Courtesy of Nóra Attalai. 86

4.4 Gábor Attalai, *Process of Balding 4*, 1970. Vintage Gallery. Courtesy of Nóra Attalai. 91

5.1 Patrick Ireland (aka Brian O'Doherty), *Ireland: A Modest Proposal*, 1980. Collection Irish Museum of Modern Art (IMMA), Purchase, 2006. Courtesy of IMMA and the Estate of Brian O'Doherty. 100

5.2 Patrick Ireland (aka Brian O'Doherty), *Studies on O.S. Maps for the Purgatory of Humphrey Chimpden Earwicher Humunculus Rope Drawing #73*, 1985. Douglas Hyde Gallery, Trinity College Dublin. Courtesy of University Art Collections, Trinity College Dublin and the Estate of Brian O'Doherty. 101

6.1 Anna Bella Geiger, *Fígados conversando* (*Livers Talking*), from the *Viscerais* series, 1968. Courtesy of the artist. 117

6.2 Anna Bella Geiger, *Lunar I*, 1973. Courtesy of the artist. 122

6.3 Anna Bella Geiger, *Sem título (Trevas/luz)* (*Untitled (Darkness/Light)*), from the *Polaridades/Lunares* series, 1974. Courtesy of the artist. 123

6.4   Anna Bella Geiger, *Correntes culturais* (*Cultural Currents*), 1976.
      Courtesy of the artist.   129
6.5   Anna Bella Geiger, *Orbis descriptio with Six Winds*, from the
      Borderline series, 1995. Courtesy of the artist.   133
7.1   Dennis Oppenheim, *Time Pocket*, 1968–89. Courtesy of the
      Dennis Oppenheim Estate.   144
7.2   Dennis Oppenheim, *Gallery Transplant*, 1969. The Art Institute of
      Chicago. Courtesy of the Dennis Oppenheim Estate.   147
7.3   Dennis Oppenheim, *Ground Mutations – Shoe Prints*, November
      1969. Courtesy of the Dennis Oppenheim Estate.   149
7.4   Dennis Oppenheim, *Landslide*, 1968. Courtesy of the Dennis
      Oppenheim Estate.   152
8.1   Psychophysiology Research Institute artist's book and portfolio of
      cards (facsimile edition, 2009 [1970]).   159
8.2   Ina Ken'ichirō, *Weathering (Time)*, 1969. Contribution on 7
      December 1969 (first undertaking) to Psychophysiology Research
      Institute. Reproduced in *Psychophysiology Research Institute*
      (1970), p. 10.   162
8.3   Ina Ken'ichirō, *Weathering (Time)*, 1969. Contribution on 7
      December 1969 (first undertaking) to Psychophysiology Research
      Institute. Three elements (photograph, map and data sheet), as
      digitised in the CD edition of *Psychophysiology Research Institute*
      (1970/2009).   169
8.4   Psychophysiology Research Institute, original copy envelope,
      7 December 1969. Collection of Horikawa Michio. Courtesy of
      Horikawa Michio.   171
8.5   Itoi Kanji, *1970.4.27. 11:45, Dada Kan's Successful Streaking
      under the Tower of the Sun*. Contribution on 10 May 1970 (sixth
      undertaking) to Psychophysiology Research Institute. Reproduced
      in *Psychophysiology Research Institute* (1970), p. 53.   175
9.1   IBMR, *Soft-Tape*, 1966. Installation for the Biennale of Sydney, 1989.   184
9.2   Ian Burn, *Blue Reflex* series, 1967. Installation view, New York.
      Courtesy of Art & Language.   189
9.3   Art & Language, *Alternate Map for Documenta (Based on Citation
      A)*, 1972. Courtesy of Art & Language.   191
9.4   IBMR, *Comparative Models No. 1*, 1971. Collection Fabre, Brussels.   192
9.5   IBMR, *Comparative Models No. 2*, 1972. Galerie Daniel Templon,
      Paris, 1973.   194
11.1 Invitation to André Cadere's exhibition at Samangallery, Genoa,
      1975. Archive Herbert Foundation, Ghent.   225
11.2 André Cadere holding one of his bars, ICC Antwerp, 1975. ICC
      Archive, Antwerp. Photo: Bert Van Evercooren.   228

11.3   André Cadere's activity report, 1978. Archive Herbert
       Foundation, Ghent.   235
11.4   David Lamelas, *Antwerp-Brussels (People + Time)*, 1969.
       Photo: Maria Gilissen. Courtesy of the artist and Jan Mot, Brussels.   236
12.1   Hélio Oiticica, *Delirium ambulatorium*, 24 October 1978.
       Doc. No. 0066. AHO/PHO. Courtesy of Projeto Hélio Oiticica.
       © César and Claudio Oiticica.   245
12.2   Hélio Oiticica, *Tropicália*, 1967. Tate Modern. Photo by María José
       Martínez Sanchez.   246
12.3   Rasheed Araeen, *Paki Bastard (Portrait of the Artist as a Black
       Person)*, image of the artist exiting Clifton Restaurant. Private
       performance, Brick Lane, London, 1977. Photo: Elena Bozanigo.
       Courtesy of the artist.   251
12.4   Lee Wen, video stills from *Journey of a Yellow Man No. 5: Index to
       Freedom*. Fukuoka, Japan, 1995. Courtesy of the Lee Wen Archive.   256–7

Contributors

Alexander Alberro, Virginia B. Wright Professor of Modern and Contemporary Art History at Barnard College and Columbia University, is the author, most recently, of *Abstraction in Reverse: The Reconfigured Spectator in Mid-Twentieth Century Latin American Art* (2017). Some of his other volumes include *Institutional Critique: An Anthology of Artists' Writings* (2009), *Art after Conceptual Art* (2006), *Conceptual Art and the Politics of Publicity* (2003), *Recording Conceptual Art* (2001) and *Conceptual Art: A Critical Anthology* (1999). He has also published in a broad array of journals and exhibition catalogues. He is presently completing a book-length study, *At Contemporary Art's Boundaries*, that focuses on the relationship between art frameworks and the geography of globalisation.

Eva Bentcheva is an art historian and curator with a focus on transnational archives, conceptualism and performance/participation art in South/Southeast Asia and Europe. She is currently Associate Lecturer at the Heidelberg Centre for Transcultural Studies, and Postdoctoral Researcher/Publications Coordinator for the international project 'Worlding Public Cultures: The Arts and Social Innovation'. She completed her Ph.D. in art history at the School of Oriental and African Studies (SOAS), University of London, on 'The cultural politics of British South Asian performance art, 1960s to the present'. Her previous positions have included Adjunct Researcher for the Tate Research Centre: Asia in London; the Paul Mellon Centre for Studies in British Art; and the Goethe-Institut Fellow at Haus der Kunst in Munich, where she cocurated the exhibition *Archives in Residence: Southeast Asia Performance Collection* in 2019. She was coeditor of a guest-edited issue of the journal *Southeast of Now: Directions in Contemporary and Modern Art* on 'Pathways of performativity in contemporary art of Southeast Asia' (2022).

Inesa Brašiškė is an art historian and curator based in Vilnius, Lithuania. She graduated from Modern and Contemporary Art: Critical and Curatorial Studies (MODA) at Columbia University. Her research interests span postwar European and American art and avant-garde film. She recently coedited *Jonas Mekas: The*

Camera Was Always Running (2022), and cocurated the exhibition *Jonas Mekas and the New York Avant-Garde* (National Gallery of Art in Vilnius, 2021). She is currently completing extensive research on André Cadere (1934–78), coediting a book of essays on his work and preparing the first monograph on the artist. Brašiškė has taught at the Vilnius Academy of Arts; organised symposia, including 'The Post-Socialist Object: Contemporary Art in China and Eastern Europe' (Columbia University, 2017) and 'Jonas Mekas Expanded' (National Gallery of Art, Vilnius, 2022); and initiated the continuous lecture series *Thinking Contemporary Art* (www.thinkingcontemporaryart.lt). She regularly contributes to academic publications, catalogues and journals, and presents her research at international conferences and symposia. In her role as curator she has organised exhibitions and film programmes based on the work of Babette Mangolte, Sharon Lockhart, Marie Menken, Jonas Mekas and others.

Katalin Cseh-Varga currently works as a Hertha Firnberg Fellow at the Academy of Fine Arts in Vienna. In the academic year 2020/21 she was a visiting professor for east European art history at the Humboldt-University, Berlin. Her most recent book, *The Hungarian Avant-Garde in Late Socialism: Art of the Second Public Sphere*, was published in 2023. Her research focuses on the theory of public spheres in the former Eastern Bloc, the intellectual history of really existing socialism, archival theory, creative practices of Hungarian *samizdat*, and performative and medial spaces of the Hungarian experimental art scene from the late 1960s to the early 1990s. Her publications include 'The troubled public sphere: Understanding the art scene in socialist Hungary', in *New Narratives of Russian and East European Art: Between Traditions and Revolutions* (2020); *Performance Art in the Second Public Sphere: Event-Based Art in Late Socialist Europe* (coedited with Ádám Czirák, 2018); and 'Documentary traces of Hungarian event-based art', in *Promote, Tolerate, Ban: Art and Culture in Cold War Hungary* (2018).

Larisa Dryansky is Associate Professor of Contemporary Art History at Sorbonne University. Her research focuses on the intersections of art, science and technology in postwar and contemporary art, and on technological images (photography, film, video). Her current book project is an investigation of artists' engagement with the concept of anti-matter, a topic introduced in her essay 'Another matter: Antimatter and the dematerialization of art', in *Conceptualism and Materiality* (2019). Her first book, *Cartophotographies: Du land art à l'art conceptuel* (2017), addressed the combined uses of photography and cartography in American art of the 1960s and 1970s. She has coedited several volumes, including, recently, *Repenser le médium: Art contemporain et cinéma* (2022). From 2014 to 2016 she was Senior Fellow in charge of contemporary art programmes at the French National Art Institute (INHA).

Dária Jaremtchuk is Associate Professor of Art History at the School of Arts, Sciences and Humanities at São Paulo University, Brazil. She is also a contributor to the Graduate Program in Visual Arts at the School of Communication and Arts (ECA/USP) in the Department of Visual Arts, where she teaches courses on contemporary art. In 2019, she won the Fulbright Brazil Distinguished Chair at Emory University. She is currently researching the relocation of Brazilian artists to New York during the Brazilian military dictatorships of the 1960s and 1970s and the artistic exchange between Brazil and the United States at that time. She is the author of '*Políticas de atração': relações culturais entre Estados Unidos e Brasil 1960–1970* (2023).

Eve Kalyva is a lecturer at the University of Kent and codirector of the research group 'Global Trajectories of Thought and Memory: Art and the Global South' at the University of Amsterdam. She works on conceptual and contemporary art, activism and politics, image and text relations, museum pedagogies, exhibition design, and decolonial praxis. She is author of *Image and Text in Conceptual Art: Critical Operations in Context* (2016), and has published in *Parallax, Latin American Research Review, Social Semiotics* and *Latin American and Latinx Visual Culture.*

Christa-Maria Lerm Hayes is Professor of Modern and Contemporary Art History at the University of Amsterdam, and recently served as Academic Director of the Amsterdam School for Heritage, Memory and Material Culture. Until 2014 she led the Ph.D. programme of the Faculty of Art, Design and the Built Environment at Ulster University, Belfast. Her books include *W. G. Sebald's Artistic Legacies: Memory, Word and Image* (2022); 'Introduction, or the crossdresser's secret', in *Brian O'Doherty/Patrick Ireland: Word, Image and Institutional Critique* (2017); *Post-War Germany and 'Objective Chance': W. G. Sebald, Joseph Beuys and Tacita Dean* (2011); *Joyce in Art* (2004); and *James Joyce als Inspirationsquelle für Joseph Beuys* (2001). She has curated exhibitions internationally. She is Editor-in-Chief of the Brill book series, Research/Art/Writing.

María José Martínez Sanchez is Associate Dean of Research at the Scott Sutherland School of Architecture (RGU). She is a qualified Architect in the UK (ARB/RIBA) and has a professional background in performance design. Her design and arts practice has been presented at the Museum of Contemporary Art Reina Sofía, the Prague Quadrennial of Scenography, the Dance Venice Biennale and the Venice Biennale of Architecture. She has extensive experience in interdisciplinary teaching-led research in Architecture undergraduate and postgraduate programmes, focusing on collaborative live projects. She is the author of *Dynamic Cartography: Body, Architecture and Performative Space* (2020).

Elize Mazadiego is an art historian working on global modern and contemporary art, with a focus on Latin American art and its transnational contexts. She is an assistant professor in world art history in the Institute for Art History at the University of Bern. From 2019 to 2023 she was a Marie Skłodowska Curie Fellow at the University of Amsterdam within art history and the Amsterdam School of Cultural Analysis. She is the author of *Dematerialisation and the Social Materiality of Art: Experimental Forms in Argentina, 1955–1968* (2021), which won the 2022 Best Book Award in Latin American Visual Culture Studies from the Latin American Studies Association (LASA). Her work is featured in *Arts*, *Latin American and Latinx Visual Culture*, *Stedelijk Studies*, *Frieze*, *ArtNexus* and *E-tcetera*.

Jennifer Sarathy is an art historian whose work surveys interventions in urban and rural landscapes in 1960s and 1970s Britain. Her research analyses how representations of the land and alternative mapping practices related to postcolonial debates over British national identity, citizenship, gender and race. She holds a B.A. in art history from Johns Hopkins University, Baltimore, an M.A. in Southeast Asian studies from the National University of Singapore and is a doctoral candidate in art history at the Graduate Center at the City University of New York.

Ann Stephen is an art historian and senior curator of art at Chau Chak Wing Museum, University of Sydney. She has curated and published on modernism and conceptual art, including such titles as *On Looking at Looking: The Art and Politics of Ian Burn* (2006), *Light & Darkness* (2021) and *Ian Burn: Collected Writings* (2023). She coedited, with Andrew McNamara and Philip Goad, *Modernism & Australia: Documents on Art, Design and Architecture 1917–1967* (2006), *Modern Times: The Untold Story of Modernism in Australia* (2008) and *Bauhaus Diaspora* (2019).

Reiko Tomii is an independent art historian and curator who investigates post-1945 Japanese art, which constitutes a vital part of world art history of modernisms. Her early works include her contribution to *Global Conceptualism* (Queens Museum of Art, 1999), *Century City* (Tate Modern, 2001) and *Art, Anti-Art, Non-Art* (Getty Research Institute, 2007). She is codirector of PoNJA-GenKon, a listserv group of specialists interested in contemporary Japanese art. In this role she has organised a number of symposia and panels in collaboration with Yale University, Getty Research Institute and other major academic institutions. In another collective undertaking, she has collaborated with Asia Art Archive in America on the Ponja Wikipedia Initiative (PWI) since 2021. Her most recent publication, *Radicalism in the Wilderness: International Contemporaneity and 1960s Art in Japan* (2016), received the 2017 Robert Motherwell Book Award. In 2019, based on the book, she curated *Radicalism in the Wilderness: Japanese Artists in the Global 1960s*, which highlighted three practitioners – Matsuzawa Yutaka, The Play and GUN – at the Japan Society Gallery in New York. In 2020, she received the Commissioner for Cultural Affairs Award from the Japanese Government for cultural transmission and international exchange through postwar Japanese art history.

Alena J. Williams is Assistant Professor in the Department of Visual Arts at the University of California, San Diego. Her research areas include modern and contemporary art, the rhetoric of visual culture and the epistemology of the image. A 2016 Hellman Fellow, she was a visiting scholar at the Max Planck Institute for the History of Science in Berlin (2017), a Deutscher Akademischer Austauschdienst (DAAD) Fellow at the Institute for the History and Theory of Design at the Universität der Künste Berlin (2018), and a Society Fellow of the Cornell Society for the Humanities (2019–20). Between 2018 and 2019 she was a faculty coinvestigator for *Interrogating the Archive: Shared Research Methodologies at the Intersection of Aesthetics and Authenticity*, an interdisciplinary research group on archival experimentation and decolonial practices at University of California San Diego. From 2010 to 2013 Williams curated *Nancy Holt: Sightlines*, an international travelling exhibition on American artist Nancy Holt's land art, films, videos and related works from 1966 to 1080 for the Miriam and Ira D. Wallach Art Gallery at Columbia University in New York.

Acknowledgements

This book is dedicated to the artists whose work first inspired this project. While there are too many to name here, I wish to extend a special thanks to Anna Bella Geiger. In addition to providing the image for the cover, she has been very generous with her insights on the relationship between art, mapping and spatiality. I am deeply grateful to the authors in this volume for their sustained involvement, especially during the most precarious of times in 2020. Your intellectual engagement, collaboration and commitment to this project have been vital to the making of the book. My sincerest appreciation to Emma Brennan and Alun Richards at Manchester University Press for their support of the project, as well as to the series editors for including this book in Rethinking Art's Histories, and to the anonymous reviewers for their rigorous feedback. Finally, warm thanks to the artists, estates and institutions who generously provided permission to publish reproductions of artworks.

Introduction: Maps, spatiality and conceptual art

Elize Mazadiego

Mapping presumes a scientific ordering in what Doreen Massey calls the 'taming of the spatial', but also involves what Denis Cosgrove describes as 'visualizing, conceptualizing, recording, representing and creating spaces'.[1] These two lines of thought point to mapping as an engagement with space and spatiality. In essence, it is a cognitive and embodied activity – a spatial practice or process – that explores as much as it shapes and inscribes the contours of our world. Ubiquitous in conceptualism are acts of mapping that suggest a key moment when art was working through issues of space, but also epistemologies of knowing and understanding the world. This volume provides a selected overview of artists and works from the late 1960s to the 1990s that use cartographic language and other forms of spatial representation. It surveys and registers conceptualism's critical engagement with space as artists, critics and dealers attempted to chart space, mediate it, give it form, expand it, transcend it or make it obsolete. The essays within this collection underscore the significance of spatiality within conceptualism, ultimately shedding light on the philosophical and political stakes in such artistic experiments.

Conceptualism's affinity for maps and mapping was duly noted in 1981 by *New York Times* critic Roberta Smith, who stated 'At a certain point around 1973, it was probably difficult to find an artist working in the Conceptualist or Earthwork mode who had not used a map at least once.'[2] Film theorist Peter Wollen made a similar observation in 1999 when he explored a shared 'fascination with maps' between conceptual artists and members of the Situationist International (SI).[3] More recently, art historian Sophie Cras reiterated that maps were 'a privileged artistic theme in the 1960s'.[4] Even geographers, such as Denis Wood and Denis Cosgrove, have registered conceptual art's interest in maps and cartography.[5]

For Cras, maps 'suited conceptual artists' search for non-expressive, scientific-looking images, closer to documentation than to art and supposedly able to efficiently transmit information'.[6] Likewise, Wollen foregrounded conceptual art's maps as primarily documentation, or the 'semiotic code' to convey the work's information, as well as conceptually reconstruct the work.[7] Both scholars advance the view that maps were one of many indexical models, such as photographs, texts and diagrams, that served to record and communicate artists' conceptual strategies, processes or performances.

This position upholds that maps were primarily employed as a transparent means of inscription and a denotational image – similar to the operation of photography and language in conceptual art. As Liz Kotz argues, the model of communication that informed conceptual artists in the United States was rooted in cybernetics, systems theory and mass communication technologies that 'hinged on the processes of "information transmission"'.[8] Along similar lines, Eve Meltzer points to structuralism's influence in conceptual art's 'scientistic aesthetic in which the artworks were abstracted down to its "essential" aspects and conveyed through linguistic data or structural system'.[9] It was in the 1960s, with geographers such as Arthur H. Robinson and J. L. Morrison, that cartography was perceived as primarily a science of communicating information.[10] This aligns with artist Douglas Huebler's position that the map was another linguistic form that, in one respect, factually 'tell[s] people where they are'.[11] At the same time, Hubeler's works, such as *Location Piece No. 1: New York–Los Angeles* (1969), call into question the pure indexicality of maps, revealing the extent to which maps project far more than the pictorial depiction of geographic information. While maps were part of a system of documentation, and even functioned as a style in what Benjamin Buchloch referred to as an 'aesthetics of administration', such analysis tends to eclipse conceptualism's more idiosyncratic and complex explorations of space. This volume shows how conceptual artists, far from affirming cartographic objectivity, often sought to critique and expand established ideas about mapping.

The repurposed, modified or manipulated standardised maps prevalent in conceptual artworks account for a common set of cartographic pieces, in which the map was a material basis for their artistic interventions. One only needs to think of On Kawara's often discussed *I Went* series, or lesser known works such as Claudio Perna's *República de Venezuela, mapa ecológico* (*Republic of Venezuela, Ecological Map*; 1975) or *Correntes culturais* (*Cultural Currents*; 1976) by Anna Bella Geiger, discussed in Chapter 6 (pp. 129–30). However, On Kawara's *Location* (1965), in which the artist painted in white type on a black canvas the precise geographic coordinates of an obscure location in the Sahara, presents another form of spatial visualisation.[12] The operation of the map – an abstract notational system to describe and represent a place otherwise beyond our field of vision – is rendered with words rather than the typical graphic image. This example points to the equivalence drawn between language and image, but also broadens our definition of the map to include other cartographies within conceptualism.

The contributors to this volume alternate between reading work where the conventional map was central and other myriad forms that visually and conceptually refer to real, physical space. Works featured in this book, such as Nancy Holt's large-scale sculptural *Sun Tunnels* (1973–76) or Adrian Piper's *Hypothesis* series (1968–69) combine diagrams, charts, photographs and other forms that effectively draw spatial relationships to convey designated spaces. While these examples may not be the scaled renderings of geographical facts, they do fulfil cartography's basic function conceivably to measure and represent space. In this respect, this book does not limit conceptual art's maps to a specific type of notation or presentation, but includes a wider spectrum of spatial representations that have yet to be accounted for in the history of conceptualism. It places emphasis on conceptual art's *cartographies* – an evident practice of mapping or *charting space* in diverse modes, productions and processes.

Shiomi Mieko's *Spatial Poems* (1965–75) is one such example. Described as 'nine global events', the work conceptually connected artists across space in several international networked performances.[13] For each event, Shiomi mailed a typed event score to Fluxus artists and friends scattered across the globe, with the request to return some form of documentation of their performance (see Figure 0.1). From her responses, she produced a book and art objects with multiple maps marked with the location and action of each participation (see Figure 0.2). Apart from the actual maps used in *Spatial Poems*, its disparate elements (score, performance, mailings) come together to form a complex cartography, with multiple scales that encompass space that is both material and conceptual. On one level, *Spatial Poems* is a graphic depiction of Fluxus's dispersed geography, visualising the group's international ambitions and an emerging spatiality in the postwar art world, predicated on a network of relations and system of communications. On another level, art historian Midori Yoshimoto reads *Spatial Poems* through the lens of Shiomi's return to Japan after living in New York and rearing her young children. Yoshimoto observed 'the global dimension of *Spatial Poem* [*sic*] enabled Shiomi to transcend the physical and temporal constrictions on her life'.[14] While the work is a rendering of the artist's spatial condition, characterised by relative distance, her cartography produces a liberating social space formed through her artistic relationships.

From these cartographic practices the book elaborates on conceptualism's spaces, effectively moving beyond initial readings of its maps as transparent transfers of external information to understand these objects' larger significance and entanglement with social, political and historical contexts. Reading conceptual works more closely, this volume foregrounds artists' mappings as interrogations of space and spatiality that ultimately probed the multiple dimensions of the world in which they lived – but also sought to reformulate

SPATIAL POEM No.2

Around the time listed below
what kind of direction are you moving
or facing toward ?
— either performance or spontaneous —
please send me a report about it
which will be edited on a world map

New York ············ 5:00 pm, Oct. 15, 1965
Amsterdam ········· 11:00 pm, Oct. 15, 1965
Copenhagen ········ 11:00 pm, Oct. 15, 1965
Paris ················· 11:00 pm, Oct. 15, 1965
Japan ················ 7:00 am, Oct. 16, 1965
Stockholm ··········· 11:00 pm, Oct. 15, 1965
London ············· 10:00 pm, Oct. 15, 1965
Scotland ············· 10:00 pm, Oct. 15, 1965
Vienna ············· 11:00 pm, Oct. 15, 1965
Nice ··············· 11:00 pm, Oct. 15, 1965
Rome ··············· 11:00 pm, Oct. 15, 1965
Moscow ············· 1:00 am, Oct. 16, 1965
Berlin ··············· 11:00 pm, Oct. 15, 1965
Los Angeles ········ 2:00 pm, Oct. 15, 1965
Montreal ············· 5:00 pm, Oct. 15, 1965
India ··············· 3:30 am, Oct. 16, 1965
Barcelona ··········· 11:00 pm, Oct. 15, 1965
Cologne ············· 11:00 pm, Oct. 15, 1965
Prague ············· 11:00 pm, Oct. 15, 1965
Chicago ············· 4:00 pm, Oct. 15, 1965
Mexico city ········ 4:00 pm, Oct. 15, 1965
Brazil ··············· 7:00 pm, Oct. 15, 1965
Iran ················· 1:30 am, Oct. 16, 1965
Sydney ············· 8:00 am, Oct. 16, 1965
Hawaii ············· 0:00 pm, Oct. 15, 1965
Greenland ··········· 7:00 pm, Oct. 15, 1965

etc.   simultaneous

Chieko Shiomi
7-1 Mizuho-juza
Kitanagase, Okayama
Japan

• Please write in print hand or use typewriter

0.1 Mieko Shiomi, *Spatial Poem #2* ('Invitation'), from *Spatial Poems*, 1965–75.

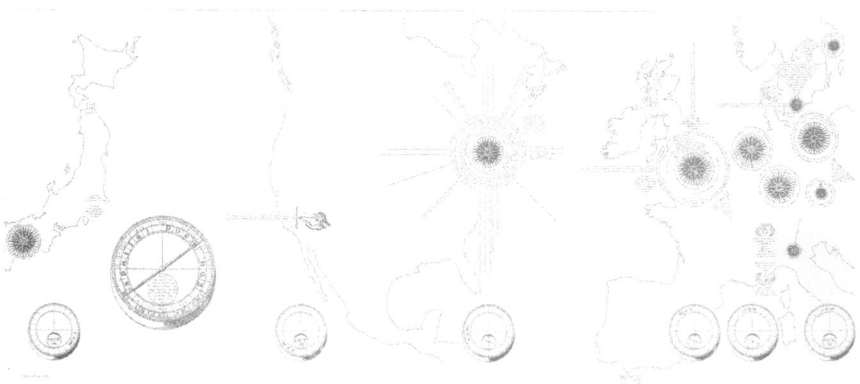

Mieko Shiomi, *Spatial Poem #2* ('Fluxatlas'), from *Spatial Poems*, 1965–75.   **0.2**

them. In this regard, conceptualism's cartographies and its diverse spatial practices are then sites to formulate artists' politics as they graph new heterogeneous spaces, potentially upsetting prevailing constructs and systems.

Conceptualism's spatial turn

In an interview with Douglas Huebler in July 1969, Patricia Norvell wondered to what extent the recent landing on the moon had changed the artist's thinking, particularly in terms of one's 'orientation or concept of place'.[15] Huebler's response that 'our view is getting much more cosmic' indicates a new and expanded sense of spatial awareness by the late 1960s.[16] The same year, Jennifer Licht, associate curator at the Museum of Modern Art (MoMA), commented that 'space – sensorial, social ecological, extraterrestrial' was 'the central issue of our time' and one catalyst for her show *Spaces*.[17]

The MoMA exhibition involved five artists – Michael Asher, Larry Bell, Dan Flavin, Robert Morris and Franz Erhard Walther – and the group Pulsa, to create a work *in situ* that shaped, manipulated, activated and ultimately presented 'space' as art.[18] The museum divided their ground-floor Garden Wing into rooms in which each artist could construct an ephemeral, site-specific installation or environment. For example, in Asher's *Untitled* piece, the artist lowered the room's ceilings; dimmed the lighting; and lined the walls, ceiling and floor with acoustical board that absorbed all sound. His intended effect was to remove any perceptual distractions, allowing the visitor to focus on the spatial experience. Dan Flavin's *Untitled (For Sonja)* installed fluorescent light on two opposing walls that flooded the physical space with hues of green and yellow. For Licht, this work made the 'immaterial' and 'invisible' field of space perceptible via phenomenological reception. Space and its context, however, remained relatively limited to its physical attributes as artists drew attention to size, scale, dimension, light, temperature and sound. This literal approach aligned with site-specific work's early formation, which defined space according to its basic physical conditions.[19]

The example of *Spaces* highlights the extent to which space was becoming a central feature within art and artistic discourse by the late 1960s. As Licht outlined in her catalogue essay, artists' investigations of 'actual, real space' mirrored a concurrent 'interest in the idea of space'; she cited the theories of Gaston Bachelard and Richard Buchminster Fuller, experimental compositions by John Cage and Karlheinz Stockhausen, and the architecture of Frank Lloyd Wright and Ludwig Mies van der Rohe.[20] Underpinning her exhibition was also a genealogy of artistic avant-garde movements that dealt with three-dimensional space, from Kurt Schwitters to Marcel Duchamp and later Allan Kaprow's 'environments'. These historical precedents were evidence of an integration of physical space into works of art. The artists in *Space*, then, were 'an outgrowth of an amalgamation of larger artistic traditions with the particular cultural concerns of the present moment'.[21] In this show, however, the artists took physical space and spatial context as their central artistic material, tending to ignore its discursive elements. To some extent these works – intent on pointing to the physical conditions of space – implied an early form of institutional critique as they oriented our attention to a spatial framework, potentially exposing the once invisible exhibition space as a determining factor in the artwork's meaning and value. Yet this was not the exhibition's primary position; rather, Licht imagined the artists in the show in rather broad terms – virtually space explorers. The catalogue's cover image – a rich blue cluster of stars reminiscent of outer space – certainly evoked a correlation between the scientific space exploration that characterised 1969 and the artistic space exploration within the exhibition.

The same year, a symposium, broadcast on the New York radio station WBAI-FM and titled Art without Space, featured dealer Seth Siegelaub in conversation with a number of now canonical conceptual artists: Robert Barry, Douglas Huebler, Joseph Kosuth and Lawrence Weiner. In Siegelaub's opening remarks he premises the theme of the symposium on the basis of 'an art whose primary existence in the world does not relate to space, not to its exhibition in space, not to its imposing things on the walls'.[22] By that time Siegelaub had organised several exhibitions that took the form of a widely distributed catalogue rather than a physical show.[23] For *One Month (March 1–31)* (1969) the catalogue included textual contributions from thirty-one artists. As Siegelaub explained, he 'eliminated the idea of [gallery] space', making his gallery 'the world now'.[24] In contrast to MoMA's *Spaces*, Siegelaub's catalogue shows attempted to uproot art from its physical, locational context, or at least to situate it in a fluid and mobile space. Despite Siegelaub's opening, the artists in the symposium called into question his disregard and narrow definition of space. The artist Robert Barry asserted that nearly all artists present had work correlated to 'some kind of spatial experiences'.[25] What emerged from the ensuing dialogue was a much broader formulation of space in art and a series of realisations that conceptual art was dealing with space differently than its object-based predecessors. For Barry the experience of space was becoming less physical, whereas Huebler found language useful for perceiving space. Yet both arrive at an understanding of space (and art's use of it) as predominantly conceptual.

I bring these two instances together to show that Siegelaub, Licht and the artists within their orbit started to think spatially, sharing a preoccupation with art's relationship to space. But the nature of that relationship was open to interpretation: while Licht considered space a central 'agent in art', Siegelaub argued for its irrelevance. Counter to Siegelaub's claim that the apparent dematerialisation of art provoked an 'art without space', this book argues that conceptualism had a more nuanced perspective and close dialectical relationship to space. In particular, conceptual artists dealt with matters of space that complicated the dominant view of it as largely static, empty and abstract, and asserted understandings of it that would have larger implications for art's relation to the world. A task of this book is to make explicit art's engagements with space, suggesting that conceptualism tended towards a 'spatial turn' that addressed new, complex conceptualisations of space – from physical, institutional and geographic frameworks to social, cultural, public, private and political spheres.

Charting Space discusses this turn relative to the historical, political, social, cultural and technological developments of the period that heavily influenced conceptual artists and their work in relation to space and spatiality. While art historian Pamela Lee has argued for the pre-eminence of time in art from the 1960s, in the years following the Second World War space held the critical attention of critics, theorists and – as this book argues – artists and curators.[26] Since the war the concept of space has garnered significant attention across disciplines. Ranging from critical theory to cultural studies, there has been a recognisable spatial turn in which space became a central subject of enquiry and reflection. In *Postmodern Geographies: The Reassertion of Space in Critical Social Theory*, Edward Soja identifies the start of this shift in the 1960s with the emergence of poststructuralist thought. Prior to the mid-twentieth century the significance of space was largely 'devalued, occluded and depoliticized', and otherwise subordinate to time.[27] Soja echoes Michel Foucault, who remarked in 1976 that there was a 'devaluation of space that prevailed for generations' that 'treated [space] as the dead, the fixed, the undialectical, the immobile', whereas time was 'richness, fecundity, life, dialectic'.[28] French postwar theory was productive in shifting this imbalance. In 1967 Foucault's lecture 'Of other spaces' declared the present as 'an epoch of space' dominated by an 'experience of the world' that is 'less that of a long life developing through time than of a network that connects points and intersects with its own skein.'[29] By the 1970s space was again a focal point for Marxist philosopher Henri Lefebvre, whose book *The Production of Space* (1974) asserted that space was an active process of social production.[30] In contrast with a Euclidean notion of empty space as the background to historical and temporal events, Foucault and Lefebvre positioned space as changing, inventive and relational. Lefebvre specifically identified space whereby social and spatial relationships are dialectic, interdependent and contingent. Following this interpretation, the primordial, physical and external qualities of space give way to a generative and transformative practice of spatiality.

The significance given to space in the postwar period was presumably provoked by a radical altering of its experience. Rapid urbanisation, innovative telecommunications, the space age and low-cost travel are just some contemporaneous developments that compressed space-time and thereby changed the perception of physical, geographical space. Indeed, 1969 was remarkable for the Apollo 11 spaceflight that landed on the moon, while social and political transformations also lent themselves to new spatialities. Beginning in the late 1940s, with the independence of India and Pakistan through partition in 1947, processes of decolonisation in Asia and Africa disrupted and realigned a former imperial geography, from which emerged new independent nation-states and transregional political configurations. This postcolonial geography, along with the Cold War's bipolarisation of the globe, essentially remapped the world. Yet, globalisation and processes of capitalism rendered space unbounded and largely uninhibited by territorial and economic borders, facilitating free movement and the flow of people and capital.

As Larisa Dryansky highlights in Chapter 7, theorist Marshall McLuhan's 1964 idea of a 'global village', in which spatio-temporal distances are transcended by new telecommunications, influenced conceptual art's cartographic work.[31] Pointing to *Telexed Triangle* (1969) by Canadian artist duo N. E. Thing Company, Dryansky sees the artists' electronically transmitted message across three different locations (Inuvik, Vancouver and Halifax) as a simulation of space and time's compression, famously proclaimed by McLuhan. Inversely, Dryansky interprets Dennis Oppenheim's land works transplanting space and time as a direct critique of McLuhan's utopian thinking.

For Brazilian artist Anna Bella Geiger, Dária Jaremtchuk (Chapter 6) points to the artist's geopolitical concerns articulated in works such *O novo atlas I* (*New Atlas I*; 1977). A page from the artist book contains a drawing of a Mercator projection map alongside three other geographic maps of the world on a scale according to capitalist and colonial cultural, economic and geopolitical systems. One such drawing depicts a dimunitive Global South in juxtaposition with an exaggerated Northern Hemisphere, accompanied by the text 'Desenvolvido e subdesenvolvido' ('Developed and underdeveloped') – taxonomies that became popular in the 1960s. Her work makes visible hegemonic structures and the conceptualisations that form perceptual knowledge but also shape the physical world. For Geiger, maps enabled her 'to subvert descriptive meaning into an ideological one, by transforming certain scales and proportions with the use of distortions'.[32]

This volume situates many of the spatialising practices in conceptualism within the shifting understandings and meanings of space that occurred from the 1960s onwards. It argues for an unexamined yet intrinsic relationship among conceptualism, space and history. Like the critical theorists, conceptual artists grappled with the wild transformations of a world inherited from the modernist, industrial and colonial traditions into a globalised one. Their cartographies are efforts in making sense of the places and spaces in the world. Their works are thus critical observations about the character of their contemporary space, but also how it can be produced in new ways. In particular, many of the chapters express an interesting relationship between the abstract visual constructions of the map – the static geographic notation of space – and the social and performative operations that act on that environment to activate, modify or resignify it.

Mapping is one modality by which our material (spatial) world is conceptualised and experienced conceptually. As artists from the 1960s purported to elevate ideas and language over material objects, the shape of space increasingly took the form of conceptual information. In Eve Meltzer's discussion of the 1970 *Information* exhibition, curated by Kynaston McShine at MoMA, conceptual artists conspicuously embraced the look of information, but also a discourse of information from the field of communications engineering, with the belief that such technologies were reducing the world to data. She points to the catalogue cover picturing a collage of Xeroxed images of contemporary media and communication technologies as evidence that 'the world itself had become an information system'.[33] Concept-based work in the show, then, was a reflection of this condition, but also an effort to operate critically – potentially intervening – within such systems. One example is Hans Haacke's *MoMA Poll*, an information work that sought to undermine the governor's political position and more broadly politicise the artistic institution. Meltzer's point is that *Information* and, more broadly, conceptual art, 'broached a structuralist world-view' that perceived the world in terms of systems, with language as the important sign system that produces meaning, ultimately constituting the world.[34]

Jennifer Sarathy (Chapter 3) provides the example of *Women and Work: A Document on the Division of Labor in Industry* (1973–75), which exhibited information on the female labourers and their working conditions at the

Metal Box Company in south London. The copious amounts of data on display certainly gave the appearance of a conceptual art exhibition, but as Sarathy explains, artists Margaret Harrison, Kay Fido Hunt and Mary Kelly registered and made visible the ways in which these women's lives were abstracted by administrative details and operated within a social system of gendered socio-economic relations. At the same time, this information was critically used to map conceptually a network of spatial relations among the women labourers, their workplace, home and the city in a way that effectively draws new meanings and relations to their environments, producing what Sarathy calls an 'alternative cartography' (p. 64). *Women and Work* therefore instrumentalises information as a form of cognition and communication that produces social space.

The term 'social space' was first introduced in Henri Lefebvre's seminal book *The Production of Space*, published in 1974 in his native French and only translated into English in 1991. In this text Lefebvre took issue with structuralism's emphasis on concept and structure, arguing that 'the systematic study of language, and/or study of language as a system, have eliminated the "subject" in every sense of the term'.[35] For Lefebvre, this had larger implications for space, stating that linguistic structuralism 'reduces [social and physical space] to an epistemological (mental) space – the space of discourse and of the Cartesian *cognito*'.[36] Moving away from a narrow understanding of space as strictly an inert 'mental thing', Lefebvre argued for a dialectical relation between the mental and material. His tripartite model of 'spatial practice' (perceived space), 'representations of space' (conceived space) and 'representational space' (lived space) is the framework for understanding space as simultaneously physical and material, conceptual and lived. Lefebvre's bold proposition is that space is not the empty container of Cartesian thought or a purely mental field, but an active, ongoing process of production by human agency and its social relations. In the words of Mark Gottdiener, 'Every mode of social organization produces an environment that is a consequence of the social relations it possesses. In addition, by producing a space according to its own nature, a society not only materializes into distinctive built forms, but also reproduces itself.'[37]

For art historians Simon Sadler and Thomas F. McDonough, Lefebvre's form of social geography was in close dialogue with the SI's psychogeographies of the 1950s.[38] Indeed, SI's maps – such as *The Naked City* (1957) – and *dérives* could be conceived as avant-garde experiments in space that sought to construct new socio-spatial relations in various European cities, largely in response to their changing urban conditions. For Peter Wollen, conceptualism's cartography is characterised by its 'scientificity', which departed from such critical postures and Debordian 'passion'.[39] In contrast, this book contends that conceptualism advanced a concept of space that was an open, dynamic and relational process of production. As with the example of *Women and Work*, space is not a fixed entity or simply the static surface on which artists are making their work; rather, it is an affect of artists' conceptual mapping, which charts a different set of relations that form our world. So, while the art in this book has affinities with and contains assimilations of Lefebvre's spatial theories, it also invokes new understandings of (social) space that are at times feminist or decolonial. Given that feminist geography emerges in the 1990s, with Doreen Massey and Gillian Rose's work, much of the work we see in this volume demonstrates a practice that precedes some critical theoretical developments.[40] Furthermore, this book grapples with the question 'What is the significance of conceptualism's space-making?'. As it unfolds, contributors point to a number of consequences to this practice. As Sarathy explains in her chapter on *Women and Work*, the exhibition animated a political discourse about these women's lives in relation to the city and place of work (Chapter 3). The work of Anna Bella Geiger, featured in Chapter 6, and Rasheed Araeen's in Chapter 12, signals the various artistic attempts to think critically about the systems that order our world, but also rewrite their spatialities. As Doreen Massey argued in *For Space*

> thinking the spatial in a particular way can shake up the manner in which certain political questions are formulated, can contribute to political arguments already under way, and – most deeply – can be an essential element in the imaginative structure which enables in the first place an opening up to the very sphere of the political.[41]

New histories of conceptualism

Since the 1999 exhibition *Global Conceptualism: Points of Origin 1950s–1980s*, the history of conceptual art has been variously globalised, reconsidered, rewritten and expanded. This book is part of the continuous reassessment of the historical evaluations of the period that gives new critical and theoretical insights. *Charting Space* intervenes in established debates on conceptualism's philosophy, art of administration, institutional critique and documentary practices. Its central contribution is to consider conceptualism's social and political relevance and its particular mode of address through its spatially oriented practices. In particular, the book adds to the ongoing questions around conceptualism's relationship to topics of internationalism, globalisation, feminism and postcolonialism.

Larisa Dryansky's 2017 book *Cartophotographies: De l'art conceptuel au Land Art* (*Cartographies: From Conceptual to Land Art*) laid the groundwork for discussing conceptual art's cartography with its study of five US male artists working from the 1960s to the early 1970s: Douglas Huebler, Mel Bochner,

Dennis Oppenheim, Ed Ruscha and Robert Smithson.[42] Her important study explored the intersections between cartography and photography to discuss conceptions of time, the American landscape and spatial perspective. *Charting Space* ultimately widens the scope across artistic approaches to include other conceptual work, such as Fluxus and land art, but also across geography, gender and history, while foregrounding spatiality as a central and varied concept in conceptual artistic practices.

The book juxtaposes a range of practices and contexts that existed within conceptualism from the mid-1960s into the early 1990s in different parts of the world, demonstrating that mapping, spatial practices and thinking were not specific to the Anglo-American model of conceptual art or limited to the period between 1966 and 1972, but rather were representative of broader histories of conceptualism. The time frame extends beyond conceptual art's traditional span, roughly between 1966 and 1972, tracing its later developments into the mid-to-late 1970s and resonances into the 1980s and 1990s.[43] Many attempts have been made to connect and differentiate the former and latter periods. While conceptual artistic practices since the mid-1970s may have been bracketed under the term 'post-conceptual', conceptualism's development and evolution with subsequent generations of artists carry its history into the contemporary.[44]

Work from the later half of the 1970s is broadly characterised by conceptualism's shift away from a focused critique of high modernism towards a deepening social and political engagement.[45] However, when taking a wider view of conceptual artistic practices, this binary is complicated by a number of artists within and outside the USA and western Europe who were referencing their politics as early as 1968.[46] In the radical political climate unfolding internationally at the end of the 1960s, from the rise of authoritarian regimes in different parts of the world to the emergence of feminism and postcolonialism, conceptual artists increasingly aligned their analytical propositions with their 'real-life' conditions and concerns.[47] This book spotlights those artists who developed modes of addressing particular concrete 'worldly subject matter' – for example concerning the geopolitics within 1970s dictatorial Brazil and socialist Hungary, or the gendered, economic and racial social relations within a given city.[48] Authors Christa-Maria Lerm Hayes (Chapter 5), and Eva Bentcheva and María José Martínez Sanchez (Chapter 12) further trace these conceptualist tendencies to the end of the twentieth century, with studies on Patrick Ireland's mappings in the 1980s and Singaporean artist Lee Wen's performances in the 1990s respectively. This expanded time frame considers the longer continuum of conceptual art that stems from the late modern period into the contemporary. Recalling the work of Terry Smith and Reiko Tomii on the topic of contemporaneity, conceptualism's time frame is complicated by a complex, non-linear development. Therefore, while the book is attentive to conceptualism's temporality, it tends to privilege conceptualism's spatial, networked dimension.

With chapters focused on artists in specific yet connected localities, the contributors in this book highlight the differentiated concerns across multiple geographic and cultural contexts, especially as they relate to questions of space and place. The need for specificity becomes quite clear given the various formal and theoretical investigations during this period, from Adrian Piper's *Hypotheses* to Hélio Oiticica's *Delirium Ambulatorium*. In spite of the heterogeneity, the book weaves them together as a characterisation of conceptualism and its development across time and space. The contributors approach conceptualism from various contexts in order to provide focused studies from different locations. With the show *Global Conceptualism*, the curators drew a 'multicentered map' of art's conceptual tendency worldwide, thereby widening conceptual art's scope beyond the USA and western Europe to show articulations in Latin America, Asia, Africa and beyond that shared an 'attitudinal expression'.[49] The landmark exhibition was significant in reconfiguring the traditional topography of conceptual art. While this book similarly examines histories of conceptual art beyond the USA and western Europe, it remains limited in its geography. Even so, *Charting Space* allows us to examine the interesting and complex spatial practices conceived by artists in Latin America, Asia, Australia and eastern Europe, or by artists tied to those places but working transnationally.

Despite the various regional and transregional contexts this book covers, it does not give a comprehensive account of global conceptualism. Much work still needs to be done to unpack the global structure of conceptualism, and a revisionist history on global conceptualism is due. The purpose of this book is not to write this history, but rather to attend to the multiple, shifting discourses of space in art from the 1960s and its place within conceptualism. That said, the book gives some perspective on conceptualism's discursive construction of the global and a sense of its own geography. Given that conceptualism's emergence coincided with the very processes of globalisation, the Euro-American strand of conceptualism tended to project an international universalism and to disregard prevailing inequalities between centre and periphery.[50] The book's chapters offer another reading of conceptualism's complex global construct or world-system, viewed with a keen sense of location and its multiple registers of experience. One question this book puts forth is 'What role did works play in translating conceptualism's geography, global or otherwise?'. Reiko Tomii's chapter on the Psychophysiology Research Institute suggests that its 'space of information' was a mode to manoeuvre or disrupt conceptualism's spatial coordinates (Chapter 8, pp. 173–8).

In fact, many of the case studies here stem from contexts in the USA and Europe, and those that were nevertheless in dialogue with the West. The volume attempts, however, to highlight a shared conception of art and space that is at the same time multivalent and multi-sited. It therefore approaches conceptualism from positions of difference, with focused studies of artists working in locally specific contexts who are not necessarily consolidated but are conceptually linked. Tomii's work on the 'connections' and 'resonances' between Japan and the western art world is apt for how this volume might map similar tendencies from distinct, local narratives. In many ways the chapters in the book converge on their epistemological enquiry of space by asking the simple question 'How do we perceive, experience and know space?'. What emerges is variously bound to different ways of knowing that are localised, placing the subject and body at the centre and always in relation to space-time. Therefore, this book proposes a geography based in practice, materials and other geographic categories (cities, borders, time zones, streets etc.) or spatial metaphors. This is reflected in the thematic structure that is sectioned across concepts of space within conceptualism: social cartographies, political geographies, sites and networks, and itineraries.

Part I, 'Social cartographies', focuses on artists' examination of space's dialectical process of production in three different contexts: London's urban sphere in the 1970s; Adrian Piper's quotidian life; and the binary spaces interrogated by Art & Language, David Lamelas and Juan Carlos Romero. The chapters foreground the urban and lived practices in these works and the ways these aspects are the locus for social engagement and their potential to produce alternative or critical spaces. In Chapter 1, Eve Kalyva gives a comparative reading of three spatial works from the late 1960s by Art & Language, David Lamelas and Juan Carlos Romero. Kalyva considers how these works' reference systems orient the viewer in relation to their spatial environments as a means of investigating space and its social construction. Her reading underscores the way in which conceptual art extended beyond a self-referential posture to relate to the world. Alex Alberro's chapter traces Adrian Piper's evolving concepts of space in her work from 1967 to 1970. His analysis reveals Piper's use of space as a medium in her conceptual practice, while also tracing her move from the abstract to a dynamic social space. Alberro's chapter takes a perspective on conceptual artists who tackle the intricate relations of space and the construction of gendered and racial realities. In Chapter 3 Jennifer Sarathy draws our attention to the conceptual work of several artist collectives based in London in the 1970s that produced an alternative cartography of the city. In her close reading of *Garbage Walk* (1970), *The West London Social Resource Project* (1972–73) and *Women and Work: A Document on the Division of Labour in Industry 1973–1975* (1973–75), Sarathy elucidates how artists mapped specific facets of urban life and work to make visible London's socio-spatial order, but also to recode their structure and meaning.

Part II, 'Political geographies', is centred on the geopolitics in the practice of Gábor Attalai, Brian O'Doherty/Patrick Ireland and Anna Bella Geiger. It considers the issues of territory, hegemony and empire that shape these works. In line with Edward Said's claim that 'none of us are completely free from the struggle over geography', the chapters in this part expand on contentions 'about ideas, about forms, about images and imaginings'.[51] The section speaks to conceptual artists' mappings as a means to negotiate space and critique power. Chapter 4, by Katalin Cseh-Varga, turns to Gábor Attalai's practice between 1970 and 1971, which took the form of performative conceptualism, mail art and land art, as different articulations of spatial subversions, or what she terms 'immaterial countercartography'. Using the context of Hungary's Kádár regime and the emergence of conceptual art in eastern Europe as her frame, Cseh-Varga points to Attalai's reworking of geopolitical signs and texts as challenges to fixed ways of thinking about the world. Artistic manipulations of maps as a challenge to spatial regimes also course through Christa-Maria Lerm Hayes's contribution on the New York-based Irish artist Brian O'Doherty, working under the name Patrick Ireland, and two cartographic works from 1980 and 1985. Lerm Hayes's essay evaluates his modified maps of Ireland, alongside literature and politics, to explore the boundaries between real and imagined space. She argues that Ireland's intervention is directed towards epistemology and its power over history, culture and politics. This chapter underlines the tensions between conceived and lived space. Dária Jaremtchuk's chapter turns to Brazilian artist Anna Bella Geiger, who started working with maps in the 1970s across various media – a practice she continues today. Jaremtchuk, however, argues that Geiger demonstrated an interest in cartography and spatiality years prior, with her Visceral series in 1965, and then in 1968 with *Circumambulatio*, which explored bodily and cosmic space. Her study of Geiger's work reveals the artist's sustained thinking about space, but also highlights a turn towards more conceptual works that exercised the process of constructing spatial narratives about nation (Brazil), region (Latin America) and identity.

Part III, 'Sites and networks', explores the complex relationship among space, place and meaning, often figured through distant networks. The chapters share types of spatial reconfigurations that balance fiction with reality. This section addresses how spatial imagination was instrumental to reconceptualising conventional geographies and realising new spatial frameworks. In Chapter 7, Larisa Dryansky discusses Dennis Oppenheim's land-based works that juxtapose sites with incongruent cartographic representation as a form of spatial play. Reading this work through French philosopher Louis Marin's 1973 notion of a 'utopic non-place', Dryansky argues that Oppenheim's approach to site, space and place was one of friction that ultimately problematised ideologies of representation and indexicality.

The collective Psychophysiology Research Institute (PRI) in Japan is the subject of Reiko Tomii's chapter. Tomii posits their practice – in the form of performances, mail art and xeroxed books – as a space of information. This chapter considers how PRI conceptualised their production and its exhibition in spatio-temporal terms that in turn became a vehicle for overcoming the artists' distant locations. Tomii's contribution spotlights the networked conceptual space produced by PRI's mail art and reproductive technology as a sort of spatial imagination.

Ann Stephen considers the collaboration between Ian Burn and Mel Ramsden (IBMR) and their experiments with space, locality and meaning. Her chapter reveals how Burn's displacements, from Melbourne to London and then New York, informed IBMR's spatial awareness. In the example of their first joint work, *Soft-Tape* (1966), the sound environment was the start of a longer elaboration on how space – physical, geographical and contextual – is derived from perception.

The last part, 'Itineraries', follows the 'conceptual mapping' of several artists who position the subjective body at the centre of their spatial practices. Across three chapters, authors foreground works in which different scales of peripatetic movement are used to explore spatial relations or disrupt stable orderings. This section takes its inspiration from Setha Low's 'embodied space', a term to describe the 'experiential and material aspects of the body in space as well as the merging of body/space as a location that can communicate, transform and contest existing social structures'.[52] Along these lines, 'Itineraries' underscores the relational aspects that constitute both subject and space, with a focus on how the artist or viewer acts on conceptual and material spatial forms. In Chapter 10, Alena J. Williams addresses the tense relationship between abstract and experiential understandings of space through her analysis of Nancy Holt's conceptual work. Drawing on the artist's concrete poetry, photography, film and sculpture, she explores Holt's rich cartographic practice, which mapped the earth, the universe and the subjective body in relation to each other.

In Chapter 11, Inesa Brašiškė traces the mobility of André Cadere as a central feature of his practice but also as a larger meditation on the space of art in the 1960s. With site-specificity as an emerging backdrop, Cadere's work was ungrounded as it moved across sites and assumed its meaning from its circulation. Brašiškė argues that this implied a perspective on art's nomadic, networked space, defined as a web of moving people and places.

Artistic wanderings similarly inform the chapter by Eva Bentcheva and María José Martínez Sanchez. They present Hélio Oiticica's performative text from 1978 titled *Delirium Ambulatorium* as a basis for understanding a practice of conceptual mapping, involving the space and the body in a dialectical encounter. Bentcheva and Martínez Sanchez draw connections between Oiticica and the itinerant works by Rasheed Araeen in the late 1970s and Lee

Wen in the 1990s. They point to the resonances across artists' use of urban space to address geographies of identity, diaspora, race and politics.

The selection of case studies in this book are meant to reflect the diverse cartographies in conceptual practices emerging as of the 1960s and its many spatialities. In no way is this compilation exhaustive, but it serves to introduce the spatial as philosophically and politically signficant to conceptualism. Recalling Jennifer Licht, by 1968 'space [was] no longer an abstraction'.[53] As the conventional understandings of space shifted, artists also redefined space to include material, social and political dimensions. This book traces the ways artists sited such issues, including but not limited to the city, economics, transnationalism, the public sphere and colonisation. On these terms, space in art was not merely a static surface, the physical conditions of a place or a geographical location. Rather, artists offered new, alternative conceptualisations that broached theories of social space. Evident from this discussion is a reassessment of maps and cartography in conceptualism, as the book expands the definition of their forms and significance. This book elaborates on what Peter Wollen at first identified in conceptual art's mapping practices as 'resistance-mapping' that 'challeng[ed] the orthodoxies of power through an alternative cartography'.[54] It moves beyond this initial premise, however, to understand how such practices participate in space's perpetual production and transformation. As Setha Low contends, 'the social construction of space is the actual transformation of space – through people's social exchanges, memories, images and daily use of the material setting – into scenes and actions that convey symbolic meanings'.[55] This proposition opens up conceptualism and its works to the future – a world of relations and systems still to be determined.

Acknowledgements

I would like to acknowledge my colleagues Christian Berger, Camilla Sutherland and Simon Ferdinand who generously read versions of this introduction. I am most grateful for their insightful comments and inspiration. I would also like to thank the reviewers and series editors for their comments.

Notes

1 Doreen Massey, *For Space* (London: Sage, 2005), p. 106; Denis Cosgrove, *Mapping* (London: Reaktion Books, 1999), p. 1.

2 Roberta Smith, *4 Artists and the Map: Image/Process/Data/Place* (exh. cat.) (Lawrence, KS: Spencer Museum of Art, University of Kansas, 1981), pp. 6–7.

3 Peter Wollen, 'Mappings: Situationists and/or conceptualists', in Michael Newman and Jon Bird (eds), *Rewriting Conceptual Art* (London: Reaktion Books, 1999), p. 29.

4   Sophie Cras, 'Global conceptualism? Cartographies of conceptual art in pursuit of decentering', in Thomas DaCosta Kaufmann, Catherine Dossin and Béatrice Joyeux-Prunel (eds), *Circulations in the Global History of Art* (London: Routledge, 2015), p. 176.

5   Denis Cosgrove, 'Maps, mapping, modernity: Art and cartography in the twentieth century', *Imago Mundi* 57:1 (2005), 35–54. Other geographers have also identified conceptual art's prevalent use of maps; see Denis Wood, 'Map art', *Cartographic Perspectives* 53 (2006), 5–14.

6   Cras, 'Global conceptualism?', p. 176.

7   Wollen, 'Mappings', p. 29.

8   Liz Kotz, *Words to Be Looked At: Language in 1960s Art* (Cambridge, MA: MIT Press), p. 223.

9   Eve Meltzer, 'The dream of the information world', *Oxford Art Journal* 29:1 (2006), 115–35 (p. 124).

10   For more information on this history see Christopher Board, 'Cartographic communication', *Cartographica* 18:2 (1972), 42–78.

11   Patricia Norvell, 'Douglas Huebler: July 25, 1969', in Patricia Norvell, *Recording Conceptual Art: Early Interviews with Barry, Huebler, Kaltenbach, LeWitt, Morris, Oppenheim, Siegelaub, Smithson, and Weiner*, ed. Alexander Alberro and Patricia Norvell (Berkeley, CA: University of California Press, 2001), p. 138.

12   *Location* has also been referred to as *LAT. 31° 25´ N, LONG. 8° 41´ E.*

13   Mieko Shiomi, *Spatial Poems* (Osaka: M. Shiomi, 1976).

14   Midori Yoshimoto, *Into Performance: Japanese Women Artists in New York* (New Brunswick: Rutgers University Press, 2005), p. 166.

15   Norvell, 'Douglas Huebler: July 25, 1969', p. 150.

16   *Ibid.*, p. 151.

17   Jennifer Licht, *Spaces* (exh. cat.) (New York: Museum of Modern Art, 1970).

18   Pulsa consisted of seven individuals: Michael Cain, Patrick Clancy, William Crosby, William Duesing, Paul Fuge, Peter Kindlmann and David Rumsey.

19   For a history of this subject see Julie H. Reiss, *From Margin to Center: The Spaces of Installation Art* (Cambridge, MA: MIT Press, 2001); and Miwon Kwon, *One Place after Another: Site Specific Art and Locational Identity* (Cambridge, MA: MIT Press, 2004).

20   Licht, *Spaces*.

21   *Ibid.*

22   Excerpt in Lucy Lippard (ed.), *Six Years: The Dematerialization of the Art Object from 1966 to 1972* (Berkeley, CA: University of California Press, 1997), pp. 127–33.

23   Shows include *Xerox Book* (1968), copublished with Jack Wendler; *One Month (March 1–31)* (1969); and *July/August/September* (1969).

24   Patricia Norvell, 'Seth Siegelaub: April 17, 1969', in Alberro and Norvell, *Recording Conceptual Art*, p. 38.

25   Lippard, *Six Years*, p. 127.

26   Pamela M. Lee, *Chronophobia: On Time in Art from the 1960s* (Cambridge, MA: MIT Press, 2004).

27 Edward W. Soja, *Postmodern Geographies: The Reassertion of Space in Critical Social Theory* (London: Verso Books, 1989), p. 4.

28 This statement was made during an interview for *Hérodote* 1 (1976), as quoted in Michel Foucault, *Power/Knowledge: Selected Interviews and Other Writings 1972–77* (New York: Pantheon Books, 1980), p. 70.

29 Michel Foucault, 'Of other spaces', *Diacritics* 16:1 (1986), p. 22.

30 Henri Lefebvre, *The Production of Space*, trans. D. Nicholson-Smith (Oxford: Blackwell, 1991).

31 Marshall McLuhan, *Understanding Media: The Extensions of Man* (London: Routledge, 1964).

32 Anna Bella Geiger, 'Da artista', in *Gavetas de memória: Anna Bella Geiger* (São Paulo: Caixa Cultura, 2018).

33 Meltzer, 'The dream of the information world', p. 126.

34 *Ibid.*, 128–9.

35 Lefebvre, *The Production of Space*, p. 61.

36 *Ibid.*

37 Mark Gottdiener, 'A Marx for our time: Henri Lefebvre and the production of space', *Sociology Theory* 11:1 (1993), 129–34 (p. 132).

38 Thomas F. McDonough, 'Situationist space', *October* 67 (Winter 1994), 58–77; and Simon Sadler, *The Situationist City* (Cambridge, MA: MIT Press, 1998). For another perspective on this subject see Kristin Ross, 'Lefebvre on the Situationists: An Interview', *October* 79 (Winter 1997), 69–83.

39 Wollen, 'Mappings', p. 36.

40 Doreen Massey, *Space, Place, and Gender* (Minneapolis: University of Minnesota, 1994); and Gillian Rose, *Feminism and Geography: The Limits of Geographical Knowledge* (Minneapolis: University of Minnesota, 1993).

41 Massey, *For Space*, p. 9.

42 Larisa Dryansky, *Cartophotographies: De l'art conceptuel au Land Art* (Paris: Comité des travaux historiques et scientifiques/Institut national d'histoire de l'art, 2017).

43 The time span between 1966 and 1972 corresponds with Lucy Lippard's book *Six Years*, and has been echoed repeatedly in scholarly literature. The most recent example is Christian Berger (ed.), *Conceptualism and Materiality: Matters of Art and Politics* (Leiden: Brill, 2019).

44 Peter Osborne, *Anywhere or Not at All: Philosophy of Contemporary Art* (London: Verso, 2013); Alexander Alberro and Sabeth Buchmann (eds), *Art after Conceptual Art* (Cambridge, MA: MIT Press, 2006); Terry Smith, *One and Three Ideas: On Conceptual Art and Conceptualism* (Durham, NC: Duke University Press, 2017); Camiel van Winkel, *During the Exhibition the Gallery Will Be Closed: Contemporary Art and the Paradoxes of Conceptualism* (Amsterdam: Valiz, 2012); Nizan Shaked, *The Synthetic Proposition: Conceptualism and the Political Referent in Contemporary Art* (Manchester: Manchester University Press, 2017).

45 Andrew Wilson (ed.), *Conceptual Art in Britain 1969–1979* (London: Tate, 2016); and Catherine Morris and Vincent Bonin (eds), *Materializing Six Years: Lucy*

Lippard and the Emergence of Conceptual Art (exh. cat.) (Brooklyn, NY: Brooklyn Museum/MIT Press, 2012).

46 See for example Chapters 1 and 2 in this volume by Eve Kalyva and Alexander Alberro respectively. It should be noted that scholars of the postwar avant-garde in Latin America and eastern Europe continue to address the ways in which conceptualist practices were infused with politics as early as the mid-1960s.

47 Smith, *One and Five Ideas*.

48 Shaked, *The Synthetic Proposition*, p. 2.

49 Luis Camnitzer, Jane Farver and Rachel Weiss (eds), *Global Conceptualism: Points of Origin 1950s–1980s* (exh. cat.) (New York: Queens Museum of Art, 1999). It could be argued that Lucy Lippard and Kynaston McShine, to an extent, recognised this tendency in the 1960s, with *Six Years* and the exhibition *Information* as attempts to trace an international topography of conceptual art.

50 Zoe Sutherland, 'The world as gallery: Conceptualism and global neo-avant-garde', *New Left Review* 98 (2016), 81–111; Sophie Cras, 'Global Conceptualism?'.

51 Edward Said, *Culture and Imperialism* (New York: Knopf, 1993), p. 7.

52 Setha Low, *Spatializing Culture: The Ethnography of Space and Place* (London: Routledge, 2017), p. 94.

53 Licht, *Spaces*.

54 Wollen, 'Mappings', 45.

55 Setha Low, 'Introduction: Theorizing the city', in Setha Low (ed.), *Theorizing the City: The New Urban Anthropology Reader* (New Brunswick: Rutgers University Press, 1999), p. 112.

Part I
Social cartographies

Borderline: Mapping out (social) spaces of representation in conceptual art

Eve Kalyva

Conceptual art is easily recognised by its factual presentation. In the form of juxtaposed texts, images and diagrams, chance encounters, multiple prints and perishable materials, its appearance is free of adornment while its contents seek to stimulate one's brain as well as one's eyes. In the late 1960s and the early 1970s, many conceptual artists opted for such stylistic choices, considered 'radical' by many, in order to redefine the scope of art and to challenge the art establishment and the late modernist art discourse.

During the Cold War, Greenbergian formalism exalted the universality of aesthetic apprehension and the intuitive and unmediated signification of meaning in art. Artworks were deemed to be vehicles of expression of colour, form and feelings extricated from context and, unlike 'committed' art, bound to purity free of any social or political concerns. Equally, the modernist art critic defended the art gallery as a haven and a space of quiet contemplation set apart from everything else. Contesting such prevalent attitudes, many conceptual artists rejected the detachment of art from social reality and everyday life. Reverberating the interest of the historical avant-garde, they expanded their outlook beyond the institutions of art and employed a matter-of-fact presentation as a means to undermine the aestheticisation and commodification of art in favour of a critical view of the world.

Artists also turned their attention to the context of viewing. Context is important because very little makes sense outside it. This is true even for propositions of logic, as Ludwig Wittgenstein – favoured among conceptual artists – had argued in the 1920s.[1] Resources from analytic philosophy with regard to language, Marxist analyses of capitalist societies, and mathematical and cartographic systems were thus used to contest claims of art's apolitical universality. In addition, critically engaged artists explored the conditions of communication and how meaning and understanding are structured as processes in different institutional and social settings. Much to the dismay of the modernist art critic, their artistic practice would demonstrate that interpretation is always involved in the apprehension of art, and interpretation is never neutral.

Conceptual art shifted the scope of art in a shifting world. Artists used methodologies and references beyond the purview of the art world to challenge the aesthetic premises and institutional practices of modernism and to advance a critical view of reality. Such radical considerations were on a par with wider changes. In the art world, conceptual art pushed to the limits the inherent inability of late modernism to account for a plurality of artistic forms based on anything other than taste, and revealed how its premises were conservative, hegemonic and politically entrenched.[2] Beyond the art world, the particular historical time of conceptual art formed a turning point in western societies and global politics.

The 1960s and 1970s were a time of colour television, consumerism, Cold War propaganda, military dictatorships and the space race – as well as a time of civil rights and anti-war movements and the liberation of the so-called 'Third' World. In this context, interest in science, the media and information was also advanced through art, while the advent of technology facilitated the use of photographic and video cameras. Marshall McLuhan's 1964 book *Understanding Media* and his maxim 'the medium is the message' became very popular,[3] and exhibitions such as *Cybernetic Serendipity: The Computer and the Arts* (Institute of Contemporary Art, London (ICA), 1968), *The Machine as Seen at the End of the Mechanical Age* (Museum of Modern Art, New York (MoMA), 1969) and *Information* (MoMA, 1970) marked a new age for art. This last survey exhibition presented more than 150 artists and placed conceptual art at the endpoint of American art, after minimalism and abstract expressionism.

The discussion that follows, therefore, is conditional on different processes: the increasing inability of modernist discourse to contain the category of art in a rapidly changing world based on internalised aesthetic pursuits, the reconsideration of neutrality and universality by philosophy and communication studies, and revolutions and political upheaval around the globe. Lying at the crux of world politics, spatial ordering and mapping drew critical interest.

The cartographic works of Art & Language's *Map of an Area of Dimensions 12″ × 12″* (1967) and *Map to Not Indicate* (1967), David Lamelas's film *A Study of Relationships between Inner and Outer Space* (1969) and Juan Carlos Romero's *4,000,000 m² de la ciudad de Buenos Aires* (*4,000,000 m² of the City of Buenos Aires*; 1970) have an investigatory interest beyond the scope of art. They experiment with reference systems that are better defined, scientific or modular in relation to the predominant aesthetic theories of the time, and use cartography and different conceptualisations of framing to advance a critical enquiry beyond aesthetic apprehension. Through binary juxtapositions such as inside/outside and art/non-art, they link art with the world and investigate how space – specifically social space – is structured, understood and experienced.

They do so by negotiating ideas about representation and, more crucially, by implicating the way they are viewed. Putting forward a modular experience, they set themselves as *part* of the world and turn critical attention towards it.

Enquiring into the category of art, the framing of the artwork and our experience of it implicates both perception and classification. And in both cases, borders are important. They mark and define the limits of something and, by doing so, also mark and define how that something is understood. This is clearly explored in the works of Art & Language, Lamelas and Romero, negotiating different systems of reference, representation and interpretation of art as much as of the world. Specifically, these works generate a critical dialogue that positions the artist and the viewer in relation to physical, institutional, social and discursive environments.

An important question follows. Is it possible for artworks that scrutinise their given context to remain meaningful and critical elsewhere? To put it differently, what can we still learn from conceptual art, fifty years later? If conceptual art circulated through international networks because of its reproducible, 'dematerialised' forms, transregionality is now a key characteristic of contemporary art. One must therefore consider the effects of dislocation and the limits of critique – and how the latter can exceed the locality of the individual artworks that carry it forward and become relevant elsewhere. To identify how conceptual artworks respond to this predicament is to locate one of the contributions of conceptual art today.

The power to name

One of the main interests of Art & Language is to expose and challenge the interpretive contexts of art.[4] The group produces works that combine visual and textual elements, the latter often taking substantial form (for example essays and books), and present them in varying configurations. By blurring the limits between the work of art proper, its documentation, its description and its different versions, Art & Language aim to question how art is defined, classified and understood. A related interest is how the experience of art becomes normalised. To demonstrate and contest this process, the group manipulates the language that art critics use to talk about art. Drawing resources from analytic philosophy and Marxism, they develop a self-reflective practice of analysis carried forward by their works, while at the same time questioning their validity *as* artworks. This analytic approach not only negotiates the object in the context from which it emerges, but moreover offers an analysis of that context and our dispositions towards it.

Map of an Area of Dimensions 12″ × 12″ Indicating 2,304 ¼″ Squares (Map of Itself) (Atkinson and Baldwin, 1967; see Figure 1.1) was produced using letterpress, a technique of professional printing but also a craft, since it was done

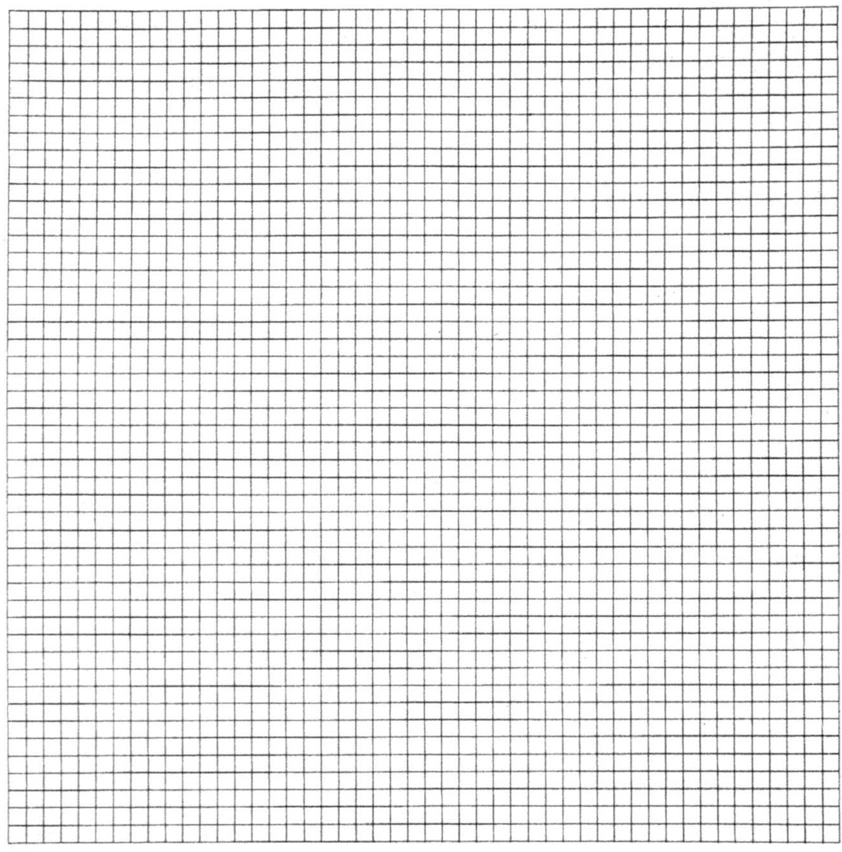

Map of an area of dimensions 12″ × 12″ indicating 2,304 ¼″ squares

1.1   Art & Language (Terry Atkinson and Michael Baldwin), *Map of an Area of Dimensions 12″× 12″ Indicating 2,304 ¼″ Squares*, 1967. Letterpress, composition: 31.6 cm × 30.5 cm; sheet: 36.8 cm × 45.7 cm.

by hand. The print consists of a dense grid of ¼-inch squares, overall sized 12 × 12 inches, and a sentence below it that provides the grid's exact description. This sentence forms the work's title, along with the added qualification 'Map of Itself'. In an art world that celebrated the intuitive understanding of art, the unique ability of the artist-genius to somehow channel his (in the majority of cases) unmediated intention into form and the inherent capacity of the viewer to somehow 'get it', Art & Language's map is a pun.

Seemingly forthcoming about its nature and artistic intent because of its title, *Map of an Area* should leave no doubt when it comes to its apprehension as precisely that. At the same time, however, the very presence of this description raises questions regarding the need for explanations. Does it tell us enough about the work? This question goes a long way in displacing the modernist premise of the 'self-evidence' of art, whether that concerns its apprehension or its aesthetic value. To be exact, the blunt self-referentiality of Art & Language's map pushes the modernist appeal to self-evidence to a tautological extreme. Recalling Wittgenstein, tautologies are meaningless, refer only to themselves and tell us nothing about the world.[5]

On a 1:1 scale, and self-described as a map of such an area, the work stands as a map of itself. Characteristically, it both demonstrates its nature and tells us that it does so. Generally speaking, self-referentiality does not cause a problem, if we recall minimalist art. However, linguistic assertion as part of an artwork does. This is not only because late modernism defended the capacity of art to communicate autonomously. Even if we accept the presence of language in an expanded field of *visual* art, the literality of Art & Language's map makes us wonder about the purpose of such a copious assertion. True, doubt rises in the mind of the viewer when faced with a new venture in art. Yet, more than doubt, this work evokes a sense of irony. To understand it, let us compare it to another example where the juxtaposition of what we see and what we read raises an eyebrow.

In 1929, René Magritte produced the painting *La trahison des images* (*The Treachery of Images*), which featured a pipe and, underneath it, a sentence reading 'This is not a pipe.' According to Michel Foucault, who was in conversation with the artist, the claim of the work is true, and *that* is problematic.[6] Its visual part illustrates a pipe, which is therefore not the real thing, while its textual counterpart confirms that what we see is *not* a pipe. This goes against the general understanding that figurative art is able to *show* reality. Furthermore, this dissonance creates distance between the pipe as the real object, the pipe as an image and the pipe as the referent of a word. At the same time, Magritte's painting shows how we become accustomed to conflating this distance and make things stand in for other things.

This 'treacherous' painting introduces language into the realm of the plastic arts – traditionally safeguarded as a realm of evocation attuned to the senses beyond language or logic – in order to destabilise it. At the same time, it destabilises language. For Foucault, Magritte's painting reverses the use of the calligram (a fashionable – at the time – form of experimental annotation that resembled the visual characteristics of its referent). Indeed, while calligrams were used to visualise and enhance meaning as in the textbook example of Guillaume Apollinaire's poem 'La colombe poignardée et le jet d'eau' (1918), we can argue that Magritte uses script here to *contest* literacy.

If Magritte's painting demonstrates how the object, its picture and its description become aligned in our process of understanding but are different in terms of ontology and unstable in terms of pragmatics, Art & Language's grid goes a step further. It shows that the art object still cannot be equated with the real thing and that literacy, visual or textual, is dubious even when what we see and what we read are in agreement and true.

Maps resolve the relationship between representation and reality based on function, and are bound to a matrix of transformation and convention that concerns scale, data accuracy, legibility, design, hierarchical organisation, navigation and coordination, among other things. In the case of Art & Language's map, the object we see *is* technically a map of what its description tells us it is, and this textual description is functionally embedded in the work as its title. Just the same, something raises suspicion, affecting the pleasure we might get from viewing this rigid work and causing trouble. By counterpoising a combination of visual and textual description against the presumed self-evident aesthetic qualities of art as proclaimed by the modernist art critic, *Map of an Area* orchestrates the ever-present anxiety behind the art-critical rhetoric. Accurate as a map, albeit lacking any other use value, it asks 'Can what we are looking at still be called art and, if so, by whom?'.

The borderline of authority is more interesting to navigate than the nature of ontology. To put it plainly, asking *how* something is art is more constructive than asking *why* something is art. Art & Language's map work draws attention to how the art world functions as a frame of reference and interpretation of art; this frame supersedes any modes of representation, denotation and linguistic assertion that artists or the public may command. It demonstrates that even when fealty to representation is bypassed and an artwork becomes self-referring and tautological, it is still not autonomous or self-evident *as* art but requires external validation to be understood as such.

This line of enquiry regarding intrinsic qualities, representation, function and validation is further explored in Art & Language's *Map to Not Indicate* (Atkinson and Baldwin, 1967; see Figure 1.2). This work also combines a diagram and a factual title; however, rather than offering the same information through different means, the two elements complement each other. The diagram shows the outlines of two non-bordering US states (Iowa and Kentucky) that are not mentioned in the text-title that runs below it, and the text-title lists locations that are not depicted in the diagram above it. These span Canada, the eastern and southern USA and the Gulf of Mexico, and include, without particular order or sense, areas such as Lake of the Woods, the Straits of Florida, Cuba, the Atlantic Ocean and the whimsical 'eastern borders of North Dakota'.[7] According to the Tate, which owns the work, *Map to Not Indicate* plays with the conventions of marking while the states of Iowa and Kentucky lose their geographic relevance and float like islands, metaphorically cast adrift from their cartographic moorings.[8] The evocation of a sense of drifting is one reaction to this work, but it is a sense that dissolves quickly enough once the viewer juxtaposes what she sees with what she reads. With a lot of empty space on the

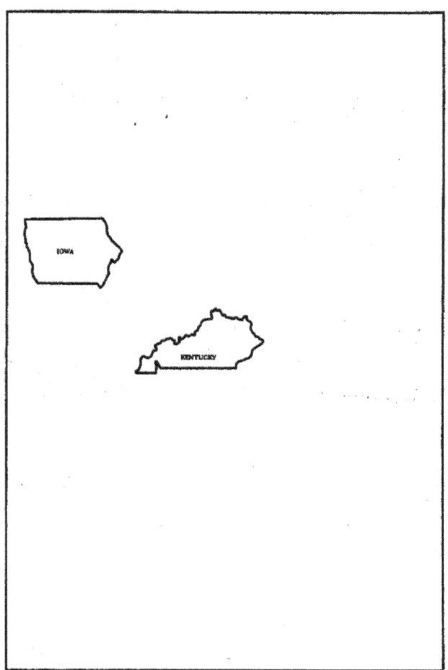

Map to not indicate : CANADA, JAMES BAY, ONTARIO, QUEBEC, ST. LAWRENCE RIVER, NEW BRUNSWICK, MANITOBA, AKIMISKI ISLAND, LAKE WINNIPEG, LAKE OF THE WOODS, LAKE NIPIGON, LAKE SUPERIOR, LAKE HURON, LAKE MICHIGAN, LAKE ONTARIO, LAKE ERIE, MAINE, NEW HAMPSHIRE, MASSACHUSETTS, VERMONT, CONNECTICUT, RHODE ISLAND, NEW YORK, NEW JERSEY, PENNSYLVANIA, DELAWARE, MARYLAND, WEST VIRGINIA, VIRGINIA, OHIO, MICHIGAN, WISCONSIN, MINNESOTA, EASTERN BORDERS OF NORTH DAKOTA, SOUTH DAKOTA, NEBRASKA, KANSAS, OKLAHOMA, TEXAS, MISSOURI, ILLINOIS, INDIANA, TENNESSEE, ARKANSAS, LOUISIANA, MISSISSIPPI, ALABAMA, GEORGIA, NORTH CAROLINA, SOUTH CAROL- INA, FLORIDA, CUBA, BAHAMAS, ATLANTIC OCEAN, ANDROS ISLANDS, GULF OF MEXICO, STRAITS OF FLORIDA.

Art & Language (Terry Atkinson and Michael Baldwin), *Map to Not Indicate*, 1967.   **1.2**
Linotype on paper, 50.8 cm × 62.9 cm.

one hand, and a dense and dull passage on the other, one is left to wonder what else this map may be up to.

Positioning and reference are important in correlating a place with its diagrammatic representation. If considered as a map, *Map to Not Indicate* observes reference but there is no logic to its organisation. The selection of locations seems random and lacks correlation between parts, which leaves the work void of a map's internal logic. Its contents may be factual and irre- futable, but the object is utterly pointless as a map. And then there is the empty space.

In his seminal book *The Production of Space* published in 1974, Henri Lefebvre demonstrates how space does not simply exist but is produced in ideological, experiential and social terms.[9] This provided the conceptual framework for practices of critical and operative cartography that aimed at revealing and evaluating how maps construct realities. Today, there is no doubt that maps affect the experience of space itself, as well as the relationships that are shaped by and articulated through that space.

Based on this tradition, Roger Pàez i Blanch outlines a typology of maps according to how they deploy empty space.[10] This includes maps that are absurd, trivial and paradoxical. An absurd map obstructs the dominant definition of space, since it is laden with meaninglessness and floating signifiers. A trivial map lacks content and upsets the basic logic of conventional mapping as a regulatory mechanism qualified by the principles, after Lefebvre, of homogeneity, fragmentation and hierarchisation. A paradoxical map cancels out representational space by collapsing the distance between the map and its depicted territory.

Pàez i Blanch classifies Art & Language's *Map to Not Indicate* as an absurd map and *Map of an Area* as a trivial map. The former is explicit about what it does not represent, highlighting the fact that all maps are incomplete since they only show certain aspects of reality. The latter is an exercise in self-referential tautology that is nonsensical and ironic in the fashion of Lewis Carroll's blank sea map in his poem 'The Hunting of the Snark' (1876). Since *Map of an Area* is on a 1:1 scale, we could add that it is also a paradoxical map, implicating a map's relation to reality and, as Pàez i Blanch has defined it, pointing out the impossibility of any unmediated understanding of the world.

Art & Language's maps become means of analysis and a pretext, if you like, to raise questions and reveal paradoxes regarding the limits of the artwork, authority and the power to name. By bringing mapping into the art world, their works recast the enquiry into the limits of representation and the relation between art and the world as a matter of institutional conditioning. More than a tautological exercise in ontology, their maps toy with conceptualisations of indication, identification, classification and description. To be certain, this frustrates the late modernist art critic who strove to defend the autonomy of a fast-changing artistic production in a fast-changing world while fending off the looming danger of politically committed art.

This is one way to carry forward an institutional and an ideological critique. In its historical context, conceptual art was informed by Marxist dialectics and the critique of capitalism and its institutions, including from anti-imperialist and feminist perspectives. By the end of the 1970s, critics and artists alike scrutinised the structuration of meaning and the premises of the (male) gaze. They demonstrated that interpretation is not neutral but is determined by ideology and codified across different registers (cf. Barthes, Berger, Sontag, Rosler and Kruger). This interrogation of the protocols of interpretation extended from the hierarchies of the gaze to social and spatial hierarchies, drawing attention to mapping as a practice that both articulates world order and alleges the power to assert it. This is in line with the critical programme of conceptual art to unmask and reject the ideological premises of late modernism. After all, modernist art during the Cold War became a vehicle of right-wing political agendas and a means of cultural imperialism and colonisation.[11]

Within the art world of the late 1960s and beyond, empty space can bear different meanings: unknowable, uncharted, neutral, full of possibilities, omissions and deletions, or ready to be populated by power structures. The contrast between what is shown and what is left out, as found in Art & Language's maps, calls out the malleable gaps in the representation of reality by artistic practices as well as by social and political ones.

Relationships of space

In 1966, the right-wing military in Argentina seized power and installed a dictatorship that proclaimed itself as the 'Argentine Revolution'. David Lamelas (b. 1946) came to the UK from Argentina in 1968 after exhibiting at the Venice Biennale the same year, and studied sculpture at St Martin's College, London on a British Council scholarship. The college was one of the hotspots of conceptual art in the country, and it was attended by artists such as Richard Long, John Hilliard, Barry Flanagan and Gilbert & George. Art & Language members Harold Hurrell and Charles Harrison were also affiliated with St Martin's. Anthony Caro gave evening classes, and experimentation was the order of the day.

A Study of Relationships between Inner and Outer Space (1969) is Lamelas's first film and a typical example of the interest in exploring artistic practice beyond the physical and institutional confines of the gallery space. Stills from the film can be seen in Figure 1.3. Shot on black-and-white 16 mm film, *A Study* lasts twenty-four minutes and is divided in two parts,

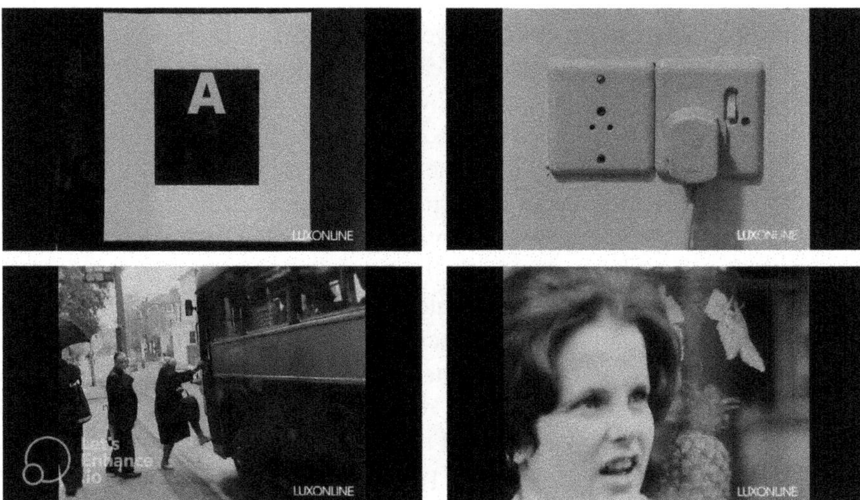

Video stills from David Lamelas, *A Study of the Relationships between Inner and Outer Space*, 1969. 24 minutes, black and white, Opt., 4:3, 16 mm film.   **1.3**

defined by the film as 'phases'. It combines voiceover, silent shots, shots from everyday city life and interviews.

Phase A, 'Inner space at the Camden Art Centre', examines the location where the film was first exhibited. It relays information about the physical dimensions of one of the venue's rooms (perhaps the room where the film would be shown), as well as illumination and noise levels. Monotonous and uninspiring, the camera traces the length of a white wall corner from floor to ceiling, zooms out from focusing on a ventilation grid and pauses over electrical wall plugs and light fixtures. It is matched by a factual voiceover.

Information is also given about the activities that take place inside the gallery, such as cleaning, answering the phone and handing out programmes. Gallery staff explain their tasks, which include showing others how to use the projector in preparation for the 'environment show'. This exhibition, *Environmental Reversal* (26 June–27 July 1969), was the exhibition for which Lamelas made the film. Regarding visitors, activities include walking and sitting, presumably to look at the art. Throughout the film, the narration is accompanied by visual confirmation.

Phase B, 'Outer space of London', focuses on the city and presents information about its layout, means of communication, transportation, population distribution and climate morphology. Structurally, each segment begins with a map and presentation of relevant information, and continues with explanatory city shots. The voiceover remains factual and is keen on statistics. We learn about the city's urban rings, railway stations, airports, motorways, tube network and bus lines; the number of dailies that London 'consumes'; and that there are also a radio station, three television channels and two mail deliveries per day. Street posters 'are one of the main ways of advertising in the public areas', the voiceover explains, and communication can also carried out using public telephone kiosks.

Prepared and shown during NASA's Apollo missions, the film concludes with street interviews about the first moon landing. Questions include whether the interviewees are excited about the event, what they think will be found there and whether they would be surprised to hear that the first man on the moon were black or Chinese. The demographics of those asked vary in terms of age, class and gender, and so do their responses. A young woman with plain long hair argues that the money would be better spent on real problems on earth, and a boy in school uniform describes the landing as a stepping-stone on the way to outer space and finding planets to inhabit, such as Mars. When asked about race, a white, middle-class man retorts that he would not be surprised if the first man on the moon was black ('negro' in the original), whereas a white, smartly dressed woman grins at the possibility of the first man there being Chinese (see Figure 1.3).

The relationships between inner and outer space that the film's title indicates unfold across different levels. The viewer watches the film inside the space it describes, at least for its debut screening at Camden, and would have traversed the city the film describes to arrive there. The viewer would also be familiar with much of the information provided, especially regarding the space race. Even if the exact facts and figures the film relays are unknown, or if opinions differ, direct experience makes Lamelas's film more relatable than Art & Language's maps.

The interest in how facts are structured and their matter-of-fact presentation is typical of conceptual art and in clear contrast to the aesthetic demands placed on art by late modernist art discourse. That said, the London audiences were becoming accustomed to diversity. Private galleries such as Lisson and Nigel Greenwood began representing conceptual artists, and publicly funded art venues were given leeway for experimentation – for example *Cybernetic Serendipity* (1968), *When Attitudes Become Form* (1969) and Ian Breakwell's *Unword 2* (1969) at the ICA. For Camden's *Environmental Reversal* in the same year, the influential art critic Guy Brett noted in his exhibition review for *The Times*: 'What Alice dreamed and the Surrealists depicted is given an environmental scale of illusion.'[12] Artworks on display included mirror installations by the Artist Placement Group; sounds of breathing, laughing and applause by Keith Arnatt; and nylon bubbles by the Eventstructure Research Group.

If conceptual art's blunt presentation has been described as anti-aesthetic, this should be understood as an attempt to oppose the value system of late modernism. According to Peter Osborne, 'strong' conceptual art practices were characterised by a particular anti-aesthetic *desire*; while overall they failed to eliminate the aesthetic as a necessary component of the artwork, they still showed that it was radically insufficient.[13] This insufficiency was made evident partly because of the new communicative demands that art had to meet in an increasingly complex world, and partly because of the institutional and social critique that many conceptual artists sought to advance through their practice.

This is not to say that artists made no stylistic choices no matter how interested they were in prioritising the non-aesthetic aspects of their artworks, nor that those stylistic choices – even when the artists who made them were disinterested in them – had no effect. This is equally true for factual presentations.

In the case of Art & Language, factuality is used instrumentally to the point of absurdity. In Lamelas's film, narration is so artificial that it becomes almost comical. Consider, for example, the observations that the green bus line disperses and collects people from the suburbs, and that telephones are used to place overseas calls and dictate telegrams but also to share information about the weather. Qualifying data in such ways creates the sense that something is being satirised. This can be the carefree way of living in capitalist societies – which can moreover be contrasted with the grim reality of the dictatorial regime in Argentina that Lamelas left behind – or, more broadly, how the experience of life in metropolitan centres becomes normalised.

The last section of *A Study* shifts perspective. It engages the actuality of the space race – a facet of the Cold War that viewers would most probably be familiar with – but instead of a factual presentation of information it shows the attitudes and opinions of different social groups. By doing so, it establishes a connection with its audience at a second level. Apart from tapping into personal experience and referencing the site of its display where the viewer is located (Phase A), the film turns to everyday life, articulates views that its audiences might share and maps socio-political developments that would probably be of concern (Phase B). This combination of factual information and opinion gives Lamelas's film a sense of exploration. Thus, *A Study* can be understood as creating a lens to look at reality; by doing so, it creates a space of representation that, turning away from purely aesthetic interests, engages lived experience.

Notwithstanding, it is not clear where the work locates itself or the artist in relation to the spaces it charts, or indeed the institutions that frame it, either within or beyond the art world. According to Lefebvre, the under-pinning of social relations is spatial.[14] In producing social relations, people also produce social space. At the same time, space is also produced by other processes such as financial activities and property relations, as well as imagination and ideas.

A Study touches on the interconnection of (social) space and (social) relations; yet its own participation in this process remains obscured, as if the choice of which facts to present is also factual. True, the film brings the outdoors inside the art gallery and, by starting off with the exhibition room and expanding outwards, sets that art gallery as a constituent of a bigger frame of reference. However, this movement relies on the viewer to correlate across the city, the gallery room and the film based on his or her own experience of them. Lacking an *inner* logic connecting its different perspectives, the film *jumps* from one site to the other – a jump that is tellingly formalised by a blank shot dividing the film's two phases, inner and outer space. Behind these gaps lies the subjective interest of the artist in bringing these perspectives together for the viewer to associate.

By allowing subjectivity to enter the picture despite its neutral appearance, Lamelas's film echoes the genius of the artist to offer a privileged view on the world as the modernists would have it. Presenting no matrix of operation, the film's choice of city locations and relayed information appears random. More to the point, there is no indication of how any set of relationships develops across these different sites and affects the artwork itself. The film may draw parallels across how people look at art, consume products and replicate views about the world. Yet it does not offer any systematic or critical way to correlate sites and behaviours. Nor does it address how the art gallery, as an additional space of representation, might conceal or ignore social reality.

Other works by Lamelas explore the relationships across the outside and the inside (i.e. of the space of art). His installation *Office of Information about the Vietnam War at Three Levels: The Visual Image, Text and Audio* (1968) was presented at the turbulent 1968 Venice Biennale, which was boycotted as fascist and capitalist by protesting students and intellectuals. It consisted of a mock set-up of an office – complete with a desk, a chair and other furniture designed by the Italian manufacturer Olivetti. A woman would enter the set and read out live transmissions about the Vietnam War that were received through a telex machine. In her absence, visitors could pick up headsets and hear recordings of news reports in several languages.

This work contrasts reality with the institutional setting of art – controlled, celebrated and upheld as a safe haven in a turbulent world. While structurally less composite than *A Study* and more clearly touching on socio-political context, is this kind of juxtaposition (i.e. through a telex machine, on a stage etc.) enough to incite viewers to reflect on wider issues, such as the alienation of art and themselves from the world? To determine this, we must identify the turning point when the critical enquiry of an artwork stops confronting its audiences and becomes an engaging intellectual exercise that nonetheless remains benign in relation to one's life choices.

If an artwork fails to expose how art becomes institutionalised, co-opted and neutralised, or if it fails to address responsibility and evoke a sense of threat for the purported neutrality of the status quo, it remains prone to elitism and to the risk of enabling, rather than destabilising, the habit of passively consuming ideas, news and worldviews. To avoid this pitfall, an artwork that juxtaposes different sites should also make it clear how these interconnect physically, behaviourally and discursively, and relate this process to its own mode of production. This is what the last case study attempts to do.

Practices of exclusion

Juan Carlos Romero (1931–2017) was an Argentine conceptual artist working with experimental printmaking and collage. His works often take the form of serial installations, and combine photographs, maps and newspaper clippings. Crucially, they engage a socio-political reality that was marked by the last two Argentine civic-military dictatorships of 1966–73 and 1976–83.

As part of Arte Gráfico Grupo Buenos Aires (Graphic Art Buenos Aires Group), active between 1970 and 1975, Romero gave printmaking demonstrations and workshops in public spaces, cultural centres and factories.[15] In the context of a military dictatorship, learning how to design and print posters and pamphlets, let alone in public, had political affordances.

Through his artistic practice, Romero sought to raise awareness regarding the violence, oppression and injustice he saw in his everyday life. He advocated for art beyond the elitist art institutions as an accessible means of expression and critical engagement with the world, and created works that incite viewers to reflect on their relationship with art, and art's social responsibility.

Romero's *4,000,000 m² de la ciudad de Buenos Aires* (*4,000,000 m² of the City of Buenos Aires*) (1970; see Figure 1.4) places art and the viewer vis-à-vis social reality. It was presented at the I Certamen Nacional de Investigaciones Visuales (First National Contest of Visual Investigations) at the Museum of Fine Art, Buenos Aires, in 1970 during the dictatorship of Lieutenant General Juan Carlos Onganía, which Lamelas left behind. The following year, *4,000,000 m²* was shown at the Camden Arts Centre in London.

The work consists of the blueprint of the museum floor where it was first shown, a city map and eight photographs. Its format demonstrates one way – in this case, geometrical – through which social space, its experience and its meaning become structured. Starting from inside the museum room and progressively spreading over the city, *4,000,000 m²* maps an expanding space while engaging the attitudes that its corresponding sites produce. Meanwhile, the work takes active part in this process. In more detail, the museum blueprint that *4,000,000 m²* includes is superimposed with two concentric squares,

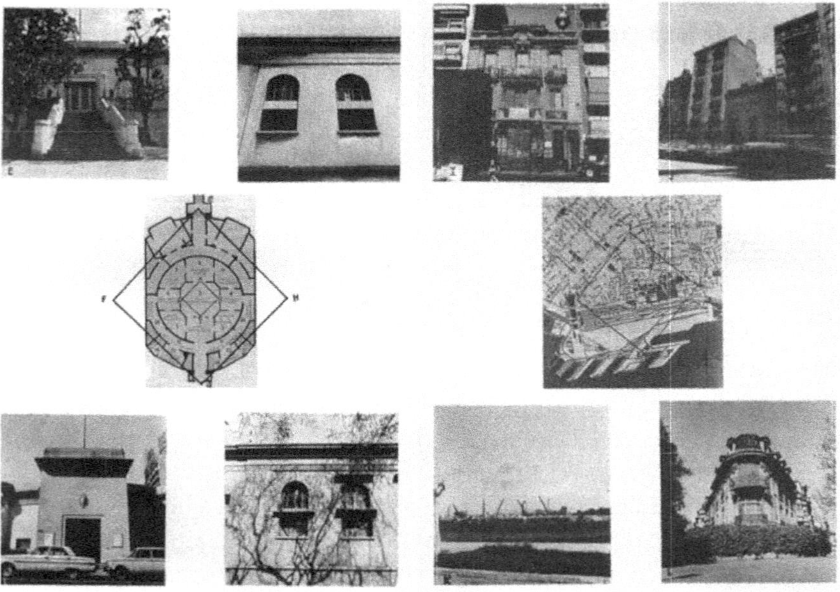

1.4   Juan Carlos Romero, *4,000,000 m² de la ciudad de Buenos Aires* (*4,000,000 m² of the City of Buenos Aires*), 1970. Text and ten photographs, 60 cm × 50 cm each.

ABCD and EFGH. The first square marks the museum room where the work was exhibited, and its points indicate the room's exits. Apart from this blueprint being exhibited on the wall as part of the artwork, it is possible that the letters ABCD were also marked on the floor of the room.[16] The second blueprint square, EFGH, encompasses the whole museum floor, and two of its points, E and G, indicate the museum's entrances. It is accompanied by four photographs of the museum's exterior, including the entrances marked E and G.

Next to this blueprint and its photographs is a city map. The map is superimposed with a third square, IJKL, and likewise accompanied by photographs from the square's corresponding points. These include a shopping mall and the port area. Apart from the arts, consumerism and fashion were high on the agenda of the military regime, which deployed a rhetoric of internationalisation, order, progress and economic growth to mask its murderous tactics and reactionary, neoliberal policies (such as the privatisation of public services and natural resources; the devaluation of wages; and the suspension of labour rights, including the right to strike). For its part, the port area, controlled by the armed forces, was infamous for its clandestine detention centres and the 'death planes' from which political prisoners were thrown alive into the waters of the La Plata River. There were more than 500 such illegal detention centres in Argentina, and some 30,000 people remain missing to this day, without counting the death toll caused by the armed conflict.

In a text accompanying *4,000,000 m²*, Romero characterised the work as a system consisting of semi-fixed parts such as streets, blocks, buildings and trees, and of mobile parts such as people, animals, water, telephone communications, radio, television, cars and incineration.[17] He moreover identified the small square inside the museum room, ABCD, as *generador* ('generator'), and the large square over the city, IJKL, as *cierre total* ('complete closure'). Through these concentric squares, the work covers a city area of 4,000,000 m², as its factual title informs us. At the same time, it encompasses multiple elements and attitudes that take place within those boundaries; yet, as Romero notes, from all the components of the system defined by the work, only people can become aware of it.

The works discussed in this chapter negotiate space at different degrees of proximity. Romero's ensemble combines a map matrix that generates a space representative of reality like Art & Language's maps, and images from the city in order to engage that reality like Lamelas's film. More clearly than these works however, Romero's *4,000,000 m²* spells out the logic of its organisation and how its constituent parts correlate. Its clearly marked squares denote physical and conceptual boundaries such as the architectural space of the art museum, the city streets, the illusion of economic progress that the civic-military dictatorship cultivated and the dreaded areas that the armed forces controlled. This structural articulation guides the viewer's attention to the processes that frame what lies inside and outside, as well as to how these spaces are defined and understood. At the same time, it enables the work to exceed its own limits and prompt a mode of critical reflection that can be applied by the viewer elsewhere.

By bringing the outside into dialogue with the inside, the work creates tension and a sense of threat. The viewer looking at the work is shown the four exits from the room in which she stands, the entrances of the museum she has visited and the high walls that protect it; but she is also shown the city, whose inhabitants may be oblivious to the grim and violent reality they live in. To enhance this sense of threat, or even compliance and cover-up, none of the work's photographs show people – the only human presence is that of the beholder. Indeed, and as Romero noted, it is not the city's architectural or other urban features that are the point of interest here, but the behaviours of those populating the city and whether they can become aware of the impact of their behaviours.[18]

Deriving from the work's three squares, a frame of reference is created at three levels: the viewer in relation to art, the art institution in relation to the city, and art in relation to everyday life. This is another way that an artwork can combine institutional and socio-political critique. Romero's *4,000,000 m²* acts as a generator not only of space but also of relationships in order to criticise the purported autonomy of art, the neutrality of its institutions and social reality. Rather than featuring distinct sites (the room of direct experience, the museum and the world), the symmetry of the concentric squares and the juxtaposition of the images of walls but also of windows, doorways and streets support the conceptualisation of a space that is continuous but becomes fragmented through practices of exclusion.

To conclude, the matrix composition of *4,000,000 m²* helps visualise an expansive space that runs across the museum and the city while drawing attention to how that space is experienced in fragmented and disassociated ways. Space is generated not only geometrically as a site, but also as an experiential and social space populated by the people who move across it, enjoy it or become deprived of it – hence the artist's references, in the text that accompanied this work, to water, animals, incineration and cars. These bring to mind the plundering of natural resources, the brutality of the army and the police, the horror of torture and the regime's punitive measures. As for cars, they could refer to a provocative lifestyle at a time of impoverishment and hunger, as well as to the fact that one could spot the agents of the military regime by their cars. Indeed, one of the work's photographs shows such vehicles parked outside the museum's entrance. Likewise, the reference to telecommunications is not coincidental. At the time, Romero worked for the State telephone company (where he was also a leading trade unionist), and the public would no doubt have first-hand, everyday experience of censorship and propaganda.

In the same critical vein as *4,000,000 m²*, Romero's cartographic *Segmento de linea recta* (*Straight Line Segment*; 1972) directly links via a straight line the National Telecommunications Company; the Buenos Aires Museum of Modern Art; the Centro de Arte y Comunicación (Centre of Art and Communication; CAYC), where Romero would regularly exhibit; and the ship *Granaderos*, then an illegal clandestine detention centre moored at the North Dock. As with the squares of *4,000,000 m²*, the use of a line here can prompt the viewer to consider the different aspects of social reality she comes across when traversing the city in daily life.

To address propaganda and the banalisation of violence more concretely, Romero utilised press clippings. His solo exhibition *Violencia* (*Violence*) took place at CAYC in April 1973. After the Peronist candidates won the elections in March, the dictatorship ended in May and Juan Perón returned from exile in June; this democratic interlude, however, was too short, and a new dictatorship soon engulfed the country. Romero's exhibition at CAYC was divided into three parts across the centre's three floors. In the first, posters containing the word 'violence' covered the exhibition room from floor to ceiling and across it. The second section presented poems and texts on violence from various philosophical, political and religious sources. Finally, the exhibition presented gruesome images and collages from the tabloid *Así*, notorious for sensationalising the socio-political repression that was rampant across the country.

Romero's works bring what would lie outside the art world inside the gallery room and back out again, exposing the concealment (and, in the case of the media, the banalisation) of the torture, murder and disappearance of thousands of people by the military regime. His cartographic works self-referentially implicate themselves by addressing both the place and the manner in which they are viewed. His silent and empty views of Buenos Aires are very different from Lamelas's busy London and more relatable than Art & Language's abstracted maps. In lieu of a factual but often tangential or ad hoc mapping, Romero's works deploy the formal logic of a mathematical formula. This supports a systematic generation of conceptual, experiential and ideological spaces beyond the work's locus.

Continuity is important. Rather than jumping across the inside and outside of the art gallery, in and out of art and from representation to a grim reality, Romero's cartographic work identifies a pattern that is not subjective and that can be applied beyond its own body. Moreover, the low complexity of its easily reproduced geometry demystifies the function of its carrier, the artwork. The latter is not, therefore, autonomous. While the work replicates how social spaces are produced and how elements are transferred across them, and while these spaces include the artwork itself (its composition, reception and function), the work only forms one instance of a view of the world. In this way, *4,000,000 m²* rejects the tendency to hide away in art as a privileged site detached from social reality, and implicates the responsibility of the viewer, whose behaviour connects and defines the different sites that the work maps. While these sites are unequal in power and potential, their boundaries are not absolute. Generating momentum through a simple correlation, the work's critical enquiry points outwards where action, and real change, can happen.

A dislocation of critique?

Borders mark and define the limits of something as well as what that something is: its essence and composition. As such, framing structures both awareness and understanding. With this in mind, conceptual art negotiated a borderline. In their historical context, conceptual artists used materials and means not traditionally associated with art, such as maps, blueprints, diagrams and street interviews. Equally, they scrutinised the relationship between representation and reality as well as between inside and outside what was considered to be the scope of art, and turned their attention to the institutional and socio-political context. They challenged the attitudes, norms and habits that regulate the experience of art, sought to reconnect art with social reality and explored how space is constructed. This last interest was with regard not only to visual space but also to discursive and social space.

Still, there is another kind of borderline we can locate. Critically engaged conceptual artists sought to demystify the creative process through works that were sample applications of a critical enquiry the viewer was cued to take on and apply herself elsewhere. This entails the viewer becoming aware not only of an artwork's subject matter, but also of its internal logic, which is part of a system that is wider than the work and of which the work forms part – be it a system of reference, classification or production. In this way, the artwork can carry forward a critique that is not internalised; most importantly, it can assume responsibility for its positioning in the social context it engages. This marks the difference between a work that refers to itself as a way of generating an enquiry beyond its borderline condition, and a tautological work that ends where it begins: with itself.

Art & Language's maps show that even when the objectivity of representation is pushed to the limits, there are still other hierarchies, external to art, that frame our understanding. Linking institutional to socio-political critique, the works of Lamelas and Romero connect the experience of art to daily life. While Lamelas's film raises questions regarding where the work stands in relation to what it represents, Romero resolves this through a matrix that is generated by the work but points outwards. In all three cases, and contesting what the late modernist art critic sought to defend, the acknowledgement that art is neither self-evident nor self-sufficient is precisely what achieves and maintains critical engagement.

Let us consider dislocation and contextual dependence. Romero's *4,000,000 m²* was presented at the exhibition *From Figuration Art to Systems Art in Argentina* at the Camden Arts Centre in February 1971, two years after Lamelas's film was shown there. The exhibition was organised by Jorge Glusberg, director of CAYC, in collaboration with Charles Harrison, a member of Art & Language, who in May of the same year organised the exhibition *Idea from England* at CAYC in Buenos Aires. Such international exchanges, typical of conceptual art's easily reproduced and 'dematerialised' objects, meant that both artists and audiences had the opportunity to engage with a diversity of practices and concerns. Regarding Romero's *4,000,000 m²*, the London audiences would be familiar with artists using non-traditional media, such as blueprints and photographs, and having preoccupations beyond colour and form, for example contesting the purported autonomy of the art gallery. In terms of the work's subject matter, the dictatorship in Argentina was ongoing and, like today, were one not to consider Romero's work in that context, much of its point would be lost.

Dislocation does not impede our understanding of a work's critical gesture if it carries, as most clearly presented by Romero's *4,000,000 m²*, a method of critique that is based on systemic logic, and that therefore makes sense and can be applied elsewhere. It is also important that the work sets itself as one reiteration of the world it presents rather than as a privileged view of it. Such a view can therefore be replaced, bringing the genius of the artist to the same level as that of the viewer; at the same time, relational positioning on behalf of the work underlines the necessity of looking at the world in order to understand the work. If conceptual art's most critical examples introduced a plurality of interpretive systems into the art world and counterpoised them with the old and tried methods of modernism, they also established that there is no other way we can look at art except in social context. Which is to say: we cannot afford *not* to look past the object in front of us.

Let this become a lesson, then, for contemporary art. At a time when 'everything goes' in terms of the means, modes, scope and sites in which art can appear, contemporary art increasingly relies on interpretive frameworks that lie outside the body of an artwork in order to legitimise its claims. Moreover, it is often characterised by transregionality, drawing multiple references from beyond the metropolitan centres of display. It thus becomes imperative to address and implicate the institutional, conceptual and socio-political frameworks that structure this plurality of voices. Otherwise, contemporary art practices run the risk of naturalising, and therefore reinforcing, the hegemonic relations they should be questioning between the sites they reference and the sites in which they display their claims.

Borderline mapping techniques as found in conceptual art demonstrate the interdependence of the carrier, the limits of critique and the limits of spatio-temporal locality. Spatio-temporal locality is defined by a work's material presence and the frameworks of classification and interpretation that define it, as well as overlapping contexts such as the material, the discursive, the social and the institutional. Critique is therefore a process, rather than an instance, that can move beyond particular applications towards a wider view of the world. However, returning to Marxist dialectics, one should remember that the instrument of critique cannot take itself outside history but must negotiate its position therein, as well as the validity of its own claims. By doing so, art can offer the tools to understand reality as a process of transformation rather than as a fixed state of affairs, and open up space for change to take place.

Notes

1 Ludwig Wittgenstein, *Tractatus logico-philosophicus* (1921), trans. D. F. Pears and D. F. McGuinness (London: Routledge, 2002).

2 Clement Greenberg, 'Seminar five', *Studio International* 189:975 (1975), 191–2; C. Harrison and F. Orton, *A Provisional History of Art & Language* (Paris: Editions E. Fabre, 1982); and Charles Harrison, 'A crisis of modernism', in *Blast to Freeze British Art in the 20th Century* (exh. cat.) (Ostfildern: Cantz, 2002), 221–4.

3 Marshall McLuhan, *Understanding Media: The Extensions of Man* (London: Routledge, 1964).

4 Since its formation in 1968, the group has had different members and affiliates: Terry Atkinson, David Bainbridge, Michael Baldwin, Harold Hurrell, Mel Ramsden, Charles Harrison, Philip Pilkington, David Rushton, Ian Burn and Terry Smith. Today, the group consists of Baldwin (b. 1945) and Ramsden (b. 1944). The names of earlier group members responsible for particular works are given in parentheses.

5 Wittgenstein, *Tractatus logico-philosophicus*.

6 Michel Foucault, *This Is Not a Pipe*, trans. J. Harkness (Berkeley: University of California Press, 1983).

7 The text-title reads: 'Map to not indicate: CANADA, JAMES BAY, ONTARIO, QUEBEC, ST. LAWRENCE RIVER, NEW BRUNSWICK, MANITOBA, AKIMISKI ISLAND, LAKE WINNIPEG, LAKE OF THE WOODS, LAKE NIPIGON, LAKE SUPERIOR, LAKE HURON, LAKE MICHIGAN, LAKE ONTARIO, LAKE ERIE, MAINE, NEW HAMPSHIRE, MASSACHUSETTS, VERMONT, CONNECTICUT, RHODE ISLAND, NEW YORK, NEW JERSEY, PENNSYLVANIA, DELAWARE, MARYLAND, WEST VIRGINIA, VIRGINIA, OHIO, MICHIGAN, WISCONSIN, MINNESOTA, EASTERN BORDERS OF NORTH DAKOTA, SOUTH DAKOTA, NEBRASKA, KANSAS, OKLAHOMA, TEXAS, MISSOURI, ILLINOIS, INDIANA, TENNESSEE, ARKANSAS, LOUISIANA, MISSISSIPPI, ALABAMA, GEORGIA, NORTH CAROLINA, SOUTH CAROLINA, FLORIDA, CUBA, BAHAMAS, ATLANTIC OCEAN, ANDROS ISLANDS, GULF OF MEXICO, STRAITS OF FLORIDA.'

8 Display caption for Art & Language, *Map to Not Indicate* (1967), Tate website, www.tate.org.uk/art/artworks/art-language-map-to-not-indicate-p01357 (accessed 11 May 2020).

9 Henri Lefebvre, *The Production of Space*, trans. Donald Nicholson-Smith (Oxford: Blackwell, 1991).

10 Roger Pàez i Blanch, 'Mapas lacunares: Activación cartográfica del espacio vacío', *Cuadernos de proyectos arquitectónicos* 5 (2014), 116–23.

11 See Eva Cockcroft, 'Abstract expressionism: Weapon of the Cold War', *Artforum* 12:10 (1974), 39–41; Victoria Combalía, *La poética de lo neutro* (Barcelona: Debolsillo, 1975); and Simón Marchán Fiz, *Del arte objetual al arte de concepto* (Madrid: Corazón, 1972).

12 Guy Brett, 'Inside out in the worlds of art', *The Times*, 14 July 1969, 11.

13 Peter Osborne, 'Art beyond aesthetics: Philosophical criticism, art history and contemporary art', *Art History* 27:4 (2004), 651–70. Original emphasis.

14 Lefebvre, *The Production of Space*, p. 404.

15 Silvia Dolinko, *Arte para todos: La difusión del grabado como estrategia para la popularización del arte* (Buenos Aires: Fundación Espigas, 2002).

16 Juan Carlos Romero, Fernando Davis and Ana Longoni, *Romero: Colección conceptual* (Buenos Aires: Fundación Espigas, 2010), p. 70.

17 *Ibid.*

18 *Ibid.*

2

Adrian Piper: In and out of conceptual art

Alexander Alberro

Beginning in April 1970, Adrian Piper executed a series of unannounced actions in New York City that she called *Catalysis* (see Figure 2.1). The artist moved through public and private spaces confronting unsuspecting passers-by while, for example, having stuffed her mouth with a towel, wearing odorous clothing or substances on her body, with balloons bulging from various parts of her frame under her attire, or carrying a 'WET PAINT' sign over a shirt soaked in sticky white enamel. These actions were meant to provoke Piper's unwitting audience, and have been understood as the crucial break with the abstractness of the artist's late 1960s work, which often used classification techniques such as grids, serial sequences and arrangements of words as media, in favour of works that can be interpreted as socially engaged interventions addressing race and gender objectification, passive and active transactions, otherness, identity, and xenophobia. Piper has, on several occasions, attributed this shift in her work to the social realities that promoted her growing political awareness and engagement in the early 1970s. As she recalled in 1973:

> In the spring of 1970, a number of events occurred that changed everything for me: 1) the invasion of Cambodia; 2) The Women's Movement; 3) Kent State and Jackson State; 4) and the closing of CCNY [City College of New York], where I was in my first term as a philosophy major, during the student rebellion.[1]

These events, she recalls, had a profound effect on her, leading her to reconsider her 'position as an artist, as a woman, and a black'.[2] Yet, the spatial relations that characterise *Catalysis* or the *Mythic Being* performances of a few years later are much more in accordance with the artist's conceptual art of the late 1960s than is usually acknowledged. The impact of the social and political realities of the late 1960s and early 1970s on Piper's work is unquestionable. But the artist's 1970s actions evolve, in many ways logically, from her late 1960s conceptual work.

Piper's early conceptual art practice, which she commenced in 1967, explored things, words, sounds and pieces of paper as concrete physical objects that

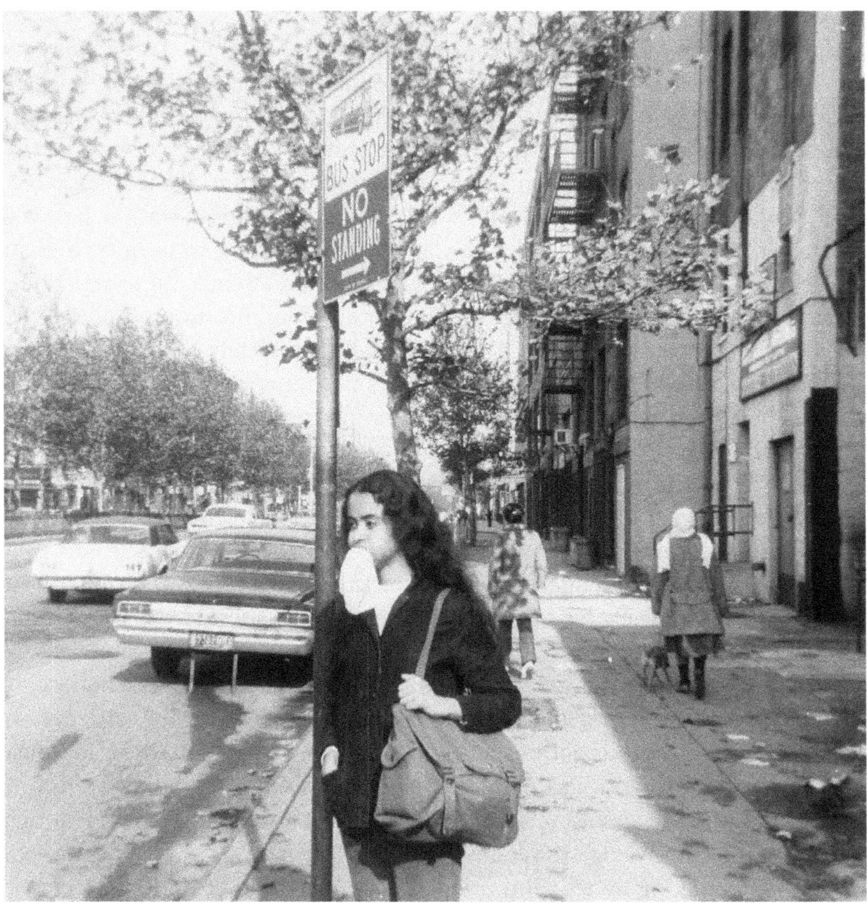

Adrian Piper, *Catalysis IV*, 1970. Performance documentation. Five silver gelatin print photographs, 40.6 cm × 40.6 cm each. Detail, photograph No. 1 of 5.   **2.1**

referred both to themselves and also outwards, to the world of abstract, symbolic meaning. By 1968 the artist had recognised the parallels between her work and that of Sol LeWitt. Beginning in the mid-to-late 1960s, LeWitt's art gave primacy to the concept; all decisions about execution were made in advance. The idea, LeWitt writes in 'Paragraphs on conceptual art' (1967), functions like 'a machine that makes the art': a logical operation of predetermined rules for decision-making that 'eliminates the arbitrary, capricious, and the subjective as much as possible.'[3] While largely rejecting the importance LeWitt placed on the perceptual presentation of the end product and its value in relation to the intellectual process that orders sensory impressions into cognitive categories, Piper found that her older peer's notion of conceptual art generally tended to corroborate and strengthen her own. This was especially true of LeWitt's emphasis on the prominence of the conceptual aspect of the creative process. For the kinds of interests Piper was developing, it was essential that the generative concept be fully developed before the piece was made. Piper's primary concern became 'the construction of finite systems', defined as 'systems that serve to contain an idea within certain formal limits and to exhaust the possibilities of the idea set by those limits'.[4] This, the artist believed, was the best way to prevent the potentialities of a concept from extending to infinity, thereby presenting her with the conflicting choices of either attempting to satisfy her curiosity about the notion by pursuing it for an indefinite amount of time, or else ignoring the limitless aspect of the thought completely.

The difficulty of having to decide when a permutation was part of the original concept, and when it veered into generating another idea altogether – with its own separate set of possibilities – soon emerged. Piper tried to resolve the problem by putting aside new ideas for later investigations. She was also aware of the gulf between concepts and their manifestation in media. Accordingly, she would only settle on the final system of the artwork when she was fully confident that she had reduced the characteristics of the physical form to those most truthful to the evolved thought. In the crystallisation of the art idea, she sought to discern and mobilise the form that most effectively conveyed it.

Piper evidently recognised that she has little to no control over a number of elements that enter into the production process. The spectator (or reader as the case may be) has various options upon encountering her work. One is to refuse to consider the artwork's assembled system in its entirety, thereby rejecting perceptual (not to mention conceptual) information altogether. Another option is to acknowledge the logic that underpins and in turn generates the piece, while making no effort to infer from it. Still another option is to grasp the operation of the system, while deriving from it a highly idiosyncratic set of implications. In the first and second instances, there is little that Piper could do other than accept the validity of those responses. Although in her writings she indicates her frustration at the thought of her artwork being reduced, she came to accept this result in an objective way. After all, subjects see things differently, and clearly it is impossible for her to impose her own subjective perspective of her work on anybody (let alone everybody) else.

Piper seems to have found the third type of response to be the most valuable and desirable. For one thing, this option generates many new ideas, for which she has only to find a more concisely realisable form than the existing one. For another, it broadens her naturally subjective perception, and in the combination of two or more personal visions, she finds a greater critical objectivity, which she attempts to retain about her work and general development as a whole. Her early conceptual art mobilises descriptive or representational formats such as grids, maps, linguistic patterns or serial sequences in order to integrate abstract concepts of space into a logical system of order. These techniques are used as what art historian Helmut Draxler describes as 'matrixes' to represent space.[5] As placements, or rather as spatial and temporal concretisations of the subjective, the momentary or the punctual in general, the matrixes function as 'a priori coordinate systems'.[6] Thus, for example, a collage such as *Utah–Manhattan Transfer* (1968) does not just expand the horizon by exchanging a one-inch-square field from a cropped map of a top-secret US military site in Utah with one of a comparable size of a subway map of Manhattan (see Figure 2.2). The artwork also calls into question the very operation of abstract classification tools such as cartographic diagrams, graphs, maps and grids, descriptions, or representations of space, including, in this case, the physical military site, the subway route, the empty Utah desert and the relatively dense New York City borough of Manhattan, which now all seem to converge.[7] Space, as conceived in artworks such as *Utah–Manhattan Transfer*, is encountered not ontologically, related to what exists, but conceptually and epistemologically, as a particular way of seeing and knowing the world. By early 1969 Piper had come to describe her conceptual art as 'involved with using the boundaries of specific elements of time and/or space as limitations on the infinite number of possible permutations of these elements, implied by the structure of the language used to identify them'.[8] The artist considered the potentialities of abstract symbolic formats such as language and other descriptive and representational techniques to be much greater than those of human perceptual faculties when it came to conveying 'the inherent character of an area in space'. Piper had evidently realised that these formats generate an enormous amount of information about space, and allowed 'the specificity – the particular limits – of the elements' she had chosen to work with to define the amount of information presented.[9]

That same year, 1969, Piper wrote what seems in retrospect to be a crucial, manifesto-like text: 'Idea, form, context'. The document proposes three central premises: (1) that 'good ideas are necessary and sufficient for good art'; (2) that artistic 'form is separate from, but necessary for, the realization of an idea' in art; and (3) that context, generally understood as referring to spatial and temporal factors, is 'separate from, but necessary for, presenting a realized idea'.[10] From these, Piper concludes that both form and context are fundamental, but not sufficient, for the production of art. The underlying idea is what is crucial in art.[11] Yet, she continues, 'the relative importance of form and context in an idea are factors by which the general nature of certain ideas may be determined. When form is important and context unimportant', as in the case of the recent work of Donald Judd or Eva Hesse, 'the idea is generally formal in nature'. When, by contrast, both form and context are important, the 'nature' of the idea 'is generally environmental'.[12] Piper cites Steve Reich's *Pendulum Music* (1969) and Robert Smithson's *Asphalt Rundown* (1969) as works that

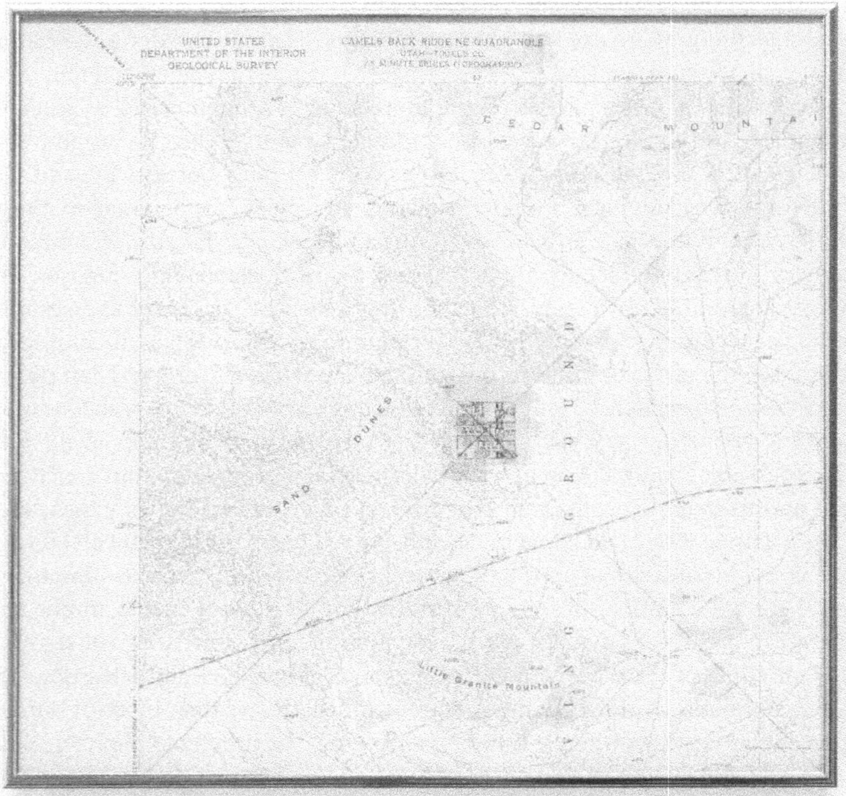

2.2   Adrian Piper, *Utah–Manhattan Transfer*, 1968. Pencil and ballpoint pen on cut-and-paste maps, mounted on two pieces of foamcore. First panel: 33.7 cm × 36 cm; second panel: 30.5 cm × 30.5 cm.

follow this premise.[13] In cases where both form and context are unimportant, she continues, 'the idea is generally conceptual'. The example Piper provides is LeWitt's *46 Three-Part Variations on 3 Different Kinds of Cubes* (1967), which she has repeatedly acknowledged as having had a very important effect on her understanding of art's possibilities.[14] However, Piper explains, 'when form is unimportant and context important, the idea is generally ideal in nature'. For Piper, this premise relates closely not only to the late 1960s art of Vito Acconci – she cites Acconci's *Points, Blanks* (1969) as an example – but also to her own recent work: she directs the reader to *Area Relocation #2* (1969).[15]

Acconci's *Points, Blanks* is one of a group of works the artist made in 1969 that involved a predetermined task executed at regular intervals across a context of time and space. In this case, Acconci (on 13 June 1969) called the Paula Cooper Gallery in New York City every ten minutes from public telephones as

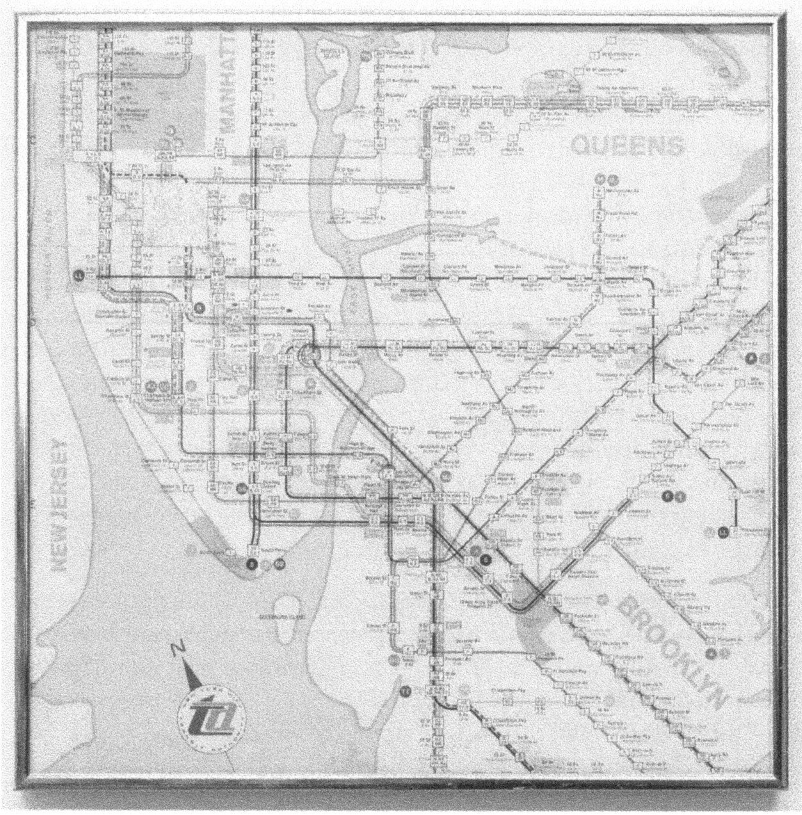

2.2

he made his way from the Upper West Side of Manhattan to the gallery's storefront location, just south of Houston Street, where the opening of a group show that included his work was in process. At 7.31 p.m., the start of the programme, Acconci called from Broadway and 100th Street; at 7.42 p.m. he called from Broadway and 90th Street; at 7.51 p.m. he called from Broadway and 84th Street, and so on until he reached the gallery in SoHo at 9.51 p.m., just as the vernissage was ending. Over the 2 hours and 15 minutes of the piece, the artist goes from functioning as a peripheral figure relative to the art public at the opening to representing the central focal point of the work. While the programme unfolded, the phone could be heard ringing in the gallery, and every call Acconci made was followed by a public announcement of the locations of his phone calls, which were also marked on a map of Manhattan. As such, *Points, Blank* actuates a descriptive approach to space. Acconci was interested in neither the unique attributes of the specific locations that he moved through nor the social relations that characterised the kinds of social forces involved in those spaces. Instead, his interest centred on the logistics of those sites as he passed through them.

Piper's *Area Relocation #2* catalyses a similar notion of space (see Figure 2.3). The artwork took the form of a public notice advertised in a local newspaper, the *Village Voice*. The public notice informed the reader that the area or space of the advert had been relocated from the headquarters of the *Village Voice* to the reader's address. The artwork was similar in kind to another work in the same series, an untitled piece in which Piper sent postcards to 170 readers of the summer 1969 issue of the magazine *0 to 9*. The postcards directed those who received them to Piper's untitled grid project in the latest issue of the journal, with the other side of each card containing an enlargement of one rectangle on the grid, 'relocated to' the recipient's address.[16] Both pieces mobilised abstract representational space indexically to relate the two-dimensional space of the printed medium with no volume at all to the reader's address, which should be distinguished from the actual location of that reader's residence. As Piper subsequently explained about this intervention:

> in fact, it's not possible to *physically* relocate an area at all. When we refer to an area in commonplace parlance, e.g. the 'area' of a playing field or a chessboard, we are actually not referring to areas in the strict sense, but rather to three-dimensional physical objects. So in its ideationality, [works such as the *Area Relocation* pieces] address a *geometrical* reality that is essentially abstract and conceptual.[17]

In other words, the relocations that are central to these works can only be accomplished when they are consummated in the mind of the receiver.

Piper would soon materialise the concept of space in her artwork itself. Her *Hypothesis* project, for instance, which she began in late 1968 and developed over the next year-and-a-half, folded her 'pure' conceptual art investigations that abstracted space and time onto a study of her body as a concrete entity that could refer to itself as well as to other physical objects. The works in the series, especially the nineteen subtitled *Situations*, employ charts, diagrams, graphs, photographs and text to explore the particularities of the artist's perspective on the surrounding world. The perspective centred on the artist's body as an element that moves through the context of space and time just like any other.[18] In the words of art historian John Bowles, Piper is figured in the series 'as a hypothesis, whose presence is neither certain nor assured'. She alternates between positions of object and subject, seeking 'reassurance of her existence in the sequence of photographed moments'. Each set of photographs – and the *Hypothesis* series as a whole – sets out to anchor 'the artist's intellectual and bodily coherence'.[19]

In seeking consonance, however, *Hypothesis* also recognises that, unlike other specific three-dimensional objects, the human body (in this case the artist's) has an affective or phenomenological relationship with the space through which it moves. The works represent and communicate that

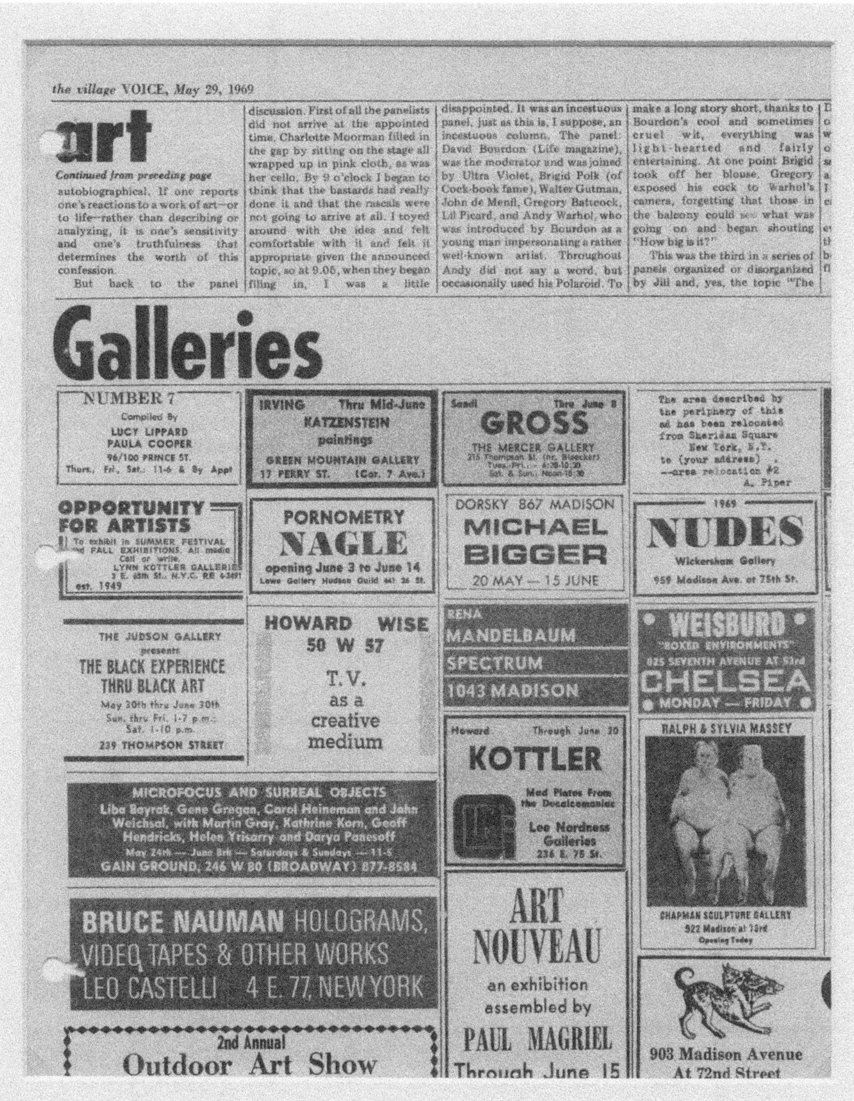

Adrian Piper, *Untitled* ('The area described by the periphery of this ad …')/*Area Relocation Series #2*, 1969. Deacidified newspaper page from the *Village Voice* with an original advertisement from 29 May 1969, 43.2 cm × 35.6 cm.   **2.3**

consciousness indexically by means of photographs, and symbolically through textual explanations, inventories of objects, charts, graphs and coordinate grids. Accordingly, *Hypothesis* documents the artist's experience and her consciousness of that experience in space and at specific time intervals as the feature that distinguishes her from other objects in the world.[20]

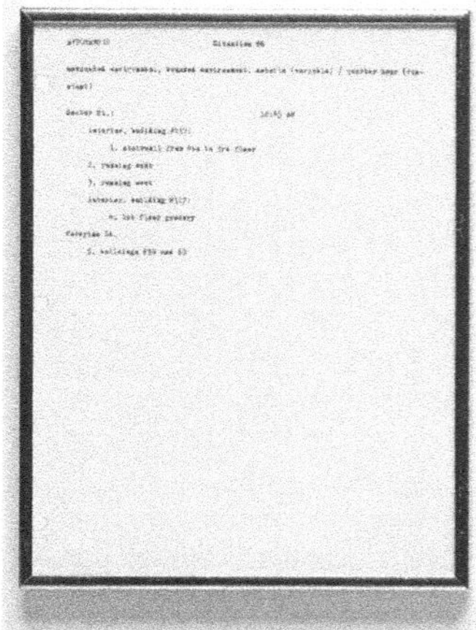

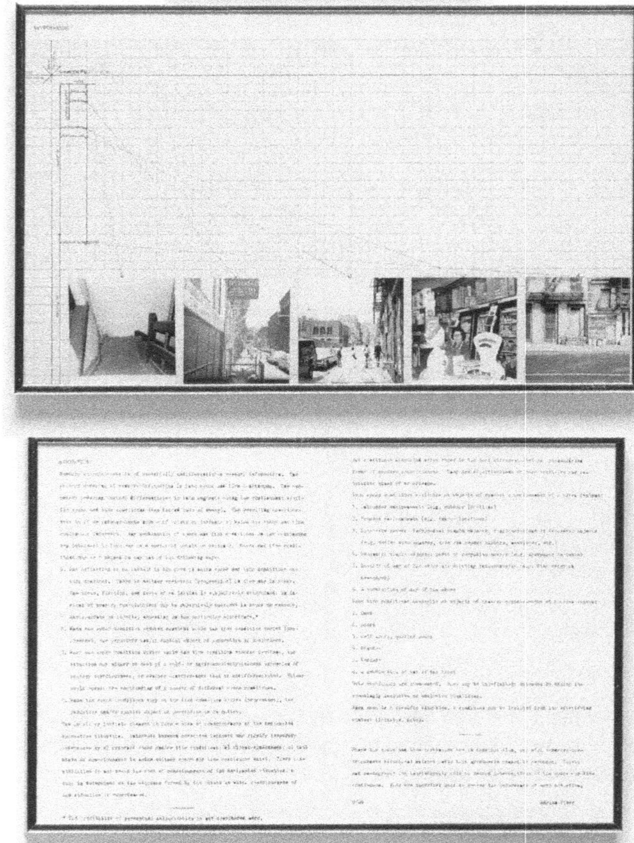

2.4 Adrian Piper, *Hypothesis: Situation #6*, 1968. Typescript on paper, silver gelatin prints and black ink on graph paper, vintage photo offset. 27.9 cm × 21.6 cm; 27.9 cm × 45.4 cm; 27.9 cm × 43.2 cm.

Piper devised a spatial and temporal scheme and took photographs of whatever came into her camera's viewfinder to make the works that make up the *Hypothesis* 'situations'. Sometimes she used measured and predetermined time intervals; other times she arbitrarily snapped the shutter. One cycle of the series, *Hypothesis: Situation #10*, depicts shots of a television every ten seconds during an advertisement for a common pain killer; *Hypothesis: Situation #15* documents furnishings in her apartment; *Hypothesis: Situation #6* captures the artist's walk from her apartment on Hester Street to a nearby grocery store on the Lower East Side of Manhattan (see Figure 2.4). Piper plotted those spaces and moments of routine domesticity on grids that functioned as space-time coordinate systems. The vertical graphs correlate space, while the horizontal ones integrate time. The photographs thus connect each instant with a particular space-time intersection as they record the phenomenological experience of the artist. Piper 'fixed her spatial relationship to the objects around her' when she snapped the camera's shutter, and the overall impression is of her scan of the surrounding space at a given point in time, suggesting what Bowles describes as her subjective presence in the work through 'the reversal of her perspective'.[21] Each individual element of the scheme indexically or symbolically represents the contents of the artist's consciousness at a particular space-time location and juncture. This is what Piper concluded was the difference between humans and inanimate objects: the latter can be located in space relative to other things, existing in their relation to each other, but only humans can relate to space, and to things in space, in a conscious and self-conscious way. That is, only humans are also *subjects*.

But insofar as Piper subsequently altered the chronological order of some of the photographs in the *Hypothesis* project, randomly rearranging them and thereby shifting the artworks' representation of reality, she set this project in relation to others, such as the *Area Relocation* series or *Utah–Manhattan Transfer*, that, as we have just seen, jumbled the descriptive or representational spaces of cartographic maps to give priority to the artist's personal conceptions of them.[22] *Hypothesis*, in other words, at once pushed towards the development of a phenomenological and social concept of space, only to be pulled back to a conceptual or representational model of space when the artist abstracted the process by rearranging the temporal sequence of the unfolding experience.

The full-fledged move into a relational concept of space, which could theorise space not only phenomenologically but also performatively, as a medium of social relations, would be developed in the *Catalysis* series, which Piper began to work on soon after the completion of *Hypothesis* in 1970 and further extended in the *Mythic Being* performances of a few years later. In these preconceived street actions, the artist's body, first in the phenomenological perception of what she described as a 'spatio-temporally immediate object', and soon in the psychogeographic and relational logic of interaction in developing a sense of self, functioned as a catalyst to bring into focus – and, in her words, to 'promote a change in' – the social spaces through which it moved.[23] Humans,

Piper's work now seemed to suggest, by producing space according to their own social, psychic and interactive nature, materialise society into distinctive forms. Yet those forms, in turn, work to reproduce the subject.

A given spatial order is internalised by the individuals it comprises. It imposes its rhythms and geographies on the bodies and psyches of the people who are subjectivised by it. From this perspective, however, space, like social contexts as a whole, is performative, always unfinished and open, made and remade on a daily basis. There can therefore be no assumption of a given coherence of spaces, or of the subject positions they produce. Identities, like the spaces and orders that catalyse them, are inherently precarious and, rather than static, are always in process – always changing. Social encounters destabilise individual difference and particularity, and place emphasis instead on the relationship between people.[24] Moreover, different individuals or social groups are placed in very distinct ways in relation to space. The degree to which one can move through it, whether walking about the streets or venturing beyond one's social circle or purview, is restricted by prevailing relations and conventions. These conceptualisations remain implicit. Subjects intuitively know their place, and what they can do where. This point concerns not only the issue of who moves and who does not – although that is an important element. It also concerns what geographer Doreen Massey refers to as the 'power in relation *to* the flows of movement'.[25] Some people, largely on account of the visible aspects of their identity – whether racial or gender-, class- or sexuality-based – are more in charge of the movement through social space than others. Some are empowered to initiate flows and movement, others are not; some are more on the receiving end of those flows and movements than others, some are effectively imprisoned by them.

Piper's works of the early 1970s emphasise that, among other things, processes of highly complex social differentiations occur within the context of social space.[26] While humans experience the world through and in space – a crucial medium in the production and development of subjectivity and identity – spaces are socially constructed, and those constructions are founded on acts of exclusion, often in contexts of unequal power relations and relations of domination and exploitation. There are differences in the degree of movement and communication, but also in that of control and initiation. Yet, to recognise that space, like identity, is essentially social and constantly struggled over and reimagined in practical ways is to understand it not as a natural, secure, ontological thing rooted in notions of closure, boundedness and permanence, but 'as the product of interrelations; as constituted through interactions', and therefore 'as always under construction … always in the process of being made' by the human beings that constitute it.[27] In short, to say that something is constructed by human forces is to say that it is within human power to change it. Which is, in the end, one of the most important insights generated by Piper's conceptualist-derived artistic practice.

Notes

1 Adrian Piper, *Out of Order, Out of Sight*, 2 vols, Vol. I, *Selected Writings in Meta-Art 1968–1992* (Cambridge, MA: MIT Press, 1996), p. 30.

2 *Ibid.*, p. 31.

3 Sol LeWitt, 'Paragraphs on conceptual art', in Alexander Alberro and Blake Stimson (eds), *Conceptual Art: A Critical Anthology* (Cambridge, MA: MIT Press, 1999), p. 12.

4 Piper, *Out of Order*, Vol. I, p. 5.

5 Helmut Draxler, 'Structures of response: Adrian Piper's transformation of minimalism', in M. Sullivan (ed.), *Structures of Response* (Berlin: S*I*G*, 2018), p. 7.

6 *Ibid.*

7 *Ibid.*

8 Piper, *Out of Order*, Vol. I, p. 15.

9 *Ibid.*

10 *Ibid.*, pp. 5–6.

11 *Ibid.*, p. 8.

12 *Ibid.*, p. 9.

13 *Ibid.*, p. 10.

14 *Ibid.*, p. 11. For Piper's acknowledgement of the importance of LeWitt's art to her artistic practice see *ibid.*, pp. 209–14.

15 Piper, *Out of Order, Out of Sight*, Vol. II, *Selected Writings in Art Criticism 1967–1992*, p. 12.

16 Adrian Piper, undated postcard, postmarked 9 July 1969, sent to Kynaston McShine, in *Information* Exhibition Papers, Museum of Modern Art, New York; quoted in J. P. Bowles, *Adrian Piper: Race, Gender, and Embodiment* (Durham, NC: Duke University Press, 2011), p. 277n18. As Bowles observes, 'The text draws the reader's attention to the project's contextual conditions and their realization. Reading the postcard or the magazine project creates an event in time and space that depends as much upon its reception in the "here and now" as on the moment when the artist made it' (p. 130).

17 Adrian Piper, personal correspondence with Nizan Shaked, 14 November 2016; quoted in Nizan Shaked, 'Propositions to politics: Adrian Piper's conceptual paradigms', in C. Butler and D. Platzker (eds), *Adrian Piper: A Reader* (New York: Museum of Modern Art, 2018), p. 78n20.

18 Piper, *Out of Order*, Vol. I, p. 19.

19 Bowles, *Adrian Piper*, p. 84.

20 Adrian Piper, *The Hypothesis Series* , Walker Art Center, Minneapolis, T. B. Walker Acquisition Fund © Adrian Piper Research Archive (APRA) Foundation Berlin, 1968–70.

21 Bowles, *Adrian Piper*, p. 86.

22 *Ibid.*

23 Piper, *Out of Order*, Vol. I, p. 32.

24 See Kobena Mercer, 'Contrapositional becomings: Adrian Piper performs questions of identity', in Butler and Platzker, *Adrian Piper*, p. 103.

25 Doreen Massey, *Space, Place, and Gender* (Minneapolis: University of Minnesota, 1994), p. 149.

26 Adrian Piper, 'It's not all black and white', *Village Voice*, 9 June 1987, 6.

27 Doreen Massey, *For Space* (London: Sage, 2005), p. 9.

3

Remapping the public sphere: Conceptual art in 1970s London

Jennifer Sarathy

In the 1970s, artists working in London combined conceptual models of production and display with collective methodologies and alternative exhibition practices. They extended the movement's challenge to traditional art world models while remapping public space and critiquing and recoding the city's social geographies. This chapter examines three site-specific interventions in London: the Polygonal Workshop's *Garbage Walk* (1970), which charts the experience of garbage in the city's streets following a dustmen's strike; Stephen Willats's *West London Social Resource Project* (1972–73), which incited local populations to 'construct new cognitions' through their awareness of social behaviour in public and private spaces; and Margaret Harrison, Kay Fido Hunt and Mary Kelly's *Women and Work: A Document on the Division of Labour in Industry 1973–75* (1973–75), which documented gender-based labour inequalities in Bermondsey, south London.[1]

These projects retain conceptualism's focus on information and ideas over the creation of unique art objects and its radical questioning of the traditional role of the artist, offering experimental methods of production and distribution. They relate to what Seth Siegelaub has described as 'the use of banal, everyday information as commentary' and 'the systematic analysis of the visual aspect of our physical and intellectual environment', but rather than simply drawing attention to phenomena, information is mobilised to incite public debate and social change.[2] Although the compilation and display of documentation and information have been associated with an 'aesthetics of administration',[3] these projects diverge from early conceptualism to emphasise social content and the collaborative production of data, which are used to literally and conceptually map new sites for public discourse outside established institutions, exploring and contesting social norms and legal codes.

The public sphere is a useful concept to understand the impact of these projects as, first, it outlines where public and private realms meet and boundaries between them are negotiated; second, the public sphere speaks to the transformation of individual needs into collective terms and charts the formation of communities in relation to the State and institutions; third, it is substantiated and shaped by law, and thus records the shift from discourse to the codification of societal customs; and fourth, the public sphere is also determined by class relations and economic production.[4] As Doreen Massey has written, 'space can be more helpfully conceptualised as the product of the stretched-out, intersecting and articulating social relations of the economy. Not only does this integrate "the social" and "the spatial" from the moment of initial conceptualisation, it also introduces – directly into space itself – the issue of social power.'[5] Like cartography, the public sphere at once evokes the symbolic and spatial orders, and while the public sphere is not necessarily a place, it is a notion attached to places and geographies defined by real physical boundaries and the experience of people within spaces. While Jürgen Habermas described a historically determined dominant bourgeois public sphere, subsequent re-evaluations have argued for a more fluid and pluralistic conceptualisation of the public sphere, comprising diverse publics and counterpublics that can contest universalising (and masculinist) norms.[6] Avoiding the universalising abstraction of conceptual art and its tautological focus on conditions of the art world, these three projects are constituted by the collective experiences of unique social spaces, inciting and recording discourse to form alternative public spheres. In doing so, they challenged centres of art world power in London and actively contested dominant social norms and legislation through the collective production and display of information.

Garbage Walk

Garbage Walk was a multifarious project initiated by Mexican artist Felipe Ehrenberg and Austrian artist Richard Kriesche, members of the newly formed international artist collective in London, the Polygonal Workshop.[7] The project responded to the monumental piles of garbage that covered the streets of London beginning in October 1969 following a dustmen's strike over wages. Ehrenberg and Kriesche began by spray-painting lines on and around the growing piles of garbage, using photography to record their growth and eventual disappearance. Kriesche's photographs were produced daily until the strike ended, and were arranged serially, registering the appearance and disappearance of personal and industrial refuse. His photographs underscore the temporal span of the strike and emphasise the conceptual parameters of the artwork.[8] By contrast, Ehrenberg's more sporadic images capture the performative and multivalent nature of the project and its expansion into a broader social field, depicting the artists at work, piles of trash filling the streets, and tenacious Londoners navigating through the garbage.[9]

The artists also collected fragments of film from the rubbish piles of production companies near Wardour Street that Ehrenberg edited together with original black-and-white 16 mm footage and titled *La Poubelle; or, It's a Sort of Disease II* (1970) (a still from which can be seen in Figure 3.1).[10] *La Poubelle* forces a reckoning with the social crisis, recording the impact of the public negotiation between collective labour and the State on public space. The work also draws attention to the experiential realities of labour – not just of the dustmen, who are shown at the end of the film cleaning and burning the garbage – but of the labourers who produce the commodities that become garbage, represented by textile workers in factories seen in portions of found film. Forcing a visceral reaction, the film uses disorienting close-ups of unthinkably large piles of trash and panning shots that reveal the overwhelming of space and architecture by garbage, stressing its 'physical existence'. The phrase 'physical existence' is repeated in the film's soundtrack, contesting an understanding of the strike as an abstract conflict of labour that can be ignored. The film criticises the acceptance of the continued state of disorder by the public and the lack of discussion about the strike at the time; it forces the taboo of private waste spilling into the public to be recognised and draws attention to the daily

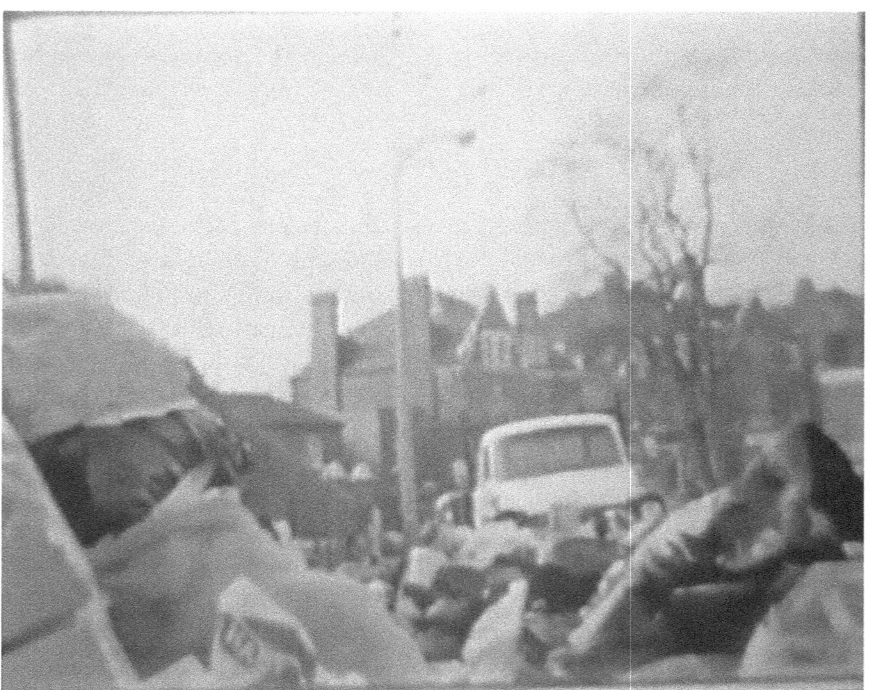

3.1   Felipe Ehrenberg, still from *La Poubelle; or, It's a Sort of Disease II*, timestamp 00:19, 1970.

unseen labour of municipal workers.[11] Reflecting this attitude, and his general approach to art-making, Ehrenberg asserted in the film's narration that 'art is anything that breaks with your programmations, anything that jolts you, pushes you, catalyses you, out of a set mode of behavior'. In the film it is both the shock of the oppressive landscape of garbage and its relationship to the realities of consumer culture that are meant to activate the viewer.

While *La Poubelle* is evidently related to the Brechtian and Debordian experimental films of the 1960s and 1970s, it can also be seen as part of a conceptual remapping of space that made visible a geography of lived experience devastatingly altered by social conflict and capitalist production. Like Ehrenberg and Kriesche's photographs, it functioned as a document within a larger series of events that sought to incite public discussion and potentially establish 'lines of communication within a community or between communities'.[12] In October 1970, after the streets were eventually cleared, the Polygonal Workshop organised a walking tour, now known as *Garbage Walk*, that followed a crooked path along the traced piles of garbage from the Leicester Square tube station to Shaftesbury Avenue near Grape Street, with a stop at the Sigi Krauss Gallery and frame shop at 29 Neal Street in Covent Garden.[13] The black-and-white invitation consists of a mapped route and typed text declaring 'on October 13, 1970, a systematic record of twelve rubbish piles was started. The transformation of these piles was marked by a white line and photographed every two days. You are invited to follow the route (see map) and observe the results in the company of the investigators.'[14] While *La Poubelle* is peripatetic, punctuated by panning shots and footage taken from the window of a moving vehicle that underscore the scale of the crisis, the map and walk emphasise the experience of living within particular spaces and geographies, inviting participants to recreate the garbage imaginatively once it was gone – reminding them that, although the strike had been mediated, the labour of dustmen underlies our experience of public space. This imaginative and conceptual component of the artwork is articulated by Ehrenberg's *Vanishing Rubbish Pile* (1970). The artist's book features images of garbage on stacked pages that become progressively slimmer from bottom to top, forming a simulated pile of trash. Segments of garbage were also given to individuals who then became 'a fragment of the vanishing rubbish pile' and were registered to receive news from the Polygonal Workshop, forming an extended network of rubbish and participants.[15]

Garbage Walk was followed by the exhibition *The 7th Day Chicken*, which was installed for a week in February 1971 at the Sigi Krauss Gallery. In the front room, the group arranged upright concrete sewer tubes that were used as podiums to display various packaged foods from a supermarket, including a raw chicken that decomposed over the course of the week, critiquing commodity culture's role in creating waste. In the back room, the artists projected

La Poubelle and made available the full documentation of the garbage and its social impact collected over the year, including photographs, notes taken during the strike and audio that recorded encounters with people made while the artists were filming and spray-painting in the streets.[16] Visitors were encouraged to participate by adding to the exhibition display. The artists were also present in the gallery during working hours, making themselves available to 'serve the public' – to talk and argue with visitors.[17]

The exhibition was described as chaotic and highly participatory, with enthusiastic, vehement and befuddled responses from critics and the public.[18] The Polygonal Workshop, therefore, served to instigate an absurdist debate with no set outcome, with the eventual meaning of the work to be determined by participants in various stages of the project and by visitors to the exhibition. Ehrenberg firmly believed in collective artistic practice, declaring 'artistic work – a result of group effort – could coherently form a part of the struggles of the majority, as one more weapon in the fight for the liberation of our people', and describing a transcendence of the world of the visual arts towards a more revolutionary extension of artistic practice into a democratic public sphere.[19] The 'art' itself, from the rotting chicken to the multimedia documentation of the garbage strike, acted primarily as provocations that forced the issue of labour and garbage into the public sphere, bringing attention to the ways in which capitalist production and consumption shapes the constitution of social space.[20] While aspects of *Garbage Walk* and related works are firmly rooted within and respond to the discourse of conceptual art, the project extends conceptualism's challenge to the traditional role of the artist and the institution through its desire to impact collective social conditions; its dispersed geographical footprint; and its collaborative, open-ended structure.

The artist as conceptual designer

Stephen Willats's *West London Social Resource Project* also situated the artist as 'instigator' of an artwork produced collaboratively over time with members of the community in order to enact social change, reflecting the artist's longstanding belief in the extension of art into social space and the importance of participation to cultural production.[21] The project selected four small areas of west London that were in close proximity, linked by a central road.[22] Each area was socio-economically distinct, representing working-class (Area 1), lower-middle-class (Area 3), middle-class (Area 2) and upper-middle-class (Area 4) communities.[23] Contrasting later works by Willats that look at isolated housing blocks, *The West London Social Resource Project* placed different communities in dialogue to confront established social patterns that were engrained in geographical and architectural spaces.[24] The project took nearly six months to produce and proceeded in several stages, asking participants to analyse and then consider modifying local spaces and associated social behaviours.[25] Responses were compared publicly to inspire collective discussion and self-reflection.

In the first stage, Willats mobilised volunteers from the art world who recruited and liaised with local participants from the different areas.[26] Participants from each of the four communities were given printed *West London Manuals* comprising sixty problems that asked them to analyse their interpersonal relationships, individual living environments and surrounding public spaces. One section of the *West London Manual* had participants describe and then draw areas of their homes, asking how members of the household used them during the day. Another section contained 'Description Sheets', including photographs of architectural elements such as storefronts, gates, doors and telephone booths from within the project areas.

Participants were asked to describe the function of these features to aid them in building 'mental models' of their social environments.[27] Some responses to the 'Description Sheets' focused on aesthetics, describing features as 'pleasant to look at' or 'fancy', while many directly linked architectural elements to class status, identifying certain spaces as 'middle class' or as having 'wealthy owners'. In others, images of particular places were associated with personal memories. These varied subjective responses were compared and contrasted when the completed *Manual* sheets were displayed on large boards in nearby public libraries (see Figure 3.2). These displays testified to the complex layers of experience and social conditioning that shape personal and communal spaces and allowed participants to view, analyse and vote on the responses. The boards featured bold-type headings and neatly arranged response sheets, invoking the aesthetic of conceptual art; however, they equally resembled local community message boards and mobile agitprop displays.

Following the first round of analysis, a second set of questions in the *London Re-Modelling Book* asked participants to reconceptualise existing mental models of their social and physical environments, and to propose alternatives they felt could better fulfil their individual and communal needs (see Figure 3.3). One sheet from the *London Re-Modelling Book* contained two prompts that asked participants first to 'Describe, draw, make a map of how you think your house, garden etc. should relate to your neighbours', and then to 'Describe and make a plan of a garden or open space that could be used by all the people in your neighbourhood showing how it would function.' The responses reimagined how public spaces and infrastructure could better serve the community, attesting to how the project effectively inspired participants to re-evaluate their immediate social spaces. The second round of responses was compiled and analysed by 'specialists' and was once again presented on boards in public libraries where proposals to modify public spaces were discussed and voted on. Analyses of responses were also shared with the community

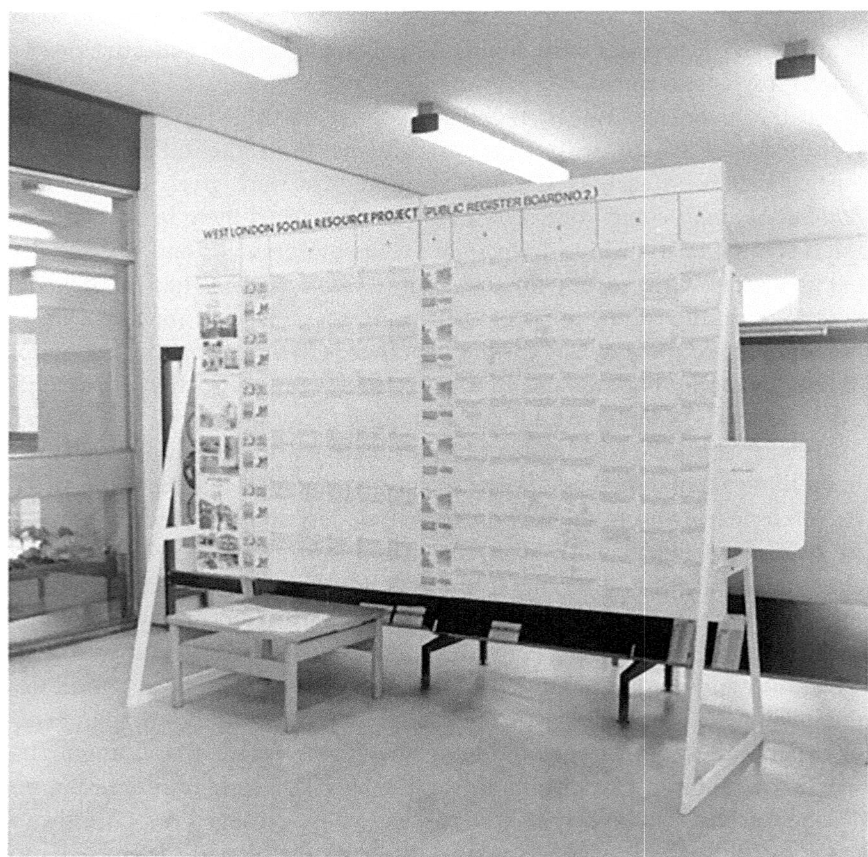

3.2   Stephen Willats, *The West London Social Resource Project*, public register board no. 2 at a local library, 1972.

in supplementary printed materials, turning experience into data that could inform future interactions within and between the four communities. While the artist designated the overall structure of the project, its meaning was solely determined by these two rounds of public analysis and discussion within the local environments that the participants had been asked to analyse self-consciously. By structuring *The West London Social Resource Project* around the self-determining experiences of participants, Willats redefined the role of the conceptual artist as closer to a 'Conceptual Designer' (a title he adopted around 1965), who radically and directly intervenes in the fabric of society itself, challenging established methods of production and distribution and the passive role of viewers.[28]

Final results of *The West London Social Resource Project* were also displayed on what Willats termed 'Public Monitors': semi-architectural displays filled

SHEET FIVE.
DESCRIBE, DRAW, MAKE A MAP OF HOW YOU THINK
YOUR HOUSE, GARDEN ETC SHOULD RELATE TO
YOUR NEIGHBOURS.

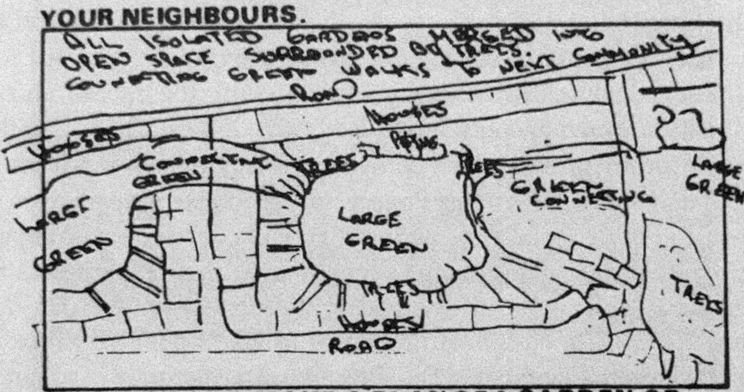

DESCRIBE AND MAKE A PLAN OF A GARDEN OR
OPEN SPACE THAT COULD BE USED BY ALL THE
PEOPLE IN YOUR NEIGHBOURHOOD SHOWING HOW
IT WOULD FUNCTION.

Stephen Willats, *The West London Social Resource Project*, Sheet 5, k, from the *West London Re-Modelling Book*, Project Area 2, 1972.

with slides, serial photographs and sheets of text that presented the work to a secondary art audience. The most prominent of these was installed at Gallery House,[29] where Willats also displayed *West London Wasteland* photographs, documenting the interstitial urban 'wastelands' that existed between isolated tower blocks in west London.[30] These photographs explore intersections among geography, architecture and socio-cultural experience, and consider how public housing in London is affected by the abstracted ideology of the State.[31] Willats writes 'Perhaps one of the most powerful expressions by our society of prevailing social consciousness is embodied in both the interior and exterior environment in which people actually lead their domestic lives.'[32] Rather than simply drawing attention to these competing forces, however, projects such as *The West London Social Resource Project* strove to make individuals conscious of their role in these social systems and their embeddedness within particular geographic locations, giving them agency to alter their experiences and collective spaces. As Roy Ascott declared in the first issue of Willats's *Control* magazine, 'To control one's environment is to assert one's existence. In controlling my identity I define it.'[33] This alternative cartography of urban space is illustrated by Willats's diagram, 'West Waste London Lands', where geography is based on localised spheres radiating outwards, providing a compelling map of how the collective mobilisation of individual communities can relate to the dominant public sphere.[34] The reduced role of the artist was also central to this project. Willats explains 'all "art" is dependent on society – dependent on the relationships between people and not the sole product of any one person … the divestment of authorship is seen as more relevant to an emerging culture founded on networks of exchange, fluidity, transience, and mutuality'.[35] These terms can equally be applied to the kind of space his work conceptualises – a cartography based on fluidity, transience, exchange and mutuality.

Feminist geography and *Women and Work*

The expansive information and printed matter produced by *The West London Social Resource Project* is mirrored by Harrison, Hunt and Kelly's *Women and Work: A Document on the Division of Labour in Industry 1973–75*. This collaborative project perhaps most clearly evidences the relationship among data, legislation and the experiences of individuals as they traverse socially coded public and private spaces. *Women and Work* analysed the gendered differentiation of jobs and wages at the south London, Bermondsey branch of the Metal Box Company following the 1970 Equal Pay Act, which aimed to establish gender and wage parity in the workplace.[36] The project stemmed from the artists' seminal involvement with the Women's Workshop of the Artists Union,[37] and overlapped with Kelly's work on *Nightcleaners* (1972–75), an activist film that documented and campaigned for the unionisation of nighttime women office cleaners.[38] Aligning with the objectives of these endeavours, *Women and Work* compiled and analysed large quantities of information, including relevant legislation, job descriptions and compensation statistics divided by gender, to evaluate the implementation of the Equal Pay Act at the Metal Box Company since 1970.[39] Hunt, Harrison and Kelly also interviewed more than 150 women on the site, accumulating additional data sourced from the factory workers. The women were featured in a large grid of portraits hung in the exhibition and their names were printed in long columns in the first pages of the catalogue and on the introductory wall of the South London Gallery. While the portraits humanised the workers, the list of their names shifted their subjectivities into linguistic order, placing their experiences at the centre of the data and information on display.

The *Women and Work* installation was described, even by a positive reviewer, as 'severely factual' with 'an abundance of information, a thunderstorm of facts' mirroring the text-only catalogue.[40] Indeed, the exhibition highlighted the presentation of information, with documents arranged in long lines on the bare white walls of the gallery, adopting the then-dominant approach of conceptual art. Exhibition materials included closely cropped photographs of work processes, photocopied factory documents and trade union reports. Data, ranging from job descriptions to summaries of relevant legislation, and timetables of workers' home and work routines, was presented on neatly typed sheets mounted on board.[41] The work thus intentionally adopts an administrative, legalistic and authoritative aesthetic, enabling it to serve as a multifarious document, factually presenting what emerged as clear gender inequalities and efforts to offset the effects of the Equal Pay Act. The documentation recorded, for instance, revised job gradings that overwhelmingly favoured men, and the subsequent reduction or elimination of part-time work that primarily affected local, middle-aged, married women.[42] The exhibition made mundane factory records available to the public – ranging from individual rate sheets to historic box pricing, job descriptions, accident reports, signed medical reports and analyses of component designs used by the company. These documents presented together – on mounted panels and in informational booklets – revealed the myriad ways that data both reflected and helped to transform social experience through labour relations and the codification of laws.[43] Presenting these documents in the South London Gallery made the company's internal and normally invisible bureaucracy visible, resonating most with the workers whose experiences were directly represented by the data on display.[44]

While the austere, serial panels of text and image in the exhibition evoked the authority of conceptual art, *Women and Work* underscored Hunt, Harrison and Kelly's commitment to content and social purpose in art – in a direct assault on the self-referentiality of conceptualism at the time.[45] In contrast to the often-abstract intellectual content of conceptual art, *Women and Work* demonstrated a clear concern to humanise the experience of women workers. Rosalind Delmar remarked that although the exhibition at first appeared somewhat 'colour-less', the side-by-side films of women and men that recorded the whirring and clanking of the factory amplified the embodied aspects of labour.[46] The gridded portraits of the women participants, photographs of workers of both genders, and materials that recorded their physical presence and daily routines (such as punch cards taken from the factory) all further concretise their experiences. This approach supplements the heavily abstracted data on view, in a manner prescient of Kelly's *Post-Partum Document* (initiated in 1973). Furthermore, data were not meant to be passively absorbed by viewers. Like the exhibitions organised by Willats and the Polygonal Workshop, the South London Gallery provided a forum for public dialogue where the information provided could be discussed and interpreted by individuals and the community that had participated in the project. As described by Delmar, the use of a variety of media, from film to audio, photography, photocopied factory documents and statistical tables displayed on the walls and in separate niches and on study desks, transformed the gallery into 'a mixture of sites – library, viewing theatre, display center' (see Figure 3.4).[47] The exhibition thus created an unorthodox laboratory where the community could work through information that extended public

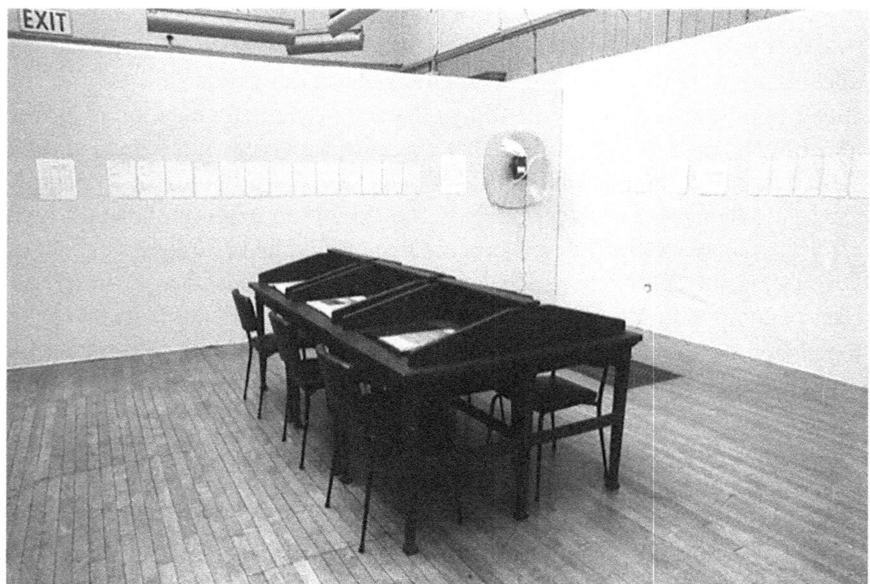

3.4   Margaret Harrison, Kay Fido Hunt and Mary Kelly, *Women and Work: A Document on the Division of Labour in Industry 1973–75*, installation view at the South London Gallery, 1975.

debates over legislation and gender equality in the home and workplace into a geographical area occupied by affected workers.[48] This format echoed the structures of the feminist movement that, as outlined by Judith Mastai, used 'community-based study and support groups which aimed to provide a place for women's voices to be heard through local discussion of shared experiences and study of important texts which formed the basis for analysis and debate about class, society and women's roles'.[49]

The physical location of the South London Gallery was essential to *Women and Work*'s critical use of documentation and data, as it was where the women lived and laboured, establishing an alternative and localised site for discourse.[50] The work also developed an alternative cartography that was explicitly feminist in orientation: the project map in the exhibition centres on south London, using pins to indicate where the women workers lived in relation to the factory (see Figure 3.5). The map spatialises the daily home and work routines recorded by the project, marking but also connecting the arenas of domestic and public labour, emphasising that the unequal division of labour in industry was 'underpinned by the division of labour in the home'.[51]

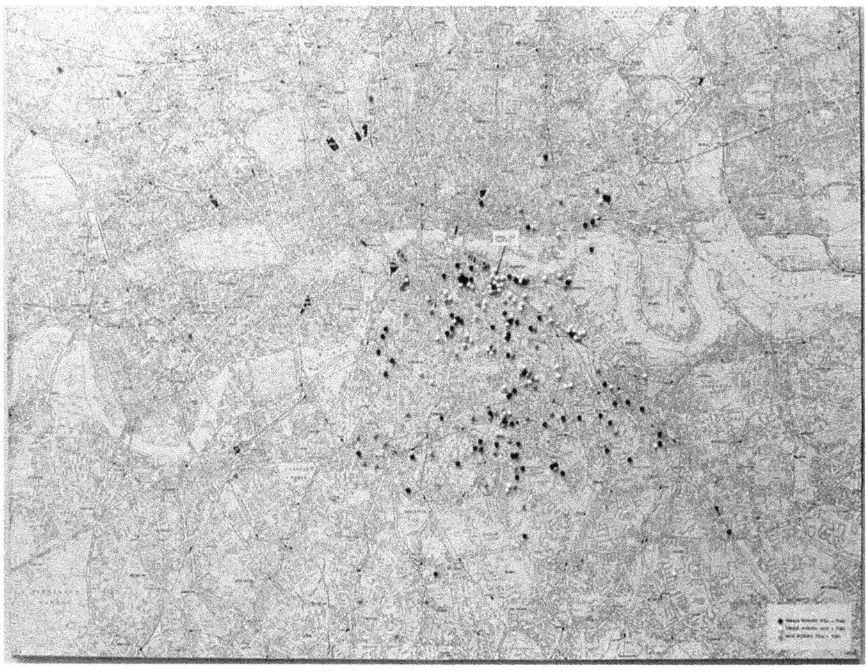

Margaret Harrison, Kay Fido Hunt and Mary Kelly, map from the exhibition *Women and Work: A Document on the Division of Labour in Industry 1973–75*, 1975.   **3.5**

Remapping social space

Both *Garbage Walk* and *The West London Social Resource Project* navigate the spaces between the public and private, breaking down barriers between the two. In *Women and Work*, the negotiation between public and private labour is implicitly gendered, denoting a central aspect of the feminist challenge to existing institutions and social structures.[52] This concern is epitomised by the assertion that 'the personal is political'. The recognition of women as labourers in and out of the home and the belief that change in social relations must also extend to the private realm became central to women's liberation struggles, with *Women and Work* serving as an important historical marker of these debates.[53] As the map and locational specificity of *Women and Work* illustrate, these social relations are also fundamentally spatial. Feminist geographers have shown that not only are the social and the spatial intertwined; geography, space and gender are deeply interconnected and implicated in their mutual construction.[54] Linda McDowell and Joanne P. Sharp summarise:

> Spatial relations and layout, the differences between and within places, the nature and form of the built environment, images and representations of this environment and of the 'natural' world, ways of writing about it, as well as our bodily place within it, are all part and parcel of the social constitution of gendered social relations and the structure and meaning of place … Physical and social boundaries reinforce each other and spatial relations act to socialise people into the acceptance of gendered power relations.[55]

Although *Garbage Walk* and *The West London Social Resource Project* do not consider the inarguable centrality of gender to the spaces they examine, all three interventions work towards the creation of a more participatory, discursive public sphere, consisting of multiple publics that can challenge social and political norms through self-conscious debate and discussion, or what Seyla Benhabib has termed 'practical discourse'.[56] While European geography has traditionally been determined by the universalising vision and priorities of upper- and middle-class white heterosexual men,[57] *Women and Work*, *Garbage Walk* and *The West London Social Resource Project* establish alternative cartographies that include the collective experiences of small communities and spaces that have normally been excluded from or underrepresented in the public sphere. These works suggest a new constitution of socio-cultural space that answers feminist critiques of the hierarchical structures of power governing the formation of public identities.

It must be noted, however, that while these projects draw attention to social conditions, class and gender, considerations of race were notably absent.

Despite the participation of immigrant women of colour in *Women and Work,* following the goals of the feminist movement at the time, it represented them within one collective framework.[58] Similarly, while Ehrenberg later remarked upon the racial bigotry that prompted his family's move from London to the countryside in Devon, his earlier projects in the city draw upon the universalising rhetoric of 1960s counterculture.[59] For Willats, his choice of communities, focus on class relations and the abstraction of individual subjects into 'models' overrode a concern for the racial anxieties that progressively plagued London in the 1970s.

Consequently, these projects do not fully address the crisis of the public sphere in the city at the time. They are, however, instructive and compelling examples of how conceptualism, shaped by collaborative production, could inform radical artistic interventions in society outside traditional art world spaces. Together recording the impact of labour, class and gender on the urban geography of London, all of these projects make visible the experiences of diverse communities, and through the presentation of maps, information and documentation they incite public discourse that emerges *from* and is debated *within* the spaces of each community. As Roberts and Crossley have explained, this intervention can be seen in relation to a Foucauldian reading of 'public reason', where the making visible of all of the heterogeneous properties that construct a space can disrupt meaning, allowing alternative rationalities to be constructed.[60] These projects simultaneously shifted the geography of the London art world outside established institutions, working directly in the streets, in homes and public libraries, and in the experimental venues of the Sigi Krauss Gallery and the South London Art Gallery,[61] to offer compelling models for the collective production and distribution of art and information that extended the critiques wrought by conceptual art to remap physical and social space.

Notes

1 While this discussion focuses on the context of London, these artists were part of various international networks that influenced their approaches. See Jo Applin, Catherine Spencer and Amy Tobin (eds), *London Art Worlds: Mobile, Contingent, and Ephemeral Networks, 1960–1980* (University Park: Pennsylvania State University Press, 2018).

2 Michel Claura and Seth Siegelaub, 'L'art conceptuel', in Alexander Alberro and Blake Stimson (eds), *Conceptual Art: A Critical Anthology* (Cambridge, MA: MIT Press, 1999), pp. 286–90.

3 Benjamin H. D. Buchloh, 'Conceptual art 1962–1969: From the aesthetic of administration to the critique of institutions', *October* 55 (1990), 105–43.

4 Jürgen Habermas, *The Structural Transformation of the Public Sphere: An Inquiry into a Category of Bourgeois Society*, trans. T. Burger and F. Lawrence (Cambridge, MA: MIT Press, 1991). My discussion of the public sphere draws from the writings of Doreen Massey, particularly *Space, Place, and Gender* (Minneapolis: University of Minnesota Press, 1994), and responds to pluralist postmodernist conceptualisations of the public sphere offered by Ernesto Laclau and Chantal Mouffe. See also Craig Calhoun (ed.), *Habermas and the Public Sphere* (Cambridge, MA: MIT Press, 1992); and N. Crossley and J. M. Roberts (eds), *After Habermas: New Perspectives on the Public Sphere* (Malden, MA: Blackwell, 2004).

5 Doreen Massey, *Spatial Divisions of Labour: Social Relations and the Geography of Production*, 2nd edn (London: Macmillan, 1995), p. 2.

6 Seyla Benhabib, 'Models of public space: Hannah Arendt, the liberal tradition, and Jürgen Habermas', in Calhoun, *Habermas and the Public Sphere*, pp. 89–120; Nancy Fraser, 'Rethinking the public sphere: A contribution to the critique of actually existing democracy', in Calhoun, *Habermas and the Public Sphere*, pp. 109–42; Massey, *Space, Place, and Gender*; Oskar Negt and Alexander Kluge, *Public Sphere and Experience: Toward an Analysis of the Bourgeois and Proletarian Public Sphere* (London: Verso, 2016).

7 The Polygonal Workshop was founded by Ehrenberg, Kriesche and Rodolfo Alcaraz. It later included Peter Axmann, Peter Conn, Serge Halsdorf, Roy Lekus and Rudolfine Well. For an overview of the Polygonal Workshop in the context of Ehrenberg's practice see Carmen Juliá, 'Mapping the city: Felipe Ehrenberg in London, 1968–71', in Applin, Spencer and Tobin, *London Art Worlds*, pp. 55–75.

8 Richard Kriesche, 'Correspondence with the author: April 12, 2019', *Projekt14: The Garbage Strike 1970/1*, available at www.medienblock-richard-kriesche.at/Projekt14/ (accessed 21 May 2022). Conrad Atkinson created a similar project, *Garbage Strike* (1970), also shown at the Sigi Krauss Gallery.

9 See Oliver Debroise, Tatiana Falcón and Cuauhtémoc Medina, *La era de la discrepancia: Arte cultura visual en México* (*The Age of Discrepancies: Art and Visual Culture in Mexico 1968–1997*), 2nd edn (Mexico City: Universidad Nacional Autónoma de Mexico, 2014), p. 170. The sustained use of photography to document the effects of social systems is reminiscent of Hans Haacke, but its use in conjunction with the more open-ended, collaborative and performative actions of the project equally align *Garbage Walk* with the spirit of Fluxus and Happenings.

10 Ehrenberg edited the film in Paris with the assistance of Polygonal Workshop member Peter Conn. An original soundtrack was provided by Conn's friend, Italian composer Cesare Massarenti.

11 In this regard *Garbage Walk* can be compared to Mierle Laderman Ukeles's *Maintenance Art Performances*, which similarly make the labour of maintenance visible, disrupting the normative functioning of the public sphere. See Helen Molesworth, 'House work and art work', *October* 92 (Spring 2000), 71–97.

12 This statement was made by Ehrenberg retrospectively, describing his lifelong interest in art becoming part of the fabric of society and his belief in collaborative practices. Martha Gever, 'Art is an excuse: An interview with Felipe Ehrenberg', *Afterimage* (April 1983), 12.

13 The Sigi Krauss Gallery served as a hub for countercultural experimentations prior to the establishment of Gallery House in 1972, which Krauss ran with Rosetta Brooks until August 1973. Despite these ventures being short-lived, their impact on the London art world cannot be underestimated. Antony Hudek, Alex Sainsbury and Elizabeth Stanton, *This Way out of England: Gallery House in Retrospect* (London: Raven Row, 2017).

14 Kriesche, *Projekt14: The Garbage Strike 1970/1*.

15 Felipe Ehrenberg and Fernando Llanos (eds), *Felipe Ehrenberg: Manchuria país periférico* (Mexico City: Editorial Diamantina, 2007).

16 Valerie Fraser, Michael Asbury, María Iñigo Clavo and Isobel Whitelegg, 'Interview with Felipe Ehrenberg at the University of Essex on the eve of "Xocoyotzin, the Penultimate"', *Arara* 8 (2010), 9.

17 Issa Ma. Benítez Dueñas, 'Reconstructing emptiness and recovering space: The conceptual Ehrenberg', in Felipe Ehrenberg and Fernando Llanos (eds), *Manchuria: Visión pereférica* (Mexico City: Editorial Diamantina, 2007), p. 25.

18 Sigi Krauss, 'Letter from Sigi Krauss Gallery to the press, responding to John Rydon's refusal to cover the exhibition', personal archives of Sigi Krauss, n.d.; Sigi Krauss, phone conversation with author, 1 April 2019; Fraser *et al.*, 'Interview with Felipe Ehrenberg', p. 9; Hans Ulrich Obrist, 'Felipe Ehrenberg', in Karen Marta (ed.), *Conversations in Mexico* (Mexico City: Fundacion Alumnos 47, 2016), pp. 338–9.

19 Felipe Ehrenberg, 'In search of a model for life', *ARTMargins* 1:1 (June 2012), 125.

20 Kriesche's later projects show a similar interest in the documentation of economic, political and social systems in immersive and architectural installations that challenge the perception of viewers. Richard Kriesche, 'Medienblock: Richard Kriesche', available at www.medienblock-richard-kriesche.at; Peter Pakesch and Richard Kriesche, *Richard Kriesche, Capital + Code anlässlich der Ausstellung Richard Kriesche, Capital + Code, Kunsthaus Graz am Landesmuseum Joanneum, 15.11.2008–22.02.2009* (Cologne: König, 2008).

21 Stephen Willats, *The Artist as an Instigator of Changes in Social Cognition and Behaviour* (London: Occasional Papers, 2011). Willats describes his focus after 1965 as redefining a 'new physical and social territory for an artwork to operate within' (p. 8). This change informed his alternative pedagogy, and influenced his establishment of *Control* magazine in 1965. See also Stephen Willats, 'The representation of social reality', in *Concerning Our Present Way of Living* (Oxford: Museum of Modern Art, 1978), 3–4.

22 The project areas were located along Greenford Road, with Project Area 4 to the north and Project Area 2 to the south. Project Area 1 was located on the southwest corner of Perivale Park, with Project Area 3 situated close by, directly south of the park.

23 Area 1 was part of the geographic area of Greenford; Area 2 corresponded with Osterley Park, Area 3 with Hanwell and Area 4 with Harrow. The project mapped these individual locations, but also the spaces that connected and divided them. Willats records that there were forty-seven participants. No responses were received from Harrow, the upper-middle-class development, despite initial interest. For a detailed description see Willats, *The Artist as an Instigator*.

24 *Ibid.*, pp. 34–7, 43.

25 The structure and intentions of the project were shaped by Willats's longstanding studies of cybernetic and systems theories. For example, he uses speculative modelling to map complex socio-economic systems conceptually, with the goal of initiating more democratic, open-ended and non-hierarchical patterns of communication. Stephen Willats, *Speculative Modelling with Diagrams* (Utrecht: Casco, 2007).

26 The volunteers included 'specialists in disciplines', such as a photographer, a sociologist, a cybernetician and a team of women called the 'West London Super Girls' who were responsible for recruiting and interviewing potential participants. This catchy anonymising of his female collaborators reflects the still-evolving gender dynamics of the 1970s London art world.

27 Willats, *The Artist as an Instigator*, pp. 48–55.

28 Grant H. Kester has described Willats's work as 'dialogical', emphasising its collaborative and discursive relationship with participants. Grant H. Kester, *Conversation Pieces: Community and Communication in Modern Art* (Berkeley: University of California Press, 2014). See Stephen Willats, 'Notice (1967)', available at www.stephenwillats.com/texts/notice-1967/ (accessed 21 May 2022); and Bronač Ferran, 'Stephen Willats interviewed by Bronač Ferran', *Interdisciplinary Science Reviews* 42:1–2 (2017), 201–13.

29 Willats also ran his pioneering Centre for Behavioural Art at Gallery House between May 1972 and March 1973. The centre provided a space for intellectuals and artists to discuss and experiment with cybernetic, behavioural and systems theories, and social psychology. See Anthony Hudek, 'A porous entity: The Centre for Behavioural Art at Gallery House, 1972–3', in Applin, Spencer and Tobin, *London Art Worlds*, pp. 39–54.

30 Willats argued that these 'wastelands' provided an escape from the determinism of domestic architecture. In addition to being featured on the Gallery House Public Monitors, the 'wastelands' were also pictured and captioned on the cover of the *West London Manual*. Willats explored these spaces in later works, including *The Lurky Place* (1978) and *Pat Purdy and the Glue Sniffers Camp* (1981–82). See Tim Holert, 'Capsules out of control: Stephen Willats and the heuristics of the margins', in Stephen Willats (ed.), *Art Society Feedback* (Nuremberg: Verlag für moderne Kunst, 2010).

31 Stephen Willats, *Between Buildings and People* (London: Academy Editions, 1996), p. 7.

32 Stephen Willats, 'Physical reality and social consciousness', in *Concerning Our Present Way of Living*, 7.

33 Roy Ascott, 'Untitled statement', *Control* 1 (1965).

34 Stephen Willats, *Speculative Modelling with Diagrams* (Utrecht: Casco, 2007), pp. 1–2.

35 Stephen Willats, *Art and Social Function: Three Projects* (London: Ellipsis, 2000), p. 7.

36 The area was selected as it had been a centre of workshop industries employing women over the past century. Hunt was also born in and lived in south London,

and generations of women in her family were working-class labourers in the area. Kay Fido Hunt, 'Statement', in Clive Phillpot and Andrea Tarsia, *Live in Your Head: Concept and Experiment in Britain 1965–75* (exh. cat.) (London: Whitechapel Art Gallery, 2000), pp. 108–9; Mary Kelly, 'A brief history of the Women's Workshop of the Artists Union 1972–3', in Judith Mastai (ed.), *Social Process/Collaborative Action: Mary Kelly 1970–1975* (Vancouver: Charles H. Scott Gallery, 1997), pp. 77–80.

37 Kelly, 'A brief history'; Rozsika Parker and Griselda Pollock (eds), *Framing Feminism: Art and the Women's Movement 1970–85* (London: Pandora, 1987).

38 See Mastai, *Social Process/Collaborative Action*, pp. 95–104; Siona Wilson, *Art Labor, Sex Politics: Feminist Effects in 1970s British Art and Performance* (Minneapolis: University of Minnesota Press, 2016).

39 Margaret Harrison's later project *Homework* (1970) also addresses the repercussions of the 1970 Equal Pay Act and related legislation affecting non-unionised women workers. See Margaret Harrison, 'On the home front', Tate website, www.tate.org. uk/tate-etc/issue-29-autumn-2013/on-home-front (accessed 21 May 2022).

40 Marina Vaizey, 'Personal print', *The Sunday Times*, 25 May 1975.

41 Margaret Harrison, Kay Fido Hunt and Mary Kelly, *Women and Work: A Document on the Division of Labour in Industry* (London: South London Gallery, 1975); Mastai, *Social Process/Collaborative Action*, pp. 79–82.

42 Harrison *et al.*, *Women and Work*; Mastai, *Social Process/Collaborative Action*, pp. 87–9; J. Watts, 'Pandora's tin box', *Guardian*, 19 May 1975.

43 For example, through the inclusion of documents such as the agreement between the Metal Box Company and the Workers Union. Tate Archives, *Women and Work*, TGA 20025/1/1.

44 This echoes Willats's belief that the language of his projects needed to speak directly to participants and local audiences.

45 Mary Kelly, *Imaging Desire* (Cambridge, MA: MIT Press, 1998), pp. 33–4, 187; Douglas Crimp, 'Douglas Crimp in conversation with Mary Kelly', in Margaret Iverson, Douglas Crimp and Homi K. Bhabha (eds), *Mary Kelly* (London: Phaidon, 1997), p. 11; Hunt, 'Statement'; Carmen Juliá, 'Margaret Harrison: *Homeworkers* (1977)', Tate website, www.tate.org.uk/art/artworks/harrison-homeworkers-t13631 (accessed 21 May 2022).

46 Rosalind Delmar, '*Women and Work: A Document on the Division of Labour in Industry*', *Spare Rib* 40 (1975), 32–3; reprinted in Parker and Pollock, *Framing Feminism*, pp. 201–2.

47 *Ibid.* For more on feminist collaboration see Amy Tobin, 'I'll show you mine, if you show me yours: Collaboration, consciousness-raising and feminist-influenced art in the 1970s', *Tate Papers*, available at www.tate.org.uk/research/tate-papers/25/ i-show-you-mine-if-you-show-me-yours (accessed 21 May 2022).

48 The exhibition seems to have been well received by the public. Letters to the gallery appreciated that the exhibition related to the surrounding community and to society more generally, although many weren't sure if it could be considered 'art'. South London Gallery Archives, London, 'Assorted letters from the public', 1975.

49 Mastai, *Social Process/Collaborative Action*, p. 17.

50 Tobin, 'I'll show you mine', discusses the importance of collaborative exhibition organising for women artists.

51 Laura Mulvey, '*Post-Partum Document*: Mary Kelly', *Spare Rib* 40 (1976); Mastai, *Social Process/Collaborative Action*, p. 89.

52 Helen Molesworth describes this mediation between the public and private as a pivotal feature of early feminist artwork, particularly of Mierle Laderman Ukeles's *Maintenance Artworks*. See Helen Molesworth, 'Cleaning up in the 1970s', in Michael Newman and Jon Bird (eds), *Rewriting Conceptual Art* (London: Reaktion Books, 1999), pp. 107–22 (later version published as Molesworth, 'House work and art work').

53 Nancy Duncan, 'Renegotiating gender and sexuality in public and private spaces', in Nancy Duncan (ed.), *BodySpace: Destabilizing Geographies of Gender and Sexuality* (London: Routledge, 1996).

54 Massey, *Space, Place, and Gender*; Linda McDowell and Joanne P. Sharp, *Space, Gender, Knowledge: Feminist Readings* (London: Arnold, 1997).

55 *Ibid.*, pp. 2–3.

56 Benhabib, 'Models of public space'.

57 Gillian Rose, *Feminism and Geography: The Limits of Geographical Knowledge* (Minneapolis: University of Minnesota Press, 1993). See also Women and Geography Study Group, 'Why study feminist geography?', in Women and Geography Study Group and Explorations in Feminism Collective (eds), *Geography and Gender: An Introduction to Feminist Geography* (London: Hutchinson, in association with the Explorations in Feminism Collective, 1984), pp. 19–23.

58 Wilson notes a similar 'blind spot' in relation to *Nightcleaners. Art Labor, Sex Politics*, p. 51.

59 Fraser *et al.*, 'Interview with Felipe Ehrenberg'; Obrist, 'Felipe Ehrenberg'.

60 Roberts and Crossley, *After Habermas*, p. 13.

61 Applin, Spencer and Tobin, *London Art Worlds*.

Part II
Political geographies

The multifaceted Hungarian artist Gábor Attalai started to engage with maps and cartography in his work in 1970–71.[1] The series entitled *Continental Change* is a simple yet resourceful montage of the world atlas. *Continental Change I* (1971) is a modification of the cartography of the globe as we know it, with the help of scissors, glue, paper and the typewriter. The montages *African Ocean, South-American Ocean, Transfer of Sweden, Transfer of Japan, Big Square Lake, Big Triangle Gulf, Round Lake, Big Star Lake* and *Amerasia* all formed part of the first collection of map transformations.[2] In the *African* and *South-American Ocean* pieces, only the contours of the continents remained; the land was 'flooded' by saltwater, leaving a narrow frame of islands – the shape of which was reminiscent of the former mainland shapes of Africa and South America. Wandering peninsulas and insular states manifested themselves in the *Transfer of Sweden* and *Transfer of Japan*; here, Sweden took on the geographical position of Italy, while Japan covered the whole of Great Britain (see Figure 4.1).

The insertion of geometrically shaped lakes onto the maps looks more artificial than the other 'geographical modifications' ('geographische Änderungen'),[3] where countries and geographical formations familiar to our view of the world atlas appear in unexpected locations. Attalai assigned a huge square-shaped lake to central Spain; placed a triangular lake across the borders of Germany and Poland; located a circular lake at the shared border of Hungary, Romania and the former Yugoslavia; and put a lake shaped like a five-pointed star across significant territories of the then Soviet Union (see Figure 4.2).

With the erasure of the Atlantic Ocean and Europe, the artist created a new continent named Amerasia. In this new landmass, Canada, the United States and Mexico became neighbours of Siberia and Iran. These examples of creative 'countercartography'[4] that challenge spatial narrations 'as … stor[ies] of domination and resistance'[5] point to the constructed nature of territories and borders, including the attribution of meaning inscribed into space to reflect order in society, politics and culture. This order determines our material and immaterial rootedness within these structures. Juggling – or

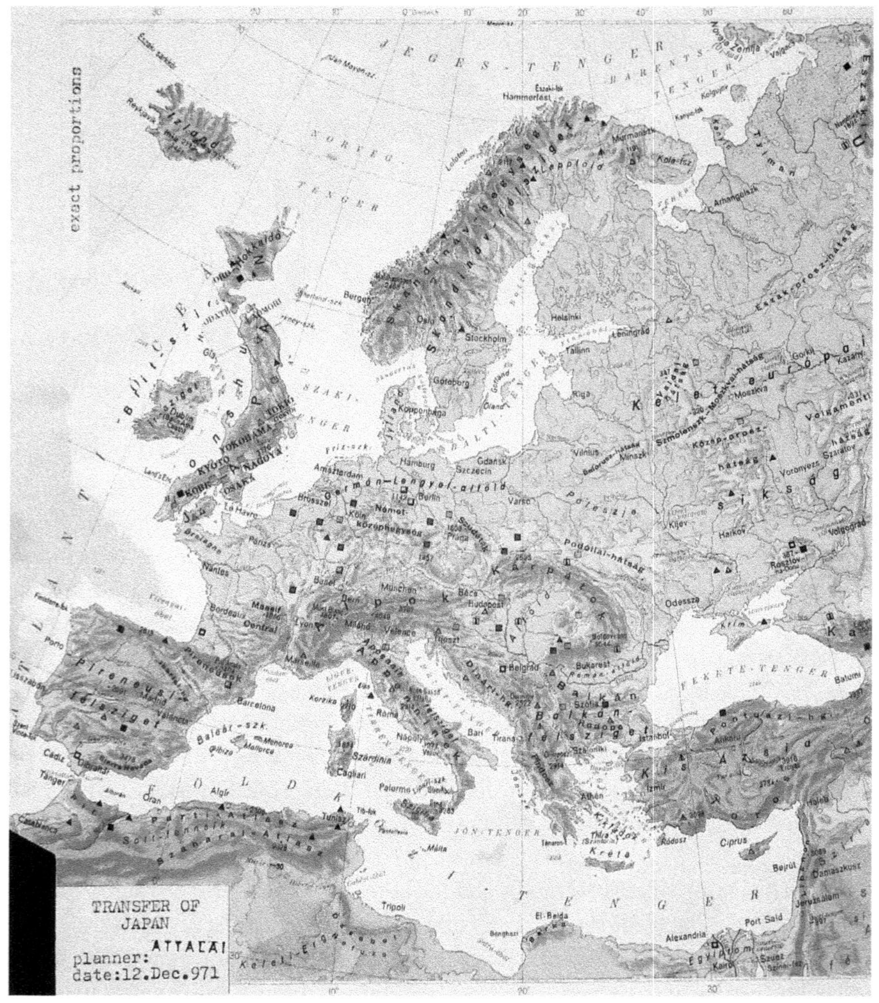

4.1   Gábor Attalai, *Transfer of Japan, Continental Change I*, 1971.

overthrowing – spatial structures in the form of these map collages could, in the words of Latin Americanist Raymond B. Craib, be understood as 'dialogic and politically empowering', through a process in which the actors who are restructuring or even reinventing the maps are 'active agents and historical subjects'.[6] Craib analyses technological, epistemological and artistic appropriations of the map in the colonial context and its aftermath, and draws our attention to the variety of stories that can complicate and challenge colonialism.[7] He imagines 'countercartographies' to be forums of dialogue 'between tradition and modernity, among the past, present and future',[8] while simultaneously

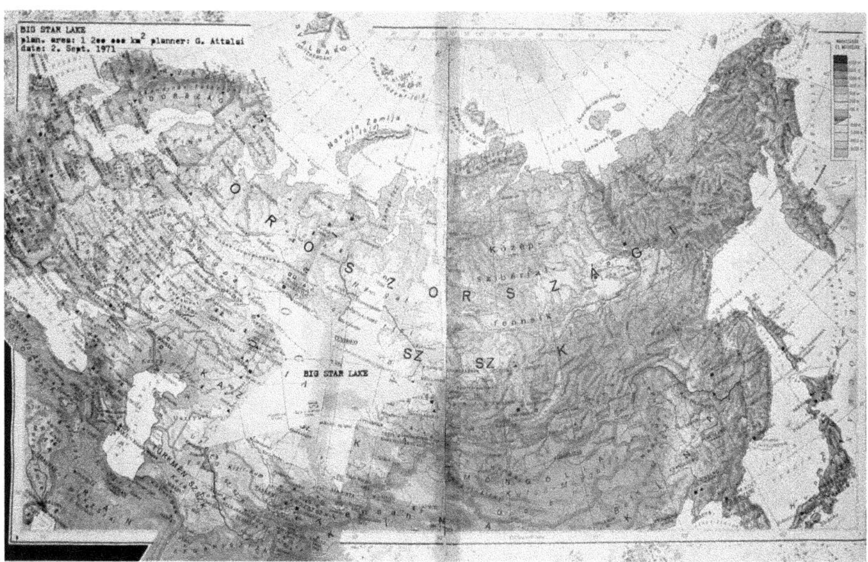

Gábor Attalai, *Big Star Lake, Continental Change I*, 1971.   **4.2**

taking care not to equate creative modes of decolonisation with independence or heroic action.[9] Craib's approach to countercartographies points to space as 'made', and highlights the power that is attached to shaping space. Any creative act of transforming space, even if it only involves the manipulation of representations of space, raises a voice against geopolitical and spatial regimes with monopolising ambitions. As the case of Gábor Attalai will reveal, it is especially interesting to examine artworks that explicitly address the issue of spatiality in geopolitical constellations with a (more or less) evident monopoly over borders and territories.

Craib argues that, during the Cold War, we witnessed the compartmentalisation of the globe into ideologically divided areas, culturally associated territories and areas categorised by their respective 'stages of development'.[10] By the 1940s the worlds that arose from this design of space and place were already subject to critical mapping strategies developed by intellectuals and artists. By exemplifying the maps made by Joaquín Torres-García, Arno Peters and Buckminster Fuller, Craib makes it clear that 'maps were used repeatedly as a means to challenge particular ways of "thinking" the world'.[11] The maps and spatial interventions by Gábor Attalai subverted and/or undermined the space guarded by the Cold War's superpowers and Hungarian State socialism.

In this chapter, I discuss Attalai as a countercartographer, both as an internationally mobile artist,[12] and through his work (mail art, correspondence and performative conceptualism), which is distinguished by its mobility and the notable way it defies conventional artistic categorisation.[13] The border crossings inherent to Attalai's art practice are visible both in his mail art and exceptionally intense art correspondence activity, and in his work transgressing the boundaries of conceptual art, project art, land art and process art.[14] The artworks discussed in this chapter also demonstrate a tendency towards spatial modification, and can therefore be read as a form of challenge to space, spatial codes and fixed structures. Immaterial countercartography, which forms the theoretical backdrop to this text, is the artistic process of engaging with space as creative opportunity – it is the performative act of challenging vertical spatial constellations. The maps and spatial interventions by Attalai discussed here thus demonstrate a 'counterhegemonic potential'.[15]

The chapter will explore how the immaterial countercartographies in Attalai's oeuvre disturb habitual expectations of space and its appearance. These expectations are scrutinised on three levels: the surface of the body, the urban space and the world atlas. In the early 1970s Attalai produced process-based artworks with a certain continuity in terms of spatial subversion. *Continental Change*, the transformation of the atlas, was an act of deconstruction and construction that drew new contours for countries and continents in a counterhegemonic manner. Here, the countries and continents represent geopolitical entities of power and ideology that Attalai disregards with his map collage.

The *Continental Change* series was a natural consequence of Attalai's desire to extend the scope of his recent land art works, the so-called *Schnee-Arbeiten* (*Snow Works*, 1970–71).[16] In these pieces Attalai used the snow-covered steps of Budapest as the initial point of his intervention and shovelled geometric shapes into the snow that became visible as examples of land art only when viewed from a distance. Compared to the map collages, the *Snow Works* were temporary spatial interventions in a more local urban space.[17] When carving out a space of his own, Attalai turned his given surroundings into an autonomous work of art. The fleeting 'monuments' of the countercartographer were the communist monuments' apparent opposites in terms of permanence and power at the time. At around the same time, Attalai conducted body art actions analogous to the *Snow Works*, where the act of carving into space had a substantial role.[18] In *Kopaszítás* (*Balding*, 1970), Attalai shaved stripes into a man's hair – an action documented by a series of photographs.[19] *Balding* addresses the most intimate 'space' of the three conceptual land art pieces – the body. Besides applying geometric shapes to a 'natural' surface, *Balding* may be interpreted as carrying the message that each individual's body is their own, and should not be at the mercy of outside forces. The motto 'My body, my territory', the basic idea of *Balding*, counteracts socialist biopolitics and introduces a unique land artwork.

In this chapter I analyse Attalai's mapping strategies against the background of (event-based) conceptual art's triumphal procession behind the

Iron Curtain. First, I discuss the historical and cultural-political context of the Kádár regime in Hungary from the mid-1960s until the mid-1970s, in terms of its effect on the emergence and existence of neo-avant-gardist tendencies. I also outline the relationship between Attalai and the socialist politics of the time. After this introduction, I explore the tendencies of conceptual art in east, central and southeast Europe in the same period, the climax of this art form, and how it spread across the Soviet zone of influence, including Hungary.[20] In this context it is important to consider constellations – such as the local and global communication of conceptual art – that created favourable conditions for the emergence of immaterial countercartographies. I continue with an exploration of the interrelatedness of conceptual art and immateriality, followed by a discussion of the relationship of conceptualism, internationalism and institutional critique. The central comparative analysis of the chapter deals with Attalai's spatial intervention on three levels: the body/skin, the urban space and the map collages. Together, these three case studies – *Balding, Snow Works* and *Continental Change I* and *II* – reveal the artistic empowerment of immaterial countercartography as a plea against (political) fixations of space and place.

Art between repression and permission: A decade of the Hungarian Kádár regime (1965–75)

As a consequence of the period of transition from the Khrushchev to the Brezhnev era, the Soviet Union's conflict with China, and the promotion in Hungary of a more liberal government structure by János Kádár – the leader of the Magyar Szocialista Munkáspárt (Hungarian Socialist Workers' Party) – experimental tendencies in the Hungarian art world began to flourish in the mid-1960s. The four main institutions and policymakers of art regulation[21] operated with 'flexible aesthetic categories' and a method of control that oscillated between differentiation and centralisation.[22] The period between 1965 and 1968 can be regarded as the 'golden' years of Kádárian socialism, as during this time the State established high living standards coupled with the so-called 'Új Gazdasági Mechanizmus' (New Economic Mechanism). The aim of this economic plan was to reduce economic shortages and to emphasise the satisfaction of consumer needs in the spirit of allowing a moderate amount of competition and entrepreneurship.[23] This financial reform demonstrated the open-mindedness of the Kádár regime at the time, supported by the spirit of the intellectual currents of 1968 that promised a general reform of the socialist systems across central and eastern Europe.[24] To the Soviet Union, this promise went too far, and ultimately required the military invasion of Czechoslovakia in 1968, with the involvement of Hungarian troops alongside those from other Warsaw Pact countries.[25]

Instead of looking outwards, the Soviet Union then tried to motivate its satellite states to collaborate with each other in the realms of economics, technology and science. The main obstacle that acted to restrict these exchanges was the outbreak of the energy crisis in the early 1970s and the socialist countries' intensified cooperation with the 'West'. It was within this framework that the international contacts with western Europe and the United States that Attalai and his fellow artists established began to flourish. In the preparation phase of the human rights agreement in the Helsinki Accord (1975), the Soviet Union's influence over Hungary weakened.[26] Kádár had proved himself to be a master of manoeuvre between the superpowers and had tried to widen Hungary's autonomy. He could not imagine losing control in his own country, however, and continued to govern in a state of dualism. This meant Kádár clearly abandoned open criticism of the regime and the possibility of pluralism in Marxist thought, but was willing to transform the system of political institutions and to review the standards of ideology.[27]

At around the time that the party turned against critical sociologists and philosophers who had publicly expressed objections to Hungary's involvement in the invasion of Czechoslovakia in 1968,[28] those in charge of cultural politics introduced systematic 'warfare' against unconventional and non-conformist art.[29] The direction – which started with the closure of the legendary IPARTERV shows (1968 and 1969) that had presented the Hungarian manifestations of international contemporary art[30] – reached its peak with the party's forceful shutdown in 1973 of the artist community and summer workshop of the Chapel Studio in Balatonboglár. After 1973 a process of slow easing began, which lasted throughout the second half of the 1970s.[31]

Attalai's double life as an internationally active neo-avant-garde artist and a reliable contract worker of the Iparművészeti Vállalat (Company of Applied Arts), and the Hungarian authorities' mostly indulgent treatment of his experimental networking activity, reflect the complexity of the Kádár regime's permissive-repressive politics. After graduating from the Magyar Iparművészeti Főiskola (Hungarian Academy of Applied Arts) in 1958, Attalai began to work for the State-owned Company of Applied Arts. Almost in parallel, he joined the art-focused self-education group Zuglói Kör (Zugló Circle, 1958–68), based in the Budapest apartment of painter Sándor Molnár.[32] Members of this circle shared passionate discussions, readings and translations about surrealism and modernism from a transnational perspective that questioned the division of eastern and western Europe.[33] At around the same time Attalai was also an active participant in the apartment exhibitions and similar events staged by the salon of music enthusiast Pál Petrigalla.[34] The artist frequently visited these alternative sites because he regarded the official cultural landscape of Kádárian Hungary as grey and boring. In the mid-1960s Attalai successfully convinced painter Imre Bak to engage actively in the direct acquisition of information from artists abroad.[35] Attalai's (party-conforming) expertise was in textiles, and brought him not only the position of president of the Képzőművészeti Szövetség Textil Alosztálya (Textile Section of the Union of Fine Arts), but also some State-funded trips to western metropoles – which were often combined with visits to museums of modern art. Polyartist Gyölgy Galántai suspects that it was the elegant, non-provocative way in which Attalai infiltrated the regime that explains his peaceful coexistence with the cultural politics of the time.[36] Attalai's open-mindedness – and comparative freedom – is expressed in his combination of textile, photography, land art and non-artistic materials. These features and genres appeared in an intense way in his performative conceptual art that, to Attalai, represented a freedom of dialogue among materials, art forms, attitudes and art worlds.[37]

Conceptual art in eastern Europe and in Hungary

Conceptual art, 'the basic premise [of which] is that ideas can be the material of art',[38] appeared almost simultaneously in many countries around the globe.[39] Zöe Sutherland, a scholar of the politics and aesthetics of contemporary art, describes conceptual art as 'globally "spontaneous", in the sense that [it] lacked any single organizational pole and conscious referent'.[40] Mostly because conceptualism's core features were 'dematerialization and ephemeralization',[41] it travelled well and was an ideal mode of expression for artists who lacked the necessary resources to produce expensive artworks. While conceptual art's criticism of the capitalist art market was of secondary importance to artists working behind the Iron Curtain, they could identify with the institutional criticism inherent to the art as an idea.[42]

In eastern Europe, high art techniques and art's mode of traditional display were increasingly regarded as obsolete, and often equated with belonging to the official, State-regulated art system.[43] Conceptual artists of the region valued the 'potential for the work to be communicated and distributed widely, rapidly, cheaply', not least because these qualities brought the promise of belonging to an imagined global collective.[44] The international wandering of artists, artworks and mail in east, central and southeast Europe was an alternative act of constructing maps *per se*. Besides participation, practising conceptual art in the Soviet zone of influence meant, in the words of Boris Groys, a 'second way of looking at things'.[45] It could help artists to overcome the implicitness of modernism, to criticise and reflect on the context of art production and infrastructure, to articulate 'a certain disbelief in the guiding role of subject-ivity', and to make 'art outside the system of linguistic and other conventions'.[46] The hegemonies and aesthetic fixation imposed on east and central European neo-avant-gardists increased their affinity for expression based on a con-cept. Opposed to following guidelines, they viewed developing a concept as the artist's own decision – and as such, as representing autonomous agency. The idea of packing the maximum meaning into the minimum amount of material was irresistible to conceptual artists operating under socialist rule. Countercartographies, such as Attalai's *Continental Change*, carried in their two-dimensional format the ambitious suggestion of a global spatial transition. Also, the series of map collages represents a balancing out of the relationship between the local and the global: the globe's geography seen and 'edited' from Attalai's local point of view was sent on a journey to the western side of the Iron Curtain.[47] Equally balancing is the art historian's role, who should be careful not to reduce eastern European, as well as Hungarian, conceptual artists to political subjects,[48] and simultaneously not to ignore the overtly politicised setting of the State socialist zone and its place in an ideologically divided world order.[49]

Both the contemporary and the retrospective perception of conceptual art in Hungary were strongly shaped by the activity of Hungarian art historian, curator and networker László Beke. Beke was an important personality in managing and 'curating' conceptual art in Hungary. György Galántai characterised Beke as a 'projektművész' ('project artist') because of his intense conceptually inspired activity in the early 1970s.[50] He organised numerous meetings and exhibitions while simultaneously selecting and coordinating artworks and artists for further international circulation through his mainly European art network.[51] Like Attalai, Beke also proactively built his connections and turned them into events.[52] Most of his (co-)organised art events had their origins in a call for participation, and he collected materials from neo-avant-gardists that reflected on a single idea or concept, such as *Elképzelés* (*Imagination*, 1971);[53] the 1973 *Tükör* (*Mirror*) exhibition in Balatonboglár;[54] and the international show entitled *Kép/vers* (*Visual/Poem*), which was staged in Budapest in 1974.[55] Beke had a clear interest in 'the passage from idea to material', and indeed in any form in which the idea could take shape.[56] Inspired by the institutional critique of conceptual art, Beke established the *World-Famous World Archives of Ideas, Concepts, Projects etc.* in his Budapest flat. Art historian Klara Kemp-Welch describes this unconventional curatorial undertaking in the following way:

> He [Beke] made 'a regular show each month of another artist with the same black ring-binder', turning the small room where he lived with his family into a gallery to which he would invite one or two people at a time to see the project. Beke estimates having shown the piece to a circle of around 80–90 people in this way, recalling the irony of the space being so cramped while the activities presented were worldwide … Later on, the project was condensed into the form of a portable book of some 80 pages that could be presented in different locations, sometimes by Beke but also at times taken on trips by Dóra Maurer.[57]

This example shows how well connected Beke was, and the kind of inventive actions he took to show the interconnectedness of international conceptual tendencies across the blocs. Furthermore, the *World Archives* opposed the traditional gallery and museum space with its experimental spatial setting: the private became public. The exhibited material appeared in a notebook format that underlined the mobile, travelling form of conceptual art in Hungary. This characteristic of mobility reoccurs in Attalai's immaterial countercartographies, since *Balding, Snow Works* and *Continental Change I* and *II* reached their audiences as small photographs.

The Beke archive has historiographical significance, too, because it reveals the Hungarian networker's self-institutionalisation and self-historicisation in ways that also affected the wider history of conceptual art in Hungary. Beke's *Imagination* initiative, a forerunner of the *World Archives* project, is often referred to as the foundational moment of the Hungarian discourse on conceptualism. On 4 August 1971, Beke put out a call to twenty-eight Hungarian artists to send him pieces related to the equation of art as the documentation of imagination: 'a MŰ = az ELKÉPZELÉS DOKUMENTÁCIÓJA' ('the ARTWORK = the IMAGINATION's DOCUMENTATION'). The call's header included a Lawrence Weiner citation, which read as follows: '1. The artist may construct the piece / 2. The piece may be fabricated / 3. The piece may need not to be built.'[58] This citation is a clue to Beke's source of information on conceptual art, and it served to orient artists on the kind of pieces he hoped to find. The goals of his call were to create an overview of current art tendencies and to overcome the barriers to exhibiting and publishing experimental art.[59] The call and a reflection on its results published by Beke a year later suggest that conceptual art in Hungary appeared in parallel with conceptualism in the West, and that its tools were characterised by 'lightness and variety' and 'strong' engagements with 'social problematics'.[60]

Among the addressees of the call was Gábor Attalai, who responded with a film proposal he had developed based on an earlier art project, entitled *Negatív csillag* (*Negative Star*, 1971); see Figure 4.3). In its original form as a land art piece, Attalai shovelled the shape of a star into the snow covering the steps on the bank of the River Danube next to the Erzsébet híd (Elisabeth Bridge) in Buda. The size of the star was about 80 m², making it visible from the Pest side of Budapest, and it was photographically documented. The artist planned to repeat the same action for the film camera. However, Attalai's 'act of shoveling' and the reaction of passers-by recorded on film remained just a proposal.[61] In the communist setting, the symbol of the five-pointed star confirmed a political 'sensitivity' to which the recording of the reactions of passers-by would have added a socio-critical dimension.[62] The five-pointed star – a symbol of communist ideology – belonged among the most reproduced icons of State socialism. How would unconventional interference in a familiar urban setting

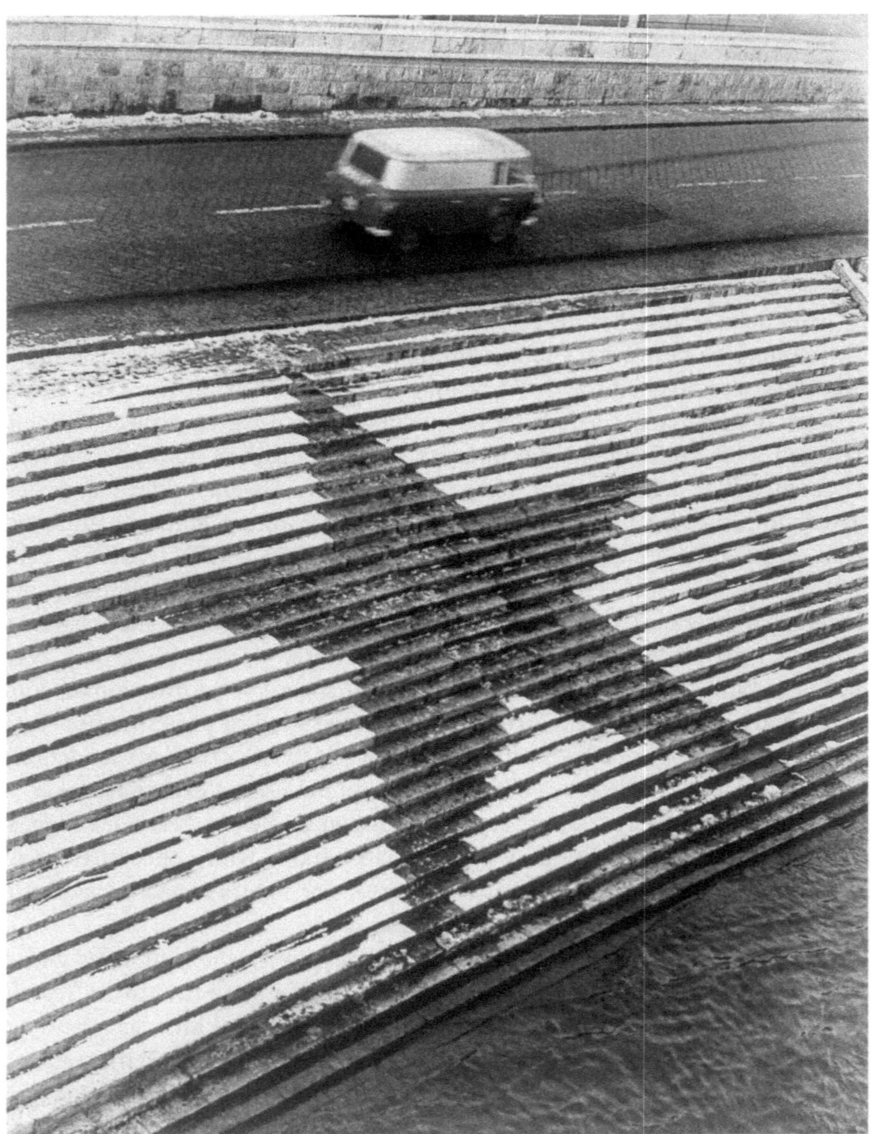

4.3   Gábor Attalai, *Negative Star* (from the *Negative Sculpture* series, *Star & Snow*), 1971, bank of the River Danube, Budapest. Silver print, 80 m², 298 mm × 230 mm.

affect people? Would the shape be regarded as sheer provocation or would it be completely ignored? *Negative Star*, if it had been realised, could have underlined political counterhegemony, since it offered a politicised symbol for free interpretation. Moreover, a film might have captured the reaction to this environmental intervention as more of a process than as a temporary image, cut out from reality. Seeing *Negative Star* as a film might have brought the observer closer to the mobility of the fleeting experience of an (un)conventional urban intervention.

On the immateriality and internationality of conceptual art in Hungary

The importance of de/immaterialisation and the ephemerality of conceptual art (also mentioned by László Beke) had, among others, one major source of inspiration in Hungary: Harald Szeemann's *Live in Your Head: When Attitudes Become Form* (1969). When asked about his first encounter with conceptual, 'dematerialised' art, Attalai recalls the effect Szeemann's exhibition and catalogue had on him.[63] *When Attitudes Become Form* and *documenta 5* (1972), also curated by Szeemann, marked a shift '[f]rom art as object … [to] art as event'.[64] The production of art as a single object was no longer as important as the attitude of the artist on display through the creation of situations. Artists who exhibited at *When Attitudes Become Form* thus concentrated on demystifying the process of art production, in which bodies and intellectual exercises interacted with each other, overwriting the dominance of the gaze and passive perception.[65]

A number of artists referred to Szeemann's show as the most important reference point of Hungarian conceptual art. A generation of artists whose activity was restricted in Kádárian culture recognised in *When Attitudes Become Form* 'a compatibility with western tendencies'.[66] Among the features of conceptual art promoted by the exhibition was the notion of fleetingness. In addition, Hungarian neo-avant-gardists, among them Imre Bak, were fascinated by the idea that no expensive and complex equipment was necessary to produce conceptual artworks. That comprehensive technical knowledge and tools were optional, but not required, made Bak think that it should be financially and politically isolated artists who had invented conceptualism.[67] Since the material was secondary, the limits on the production and circulation of dematerialised artworks were less restrictive. Although almost all works inspired by conceptual art in Hungary had a material carrier form (most often a photograph), the essence – the action behind conceptual art – remained immaterial, as in the cases of *Negative Star* and *Balding*.[68] Approaching art as an intellectual exercise or an experience in minimalist form released creative energies in artists such as Gábor Attalai and networkers such as László Beke. The form of the exhibition was revolutionised through the mobility and ephemerality of these pieces. Since most conceptual art travelled efficiently via the international postal system through this art's envelope format, it was ideal for intensifying exchange and expanding the reach of art that would otherwise have been excluded from publication.

In the context of shifting borders and overcoming spatial barriers, Lucy Lippard's book *Six Years: The Dematerialization of the Art Object from 1966 to 1972* (1973) has to be mentioned.[69] At the beginning of her monograph *Networking the Bloc: Experimental Art in Eastern Europe, 1965–1981* (2018), Klara Kemp-Welch refers to Lippard's publication, which she observes to have summarised and possibly even popularised the 'spirit of connectivity'. An art with a focus on the idea undermined institutionalised structures of exhibiting, and its publications appeared 'all over the place'.[70] Retrospective exhibitions such as *Global Conceptualism: Points of Origin, 1950s–1980s* (1999), or the volume *Unconcealed: The International Network of Conceptual Artists 1967–77* (2009),[71] have slowly turned scholarly attention towards exchange and the mobile nature of conceptual art.[72] Examples of Hungarian conceptualist tendencies were exhibited, for instance, in the Wrocław-based Galeria Sztuki Najowszej (Recent Art Gallery) in 1976,[73] and were presented in the form of 'a survey of contemporary Hungarian art put together by Dóra Maurer and László Beke' in the March/April 1973 issue of the British publication *Schmuck*.[74]

Indeed, Gábor Attalai is himself a good example of the spirit of connectivity Kemp-Welch refers to. As a countercartographer, he started with study trips relatively early on in his career, having travelled to the German Democratic Republic in 1962 and 1964, and then to West Germany and Switzerland in around 1968.[75] In the mid-1960s he began to correspond with various artists, including, for instance, Joseph Beuys, Jasper Johns, Robert Indiana, Gilbert & George, Donald Judd, Walter Auer, Paul Maenz, and Christo. Although most of these contacts were not extensive, Attalai nevertheless regarded them as important because they gave him the sense of being in the midst of the international contemporary art scene.[76] Some of his works were bought from abroad,[77] and he was also regularly published in *Flash Art* magazine.[78] A number of Attalai's conceptually inspired art projects eroded the spatial fixations of State socialisms and the borders imposed on experimental art. Some of them explicitly deal with maps, as was the case with the *Continental Change* series, while others are less straightforward and could be viewed as more abstract approaches to cartographies, as was the case with Attalai's atypical land art works. While land art for neo-avant-gardists usually centred around the 'issue of nature, ecology, and natural environment',[79] Attalai's approach to urban space and the atlas was more of an interference with accepted spatial structures. His land art was a formal experiment, and a disruption of the known. What he shared with fellow land art practitioners from eastern Europe were the limitations imposed by 'national traditions' and a 'cosmopolitan stance'.[80] Attalai was not only thinking and acting internationally in his art, but also 'distanced [himself] from the assumptions of ideal national landscapes'.[81]

On a few occasions, Attalai was able to exchange the post for his own body as a carrier and supplier of immaterial countercartography. For example, he created relatively simple *Transfer Paintings* in black and white in order to tear these artworks apart. Some pieces of the torn-apart paintings he kept in his own possession, while other pieces were taken on Attalai's journeys across Europe. When he went on his trips to cultural capitals on the other side of the Iron Curtain, Attalai made minor interventions in the urban space by placing some of his painting fragments near iconic museums such as the Louvre, the Rijksmuseum and the National Gallery in London. Their diminutive size made them almost invisible next to the grandiose buildings with their towering status.[82] On the one hand, these actions can be understood as a criticism of institutions, museums and painting alike, because they represented a countercanon that might never enter the temple of internationally recognised art history. On the other hand, *Transfer Paintings* tested the mobility, or rather the transition, of the artwork from one cultural space into another. While the execution of this series of actions was more local, Attalai's interest in spatial interventions tended to expand in scope. His high volume of mail correspondence suggests the self-promotion of a confident artist who lacked institutional support; for example, his correspondence with Carolee Schneemann reveals an unrealised project: in 1972 Attalai contacted Schneemann with the proposal to put together a global archive of female breasts.[83] Dávid Fehér saw in this proposed undertaking a continuation of the 'map transformations' of the years 1970 and 1971, since the letters Attalai wrote were addressed to female artists across the globe.[84] The fetishisation of the female body, reducing it to a single two-dimensional object of desire, was one aspect of this work. Another important characteristic of the project was the artist's intention to create alternative maps as part of his overarching desire to challenge space as we know it. *Continental Change*'s main idea was to treat the atlas as a playground of possibilities, and to expand localisation by shifting borders. Similarly, the proposed atlas of female breasts could have been a revitalised and revised map, marked by a spatial arrangement based on alienated and fetishised images, and irony.

Immaterial countercartographies in Gábor Attalai's work

As anthropogeographer Severin Halder and critical cartographer Boris Michel have put it, 'maps are by no means just representations of reality'.[85] Attalai's cartography-related projects seem to confirm that '[m]aps articulate statements that are shaped by social relations, discourses and practices, but these statements also influence them in turn'.[86] Beyond the inventiveness and aesthetic value of *Continental Change*, *Balding* and *Negative Star*, these 'maps … are full of "ifs", "buts" and question marks but also of desired worlds'.[87] Attalai's artworks restructure and reinvent space on three different levels (the body, the urban space and the atlas), and are to be understood as responses to their context of creation. To Halder and Michel, maps cannot exist without a political statement, and if questioning and experimenting with seemingly stable physical surroundings is a political act, then Attalai's countercartographies can be said to count as such as well. Furthermore, the Hungarian conceptualist regards maps as 'signs and texts and, by being signs and texts, they should be read critically'.[88] By relying on a series of actions, *Balding, Negative Star* and *Continental Change I–II* deconstruct reality (as represented by the body and urban space) and its representation (the atlas) down to its constituent parts, in order to create new structures. Attalai's immaterial countercartography thereby turns space and place into creative opportunity.

Gábor Attalai's body art pieces demonstrate a strong interest in modifying physical conditions. In 1970, he created the *Balding* series, documenting the shaving of a man's head (see Figure 4.4). The series consists of four photographs turned into coloured drawings, with the head as the theme of each image. The photographs show the process of the hair's disappearance as more and more stripes are cut into the person's hair until all the hair is gone and a bald head remains. This transformation is an intimate countercartography piece dealing with the human body as a given object that offers itself for physical intervention. The (hair-covered) head is a surface that is in the process of being transformed into bare territory – a blank area. The intimate flesh is treated like an object not all that different from any land that has been conquered and formed by human intervention. Besides referencing hard-edge painting and minimal art, *Balding* carries parallels to a land art intervention on a bigger scale, namely *Negative Star*.[89]

Negative Star was part of the *Snow Works* series, like *Negative Horg* (1971) and *Square & Caro* (1970), reminiscent of the style of contemporary geometric abstraction executed in different places across Budapest.[90] The fleetingness of these works was not only determined by the fact that they were the outcome of Attalai's physical action, but also by the nature of snow as a temporary weather occurrence. The five-pointed star of *Negative Star* took a suggestive symbol of communism as an analytical motive or a sign and inserted it into a critical setting of conceptual art. To Attalai, this countermonument was a gesture-like intervention, but not a direct political provocation.[91] The common denominator between *Balding* and *Negative Star* is the act of carving out (shaving and shovelling) and transforming a space through a series of actions. Attalai's bodily interventions had a certain coherence; for example, in another work he pressed the award for Szocialista Kultúráért (Socialist Culture) into his arm, leaving a negative imprint of the star (and millet plant) on his skin.[92] Not only are *Negative Star* and the stamping action analogous in form; both deal with Attalai's relation to the Kádár regime and the ideology of socialism, which the artist could neither avoid nor negate.[93] Together, *Balding* and *Negative Star* demonstrate that space and place could not be completely colonised, and show that there is a possibility on different scales of space to enact agency – to act in a self-determined manner.

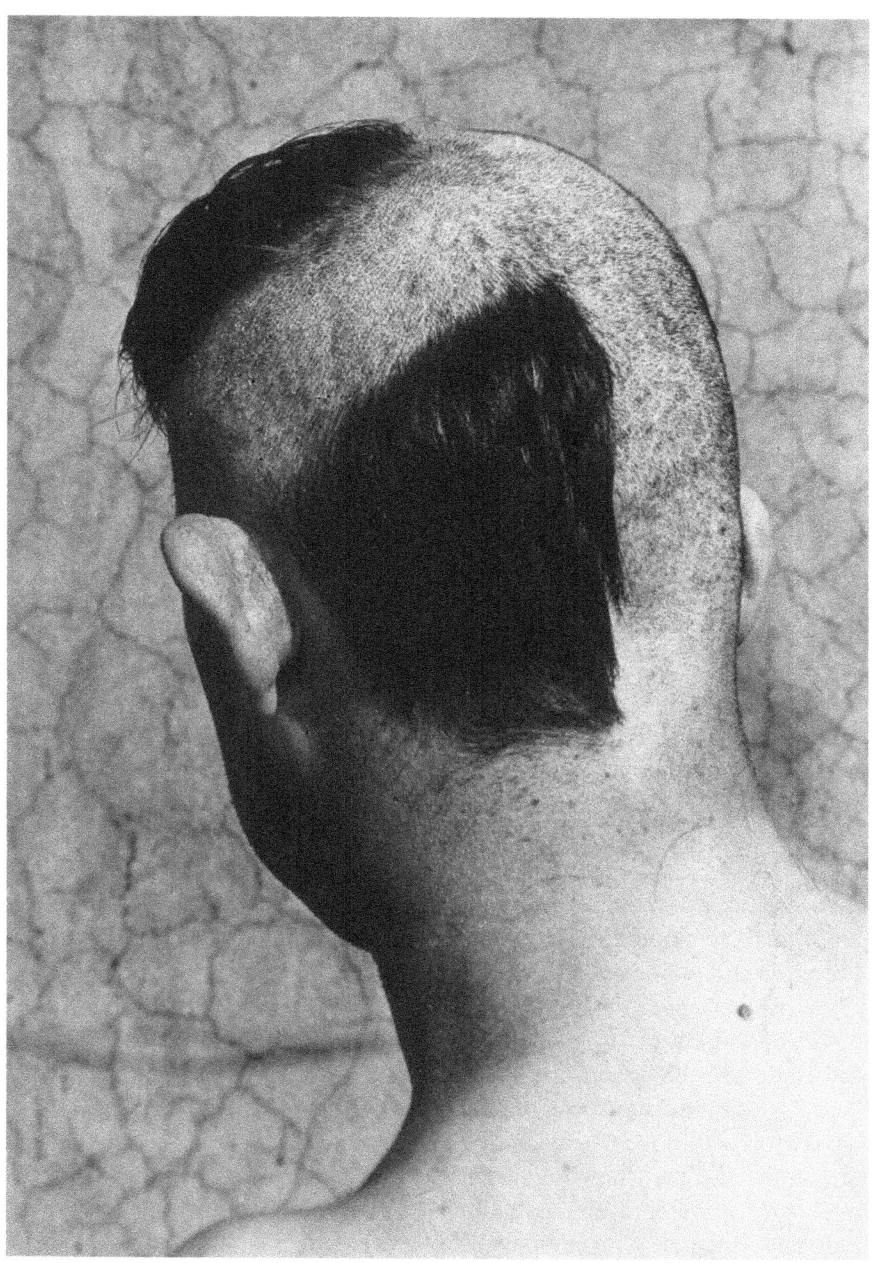

Gábor Attalai, *Process of Balding 4*, 1970. Silver print, 195 mm × 146 mm.

4.4

The *Continental Change* series expressed a desire to expand the transformations of space and surface to the atlas. In a sense, Attalai's land art of the early 1970s reached a peak in these map collages. The artist left the intimacy of the body (as seen in *Balding*) as an experimental terrain of spatial engagement. Attalai even stepped out of the urban space (as in *Negative Star*) as though he had crossed the national border with his 'conquest' of the postal system. *Continental Change* follows along the lines of the countercartographies offered by *Balding* and *Snow Works*: space was an opportunity and forum of agency. Moreover, the seriality of *Balding* and the *Snow Works* continued in *Continental Change*, while the act of process and its tools were minimised. In terms of conceptual art's institutional criticism, and through the act of decolonisation, the world map was dissociated from the geopolitics of the Cold War. What Attalai pointed out with his countercartographic gesture is that maps are not exclusively the property of global players, but belong to each of the globe's inhabitants. This reading echoes geographer James R. Akerman's understanding of decolonising the map, when he commented that this 'would entail processes and practices by which colonized peoples become more engaged or reengaged in mapping their spaces and territories'.[94] In *Continental Change I*, continents switch positions while oceans and lakes appear in surprising forms and locations, and the plan for *Continental Change II* completely merges continents, turning them into 'Asian-America', 'Australian-African-South-America' and 'Europe-Asia-America'. In this latter case, Attalai applied a somewhat brutal collage technique, cutting Africa in half and renaming it 'Half-Africa'.[95] The Hungarian artist thus freed the continents of their geographic stasis and consciously ignored and abolished borders. *Continental Change I* and *II* treat the world map as a fluid construct, highlighting its fragility and malleability. To Attalai, spaces and surfaces of all kinds represented a call for creative exposure and (re)invention.

Many of Gábor Attalai's body art works and spatial interventions created a fruitful symbiosis of conceptual art and event-based immateriality. This association resulted from the shared ephemerality of conceptual and event-based art, the main purpose of which was to overcome their limitations. The navigation within the permissive-repressive Kádárian system was a tiring task for Attalai and his fellow neo-avant-gardists, who turned their own realities into open spaces full of possibilities. Countercartographies secured Attalai a distinguished spot in the network of internationally active conceptualists. Challenging spatial narrations were rarely without political undertones, and the politics of Attalai's critical cartography lay at the crossroads of a singular personal agency, and the rejection of views of the body, the city and the globe as immutable.

Notes

1 Forschungsstelle Osteuropa Archive Bremen (FSO), Groh-Collection, letter from Gábor Attalai to Klaus Groh, 10 May 1972.
2 *Ibid.*
3 *Ibid.*
4 Raymond B. Craib, 'Cartography and decolonization', in James R. Akerman (ed.), *Decolonizing the Map: Cartography from Colony to Nation* (Chicago: University of Chicago Press, 2017), p. 54.
5 *Ibid.*, p. 32.
6 *Ibid.*
7 As cultural historian Beáta Hock has stated, inspiration for a critical art historiography of east central Europe from postcolonial studies is not uncommon in recent scholarship. Beáta Hock, 'Introduction – globalizing East European art histories: The legacy of Piotr Piotrowski and a conference', in Beáta Hock and Anu Allas (eds), *Globalizing East European Art Histories: Past and Present* (New York: Routledge, 2018), p. 7.
8 Craib, 'Cartography and decolonization', p. 33.
9 *Ibid.*, pp. 37–8.
10 *Ibid.*, pp. 48–9.
11 *Ibid.*, pp. 49–50.
12 Attalai was 'operating "outward" from Hungary'. Dávid Fehér, as quoted in Klara Kemp-Welch, *Networking the Bloc: Experimental Art in Eastern Europe, 1965–1981* (Cambridge, MA: MIT Press, 2018), p. 131.
13 FSO, Groh-Collection, Klaus Groh, 'Text on Gábor Attalai's work', unpublished MS, 1975. See also Klaus Groh, '"Andere" kreative produktion in Osteuropa', *Osteuropa: Zeitschrift für die Gegenwartsfragen des Ostens* 22 (November 1972), 754–61. In 1972 and 1973, together with other neo-avant-garde artists of his generation, Attalai regularly visited lectures on quantum technology, cosmology and astronomy at the Society for Dissemination of Scientific Knowledge in Budapest. Sándor Hornyik, *Avantgárd tudomány? A modern természettudományos világkép recepciója Gyarmathy Tihamér, Csiky Tbior és Erdély Miklós munkásságában* (Budapest: Akadémiai Kiadó, 2008), p. 77.
14 At the time, Attalai himself referred to this art as LCP-art (land, concept and project art). Groh, 'Text on Gábor Attalai's work'.
15 Craib, 'Cartography and decolonization', p. 54.
16 Attalai, letter to Groh; Groh, '"Andere" kreative Produktion in Osteuropa', p. 755.
17 Both the *Snow Works* series and Attalai's seminal conceptual action *Negative Star* carry different titles in different sources. In the body of the text I apply the most commonly used names, while I have kept the title *Negative Star* in the caption to Figure 4.2 as it was transmitted by the rightsholder.
18 Dávid Fehér, 'Transzfer ideák: Megjegyzések Attalai Gábor konceptuális művészetéhez', in Attalai Gábor, *Konceptuális művek/Conceptual Works 1969–85* (Budapest: Vintage Galéria, 2013), pp. 2–9.

19 In the documentation of the Vintage Gallery Budapest it is named in English as *Process of Balding*.

20 To art and media historian Miklós Peternák, the early era of conceptualism in Hungary was the period between 1966 and 1968, followed by an expansion from 1970 to 1971 in individual works. Peternák defined 1972–73 as a peak of conceptual art. That the definition reached a consensus after 1976 may have been the consequence of art historian István Hajdu's comprehensive attempt to compare international (or rather 'western') origins and understandings of the phenomenon with their Hungarian counterpart published in 1975 and 1976. Emese Kürti, 'Ezoterikus avantgárd: A koncept/konceptuális paradigma', *exindex*, www.exindex.hu/index.php?l=hu&page=3&id=934 (accessed 30 January 2020); István Hajdu, 'Concept Art: Kísérlet egy műfajtalan műfaj rendszerezésére', www.c3.hu/collection/koncept/images/hajdu.html (accessed 30 January 2020).

21 'Four main institutions dictated and shaped the Hungarian art scene between 1964 and 1989: the Ministry for Culture (*Művelődési Minisztérium*), the Association of Hungarian Fine and Applied Artists, the Art Fund and the Lectorate for Applied and Fine Arts (1963–2007: *Képző- és Iparművészeti Lektorátus*). Ideology and regulations were set by the Ministry of Culture and the Party's Central Committee (*Központi Bizottság*) and Political Committee (*Politikai Bizottság*). György Aczél, who played an essential role in the Ministry, the Central Committee and the Political Committee, had an especially large influence on what kind of art could be produced in Hungary between 1967 and 1982 with his three Ts, "ban-tolerate-promote", approach.' Katalin Cseh-Varga, *The Hungarian Avant-Garde and Socialism: The Art of the Second Public Sphere* (London: Bloomsbury, 2023).

22 Melinda Kalmár, *Történelmi galaxisok vonzásában: Magyarország és a szovjetrendszer, 1945–1990* (Budapest: Osiris, 2014), pp. 119–21, 125, 127–8, 205.

23 *Ibid.*, pp. 250–2.

24 Tamás Krausz, '1968 – a történelmi örökség sokfélesége: A kelet-európai "eset"', in Eszter Bartha and Tamás Krausz (eds), *1968: Kelet-Európa és a világ. Kelet-Európai tanulmányok III* (Paris: L'Harmattan–ELTE BTK Kelet-Európa Törtnénete Tanszék, 2009), pp. 9–18.

25 Kalmár, *Történelmi galaxisok vonzásában*, p. 297.

26 *Ibid.*, pp. 339, 353, 357, 361, 451.

27 *Ibid.*, pp. 374, 380, 382–3, 398, 400, 407.

28 *Ibid.*, pp. 321–2.

29 Mónika Zombori, 'Stúdió kiállítások a korabeli dokumentumok tükrében. 2. Rész: A hetvenes évek', *artmagazin* 83 (2015), 60–5.

30 Flóra Mészáros, 'Berobbant az Iparterv-csoport: Beszélgetés Sinkovits Péter művészettörténészek, az 1960-as évek végén rendezett Iparterv-tárlatok kurátorával', *Új művészet* 4 (2019), 9–10.

31 Zombori, 'Stúdió kiállítások a korabeli dokumentumok tükrében', p. 61.

32 Dávid Fehér, ' "Nem hiszek a túl direct dolgokban …": Beszélgetés Attalai Gáborral', *Ars Hungarica* 3 (2011), 110–22.

33 Edit Sasvári, 'A balatonboglári kápolnatárlatok kultúrpolitikai háttere', in Júlia
    Klaniczay and Edit Sasvári (eds), *Törvénytelen avantgárd: Galántai György
    balatonboglári kápolna műterme 1970–1973* (Budapest: Artpool-Balassi, 2003),
    pp. 9–38.
34 Fehér, 'Nem hiszek a túl direct dolgokban …', pp. 113–15.
35 *Ibid.*, pp. 113, 117.
36 Katalin Cseh-Varga, interview with György Galántai, 21 August 2014.
37 Beáta Hock, 'Attalai Gábor', *Artpool*, www.artpool.hu/Attalai/Hock.html (accessed
    4 February 2020).
38 Michael Crane, 'The origins of correspondence art', in Michael Crane and Mary
    Stofflet (eds), *Correspondence Art: Source Book for the Network of International
    Postal Art Activity* (San Francisco: La Mamelle, 1984), p. 107.
39 Kürti, 'Ezoterikus avantgárd'; Zöe Sutherland, 'The world as gallery: Conceptualism
    and global neo-avant-garde', *New Left Review* 98 (March–April 2016), 81–111.
40 Sutherland, 'The world as gallery', p. 84, where she draws our attention to the still
    important New York-based hegemony of conceptual art's origins, personified in
    Joseph Kosuth and the Art & Language group.
41 Crane, 'The origins of correspondence art', p. 107.
42 'Conceptual art challenges traditional aesthetics by rejecting the virtuosity of
    artworks based on physical qualities, style, technique, or permanence as a master-
    piece. It also challenges the marketplace of art by producing ideas as art versus
    objects to be sold as art.' *Ibid.*
43 Zdenka Badovinac, Eda Čufer, Cristina Freire *et al.*, 'Conceptual art and eastern
    Europe: Part II', *e-flux* 41 (January 2013), www.e-flux.com/journal/41/60238/
    conceptual-art-and-eastern-europe-part-ii/ (accessed January 30 2020).
44 Sutherland, 'The world as gallery', p. 111.
45 Zdenka Badovinac, Eda Čufer, Cristina Freire *et al.*, 'Conceptual art and eastern
    Europe: Part I', *e-flux* 40, www.e-flux.com/journal/40/60277/conceptual-art-and-
    eastern-europe-part-i/ (accessed 30 January 2020).
46 *Ibid.*
47 According to Attalai, letter to Groh, the *Continental Changes* pieces were sent to
    Roger D'Hondt as well as to Groh.
48 Art and culture historian Emese Kürti fostered local narratives of conceptual art
    based on micro-histories. Kürti highlighted the historiographic traps of accepting a
    purely socio-critical, activist and subversive interpretation that sheds light on only
    one dimension of conceptual art in the geopolitical region. In the case of Hungary,
    the form of engagement with art as an idea had already been debated based on
    the influence of Ludwig Wittgenstein and Joseph Kosuth's intellectual radicalism
    and the impact of the transcendent, existentialist and mythological philosophy
    of Béla Hamvas. George Lukács also appears as a reference to some Hungarian
    conceptualists as an alternative, non-Kádárian, approach to leftist ideology. Kürti,
    'Ezoterikus avantgárd'; Éva Körner, 'Az abszurd mint koncepció: Jelenetek a magyar
    koncept art történetéből. I. rész', *Balkon* 1 (1993), 22–5.

49 Dávid Fehér still emphasises the political undertone of eastern and central European conceptual art. Dávid Fehér, ' "Kiáltás egy sötét szobából": Megjegyzések Halász Károly konceptuális műveihez és akcióihoz', in Sándor Pinczehelyi (ed.), *Hopp-Halász Károly* (exh. cat.) (Pécsi Galéria és Vizuális Művészeti Műhely (Pécs Gallery and Visual Arts Workshop), 2011), pp. 53–61.

50 György Galántai, 'Hogyan tudott a művészet az életben elkezdődni? Adalékok a boglári történethez', in Klaniczay and Sasvári, *Törvénytelen avantgárd*, p. 70.

51 '[Beke] was at the heart of the European network at this early stage in the 1970s, while being less concerned with the North American scene'. Kemp-Welch, *Networking the Bloc*, p. 209.

52 Between 1966 and 1978, Attalai was the subject of solo exhibitions in Göteborg, Oldenburg, Bad Salzdefurth, Rio de Janeiro, Reykjavik, Warsaw, West Berlin, Antwerp, Aalst, Wrocław, Brescia, Milan and Haarlem. Dávid Fehér, 'Biográfia', in Attalai, *Konceptuális művek* (unpaginated).

53 László Beke, *Elképzelés: A Magyar konceptművészet kezdetei. Beke László gyűjteménye, 1971* (Budapest: Nyílt Struktúrák Művészeti Egyesület OSAS–tranzit. hu, 2008).

54 Kemp-Welch, *Networking the Bloc*, pp. 209, 212–13.

55 *Ibid.*, pp. 294–6.

56 *Ibid.*, p. 213.

57 *Ibid.*, p. 215. See also Klara Kemp-Welch, 'Autonomy, solidarity and the antipolitics of NET', in Urška Jurman, Christiane Erharter and Rawley Grau, *Extending the Dialogue: Essays by Igor Zabel Award Laureates, Grant Recipients and Jury Members 2008-2014* (Ljubljana: Archive Books/Igor Zabel Association for Culture and Theory, 2016), pp. 46–57; and Galántai, 'Hogyan tudott a művészet az életben elkezdődni?', p. 70.

58 László Beke, 'Call for participation', in Beke, *Elképzelés*, p. 1.

59 László Beke, 'Az "ELKÉPZELÉS"-ről', in László Beke (ed.), *Ahogy azt Móricka elképzeli, levél barátaimhoz* (Budapest: László Beke, 1972); reprinted in Beke, *Elképzelés*, pp. IX–XVI.

60 Beke, *Elképzelés*, pp. IX, XIII. Elsewhere Beke admits that *Imagination* had a 'slightly' socio-critical dimension. László Beke, 'A magyar konceptuális művészet szubjektív története váziat', in Deréky Pál and Müllner András (eds), *Né/ma? Tanulmányok a neoavantgárd köréböl* (Budapest: Rácio, 2004), pp. 227–39.

61 Gábor Attalai, letter to László Beke, in Beke, *Elképzelés*, p. 3.

62 Fehér, 'Transzfer ideák', p. 3.

63 Fehér, 'Nem hiszek a túl direct dolgokban …', p. 116.

64 Caroline A. Jones, *The Global Work of Art: World's Fairs, Biennials, and the Aesthetics of Experience* (Chicago: Chicago University Press, 2017), p. 165.

65 Harald Szeemann, 'Zur Ausstellung', *When Attitudes Become Form (Works, Concepts, Processes, Situations, Information)*, 22 March–27 April 1969, www.kunsthalle-bern.ch/ausstellungen/1969/when-attitudes-become-form/#&gid=1&pid=8 (accessed 2 February 2020).

66 Kürti, 'Ezoterikus avantgárd'.

67 *Ibid.*

68 Caroline A. Jones argues that the shift from art as object to art as experience/ event was accompanied by a philosophical discourse including such thinkers as, for instance, Karl Marx, Theodor Adorno, Martin Heidegger, Walter Benjamin, Jacques Derrida, Michel Foucault, Maurice Merleau-Ponty, Jean-François Lyotard, Noam Chomsky, Alain Badiou and Jacques Rancière. Jones, *The Global Work of Art.*

69 Lucy Lippard (ed.), *Six Years: The Dematerialization of the Art Object from 1966 to 1972* (Berkeley: University of California Press, 1973).

70 Kemp-Welch, *Networking the Bloc*, pp. 5–6.

71 Sophie Richard, *Unconcealed: The International Network of Conceptual Artists 1967–77. Dealers, Exhibitions and Public Collections*, ed. Lynda Morris (London: Ridinghouse, 2009).

72 Kemp-Welch, *Networking the Bloc*, pp. 5–6; Ksenya A. Gurshtein, 'TransStates: Conceptual art in eastern Europe and the limits of utopia' (Ph.D. dissertation, University of Michigan, 2011); Sutherland, 'The world as gallery'.

73 Anna Markowska, 'This glass must be wiped clean: The complicated history of the Recent Art Gallery (1975–1980) at the Pałacik Academic Culture Centre', in Anna Markowska (ed.), *Galeria Sztuki Najowszej: Awangarda nie biła braw cz. 1/The Recent Art Gallery: The Avant-Garde Did Not Applaud, Part 1* (Wrocław: Wrocław Contemporary Museum, 2014), pp. 258–317.

74 Kemp-Welch, *Networking the Bloc*, pp. 115–16; Klara Kemp-Welch and Cristina Freire, 'Introduction: Special section/artists' networks in Latin America and eastern Europe', *ARTMargins* 1:2–3 (June–October 2012), 3–23.

75 Fehér, 'Nem hiszek a túl direct dolgokban …', p. 115.

76 *Ibid.*, p. 118.

77 *Ibid.*, p. 122.

78 Fehér, 'Transzfer ideák', p. 4.

79 Maja Fowkes, *The Green Bloc: Neo-Avant-Garde Art and Ecology under Socialism* (Budapest: Central European University Press, 2015), p. 18.

80 *Ibid.*, p. 22.

81 *Ibid.*

82 Fehér, 'Transzfer ideák', p. 5; Hock, 'Attalai Gábor'.

83 Fehér, 'Transzfer ideák', p. 9.

84 *Ibid.*

85 Severin Halder and Boris Michel, 'Editorial: This is not an atlas', in kollektiv orangotango (ed.), *This Is Not an Atlas: A Global Collection of Counter-Cartographies* (Bielefeld: Transcript Verlag, 2019), pp. 12–21.

86 *Ibid.*

87 *Ibid.*

88 *Ibid.*

89 Fehér, 'Transzfer ideák', p. 5.

90 *Ibid.*, p. 3.
91 Fehér, 'Nem hiszek a túl direct dolgokban …', p. 121.
92 Hock, 'Attalai Gábor'.
93 *Ibid.*
94 James R. Akerman, 'Introduction', in Akerman, *Decolonizing the Map*, p. 8.
95 FSO, Groh-Collection, 5/VIII/1971, Gábor Attalai, 'Continental change work II (plan)'.

Brian O'Doherty/Patrick Ireland: A modest proposal to decolonise Ireland

Christa-Maria Lerm Hayes

The wish to reach an 'art without space', as expressed by Seth Siegelaub and quoted in the introduction to this volume, appeared to another New York-based art practitioner as a privilege. It was a privilege that Brian O'Doherty (born in Ireland in 1928) did not wish to acquire, and in any case couldn't – from the point of view of his socio-political positioning – afford. O'Doherty's medical training made him realise that the physical domain – the body and the space that it inhabits – is needed for conceptual artists to think about and develop their works. This is one brief reading of what is arguably O'Doherty's best-known intervention in conceptual art's history: the *Portrait of Marcel Duchamp* (1966), consisting of an ECG readout of the heartbeat of a colleague who was supposedly no longer producing art. One can estimate O'Doherty's thinking about privileges tied up with space (and time) when considering his many and varied professions: artist, doctor, art critic, theoretician (author of *Inside the White Cube* (1976) and *Aspen 5 + 6* (1967), and editor of *Art in America*) and programme director of the National Endowment for the Arts. O'Doherty takes a systemic, multidisciplinary approach, amounting to a social practice that aims to change the nature of certain spaces.[1] He charts space and art spaces programmatically, literally and metaphorically. That he would turn to maps is somewhat predictable; he has done so on two occasions, and this chapter sets out to scrutinise these works.

These two maps, used and modified, are of Ireland and its capital city, Dublin, respectively. The two works are *Ireland: A Modest Proposal* (1980; see Figure 5.1) and *Studies on O.S. Maps for the Purgatory of Humphrey Chimpden Earwicher Humunculus Rope Drawing #73* (1985; see Figure 5.2). In the 1980s, O'Doherty was, for his visual art practice, working under the pseudonym Patrick Ireland, adopted following the Bloody Sunday shootings by the British Army of thirteen civil rights marchers in the Northern Irish city of Derry (also called Londonderry) in 1972. In 2008, the artist chose to 'bury' this pseudonym, to mark (and maybe even to further) a stage in the 'peace process' that he felt conformed to the condition he had established when adopting the name: that until such a time as 'British military presence' was removed

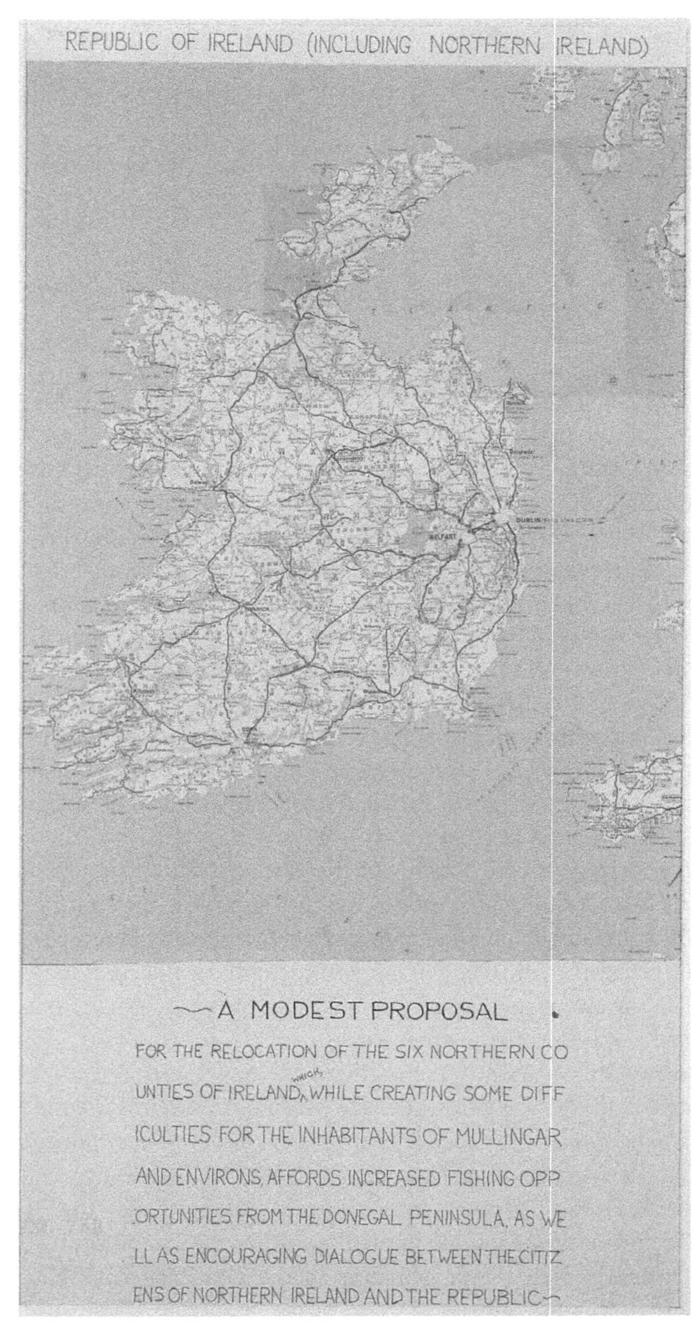

5.1 Patrick Ireland (aka Brian O'Doherty), *Ireland: A Modest Proposal*, 1980. Map collage onto posterboard, 80 cm × 42 cm.

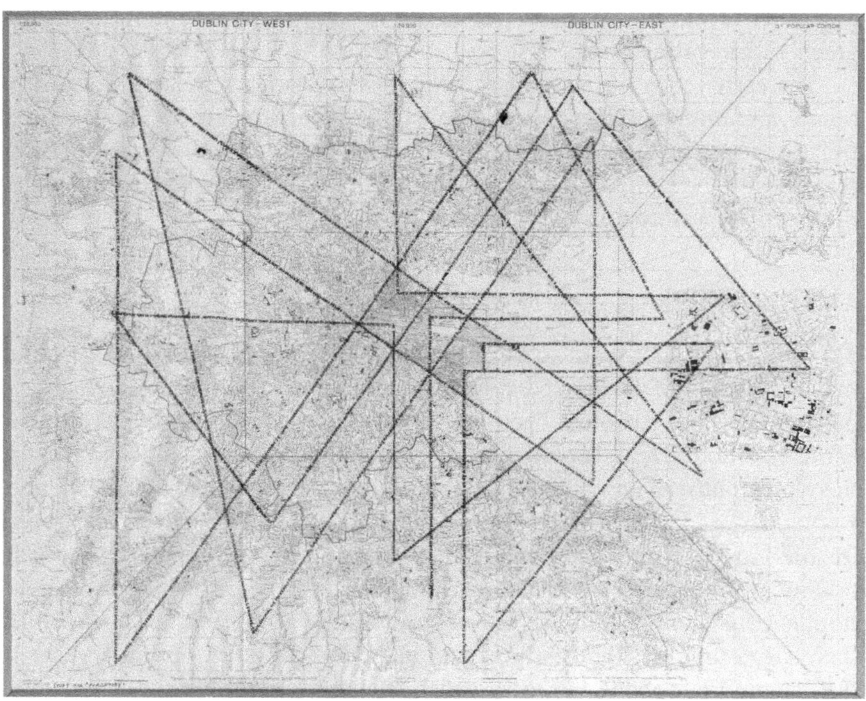

Patrick Ireland (aka Brian O'Doherty), *Studies on O.S. Maps for the Purgatory of Humphrey*   **5.2**
Chimpden Earwicher Humunculus Rope Drawing #73, 1985. Indian ink on Ordnance
Survey map of Dublin, 130 cm × 123.7 cm.

from the island he would not revert to his birth name, as the work states. The
name change was a gesture highlighting O'Doherty's Irish origins, politics and
continuing affective connections following his emigration to the USA (with
a grant to research sensory perception) in 1957: an expatriate's gesture.[2] For
a medical doctor it is not likely to forfeit the body for conceptual ends – or
to consider one to be in opposition to the other. For Patrick Ireland to forfeit
space is also unlikely.

For an artist from the rural midlands, attachment to 'the auld sod' (an affec-
tionate nickname for the country itself) – land that one was not allowed to own
under colonial rule – is vivid. And one does not need to resort to films such
as *The Field* (Jim Sheridan, Ireland, 1990) for illustration. When he was ninety,
I asked O'Doherty if he had known anyone of his current age when he was a
child – and if so, whether they had reported memories of the Irish Famine. In
the year of European revolutions, 1848, and in subsequent years, the potato
crop in Ireland had failed, and Britain still insisted on receiving grain exports.
Half the population of the island either starved to death or emigrated on so-
called 'coffin ships'. The artist responded that his elderly aunt had told him

about her recollections: she remembered seeing people with mouths stained green – from eating grass.

The early 1980s were a violent time on the island of Ireland, marked by bombs and hunger strikes, directly linked to the incomplete decolonisation of Ireland, which let the four northern counties, part of the province of Ulster, remain with the United Kingdom of Great Britain and Northern Ireland, when the Republic was established in 1921, following civil war.

A Modest Proposal

The title of the first work to be discussed here, *Ireland: A Modest Proposal*, may be thought of as directed at both the island and the artist – the matter is personal. Ireland has often been anthropomorphised: Kathleen Ní Houlihan is the traditional, female personification. Republicans who sought to reclaim the North put it in animal-related terms: 'Give the teddy back his head', goes a song. In art history, Joseph Beuys, following extensive travels all around Ireland in 1974, wrote 'The Brain of Europe' alongside the northern part of an outline of the island on a blackboard that was to become part of an installation, *Hearth* (1968–74), in Basel's Kunstmuseum. Patrick Ireland's map, rather than suggesting that the head or brain had been cut off or out, intervenes in the geography of the island more subtly; the territory of Northern Ireland is not cut off as such. While its site is covered by blue space that signifies water, its map section has been cut up and distributed in the centre of the landmass – the artist's own region of origin. Belfast ends up being located just west of Dublin. The accompanying text reads:

> A MODEST PROPOSAL FOR THE RELOCATION OF THE SIX NORTHERN COUNTIES OF IRELAND, WHILE CREATING SOME DIFFICULTIES FOR THE INHABITANTS OF MULLINGAR AND ENVIRONS, AFFORDS INCREASED FISHING OPPORTUNITIES FROM THE DONEGAL PENINSULA AS WELL AS ENCOURAGING DIALOGUE BETWEEN THE CITIZENS OF NORTHERN IRELAND AND THE REPUBLIC.

The continuing brain drain in the 1980s is one possible explanation for this solution to 'The Troubles' taking place so close by, yet – psychologically – far away across an international border with menacing checkpoints. The 1973 entry of both jurisdictions to the European Economic Community slowly created the conditions for communication, which the map work proposes: it sets out to 'encourag[e] dialogue'. This was, then, against all the odds: the Thatcher Government in Britain made it clear that it did not wish to communicate with 'terrorists', which was most painfully visible during the hunger strikes in 1982, when ten republicans – Irish Republican Army (IRA) members – died in a Northern Irish prison. Their bid to be recognised as political prisoners had been refused. While Patrick Ireland's focus was on (presumably good) communication, politicians turned the other way: from 1988 to 1994, republicans did not have a voice in the British media. What their IRA-affiliated spokespeople said was 'dubbed over' by actors in all British media coverage.[3] The intermingling of both Protestant and Catholic newcomers from the North with the southern (and, since 1921, landowning locals) in the not-very-fertile region that Ireland's work suggests, is difficult to imagine. What the work proposes is as dark as the realities: involuntary replacement and disappearance. Northern Ireland is an 'other' space, but not a heterotopia. It is a dystopia of a specific kind: an issue to which we will return.

The title adds further layers to the work's meaning. Patrick Ireland quotes Jonathan Swift's 1729 text, 'A Modest Proposal' – or, in its entirety, 'A Modest Proposal For preventing the Children of Poor People From being a Burthen to Their Parents or Country, and For making them Beneficial to the Publick'. The Dean of Dublin's Protestant cathedral, who published the text anonymously, was a high-ranking member of the ruling colonial elite. Led by his concerns for the numerous and starving indigenous Catholic population of Ireland, he made the proposal for the impoverished Irish to sell their children as meat for use in fricassee or ragout, and specified potential modes of preparation in detail. What is worse, the modest Christian's call for anthropophagy was not immediately understood by his peers and readers as the satire it was intended to be, thus proving the extent of dehumanisation prevalent in colonial Ireland at the time.

The reference to Swift in Patrick Ireland's map work exceeds the title's formulation: Swift had been inspired by the topography of the area around Belfast (Northern Ireland) for his *Gulliver's Travels*, which plays with the scale of the protagonist: a giant appears to be lying in the landscape (and satirical comments on English politics are also to be found here). In this context, Patrick Ireland's comments on 'increased fishing opportunities' and 'encouraging dialogue' can be understood as taking on Swift's tone of straight-faced satire: fishing and polite conversation conform with a jovial British self-image that belies the violent reality of Northern Ireland in 1980, just as it did in the 1720s. The visual suggestion to amputate the island's 'head' for the sake of pleasure pursuits corresponds clearly to both Swift's culinary proposal and the realities of death and destruction during the euphemistically (or satirically) named 'Troubles'.[4]

But those wishing to adhere to a jovial and sophisticated (self-)identity of the British or Protestant Northern Irish are not the only ones who might have been scandalised by Patrick Ireland's work. Seeing the map of the island of Ireland without the North is deeply unfamiliar and disturbing to inhabitants of the Republic of Ireland to this day: while UK-based news media would show both the UK 'mainland' and Northern Ireland in detail, with the Irish Republic uniformly coloured (in grey/brown, like France or Belgium, if pictured), RTÉ (the Irish Republic's TV news source) would always show the island in its entirety.[5] This, of course, owes to the political claim that the Republic has made since partition regarding the island as a whole. This mapping practice corresponds to how, for example, East German maps didn't show West Berlin (and its military complexes), while West German maps would show East Germany in as much detail as the West – with the deadly, impenetrable border a barely visible line. Or a more recent example: controversially blank sections appeared in maps of Paris, revealing that the *banlieue* districts were as alien to the map-makers as Africa was to those in the early modern era. Early map-makers loved to fill undifferentiated, 'undiscovered' sections with dragons and other scary animals in a *horror vacui* that otherwise spelled a lack of both knowledge and (colonial) power, implicitly inviting both.[6] Patrick Ireland seems to say to citizens of the Irish Republic: 'Get used to it: the North barely exists for you', belying all lip-service paid as to how much one claimed to feel for the suffering brethren in the North.

That his inserting of Northerners (and their issues) into the Republic is a deliberate and more than satirical feature of Brian O'Doherty's convictions is further illustrated by the artist's pseudonym and where he chose to 'bury' it: on the one hand, he signals that amputating the island's head hurts him (as he shares its name). On the other, he has, more recently, shown that the North belongs in the consciousness of the South: Patrick Ireland's burial took place at the Irish Museum of Modern Art, Dublin, in 2008, rather than in Belfast, as had been suggested to him.[7]

Ireland's *Modest Proposal* also implies that the 'fish' one may be able to catch in the newly 'watery' regions on the north coast may not be ordinary fare. Spinning Swift's story a little bit further, the water-world here may contain altogether more 'human' species. The Irish imagination is populated with creatures that may find their way onto land, from selkies to mermaids and the inhabitants of Atlantis or the Land of the Young, Tír na-nÓg, in Irish mythology. An underwater world that contrasts with the deceptively matter-of-fact map medium is conjured, and introduces altogether more sinister, spectral aspects in keeping with the political landscape above ground: the mute and airless Northern Ireland of 'The Troubles'. Underwater worlds or aquatopias were more recently imagined in Afro-futurist music and visual culture by the band Drexciya, and in other elaborations on the Drexciyan myth.[8] That association may seem a little far-fetched, but whom else should one trust to envision the many implications of undifferentiated or 'blank' space more acutely than the author of *Inside the White Cube*?

Brian O'Doherty had, by 1980, already written the series of *Artforum* essays that in 1986 he published as a book.[9] How the white walls of art spaces carry with them the real estate and aspirational commodity value of what is displayed within, how the body negotiates the supposedly neutral gallery space … all these questions for the first time appear in O'Doherty's writings. It is also safe to assume that, in the watery parts of Patrick Ireland's *Modest Proposal*, the multiple intertwined interests of politics and global capital are present. In the map work it is as if the indistinct surface of the sea were to inundate and fill the 'real world'. But from *Inside the White Cube* we know that – certainly for this author-artist – areas of blankness or 'whiteness' themselves are at least as forcefully inundated by all the powers of the 'real world'. His attentiveness to the unmarked white walls is arguably derived from his experience of poverty in rural Ireland, where white-washed walls were associated with everything but the riches and cultural capital that white-painted spaces then exuded in the artist's new home, New York.

Looking from both inside and out with this map work, a little bit of 'dialogue' between the Northerners fleeing the rising tides and Brian O'Doherty's old neighbours from County Roscommon may just be preferable. It may also yet be on the cards in the twenty-first century, when coercive economic and political forces have literally raised the tides. Finding similarities between atrocities from the eighteenth and twentieth centuries and relating these to water, subject to incessant flows and cycles, makes this work just as relevant for the twenty-first.

Studies on O.S. Maps

Underground forces, a gallery space, Irish political and colonial history and literature: there is much that joins the close reading above to *Studies on O.S. Maps for the Purgatory of Humphrey Chimpden Earwicker Humunculus Rope Drawing #73*. Its critique is possibly more complex, but no less pointed than the work from 1980. Brian O'Doherty grew up in Dublin and studied medicine at the Catholic University. Being invited by Trinity College Dublin (TCD) to exhibit presented certain difficulties for him: he might have liked to study there, but his family felt that this would put their collective spiritual wellbeing in danger.[10] Trinity only began to admit Catholics on an equal basis in 1979. He responds with a work called *Studies*, as studying is what the institution and this artist-researcher share, albeit so far in different spaces. The *O.S.* in the title refers to the Ordnance Survey, the British colonial enterprise of mapping Ireland – and thus, by extension, owning the land – naming and marking its 'property'. Through this title, Patrick Ireland presents TCD as 'purgatory': a space that is not mappable, and in which Protestants have abandoned belief. The artist thus 'smuggles' Catholicism into this Protestant institution – implying that it is a place of 'sinners' who need to expiate their sins before they can go to heaven. The work also reminds us that Queen Elizabeth I of England, who founded the university, was – just like the present British monarch – head of both the Church of England and the British State (which is thus lacking in a division of powers to which most democratic nations aspire).

More literally, the map work is the study for a rope drawing (rope drawing #73 to be precise), which was, indeed, realised as a one-person show in 'purgatory': TCD's art space, the Douglas Hyde Gallery (DHG) in 1985. The rope drawing that the 'study' anticipates was the focal point of this installation. Patrick Ireland's rope drawings, which he began making in 1973, have as a defining feature thin ropes spanned in such a way that they disorient the perambulating viewer, but also provide order: from a specific viewpoint, the ropes 'frame' the fields of colour in which the gallery is painted. This is advantageous for O'Doherty's alter ego, enabling him to work in art spaces and museums without exhibiting in a white-cube-as-white-cube. In this instance, the disorientation was not just the viewer's: the architecture of the DHG is brutalist, and pushes itself into the foreground to such an extent that the white-cube-undermining artist had another force to reckon with. He found it a difficult, if not 'purgatorial', place to work in.[11]

Studies on O.S. Maps implies that the (Catholic) artist is investigating the cultural origins and purposes of these maps, not taking them for granted as a means of orientation whose shape and politics may be a given. Indeed, the map of Dublin, in which TCD is centrally located, is doubled: in one part (left) overlaid with the zigzag lines – here drawn as a text in very small letters – that are to become the ropes. A coloured field that takes the shape of the letters 'HCE' is laid over the city centre: yellow in the map work, turquoise in the exhibited rope drawing. The diptych's right-hand side presents the same image on the same map, including text-lines, but cut up into a grid of twelve squares, shuffled and redistributed: a 'before and after' relating to the viewer's experience in the rope drawing. First, one is disoriented in its spiderweb-like space, then, sitting at a table, the lines quite neatly frame the letters. The text in front of the viewer on the table explains the initials: the text is from James Joyce's *Finnegans Wake*, a literary experience not known for its clarity, where HCE is the male protagonist. The right-hand page on the table even rejigs Joyce's words like the map: a scrambling of the phrases by the artist-cum-novelist Ireland/O'Doherty.

The map work does not affirm TCD's literal and figurative centrality in the city, as 'normal' maps (and people) inevitably do with this central, walled-in institution. The lines remind one of ropes used in tying ships to docks in Dublin harbour. They also crisscross the sections of the map as if the streets were Daedalus's labyrinth, where the Minotaur was held captive on Crete and where Ariadne oriented Theseus using ropes or string. Such a labyrinth is precisely what James Joyce understood his home city to be, when he gave himself the alter ego Stephen Dedalus in his early works (*Dubliners* (1914) and *The Portrait of an Artist as a Young Man* (1916)). For Patrick Ireland, in this work, Dublin becomes a constellation of coordinates similar to the maps that aid Joyce-readers by identifying the whereabouts of the characters in *Ulysses* (published in 1922). The main Joycean reference here is, however, to *Finnegans Wake*: in the initials of the main male protagonist in Joyce's 'night book', published in 1939. Like Joyce's other works, it is set in Dublin, but transcends this frame by also constituting a world history and using many languages: an emigrant's work. Joyce named HCE as Humphrey Chimpden Earwicker (as in Ireland's title), Here Comes Everybody or other variants, in order not to fix identities: something clearly attractive to an emigrant like Ireland/O'Doherty. In *Finnegans Wake*, HCE is also Tim Finnegan, who had fallen off a ladder and lies in the Dublin landscape: very much as a reference to Swift's Gulliver. Patrick Ireland explains:

> A single continuous thread (slender rope) would lead me and you (in a kind of literal metaphor) through the labyrinth of the 'Wake' … This pleased me mightily. All you had to do [when sitting at the table] was reach out (in imagination), and touch, holding the string, – all your thoughts flowing back through the string, through the labyrinth – the purgatorial labyrinth – to the H.C.E. now perfectly framed (Alleluia) from where you sat.[12]

This dual orienting and disorienting experience is accommodated in the map work's two parts: the right-hand side's squares resemble coordinates – a logical way of ordering space on the map – but by being rearranged it also breaks the typical linearity of literature. This is entirely appropriate to *Finnegans Wake*, which has struck many readers as a hypertext *avant la lettre*. The *Wake* undermines linearity as much as possible in its overall structure: the last sentence continues in the book's first, closing the cycle of the Liffey's water, and the cycle of life and death.[13]

In the context of Dublin, rearranging the square elements of a map has implications beyond art-historical ones: the medians, as overlaid across this second city of the British Empire, are oriented towards London (or, more precisely, the Greenwich Observatory) and thus, like the clock, to British colonial power, manifested in both space and time. Although the work's right-hand side looks like a cut and folded map (nearly like one in the system that Falk map publishers patented), the artist is not aiming at a practical way of presenting the city to visitors for orientation in pre-digital times. What he is representing is the disorderly, difficult text space of the *Wake*, which stereo-typically remains one of world literature's most difficult books. The literary canon is of course studied by scholars in this eminent institution (Beckett, who studied and taught at TCD, was until recently more in the foreground than the poor Catholic from the neighbourhood, Joyce). The Catholic artist Ireland at TCD aims at – and rewrites in ways that are critical of colonial centring – the pinnacle of the Irish literary canon.[14]

Patrick Ireland has, in many artworks, used arrangements of squares in order to let lines, like the sections of the envisaged rope drawing here, traverse the grid. These works are often based on the ancient Celtic Ogham alphabet. In 1967, Brian O'Doherty began to use it as an ingenious way of combining in his art a minimal formal vocabulary with conceptualist ideas or meaning, which only language could insert. Ogham operates on the basis of horizontal and diagonal lines, which were originally (in the second half of the first millennium in Ireland and Scotland) grouped as incisions on either side of the edge of a standing stone. Within a grid arrangement, the vowels, between one and four parallel lines in Ogham, were 'liberated' from their parallel arrangement and zigzag each square, reminiscent of rope drawings: nearly ricocheting in (and thus spatialising) the individual frames while remaining readable for viewers who wish to invest the time.

At TCD, Patrick Ireland thus presents himself as someone bound to the country's ancient learning and history, to be found in fields and hedge schools (when learning was prohibited under colonial law, but where classical text nevertheless survived). This tradition predates the establishment of TCD in 1592 by Elizabeth I. The artist presents in this diptych two different ways of becoming both oriented and disoriented in Dublin and in Joyce's literature. He works as a 'map artist [to] push cartography to theorise and transcend itself'.[15] He arguably achieves this by using the normative map perspective (from above), applying markers that one might associate with precise locations (of a prostrate body), but at the same time crisscrossing the city like a labyrinth, cutting it up, turning it (via the title) into hell or purgatory, and associating it – the real, historical city and its central university – with a literary site. The coloniser's gaze is from above, 'studying' its subject in a way that can be associated now with the State's gaze from a satellite or a drone – menacing. This is explored in recent art by Hito Steyerl and Hiwa K, but their works are not the first to criticise the map as a tool of colonial power. In Northern Ireland helicopters policed republican and nationalist areas and viewed the landscape from above; travelling by road would not have been safe. Also, while far from the North in many respects, Dublin's topography was not unaffected: the loyalist Dublin (and Monaghan) bombings on 17 May 1974 scarred the Republic's capital, as did the 1966 demolition by the IRA of the central monument in the city's main artery, Nelson's Pillar in O'Donnell Street.

As the city of James Joyce's literature, Dublin is, to a greater extent than most other cities, enmeshed in the mutual and performative interrelations of fiction and non-fiction. In investigating symbolic streetscapes and using the case study of Dublin, Yvonne Whelan concludes 'that cities are indeed constructed landscapes, shaped by sets of agents that are caught up in a web of social, cultural and political circumstances'.[16] This construction has, in Dublin, been literary, and it manifests itself as a city already perceived as something like a museum: a multilayered and overdetermined, simple and confusing space that does not, in those respects, differ that much from *A Modest Proposal*'s Northern Ireland. O'Doherty, resident in the USA since 1957, was drawn to Joyce's literature as an annoyance and sparring partner for the novel-writing artist, but also as a 'surrogate Ireland', as I have argued elsewhere.[17] Maps and novels are among the tools – as compromised as their 'truth' is in both cases – of emigrants and the homesick. The two works by Patrick Ireland certainly do not use their maps as straightforward, factual givens. So how do they exceed that medium or source, and how can we conceptualise what they do?

Maps, literature and politics

Both works are so infused with literature and politics that I feel compelled to turn to both Eric Bulson's *Novels, Maps, Modernity: The Spatial Imagination 1850–2000*, and Benedict Anderson's *Imagined Communities: Reflections on the Origin and Spread of Nationalism*. To turn to Bulson's argument first: 'Joyce made the urban experience a subjective, psychological affair. The interior monologue made this possible. As readers, we experience Dublin vicariously through the minds and bodies of characters … the urban dweller protects herself from the "shock" of the metropolis by retreating inward.'[18] O'Doherty/ Ireland responds with his works – the current map works among them – to his subjective experience: this includes the experience of the emigrant, but also the artist's professional knowledge as a medical doctor and researcher into sensory perception (including its failings and deceptions). To this we can add the emigrant's interest in his home country's past and present: the knowledge that familiar cities will appear strange to someone who can only visit occasionally and who does not see change happening incrementally:

> That, in effect, is what the space of the modern novel does: it makes readers confuse orientation with disorientation and feel like they are at home in the world when they are not. Georg Lukács had this idea in mind … when he argued that the novel's fractured form is an expression of 'transcendental homelessness', a symptom of the modern condition … Joyce's *Ulysses* is more than a cultural barometer. It made the modern urban experience intelligible for so many other novelists during this period. The disorientation effect on readers was one of Joyce's best inventions … remarkable is the fact that unlike his contemporary Franz Kafka, he managed to do it by creating a hyper-rationalized space … A decade after *Ulysses* was published, Walter Benjamin argued that getting lost was the only way one could get to know a city … The Situationists understood that cartographic abstraction, which they identified with the alienation caused by capitalist abstraction, could be resisted.[19]

The provision of everyday detail and hyper-rationalised space, orientation paired with disorientation and personal links: all this is to be found in Patrick Ireland's map work. He lets maps do the work of literature, and vice-versa. What is so distinctive about the novel is:

> not that readers can be lost and then found, but that they can be both lost and found at the same time … Maps and novels have had such a long and prosperous relationship in large part because readers have treated fictional spaces like real ones … the novel has contributed to the formation of a spatial imagination for centuries.[20]

O'Doherty/Ireland would not have been satisfied with only letting the deceptively orienting map turn out to be disorienting, too. Literature and maps combine in his work to reach socio-political realities: historical and present inhuman behaviour, war and neglect. In his map works, we can appreciate the capacity of the map's spatial imagination, together with a literary one, to be taken as an intervention in the real world.

But what about art's potential socio-political efficacies, given Patrick Ireland's difficult place as an Irish artist in the USA – a declared Irish republican aiming at a critique and dismantling of colonialism? In relation to Northern Ireland, the term 'Catholic' is used synonymously with 'republican' and 'nationalist'. Nationalism and maps do not have an uncomplicated one-to-one relationship, despite the overt purpose of many maps – to show the 'nation'. Benedict Anderson, in studying the cultural imagination's role in the emergence of nationalism, has relevant things to say about the uses of the map and the museum in the colonial project and nationalism thereafter:

> The 'assumption … that official nationalism in the colonized worlds … was modelled directly on that of the dynastic states of nineteenth-century Europe … [would be] hasty and superficial … the immediate genealogy should be traced to the imaginings of the colonial state … Few things bring this grammar into more visible relief than three institutions of power … the census, the map, and the museum: together, they profoundly shaped the way in which the colonial state imagined its dominion – the nature of the human beings it ruled, the geography of its domain, and the legitimacy of its ancestry.[21]

The movement towards disorientation and scrambling map parts, or 'messing with' the 'objectively' drawn geography in Patrick Ireland's work at the times of 'The Troubles', thus goes deeper and aims at the colonial technologies used to bolster the violence: census and maps in Northern Ireland show a nearly fully segregated population, learning separately and aspiring to studying in the walled-off TCD, like Dublin Castle, as a two-centred colonial power-base, separated from what used to be 'Irishtown' – spaces outside cities where the poor Catholics lived. To cite Anderson further:

the colonial state did not merely aspire to create … under its control, a human landscape of perfect visibility; the condition of this 'visibility' was that everyone, everything, had … a serial number. This style of imagining … was the product of the technologies of navigation … photography and print, to say nothing of the deep driving power of capitalism … The final logical outcome was the logo – of 'Pagan' or 'The Philippines' [or 'Ireland';] it made little difference – which by its emptiness, contextlessness, visual memorableness, and infinite reproducibility in every direction brought census and map [and museum], warp and woof, into an inerasable embrace.[22]

Patrick Ireland uses the familiar images of maps and complicates them, taking aim at these frozen 'logos' and the power structures and assumptions they carry.

Maybe we can take these thoughts on power and space one last step further: this step has to do with the fact that both the water-filled area of Northern Ireland and Trinity College's 'purgatory' appear to be heterotopic spaces in Michel Foucault's (1967) vision, somewhat imprecisely conveyed. Michiel Dehaene and Lieven De Cauter have investigated and updated notions of this 'other' space.[23] They begin their explorations with a map: Giambattista Noli, in 1748, showed Rome with solid, black buildings, but Borromini's churches around Piazza Navona as cavities, in white. Patrick Ireland has coincidentally responded to Borromini's architecture by means of rope drawings:[24]

> the churches – are not public or private, but heterotopian. What this map so eloquently shows is the necessary connection and partial overlap between public space and heterotopian space. Heterotopian spaces are necessarily collective or shared spaces … The Piazza Navona was built on the vestiges of [the] circus of Emperor Domitian, which demonstrates that heterotopias can over time develop into public spaces.[25]

The multiply assigned functions of (map) space, as well as in-between zones in terms of public and private use and meanings: this I find remarkable here in the context of Patrick Ireland's work's social implications. The authors further

> venture to say that today Foucault's analysis reaches its obvious conclusion[: w]ithin network space, heterotopia has to a large extent changed its function. Rather than interrupting normality, heterotopias now realize or simulate a common experience of place … Today heterotopia, from theme park to festival market, realises 'places to be' in the non-place urban realm … embodies the tension between place and non-place that today reshapes the nature of public space.[26]

And they conclude:

> Besides the proliferation of heterotopias that provided normality in the (atopic) network space, we now see a proliferation of camp-like situations. The camp

> properly speaking is, according to Giorgio Agamben, not an extension of the
> law like the prison, but rather a space that is extraterritorial to the law … where
> the city is annihilated and the citizen reduced to 'bare life' … Heterotopia, so
> we argue, is the opposite of the camp and could be a counterstrategy to the pro-
> liferation of camps and the spread of the exposure to the conditions of bare life.[27]

This is clearly relevant to Patrick Ireland's *Modest Proposal*, where Northern
Ireland is treated as a camp, a dystopian space, where inhabitants' bare lives are
at stake, being moved, drowning; a space to whose existence and needs many
preferred to close their eyes. Internment took individuals 'away' without trial.
In this work, the entire province is an unseen, underwater space, vanished,
a 'black site'.[28] At a time when Brexit is redrawing the maps of the islands,
decision-makers would do well to consider these two works carefully.

As far as the TCD 'purgatory' is concerned, the walled-in university with
its colonial origins loses its privileged, heterotopian position in the city space
of Dublin – especially in the right-hand map, but also through the ricocheting
text of the left-hand side of the diptych. The academic community, with its
historically less than diverse constituency, is in effect dispersed into the mix
of Dublin's conurbation: 'others', like the artist, are taking the right to engage
within the walls with their and Ireland's diachronic manifestations of culture.
Thus, the artist's gesture is similar to the previously studied map work: Patrick
Ireland provides the academics with (much needed, one could say, for the university of the 1980s) opportunities for engagement: 'encouraging dialogue', as
the *Modest Proposal* put it.

In his two works using maps, O'Doherty/Ireland has found two formulations
that share a number of features and combine to spell his vision clearly: he has
recourse to familiar images that are being altered to provide both orientation
and disorientation as two elements that – by implication – inevitably coincide,
maybe (differently) succeed one another in our perception, but will not vanish
or be neatly distinguished as order and chaos. This is an epistemological con-
viction, one pertaining specifically to colonial history in Ireland, as well as
to efforts at decolonialisation, to which Patrick Ireland added his name and
these works. The literary references that the pieces make enforce this message,
extending the works' remit from 'merely' spatial imaginaries into the realms
of (Irish) history, culture and politics. These realms are all seen as socially
constructed and always (especially when viewed in and through art) subject to
real-world forces. Given the works' fraught context in the prolonged 'Troubles'
on the island, Ireland's – and any polarised society's – future is, these works tell
us, only to be found through understanding and accepting these messy com-
plexities, through believing that the nature of space can change – and through
'dialogue'. Through propositionally mapping otherwise, creating other spaces
(heterotopias where citizens mingle, as opposed to camps), Patrick Ireland's
works play their part in shaping this future.

Notes

1   This I argued in Christa-Maria Lerm Hayes, 'Introduction, or the crossdresser's secret', in Christa-Maria Lerm Hayes (ed.), *Brian O'Doherty/Patrick Ireland: Word, Image and Institutional Critique* (Amsterdam: Valiz, 2017), pp. 9–25.

2   Thomas McEvilley, 'A dance in the excluded middle', in Lerm Hayes, *Brian O'Doherty/Patrick Ireland*, p. 27.

3   See entry for '1988–1994 British broadcasting voice restrictions', *Wikipedia*, https://en.wikipedia.org/wiki/1988%E2%80%9394_British_broadcasting_voice_restrictions (accessed 2 November 2019).

4   I thank Eve Kalyva for the information that Juan Carlos Romero created a work, *Swift en Swift*, with reference to Jonathan Swift's literature in Buenos Aires in 1970, i.e. in a context where the canonicity of (in that case) *Gulliver's Travels* was necessary to render the critical political message of the work as 'safe' as possible. Removing the spaces between words in all caps and removing punctuation also made the reading require more effort.

5   A random image of this for RTÉ is 'Weather: Dublin', RTÉ website, www.rte.ie/weather/22259-dublin/ (accessed 17 March 2023). For British media see e.g. 'How hot is it going to be in the UK this week?', The Weather Channel, www.weather.com/en-GB/unitedkingdom/weather/video/how-hot-is-it-going-to-be-in-the-uk-this-week-heatwave-england-london (accessed 2 November 2019). This practice has changed in recent years, with the advent of satellite footage and less nation-specific weather mapping.

6   Benedict Anderson, *Imagined Communities: Reflections on the Origin and Spread of Nationalism* (London: Verso, 2016), pp. 173, 175: 'European style maps worked on the basis of a totalizing classification … the entire planet's curved surface had been subjected to a geometrical grid which squared off empty seas and unexplored regions in measured boxes. The task of … "filling in" the boxes was to be accomplished by explorers, surveyors, and military forces … the practice of the imperial states of colouring their colonies on maps with an imperial dye … As this "jigsaw" effect became normal, each "piece" could be wholly detached from its geographic context … [and became a] Pure sign.'

7   Lerm Hayes, 'Introduction, or the Crossdresser's Secret', pp. 20–1.

8   Laura Kneebone, 'Black Sea: The Drexciyan mythical ocean as a radical ecology' (unpublished paper submitted to the Art Studies Research M.A., University of Amsterdam, December 2019).

9   Brian O'Doherty, *Inside the White Cube: The Ideology of the Gallery Space* (Berkeley: University of California Press, 1986).

10 See Patrick Ireland, *Letter to Mia Lerm Hayes* (extracts from a letter, 27 March 1999). This letter was transcribed and placed beside the work at the Irish Museum of Modern Art, mounted on foamboard. At the opening of *On Shifting Ground*, Brian O'Doherty noticed a considerable number of spelling mistakes in the transcription, which he immediately corrected and signed. He also suggested that I ask the museum for what was now a work, which I did.

11 'The space was quite curious, designed by an architect who hadn't a notion about what immediate context art needs to be seen, to see us, and engage in mutual meditation. Nothing new in that … that was a self-satisfied space. It gave me a lot of problems.' *Ibid.* O'Doherty also elaborates in this letter about Thomas McGreevy, his mentor in New York, who had been a friend of Joyce's in Paris and whose 'Catholic' theory was that Finnegans Wake was 'Purgatory'.

12 'I was surrounded by the labyrinth idea as a kid in Ireland, where you never get straight answers, you always get bent answers … I wanted to make labyrinths very easy, to diminish the urgency of a solution and to emphasize a rather lax process … Mine weren't authoritarian or concerned with "ingenuity". What was there was there, including you.' Dorothy Walker quoting the artist, in Patrick Ireland, *Douglas Hyde Gallery Catalogue* (Dublin: Trinity College, 1985).

13 The grid is, of course, a main feature of the art of O'Doherty/Ireland's generation, as identified by Rosalind Krauss. She considers it to be anti-literary, which would (for the reason just given) exclude Joyce's late work (and also does not account for the approximately grid-like arrangement of text in most books). Rosalind E. Krauss, *The Originality of the Avant-Garde and Other Modernist Myths* (Cambridge, MA: MIT Press, 1985). See Christa-Maria Lerm Hayes, *Joyce in Art: Visual Art Inspired by James Joyce* (Dublin: Lilliput, 2004), p. 167.

14 This is arguably a minor canon, following Gilles Deleuze and Félix Guattari, *Kafka: Towards a Minor Literature*, trans. D. Polan (Minneapolis: University of Minnesota Press, 1986). Another element to be taken into account here is that Brian O'Doherty writes novels and has earned a place on the Booker Prize shortlist. A tension then ensues concerning the choice of the name Patrick (Paddy) Ireland: this constitutes a gesture of identification with all things that are stereotypically Irish, particularly as seen from an English perspective (and possibly transferred to US culture). There is a moment of defiance in assuming that a name that connotes being dumb and backward demands artworks that are all the more multilayered and (academically) knowledgeable – even if they share a deceptively straightforward and simple conceptual aesthetic. Behind the Iron Curtain and in other marginalised spaces, a minor canon arguably was/is of great importance. See Christa-Maria Lerm Hayes, 'Notes on activist practices behind the Iron Curtain: Liberation theologies, experimental institutionalism, expanded art and minor literature', in Nick Aikens, Susan Pui San Lok and Sophie Orlando (eds), *Conceptualism: Intersectional Readings, International Framings. Situating 'Black Artists & Modernism' in Europe* (Eindhoven: Van Abbemuseum, l'Internationale, 2019), pp. 332–51, available at www.vanabbemuseum.nl/en/research/resources/articles/conceptualism-intersectional-readings-international-framings/ (accessed 17 March 2023).

15 Simon Ferdinand, 'I map therefore I am modern: Cartography and global modernity in the visual arts' (Ph.D. dissertation, Amsterdam School for Cultural Analysis, University of Amsterdam, 2017), p. 10. Ferdinand remarks on critical cartography at pp. 19–21.

16 Yvonne Whelan, 'Symbolic streetscapes: Interrogating monumental spaces of Dublin', in Jim Hourihane (ed.), *Engaging Spaces: People, Place and Space from an*

Irish Perspective (Dublin: Lilliput, 2003), p. 105. In 2012, part of celebrating Joyce's work under the aegis of the UNESCO City of Literature, Dublin, I curated a small exhibition entitled *Joyce in the City in Dublin.*

17 Lerm Hayes, *Joyce in Art*, p. 131.

18 Eric Bulson, *Novels, Maps, Modernity: The Spatial Imagination 1850–2000* (New York: Routledge, 2007), p. 13.

19 *Ibid.*, pp. 2, 13, 14, 17. 'Without Ulysses … Woolf's London and Döblin's Berlin would have lacked the narrative techniques … [In Döblin,] Franz Biberkopf's disorientation in the city is determined as much by his four-year stint in prison as it is by the fact that the physiognomy of Berlin was literally changing right before his eyes' (*ibid.*, p. 13).

20 *Ibid.*, pp. 18, 1.

21 Anderson, *Imagined Communities*, pp. 163–4.

22 *Ibid.*, pp. 184–5. *Ibid.*, p. 182: 'a characteristic feature of the instrumentalities of the profane state was infinite reproducibility … made technically possible by print and photography … the disbelief of the rulers themselves in the real sacredness of local sites … massive … archaeological reports … illustrated books … A general logoization, made possible by the profaning process'. *Ibid.*, pp. 183–4: 'It is probably not too surprising that post-independence states, which exhibited marked continuities with their colonial predecessors, inherited this form of political museumizing … Interlinked with one another, then, the census, the map and the museum illuminate the late colonial state's style of thinking about its domain. The "warp" of this thinking was a totalizing classificatory grid … It was bounded, determinate, and therefore – in principle – countable … The "weft" was what one could call serialization: the assumption that the world was made up of replicable plurals. The particular always stood as a provisional representative of a series … This is why the colonial state imagined … a nationalist series before the appearance of any nationalists.'

23 Michiel Dehaene and Lieven De Cauter, 'Heterotopia in a postcivil society', in Michiel Dehaene and Lieven De Cauter (eds), *Heterotopia and the City: Public Space in a Postcivil Society* (Abingdon: Routledge, 2008), pp. 3–9.

24 See Christina Kennedy, 'Borromini in the rope drawings of Patrick Ireland', in Lerm Hayes, *Brian O'Doherty*.

25 Dehaene and De Cauter, *Heterotopia and the City*, pp. 6, 2.

26 *Ibid.*, p. 5

27 *Ibid.*

28 Ireland as a tiny island – and the Republic as a neutral country – is not as far away as one might think from the notion of black sites: in the late 1990s, it became known that the USA used the west of Ireland's Shannon airport for so-called rendition flights, effectively flying torture chambers and other activities of disputed legality. See e.g. 'Ireland should never have given US permission to use Shannon, says veterans' spokesman', *Irish Examiner*, 10 November 2015, www.irishexaminer. com/breakingnews/ireland/ireland-should-never-have-given-us-permission-to-use-shannon-says-veterans-spokesman-704922.html (accessed 17 March 2023).

6   The contemporary topographies of Anna Bella Geiger

Dária Jaremtchuk
Translated by Jordan B. Jones

Maps occupy a place of privilege in the poetics of Anna Bella Geiger. Despite the presumed objectivity with which they are traditionally presented, in the work of this Brazilian artist they transform into contingent and selective representations that reveal and reinforce the political, economic and ideological narratives of the information they contain. Nevertheless, the reflection I propose here analyses the presence of maps in her work not as an exclusive and isolated theme, but as a connected and integral part of the body of her work. From this perspective, we can recognise that Geiger has explored many different kinds of spaces and created specific cartographic constellations from the very beginning of her career. The discussion presented here charts a trajectory that begins with her abstract phase and encompasses the appearance (in the mid-1960s) of a subepidermal cartography, in which stains and abstract colours were transformed into human viscera. This caused her poetics to be permeated by scientific perspectives and other ideas about controlling the body that were unique to that period. In the beginning of the following decade, motivated by ritualistic and symbolic territorial explorations, Geiger created a cosmic cartography. In it, photographs of space expeditions were the basis for creating spatial polarities, and political, nationalist and identity antagonisms. Thus, only in the mid-1970s did a cartographic language appear that was focused on maps, and on the geography in which borders and territories created by the artist more directly confront asymmetries of power, hierarchies and cultural hegemonies.

Subepidermal cartography

Before her work with maps, from 1953 to 1965 Geiger had created informal abstract engravings with strong aesthetic qualities. After this period, she produced drawings and engravings in which organs and viscera are dismembered from bodies. Central to this process were procedures of containing and controlling these entrails and body parts, operations that were surreptitiously associated with the widespread use of violence and with the use of force in Brazilian society under the military dictatorship, which lasted from 1964 to 1981, in the sense of a fragmentary objectification of individuals, reducing them to manipulable parts. Viewed from this perspective, this visceral series can be seen as a subepidermal mapping of the body, thus strongly associated with repression and torture in Brazil and its mechanisms of stigmatisation.

The human organs created by Geiger appear severed and isolated from the body, especially in some metal engravings. As a way of reinforcing the volumetric quality of the entrails, the dismembered body parts stand out in space because of the artist's intervention in the printing process. In other words, the organs were cut directly into the engraving plate and printed piece by piece, thus eliminating the characteristic rectangular shape of the engraving plate. On the imprint paper, the parts that were cut and printed separately each produce small protrusions transformed into reliefs with subtle volume and texture, which stand out and rise above the surface of the paper (see Figure 6.1). To use the artist's own words:

> [A]nd then I had this overarching desire to cut out, to fragment the parts that made up color, shape, and material in order to then reorganise them, like puzzle pieces, through superimpositions subjected to the pressure of a press.

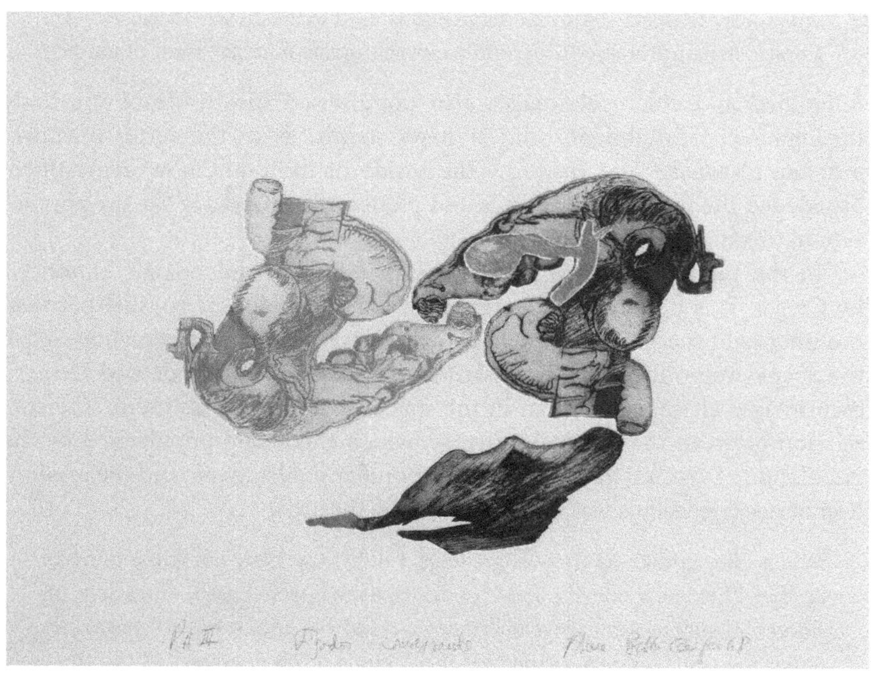

Anna Bella Geiger, *Fígados conversando* (*Livers Talking*), from the *Viscerais* series, 1968.   **6.1**
Etching in colours and relief on paper, 30 cm × 50 cm.

> This scared me when the first impressions came out – the result of this almost
> infinite fragmentation into pieces, which is possible to do in metal engraving.
> After that, I no longer had any use for the 'leftovers' – that is, the white of the
> paper. And so, at the same time (still in 1966), I began to paint visceral shapes
> on sheets of notebook paper, so I could cut them out and have them stand
> alone in terms of their tri-dimensionality.[1]

Images of human organs became common in the 1960s, especially because of
the media's constant reporting on medical advances. The body's insides became
more familiar as man began to interfere directly in its functioning, whether
through surgical advances or by performing transplants. The implantation of
organs originating from other bodies sparked debates about the irreducibility
of the body to its biological system. In 1967, South African surgeon Christian
Barnard performed the first heart transplant in Cape Town, and this feat was
replicated in São Paulo in May 1968 by cardiologist Euryclides Zerbini. Geiger
followed these events with great interest, stating:

> I'll make a point of attending the conference where he [Zerbini] will present next
> Monday. I want to hear his voice. I want to know what the transplant process
> was really like; after having created so many viscera myself, I am even becoming
> interested in Medicine. One of my plans, actually, is to create some plastic
> sculptures of viscera – with the same plastic used to create Santa Clauses – I'm
> going to make a prototype with certain movable organs and have some produced.[2]

Magnified and colourful images also popularised the inside of the body
through serial instalments sold at news stands, as in the series *Medicina
e Saúde* (*Medicine and Health*).[3] The inside of the body, now demystified,
broadened the frontiers of science and piqued the interest of the lay population in this topic.

In the 1960s, these images of consumer culture did not go unnoticed
by Geiger. It is possible to identify a formal and thematic parallel between
the images of the inside of the body and her own visceral engravings, since
the shapes reproduced in the instalments sold at news stands and Geiger's
own images all appear to float in the spaces that encompass them. The correlation between the medical universe, which was being popularised by the
circulation of visceral images printed in popular publications, and the production of her engravings was acknowledged by the artist:

> When I began making these engravings, I didn't say 'Now I'm going to make
> an eye.' They grew out of a series of drawings that were based, ultimately, on
> human elements. Nowadays every news stand has thousands of magazines
> about medicine, and everyone sees these kinds of photographs all the time.
> I did not intentionally take these as my starting point, but I don't know, all that
> must have entered my unconscious just as it did for many other people.[4]

Medical transplantation could be equated to the cutting out and printing of the viscera produced by the artist, since in the hands of Geiger the organs she produces transform into a subepidermal cartography populated by autonomous spatial forms. After all, the organs created by her pulsate and in no way recall putrefaction or repulsion. On the other hand, these brilliant objects, plastered on instalment and newspaper pages with the self-sufficiency of commodities, lead to a cold and distanced conception of the individual body, into which incisive processes such as medicalisation or torture can cut without leaving scars. As Geiger explains, the volumetric cutouts of the engravings reposition these elements of the 'collective unconscious' within another perspective.

Establishing a connection between this set of visceral engravings and the cartographies developed by the same artist in the following decades allows us to perceive continuities between creative strategies and the exploration of various kinds of spaces. The cutouts from the engraving plates were an experimental milestone that connects to her conceptual production begun in the 1970s, a moment in which she expands the scales and formats of her pieces, becoming interested in new supports such as photography, video, postcards, objects, installations etc. In this sense, the environment/installation *Circumambulatio*, created in 1972, is a reference point when we look at Geiger's production as a whole. It is important to note the reversibility between a body split into small volumetric organs from 1966 to 1967, and this other environmental body, amplified in scale, from the 1970s.

Symbolic cartography

When Geiger began her didactic activities at Rio de Janeiro's Museum of Modern Art (MAM Rio) in 1968, censorship and violence were intensifying in Brazil, at the same time that revolutions in politics and behaviour were exploding globally. In this context, it was inopportune to discuss conventional artistic techniques and supports in her role as a docent. These meetings, held outside the museum's conventional classroom spaces, covered a wide range of topics and were intended to stimulate the creativity and sensorial perception of the participants, with explorations of uncommon materials, such as industrial scraps, cardboard packaging, photographs, sand, plastic and even traditional paints.[5] Geiger added Romanian thinker Mircea Eliade and Swiss psychoanalyst Carl Jung to these practices as theoretical references, which supplied the orienting themes of the research: the unconscious and the symbolic. Both references, it should be noted, emphasise a collective corporeality, as will be seen, to the detriment of the body-as-organ, or the body-as-thing.

For Eliade, 'the Centre' is a sacred place that can be found in any microcosm, in every inhabited region. The sacred space is a real space, since 'for the archaic world, myth is real because it relates the manifestations of true reality: the sacred'.[6] Innumerable centres can exist in each microcosm, and it is in them that the sacred manifests itself completely. For the religious historian, discussing the 'Centres of the earth' means being in a sacred space and not in the 'presence of a profane, "objective" geography, somehow abstract and non-essential, a theoretical construction of a space and of a world that is uninhabited and therefore unknown'.[7]

Based on these new references, and as a result of this process developed in partnership with her students in the museological space in the MAM Rio, between April and June of 1972 Geiger exhibited *Circumambulatio*. This environment/installation formally spatialises and organises a set of fragmented and contrasting materials – some handcrafted and others not – such as audiovisual materials (with synchronised slides containing images, texts and musical excerpts), handwritten texts hung on the walls, photographs and Super-8 film (which had documented the activities of the students during the course). Among the texts chosen, one could read excerpts from various authors, such as Kazimir Malevich, Eliade, Plato, Pythagoras, Jung, Paul Klee, João Cabral, Abraham Moles etc. Also on display were phrases with excerpts from interviews with the general public about the question 'What does the centre represent for you, in Guanabara?'. Among the responses, one could read one from a thirty-seven-year-old economist:

> Central do Brasil [Station]. I like watching crowds, everyone together and at the same time, so separate, alone. Whenever I'm upset I go there; I analyse what I see in that human whirlwind and I take comfort, seeing how they go about preoccupied with themselves, with no regard for what others do or feel.

The answers varied with the places in Rio, such as the Pão de Açúcar (Sugarloaf Mountain), the Maracanã Stadium, the MAM Rio or simply the particular workplace of those interviewed. Among the twenty photographs, created from pre-existing images, one could see the Maracanã, the Milky Way, a mandala, a starfish, the Stonehenge archaeological site and even Baroque works of art.

The responses, put side by side, make it clear that the significations, even when talking about a specific geographic space – that of Guanabara – reveal that 'spaces' are experiences lived in a personal way, because they are charged with sensations, imaginations and emotions. No specific place would be capable of evoking a unanimous and common sentiment, because people experience the city in unique ways. After all, space is not an abstract, fixed or absolute concept. In *Circumambulatio* the idea of a centre is a place of individual, rather than collective, memory.

As part of the course developed by Geiger, there was an activity carried out at Marapendi Lake, very far from the centre of the city:

> We chose an abandoned lot in Barra da Tijuca, a very pretty place, where the earth is still almost in its primitive state. The first works were created with the intent of awakening the symbolic consciousness of the students. The first time the group went to this spot, we worked on the idea of one of the participants, who remained standing while she was covered in earth; another, who had brought a rope, entwined it around the mountain formed by the human figure, and the remaining end of the rope was placed in the mouth of the woman-mountain. I had given the symbol – the mountain is the navel of the earth[8] – but the perceptions came unconsciously.[9]

Geiger had asked the photographer Tomy Levinsohn to record the outside activities of the group, such as the moment with tractors on the beaches of Barra da Tijuca, and other performances executed outside the museum space.[10] Geiger used Super-8 for its mobility and capacity to 'captur[e] the space around us, internally or externally, portraying the performances in wide desert landscapes, still uninhabited, here in Rio de Janeiro', along with 'a certain "lack of quality", a brutality of the image and of color'.[11]

Cirumambulatio, along with Geiger's activities as a docent in the courses at the MAM Rio, awoke the artist's interest in exploring archetypal, symbolic and ritualistic spaces – recurring aspects in later works. In a certain sense, they also marked a new way of approaching the relationship of the body with its surroundings, which echoed in large measure the historical/political moment, even though its meanings were multiple. One can see a cosmic interaction that reconnects the body to the whole and to its symbols, and even to its city/ *polis* – far from depoliticisation, in the sense of collectivity – suggested by the organs severed into volumetric objects, ready for surgical inspection and for policies of cataloguing bodies. From this subtle reappropriation of the body as space, or of the space of the body, we can identify a new interest in territorial representation, affected by her sense of surgical cataloguing in the cartography of maps, or, in a broader sense, the cosmic dimension specific to spatial images.

Cosmic cartography

With her interest provoked by the symbology of cosmic space in *Circumambulatio*, the visual records provided by the advances in space science – like images of the lunar surface and of the earth's orbit – were the next material basis for Geiger to create a cosmic cartography, in the first half of the 1970s. *Lunar I* (see Figure 6.2) and *Lunar IV*, both created in 1973, show the image of the moon from a frontal perspective, in which it appears to be

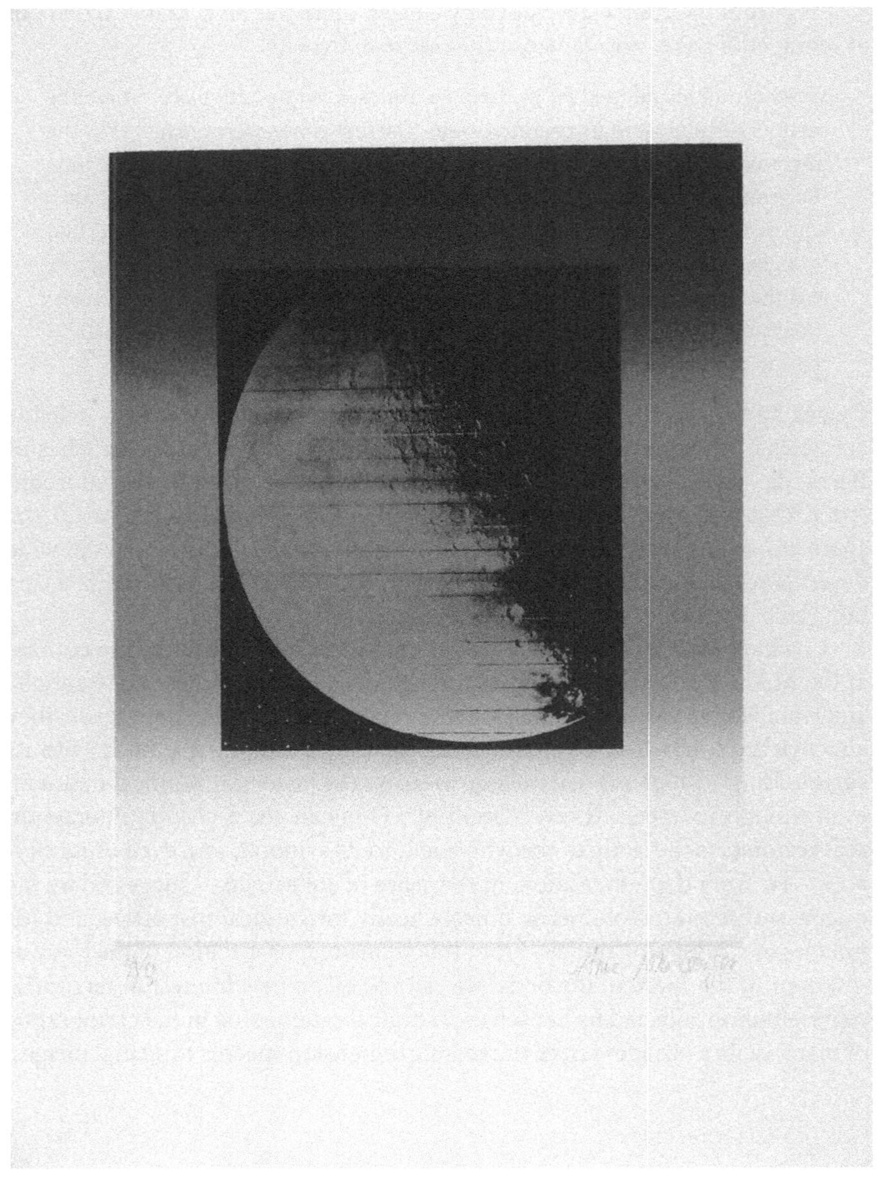

6.2   Anna Bella Geiger, *Lunar I*, 1973. Photoetching and silkscreen, 41 cm × 31 cm.

immovable in outer space, wrapped in a uniform, volatile and unbounded morphological skyscape. There is tension only in the contrast between the light and the shadow, a reference to the sun's illumination, which ends up cutting through the composition. Geiger's interest in this theme expands, and she creates a considerable number of photoserigraphies (screenprints), named *Polaridades/Lunares* (*Polarities/Lunar*).

Cold War tensions almost fade before the chromatic quality and careful impressions of these pieces. In a subtle way, the United States – protagonists against the Soviet Union in the race to the moon – are present in these representations related to the conquest of space. From material given by the United States Consulate in Rio de Janeiro, Geiger came into possession of photographs of Planet Earth and of the surface of the moon produced by NASA space missions.

In the 1974 photoengraving *Sem título (Trevas/luz)* (*Untitled (Darkness/ Light)*) (see Figure 6.3), from the *Polaridades/Lunares* series, the upper portion of the map of South America is slightly deformed, with a faint accentuation of

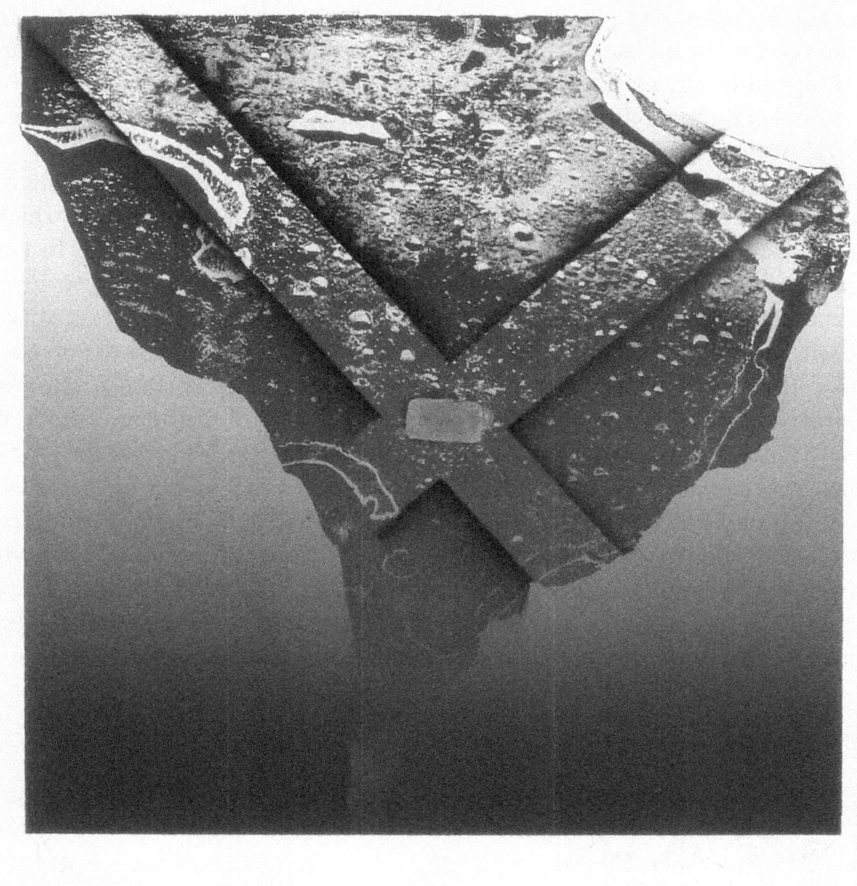

Anna Bella Geiger, *Sem título (Trevas/luz) (Untitled (Darkness/Light))*, from the *Polaridades/Lunares* series, 1974. Photoetching and silkscreen, 39 cm × 40 cm.   **6.3**

the Amazon region, and it hovers over three horizontal stripes in yellow, green and black. In Brazil in the 1960s, nationalism was a banner carried by both the cultural right and left. In the 1970s, the military exclusively assumed this role. It would only be in the *Diretas já* ('Direct Elections Now') campaigns that national symbols (such as the flag, for example) would return to the domain of the general population. In Geiger's work, the colours green and yellow – references to the Brazilian flag and to the nationalism promulgated by the military regime – share the space with a dark stripe in the lower part of the photoengraving, perhaps alluding to the growing obscurantism that fomented the growth of dictatorships throughout Latin America. The strip of earth of this continent was covered with lunar soil, which confers dryness and emptiness to the space. Front and centre in the image, two stripes cross and form an 'X' shape, further impeding access to the content represented. From the place of earthly belonging demarcated by the most reactionary nationalism during the years of the dictatorship, the map points to the borderless, arid and uninviting immensity representative of the green-yellow way, and demarcated by a symbol of impossibility, in which the ambiguity of the 'national' is confronted by a disputed territoriality and even a cosmic dimension.

Present in other works by Geiger, the 'X' shape is related to the photographic images given to her by the United States Consulate – images in which the lack of clarity would lead to their being discarded and unused. In her hands, the mark of rejection was reworked and made into something positive, becoming a symbol of a barrier to access to the spaces reproduced by the image itself, as it maps the surface from what we might call a geopolitical perspective. The neutral 'X' sign also appears between words, such as *right–wrong* and *inside–outside*, for example. The pretended neutrality of the image produced by science – but coming from a demarcated space (the United States) – by being reclaimed in its less 'precise' aspects (photos that would be discarded because of the lack of precision in the one who took them), by being reworked in its inside/outside senses, allows the cosmic or scientific neutrality to confront and be simultaneously confronted by smaller, 'national' territories. These cosmic images point, in this way, to the cartography and maps that Geiger uses, reinforcing the organ/collective and part/whole relationship.

Cartography, maps and geography

Political convulsions and processes of decolonisation substantially reconfigured the global political map, especially in the 1960s. Widely reported in the media, conflicts and events were accompanied by the reproduction of maps. It was not a coincidence that, in the same period, maps became objects of great interest to artists. While maps and the arts have had a long poetic and political relationship, this partnership became more enhanced from that point on.

Geiger uses map projections as a reference for the creation of her maps. Living with geographer Pedro Geiger (her husband) also made maps trivial representations in her home environment. With artistic appropriation, through deformations and exaggerations, she emphasises the unique meaning inherent in each of the projections used. While any representation of the earthly globe in two dimensions is an exercise of changing its three-dimensional shape, the maps produced by Geiger underscore even more visibly the disproportions implicit in the production of any transposition. She makes it clear that the act of the cartographer, who seeks to produce accurate scientific maps, reinforces previous narratives. By becoming a cartographer herself, she disobeys classical spatial epistemologies and shows that no line traced on a map is impartial.

In the collage drawing *Rio de Janeiro como centro cultural do mundo* (*Rio de Janeiro as Cultural Centre of the World*), created in 1977 and included in the artist notebook *O Novo Atlas 2* (*New Atlas 2*), we can identify two map projections: the Mercator world map and the Washington-centred azimuthal equidistant projection.[12] When placed side by side, the relativity of these representations is visible. The Mercator projection is distinguishable by the alterations in area between the representations of the Northern and Southern Hemispheres, in which the northern regions are disproportionately larger than those of the southern. The azimuthal equidistant projection, on the other hand, is recognisable because it chooses a centre for the projection – a specific point on the globe. Extending from this focal point, the regions around it are kept equidistant, but in the peripheral areas of the projection the deformations are accentuated.

Thus, when the artist places Latin America on the azimuthal equidistant projection, outlining Brazil in red, she transforms that space – historically represented as subaltern and dependent – into cultural and artistic protagonist. The relevance of the region is accentuated with the caption 'A América do Sul como centro cultural do mundo. O Brasil como centro da América do Sul. O Rio de Janeiro como centro cultural do Brasil e do mundo' ('South America as cultural centre of the world. Brazil as centre of South America. Rio de Janeiro as cultural centre of Brazil and of the world').

Choosing Latin America as a theme is not exclusive to Geiger. Revolutions and dictatorships also placed this geographic space on the agenda of intellectual and artistic debates, especially in the 1960s and 1970s. Restoring (even if only partially) a historical context to this theme allows us to recognise a political choice in the action of this artist.

According to Miguel Rojas Mix, the first person to use the term *Latin America* was the Chilean Francisco Bilbao. For Bilbao it was essential, so that South Americans could form a united front against the domination of the United States: 'only this union … will be able to halt the imperialism of the United Sates of North America, which believes in its empire as Rome believed in its own'.[13] The idea of pan-Latinism spread in the nineteenth century; Napoleon's France would instrumentalise it as a form of opposition against British interests. According to Mix, France believed it was the primary power in the Latin bloc and was keenly interested in preserving its hegemony. It was the only power that could contain the expansion of the Saxon world. The formation of a Latin America meant resistance against the Saxon domination that sought the 'exclusive dominion of the white race, [while] Latinness found its mission in the formation of a new race: the blended race, the cosmic race'.[14] In other words, the Latin identity asserted itself by capitalising on miscegenation.

Mix states further that the discourse of a Latin American identity reappears midway through the twentieth century. It was in the developmentalist context that national and continental bourgeoisies sought to assert themselves in the face of international capitals. Proposals appeared for economic integration and for import substitutions. A specific term (*pan-Latin Americanism*) was even coined in opposition to the pan-Americanism being pushed by the United States. Thus, in this moment, Latin American identity arrived on the scene of national bourgeoisie interests. The needs of local populations, such as equal rights and justice in income distribution, were ignored. The ideological construction of a Latin American identity came about only for the sake of the immediate interests of part of the population.

It was in the 1960s, though, that Latin American identity asserted itself more strongly within the left-wing political margin. Seeing oneself as a Latin American began to mean asserting discontent with the political and economic configuration. After the revolution in Cuba, many believed that other revolutions would be possible, and not just on a utopian level. Thus, the term *Latin American* gained a second meaning: the recognition of an oppressive and unjust reality. Subjugation to foreign capital needed to be fought. In the following decade, the revolutionary euphoria waned because of military regimes, but Latin American identity continued to accrue a symbolism that was considered both critical and liberating.

In the context of artistic production and art history, the dimensions of this debate extend beyond the confines of this study. It is enough to mention, however, that many colloquia and debates were promoted among critics, artists and museum directors in an attempt to strengthen ties between Latin American countries and to discuss the continent's identities. This included, for example, the 1978 Latin American Biennial, held in São Paulo – which did not extend beyond its first (highly criticised) iteration.

Within Latin America, Brazil occupies an idiosyncratic position. Colonised by Portugal, it achieved independence not through popular revolts or revolutions, but through the proclamation of the Prince Regent of Brazil – Dom Pedro de Alcântara de Bragança, son of the monarch Dom João VI (John VI), who proclaimed himself Emperor of Brazil on 7 September 1822.

Traditionally, works of art that engage with stories of conflicts between colonies and colonising powers are more recent. There is great difficulty in identifying colonising forces in this case – the ambiguity of themes such as miscegenation and the idea of a country accustomed to unproblematic assimilations of contrasts and dissension helped construct an imaginary that was at times acritical, at times utopian, regarding the structural ills of colonisation. It would be unreasonable to attempt to reconstruct the trajectory of Brazilian art in the formation of this imaginary, which would also require us to consider the various critical moments that do not fit this pattern, but the fact is that this imaginary began to be systematically altered by contemporary production, as in the cartography of Geiger, for example.

With regard to Latin America, it is commonly said that the educated Brazilian bourgeoisie preferred to turn their backs on their fellow South American neighbours and to turn directly towards Europe. It would be in the artistic exile of the 1960s and 1970s that many artists and intellectuals were to discover their Latin American identities, whether because they shared their displacement with exiles from other South American dictatorships, or whether they were treated by the artistic establishment as Latin Americans, which defines a homogenous and uniform identity for the inhabitants of this continent.

In Geiger's engravings *Local da ação n. 1* (*Place of Action No. 1*, 1979) and *Local da ação n. 001* (*Place of Action No. 001*, 1980), the world map reappears, structured by lines of longitude and latitude. But South America has its shape geometrised and the lines of longitude and latitude are interrupted when they meet this continent. 'Local da ação' ('Place of action'), written below the map, is not sufficiently capable of altering the state of suspension and dissociation in which South America finds itself with regard to its spatial and temporal surroundings.

In another composition, named *Local da ação n. 8* (*Place of Action No. 8*, 1980), the world map floats in orbit, sectioned off by three coloured stripes: brown, orange and blue. The sharpest point of a triangular geometric shape directs the viewer's eye to a specific part of the composition: the morphologically fixed landscape of South America, positioned almost in the centre of the composition.

Meanwhile, in the 1976 videos *Mapas elementares I* (*Elementary Maps I*) and *Mapas elementares III* (*Elementary Maps III*), Geiger links drawings of maps with the sound of the song 'Carta a um amigo' ('Letter to a Friend'), by Francis Hime and Chico Buarque.[15] The song lyrics address the lack of liberty, repression and figures such as Emílio Garrastazu Médici – who, in 'Apesar de você' ('In Spite of You'), was blamed by Buarque for having invented 'toda a escuridão …' ('all the darkness …'). Meanwhile, in the 1976 song-letter 'Meu caro amigo' ('My Dear Friend'), the authors cleverly work in a chance to 'send news' to theatrologist Augusto Boal and his wife, Cecília, who were in exile.

In line with the music, Geiger draws her world map to emphasise the distance between friends separated by exile. She paints the map of Brazil black when the phrase 'a coisa aqui tá preta' ('things here are looking black') is heard. By using a song with a political bent, Geiger rearticulates the relationship of the local individual – who speaks of his/her broken social connections, who sends letters to friends who have been wrenched forcibly away from home – with scientific communications capable of mapping all of the distances and all of the places, carefully laid out by the network of latitude and longitude lines. However, in the case of Latin America, this rearticulation does not establish, even to a minimal degree, the most basic of political contracts.

In *Mapas Elementares III*, one of her most well-known productions, the artist drew four anamorphic images: an amulet, a mulatta, a crutch (*uma muleta*), and a map labelled Latin America, doing so to the sound of the song 'La Virgen Negra' ('The Black Virgin').[16] Beyond the phonetic similarities between the terms (all of which contain an 'm' sound in Portuguese), all of the drawings portray cliché images, imposed identities, concepts/images established by colonisation. The Latin stereotypes are presented in an ambiguous and ironic way. One can imagine a Latin America left to its own luck, with the form of the amulet; dependent on 'external' agents (the crutch) or on divine ones (appearing in the background music, soliciting the help of the Black Madonna) in order to solve its problems; and a Latin America that continues to export exotic products, such as the mulatta.

Similarly, in the piece *Am. Latina* (*Latin Am.*, 1977), the morphologies of the sketches of an amulet, a mulatta, a crutch and a map of Latin America resemble the configuration of the continent and, still further, the words written beside each drawing, each beginning with *Am-* in Portuguese, emphasising the phonetic and conceptual similarities among the set of things drawn.

Repetition of images throughout various works is a constant of Geiger's artistic production, reminiscent of her past as an engraver in which the plates, which are now conceptual, can be reprinted, but with little or big variations. The technical operations of cutting and repeating, which are unique to engraving experiments – similar to the aesthetic 'operation', so to speak, of atomising parts – reappear in these maps as syntactic tools that reposition the signs. The very words, atomised as signs, can function as cuts and repetitions.

Between the pages of the artist notebook *O novo atlas I* (*New Atlas I*, 1977), the Mercator projection reappears, this time accompanied by three other maps created by Geiger containing geographic anamorphoses. In them there is no scale included, because the parameter used to draw the map indicates systems of economic and cultural power. In the first of these maps produced by the artist, which is juxtaposed with that of Mercator, the shape of the Middle East appears disproportionately bigger in relation to the other continents. Because it deals with the world of *petroleum*, a term indicated in the legend ('Petróleo'), the exaggeration is justified. In the next map, it is the Northern Hemisphere's turn to grow, and this time the legend explains that it deals with the configuration of the 'Desenvolvido e subdesenvolvido' ('Developed and underdeveloped') world. Finally, in the last map, labelled with the terms 'Domínio cultural ocidental' ('Western cultural domination'), the United States and Europe are amplified, while at the same time Africa and India are transformed into narrow strips of land, almost disappearing from the map. Curiously, the shape of South America was spared any thinning out and, because of the absence of Central America, is directly connected to the United States.

In the two works entitled *Correntes culturais* (*Cultural Currents*, 1975 and 1976 respectively), a different map projection serves as the foundation so that the representation of the oceans can be covered by words typed in black and white (see Figure 6.4). In the 1975 *Correntes culturais* the oceans are full of two alternately repeating phrases: 'Correntes culturais dominantes ('Dominant cultural currents') and 'Correntes culturais dependents ('Dependent cultural currents'). There is a single red, handwritten word, 'Recessiva ('Recessive'), positioned on the west coast of South America. Meanwhile, in the 1976 *Correntes culturais* the same phrases have a new plastic presentation, since the word 'dominante' ('dominant') is typed in red and alternates with the black-and-white word 'dependente' ('dependent'). This time, the word 'Recessive',

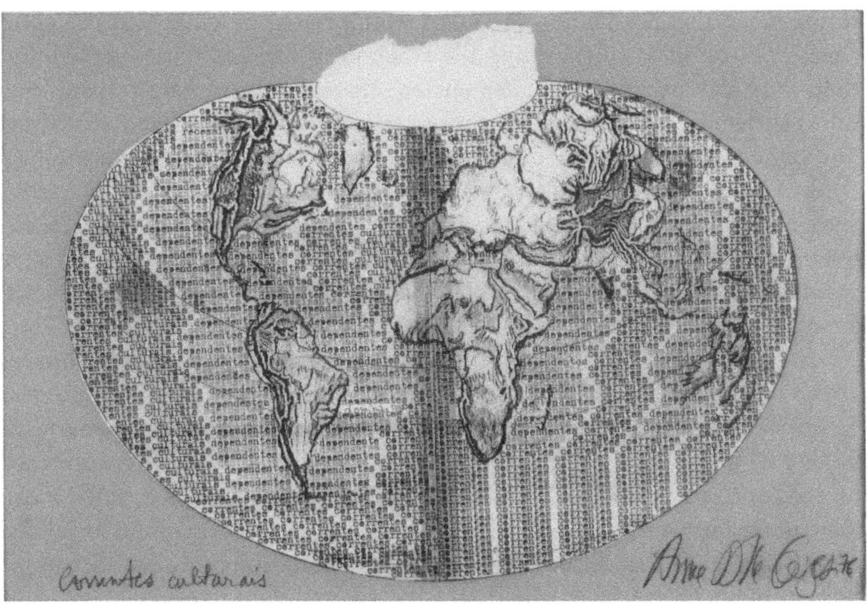

Anna Bella Geiger, *Correntes culturais* (*Cultural Currents*), 1976. Red China ink and typewriter ink on paper, 46 cm × 58 cm.

6.4

also handwritten in red, can be found in the Atlantic Ocean, near the coast of the Brazilian northeast. The ocean tides seem to chant an unaltered mantra from waves of power and subordination, which at some point nevertheless run into something that is *recessive* – something latent that, in the absence of a dominant gene, can manifest itself.

Both the 1975 and 1976 *Correntes culturais* maps appear in *O pão nosso de cada dia* (*Our Daily Bread*), an installation exhibited for the first time in 1978 and comprising a set of six postcards; a table covered in a padded white cloth, with small maps printed and embroidered on the ends; friezes of maps in white supports hung from the side walls; and a video shown on a television set.[17]

The postcards show outlines of maps of Brazil and of South (or Latin?) America cut out of the middle of slices of bread. In one of the images, a slice of bread (without any map drawn on it) is brought to the mouth, a clear reference to the sacredness of the food and to the religiousness made explicit in the title of the installation. The fusion of geographic configurations with bread, beyond symbolism, updates the anthropophagic (cannibalistic) gesture. But as, in the anthropophagic act, the one eating takes on the attributes of what is eaten, Geiger doubly affirms her Latin American identity.

In *Our Daily Bread*, the maps were retrieved from the artist notebooks *Sobre a arte* (*About Art*) and *O novo atlas I* and *II*, and transformed into patterns. Previously, reading the little notebooks facilitated an intimate and critical view of cartographic lines, and the words retained their semantic function. In the installation, the maps were printed on cloth and placed in friezes on the walls surrounding the table. Positioned as horizontal friezes, they thus acquire an artistic dimension, since the words are transformed into camouflaged lines, akin to those operations of cutting and repeating. The same maps containing cartographic anamorphoses, printed in the 1977 *O novo atlas I*, were printed on the corners of the cloth covering the table, with embroidery stitches added. However, while the information seemed irrefutable when the maps were part of the little notebook, now that they are covered in unfinished embroidery stitches, threads and loose ends they await a narrative conclusion.

The elements of this work approximate the telluric – present in the images of the bread and the softness of the padding – and technology, represented by the video and by the cold distance of the screen. Precariousness and technology continue to be coinhabitants in a representation of identity conferred on the continent. In Geiger's work, the polish and sophistication of the video exist alongside poverty and manual labour in the same geographic, social and artistic space. We can rethink, yet again, the relationship between the simple letter written to a distant friend and the great distance regulated by technology. Both spaces operate simultaneously – the small daily (im)possibility of a marginal country (the bread, the letter, the quilt) confronts the unheard possibilities of new technologies to track and map the entire surface of the planet – and even the space beyond it.

This inside/outside relationship, to use Geiger's own terms, can also be considered from a local point of view in terms of her use of cartography and its ends. While, on the one hand, the use of maps by artists in the 1960s and 1970s may be analogous to geopolitical divisions and economic interests, we should also remember that, in Brazil, public government campaigns used the map of the country as a symbolic element to reinforce nationalism. Innumerable campaigns undertaken during the military dictatorship used maps demonstrating the advance of megalomaniacal government projects, such as the construction of the Trans-Amazonian Highway. There were also campaigns that reinforced the myth of peaceful coexistence between the races and of the characteristic Brazilian passiveness, as a way of masking racism in Brazil. Maps were featured on the back covers of notebooks and instructional books, reinforcing a nationalist pedagogy.

Not by coincidence, the strong pedagogical bent identified in Geiger's works from those years has links to her motherhood and to the schooling of her four children. If we widen this domestic sphere, we can also associate them with the official (and dogmatic) education put in practice by the military regime, which supported conservative teaching methods and created courses with strong doctrinal content, such as 'Education, Morality and Civics'.

In one of the pages of the artist notebook *Sobre a arte* from 1976, we see the backs of two children – a boy and a girl – as they draw a map of Brazil. Below them is written 'IDEOLOGIA' ('IDEOLOGY'). Above the drawing (and at the top of the page) we see the configuration shown in Table 6.1 (the word *qua...dro* can be translated below as *bo...ard*). When maps are mechanically copied by children – or even by Geiger herself in the video in which she appears drawing the map of Latin America literally and with little creativity – prescribed identities are mimicked. The skill of the cartographer, charged with mechanicalness by the performative gesture of the artist, divests itself of creativity and follows previously defined models. Literacy, which follows a syllabic

Table 6.1: Extract from artist notebook *sobre a arte* (1976)

O ... Fé ... lia qua ... dro	Hi ... pó ... l i... to. Bra ... sil.
dro	bra
dra	bre
dre	bri
dri	bro
dru	bru

method lacking more complex and syntactic meaning, functions in this way as a pictorial, repetitive, and decontextualised literacy.

As we have seen here, in the 1970s Geiger had connected her maps to map projections and to geopolitics. In the following decade they faded, since the artist dedicated herself to painting, producing screens with circular and padded formats titled *macios* (*soft pieces*). Before this, some maps produced by the artist already bore dissolved national and continental borders, with a military camouflage pattern beginning to obscure them. This visual pattern can be best observed in the frieze from the installation *Mesa, friso e vídeos macios* (*Table, Frieze and Soft Videos*), presented at the sixteenth São Paulo Biennial, in 1981. When carefully observed, the green-beige camouflage that overlays the frieze does not hide the irregular contours of South America. The standardisation of times and spaces, inherent in the global economic order, appears not to have sufficient strength to flatten the particularities of that continent, which, not coincidentally, is where the artist lives.

At the beginning of the 1990s, Geiger became interested in the old drawers of metal filing cabinets, which served as the basis for the series *Fronteiriços* (*Borderlines*). Treated as receptacles, these drawers had their insides filled with encaustic (a kind of melted wax) coloured by various pigments. On the surface of the material, which hardens, the artist creates reliefs; moulds maps made of tin, lead or copper; and inserts various kinds of objects, giving birth to very peculiar worlds.

It is known that, in art history, encaustic has been used to preserve shapes and pigments, which may have led Geiger to associate it, in her works, with old texts and religious references. At the same time as the embalming seems to protect the elements added by the artist to the surfaces of the drawers, there is a certain impression that the spent quality, inherent in encaustic, suspends the maps positioned there. In *Orbis descriptio* (1995), for example, there are two parallel compartments separated by a divider. In both there are moulds of hollow maps produced on metal; on one divider we see the outline of Brazil connected to Latin America, and on the other the map of the Americas (see Figure 6.5). In the reliefs on the encaustic, created while the wax was hardening, there are many types of maps, a wide horizontal banner (which recalls a scroll), an old seal/coat of arms, and the imprint of the title of the work, *Orbis descriptio*. When the reliefs are compared, we see that the scales of the maps were inverted, since the representations of the world appear in a miniature size in relation to the proportions of the maps of the Americas and of Latin America. Added to this (above a metal half-circle) were tied lines of copper that assume the form of rays (perhaps solar rays). In the other compartment, on each end of the drawer were hung wires that represent winds.

In closing, we can assert that in the processes of creating *Fronteiriços* the artist, like a demiurge, manipulates material with fire and creates topographies

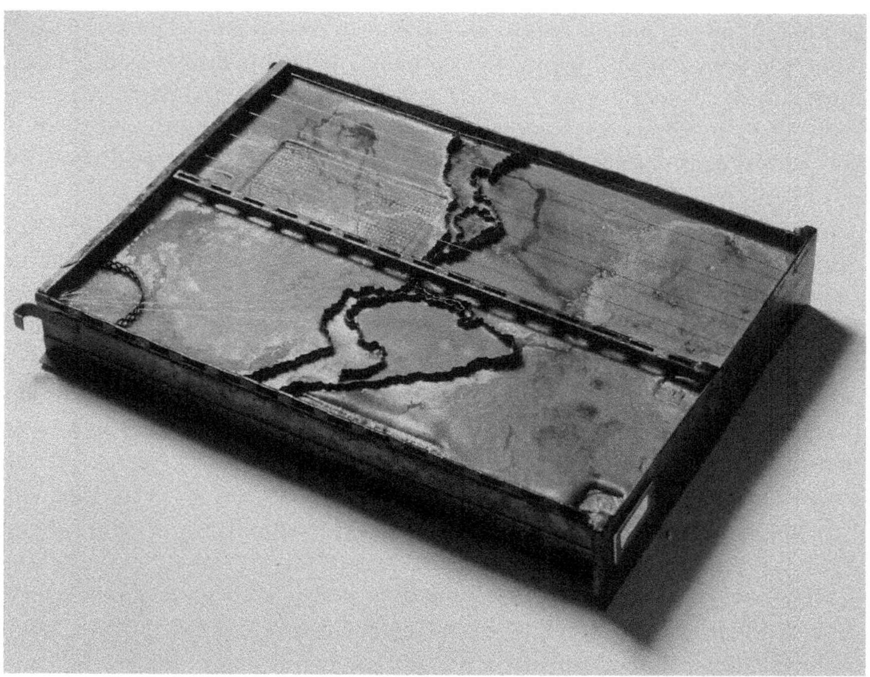

Anna Bella Geiger, *Orbis descriptio with Six Winds*, from the *Borderline* series, 1995.   **6.5**
Old iron archive shelves, encaustic, bronze plate, copper, pigments and plaster.

from personal and collective memories, while also archiving representations of her own work. Beyond the desire to preserve her work in the body of the encaustic, we see the attraction of the atemporality already expressed in the floating maps that are moulded into the surface of the encaustic. Suspended in the flow of time, these maps/moulds carry a more sublime meaning, a condition that is different from that of her initial cartography, in which the maps printed on paper or on old pages of her little notebooks presented a more mundane materiality.

It is important to note that when Geiger began *Fronteiriços* in the 1990s, and performed a kind of archiving of her own work, conceptual art was also receiving attention from historians and curators. This exercise culminated in the scanning of institutional collections in search of conceptual works in their document archives and libraries, and in the organisation of significant exhibitions of this production, such as the 1999 show *Global Conceptualism: Points of Origin, 1950–1980s* in the Queens Museum of Art in New York, and *Heterotopías: Médio siglo sin-lugar: 1918–1968* (*Heterotopias: Half a Century without a Place: 1918–1968*) in the Museo Nacional Centro de Arte Reina Sofía in Madrid in 2000/2001, for example. Part of this new historiography chose to call this Latin American production *conceptualism*, preserving the term *conceptual art* as exclusive to what was done in the Anglo-Saxon domain. About this debate, which I have intentionally avoided on account of its proportions, it is important to underscore that conceptual art was a decentralised phenomenon and that political and ethical connotations were not exclusively addressed by artists who were born Latin Americans.

The revolution in transportation and in means of communication that occurred in the 1970s intensified the transit of people and information, shortening distances and accelerating circulation, as was the case for Geiger herself – she travelled to Europe and went countless times to the United States. From this perspective, there was an international artistic debate that transcended geographical borders and that enquired about the nature of art, the role of the artist and aesthetic experience. Geiger participated actively in this discussion as an artist, as a mentor to young people in her MAM Rio courses and also as an organiser of gatherings in her home, when she met with Fernando Cocchiarale, Letícia Parente, Paulo Herkenhoff, Sônia Andrade and others to discuss topics related to the arts.

It cannot be said that Brazil remained disconnected from the great artistic centres. Intense flows of exchange can be reconstructed, as can the circulation of magazines and newspaper articles, and the publishing of books and catalogues. Museums put on exhibitions with the participation of international conceptual artists, and in their libraries – primarily those of the University of São Paulo Museum of Contemporary Art (MAC USP) and of the MAM Rio – they maintained important and up-to-date collections. In a way, considering the backdrop of the military dictatorship, these institutions represented territories that were more open to the exhibition of works of a critical nature and became spaces of opposition against institutions aligned with the authoritarian State, against art galleries, and against the boom in the Brazilian art market at the time. We must also not forget that, despite the political regime, the São Paulo Biennials continued to exhibit Brazilian and international artists every two years.

Thus, the act of Geiger's printing the term 'recessive' near Latin America and Rio de Janeiro on her maps becomes a gesture of resistance to dominant currents, whether political, economic or cultural in nature. This resistance is duplicated when we remember that Geiger preferred to use less object-bound formats and supports, such as reproductions, photographs, Super-8 film, and video – characteristics that allowed for a fluid circulation of her production among geographic spaces not bound by official art circuits. Artists from many parts of the world created new flows and gave visibility to what they produced by sending works through the mail or checking them in their luggage in order to participate in exhibitions, such as *Prospectiva* (*Prospective*, 1974) and *Poéticas visuais* (*Visual Poetics*, 1977), to cite two of the most emblematic exhibitions organised by the MAC USP, under the direction of Walter Zanini. In this way, the artistic-geographic decentralisation proposed by the cartography of Geiger highlights the geo-aesthetic turn of conceptual art, which also redrew borders on the map of the arts that had been delineated using the North Atlantic as its axis.

To conclude, we may affirm that Geiger's production allows us in equal measure to understand how artistic practices have for a long time been subversively addressing asymmetries of power, gender hierarchies, cultural hegemony, Eurocentric canons of art history and the place of production of those artists identified as Latin American women – topics very important to narratives that seek to rethink methods of decolonising the arts and rewriting art history itself. And it seems that the cartographic constellations produced by Geiger have become privileged objects in this belated revision of canons.

Notes

1 Istefania Marcarini Rubino, 'Interview with Anna Bella Geiger 2014/2015 about her visceral phase (1965–1969)', *DAPesquisa* 11:17 (December 2016), 101–12.

2 Flavio Macedo Soares, 'Eviscerando', *Correio da Manhã* (Rio de Janeiro), 14 October 1968.

3 The illustrated instalments of *Medicina e Saúde* were published by Abril Cultural in 1967, based on the Italian publication of 1964.

4 Macedo Soares, 'Eviscerando'.

5 At the end of the 1960s, the search for new creative spaces and exhibition venues became frequent in and around Rio de Janeiro. In addition to Hélio Oiticica, who exhibited his *Parangolé* capes on the grounds outside the MAM Rio in 1965, Rogério Duarte organised the Apocalipopótese (Apocalypothesis) event in 1968, which occurred at Flamengo Park, a sprawling green strip in the city, and not coincidentally the space in which, at one of its ends, the museum is located – the epicentre of the local artistic scene. On that occasion, Antonio Manuel presented his *Urnas quentes* (*Hot Ballot Boxes*), which were closed and sealed wooden boxes containing poems, texts, photographs and objects, but which relied on the actions of viewers to be opened. The artist would provide a hammer and stones so this could be done, since it was only by aggressive smashing that the contents could be discovered. And Lygia Pape put on her performance *O ovo* (*The Egg*), in which wooden cubes were wrapped in thin coloured paper or coloured plastic, which would then be ripped open by the people stationed on the inside of these structures.

6 Mircea Eliade, *Imagens e símbolos: Ensaio sobre o simbolismo mágico-religioso* (São Paulo: Martins Fontes, 1991), pp. 35–6. Owing to difficulties in locating the English version of Eliade's text, the excerpts included throughout this text are translations back from the Portuguese.

7 *Ibid.*, p. 36.

8 According to Mircea Eliade, the symbols of the Mountain, the Tree or the Pillar, situated at the Centre of the World, are widespread. 'The summit of the Cosmic Mountain is not just the highest point on earth; it is the navel of the earth, the point where creation began.' *Ibid.*, pp. 38–9. For this religious historian, 'whether spread or spontaneously discovered, symbols, myths and rites always reveal a borderline situation for man, and not just a historical situation'. *Ibid.*, p. 30.

9 'Arte visuais à procura do centro', *Jornal do Brasil* (Rio de Janeiro), 23 August 1972.

10 Geiger explained that, in addition to directing Tomy Levinsohn's photos, she also produced a few images. Anna Bella Geiger, discussion with the author (October 2002).

11 Anna Bella Geiger, 'Statement', in Fernando Cocchiarale (ed.), *Forma e imagem técnicas na arte do Rio de Janeiro: 1950–1975* (São Paulo: Paço das Artes, 2002), p. 56.

12 Geiger uses the term 'little notebooks' to refer to her artist notebooks, which could also be called artist books. Bound at the top with horizontal spirals, they offer to the 'reader' a determined narrative sequence, in which images and text alternate or are shown together. The discursive elements are present in almost all of them, characterising them by their thematic or informative aspect. However, the images are the predominant element. Despite the proposed sequence, some pages gained autonomy and transformed into individual works.

13 Miguel Rojas Mix, 'Identidade e integração na América Latina', in José Marques de Melo (ed.), *Ibero-América: Integração e comunicação* (São Paulo: Escola de Comunicações e Artes da Universidade de São Paulo, 1990). The quote from Francisco Bilbao comes from his 1856 comments recorded in Francisco Bilbao, 'Iniciativa de la América: Idea de un congreso federal de las repúblicas', *Cuadernos de cultura latinoamericana* 3 (1978), 5–27 (p. 36).

14 *Ibid.*, p. 37.

15 The lyrics are as follows: 'Meu caro amigo me perdoe, por favor / Se eu não lhe faço uma visita / Mas como agora apareceu um portador / Mando notícias nessa fita / Aqui na terra 'tão jogando futebol / Tem muito samba, muito choro e rock 'n' roll / Uns dias chove, noutros dias bate sol / Mas o que eu quero é lhe dizer que a coisa aqui tá preta/ Muita mutreta pra levar a situação / Que a gente vai levando de teimoso e de pirraça / E a gente vai tomando, que também, sem a cachaça / Ninguém segura esse rojão' ('My dear friend forgive me, please / If I don't come visit you / But since a courier just came by / I'm sending updates on this tape / Here at home they're playing soccer / There's lots of samba, lots of choro and rock n' roll / Some days it rains, and other days there's sun / But what I want to tell you is that things here are looking black / We've lots of schemes to make it through this plight / We're dealing with through pluck and pranks / And we keep drinking, 'cause without cachaça / No one can survive this grind').

16 In reality, the map is of South America. At times, the artist removes part of Central America. She states that she was not interested in using this part of the map.

17 The installation was exhibited in 1978, in the Centro Cultural Cândido Mendes (without the postcards), and in 1980, at the Venice Bienniale. In 2002 it was part of the exhibition curated by Fernando Cocchiarale, *Forma e imagem técnicas na arte do Rio de Janeiro: 1950–1975* (São Paulo: Paço das Artes, 2002).

Part III
Sites and networks

Spatial play in Dennis Oppenheim's cartographic works

Larisa Dryansky

Utopia: a map that is not on the maps.

Louis Marin (1991)[1]

According to Rosalind Krauss, a key difference between modernist and post-modernist sculpture hinges on the issue of the site. As she recounts, modernism introduced a fundamental rupture between site and sculpture. Whereas previously sculpture, following the logic of the monument, entertained a symbiotic relation with the particular place where it was erected, modernist sculpture is characterised by 'the absolute loss of the site'.[2] Against this ideal of perfect autonomy, postmodernist sculpture reinstates the site's importance. However, it does so in a paradoxical way – that is, by converting the site into its very absence, as evinced by Robert Smithson's Nonsites. Bridging these two poles – the absence of the site and site as absence – Krauss identifies an intermediary model, Constantin Brancusi's monumental ensemble at Târgu-Jiu (1938), which she describes as 'a monument whose site cannot even be localised anymore, has become an impossible fiction, an absence, a reference system that always implies that the work's place is elsewhere, a lack'.[3]

Krauss bases her argument on the fact that Brancusi did not conceive the layout of his ensemble in response to the specific characteristics of the site at Târgu-Jiu, but rather abstractly projected onto it the plan of the Parisian monumental ensemble connecting the Luxor Obelisk at the Place de la Concorde to the Arc de Triomphe du Carrousel along an axis that cuts through a flowerbed in the gardens of the Tuileries.[4] In other words, Brancusi's ensemble, while not succumbing to modernist sitelessness, does not fully belong in its place. Better yet, its very presence makes the site unreal by relating it to the shadow of a distant location. In this way, Brancusi heralds the present/absent site of postmodernism, and he does so by overlaying a map – the very emblem of localisation – onto a place completely disconnected from the map's original referent.

Although Krauss does not allude to conceptual art, her discussion of Brancusi's cartographic manipulations is reminiscent of the kind of playing with maps and locations that several artists associated with conceptual approaches engaged in. This is true, above all, of Dennis Oppenheim's cartographic pieces.

Throughout 1968 and 1969, Oppenheim produced a major series of work, variously labelled as conceptual art and land art, in which he traced on the ground of outdoor sites (wastelands, industrial sites, woods, deserts, fields, farming land) different types of maps (contour maps, floorplans, diagrams of time zones, roadmaps) pertaining to places unrelated to these same sites and, in several cases, quite distant from them. An important difference from Brancusi, of course, is that Oppenheim's pieces were ephemeral. At the same time, it might be said that, by dealing with cartographic signs directly, Oppenheim laid bare the process that remained implicit in Brancusi's approach. It is also worth mentioning that Krauss includes Oppenheim among the representatives of sculpture's postmodern shift.[5] Yet Oppenheim's use of cartography in fact complicates Krauss's narrative as well as other influential accounts of the question of the site in contemporary art.

Indeed, the idea of the absenting of the site does not quite fit what Oppenheim, for his part, often referred to as a process of transplantation: 'transplant' is the term he used to designate several of his pieces involving cartographic inscriptions. Culled from the language of both forestry and surgery, this noun evokes an organic process rather than the vanishing of the site into a non-existent entity. Similarly, Oppenheim's *Transplants* do not follow the 'move towards the dematerialization of the site' in the context of conceptual art that Miwon Kwon describes in her seminal study of site-specific art.[6] According to this view, when the notion of site-specificity first took hold in the wake of minimalism it relied on the notion that the site was a concrete, physical place and that the work was bound to it by a permanent relationship. However, the 'innocence' of this phenomenological approach was soon challenged,[7] most notably by Institutional Critique, and the 'impermanence' of the relation between art and site was emphasised.[8] Oppenheim was likewise wary of what he called 'a lot of pretentious ideas about site-specific work and the aura of a site'.[9] Neverthelesss, it would not be accurate to define his approach as a process of dematerialisation. By reprojecting a map onto the surface of the earth, Oppenheim in effect rematerialised the abstract representation that is the outcome of every mapping procedure. But because this materialisation did not coincide with the topography of the site on which it took place and, moreover, because this process often enacted a critical displacement of art spaces – as when the artist transposed the floorplans of museum galleries onto outdoor sites – neither did it submit to what the art historian Jean-Marc Poinsot has described as the 'idealist' escape from the institutional context of art attached to the original notion of site-specificity.[10]

Rather than idealism, a more relevant framework for addressing the complexity of Oppenheim's cartographic work is the French philosopher Louis Marin's contemporaneous study of Utopia.[11] Taking etymology as his cue, Marin defines Utopia not as an ideal or imaginary place, but as *another* place. Conceived by Thomas More, the author of the original *Utopia*, on the basis of the Greek *ou-topos*, the term translates literally as 'non-place'. But, for Marin, this negation does not cancel the reality of the island of More's Utopia, the model for all subsequent utopias: 'The negation does not affect the name's referent, but the name itself, which, therefore, designates an "other" referent.'[12] Neither here nor there, Utopia is in fact 'the in-determinate place'.[13] Marin also indicates that the 'utopic figure' is 'not without reference, but with an absent referent'.[14] From this point of view, the non-place of Utopia does appear to relate quite well to Krauss's postmodern site as absence and, as a point of fact, Smithson's own term for this, 'Nonsite', reads as a translation of *ou-topos*.[15] Yet Marin's 'utopics' – the term coined by the philosopher to distinguish the object of his enquiry from that which is 'utopian' – also lead in another direction. As the title of Marin's major work on this topic, *Utopics: Spatial Play* (1973), implies, the notion of utopics is inseparable from a particular conception of spatiality in which place is not so much cancelled as unmoored. More accurately, Utopia, for Marin, is a neutral space where non-congruent spaces are juxtaposed and made to interplay with one another without merging in an ideal synthesis.

It is something similar to this 'spatial play' of Utopia rather than the 'endless doubling' of site and nonsite that turns existence into 'a doubtful thing to capture', which, I want to argue, Oppenheim explored in his cartographic pieces.[16] Particularly relevant in this respect is what Marin says of the polemical nature of utopic constructions whose purpose is not to resolve tensions but to exacerbate them. In a comparable way, Oppenheim thought of his connection to the site as one in which '[t]here has to be friction'.[17] Marin's depiction of the ground of Utopia as a battlefield and 'the deserted space of contradiction' can also serve as an entry point to address Oppenheim's fascination with war, for which he found a perfect outlet in the derelict sites of wastelands and deserts.[18] Finally, for there to be 'spatial play' there has to be a space or interval, however minimal, between the realities thus brought into contact.[19] By using cartography to juxtapose distant locations, Oppenheim in a sense illustrated the collapsing of space and time precipitated by the development of telecommunications in the 1960s. Yet, rather than simply embracing this movement, Oppenheim's interplay of not just distant, but also contradictory, spaces demarcates his utopic position from 'global village' utopianism.

Non-localisation

The complexity of Oppenheim's approach to issues of situatedness and place is apparent already in his very first cartographically inspired pieces. In 1967, the artist, after having relocated to New York from the West Coast the year before, produced the *Site Markers* series, a group of works inspired by the methods of surveyors. For each piece, Oppenheim selected a place in the urban environment, in and around New York and Long Island City, which he then proceeded to claim as an artistic 'site'. He authenticated his claim through documentation: a black-and-white photograph of the site, a map indicating its location and a detailed description – to which he added an aluminium stake. The process is reminiscent of the ready-made – with the important difference that, in this case, the artist designated not an object but a place. At the same time, place here takes on an elusive quality. It is significant in this respect that Oppenheim picked unremarkable sites. Moreover, neither the blank tone of his descriptions nor the blandness of his photographs is of much assistance in providing a sense of place. As for the stake, its function is purely symbolic. Fabricated in a second stage, 'rather precious' – in some cases plated with gold – it was meant not to be driven into the ground but to substantiate the artist's transaction with the collector. As it is, the piece did not stop with the artist's claiming of the site but involved a 'transfer' of property to the buyer, as indicated by the fact that the documentation accompanying the piece includes a blank space to indicate the 'holder date of transfer'.

'Energy used in making objects is now used in locating them. This art occupied eight months of my life – I began to travel.'[20] Such is Oppenheim's account of the making of the *Site Markers*. However, with this travelling of the artist, which finds an extension in the piece's relocation to the buyer's collection, localisation itself becomes indeterminate. In this sense, Oppenheim's nondescript sites bring to mind the non-localisation of Utopia, which, according to Marin, is equally the result of an itinerary:

> Utopia stems from metaphor, understood in the Greek sense of displacement. It appears in the space generated by an itinerary. The utopic non-place … is at first the vacating of all places, which travel opens up with its movement from one place to another, one moment to another, between going and coming.[21]

Oppenheim explored this experience of non-localisation and ' "in-between" zones' further in a group of works dealing with borders, which he executed in Maine, close to Canada, during the winter of 1968.[22] By manipulating cartographic conventions, the artist brought to light geographic and political non-places that eschew both spatial and temporal localisation. Driving a snowmobile over the frozen waters of the St John's River, Oppenheim, in *Time Line*, traced the otherwise invisible line separating the USA and Canada, which, at that site, also corresponds to a temporal demarcation between two time zones: one on either side of the border. In addition to pointing at the arbitrariness of borderlines, Oppenheim here delineated a utopic space that exists in two times and two places at once. Simultaneously, the furrow traced by the snowmobile drove a wedge between the two sides of the border, similar to the *limes*, or frontier of the Roman Empire, 'tracing a path between two sides that will never join up', which, according to Marin, is an early incarnation of utopic space.[23] Similar concerns produced *Boundary Split*, for which Oppenheim set out to split a border with a chainsaw by making a series of cuts in the ice of the same St John's River, perpendicular to the time line between the countries it connects.

But it is with *Time Pocket*, as the art historian Xavier Vert rightly observes, that Oppenheim came closest to the original model of Utopia (see Figure 7.1).[24] Indeed, *Time Pocket* recalls the island that is the site of More's Utopia. For this piece, Oppenheim, still working in the area close to the border with Canada, plotted the International Date Line onto a frozen lake with an island in its centre. Because of this island, the line had to be truncated. In this way, Oppenheim metaphorically produced a 'pocket' in time: that is, a suspension of the temporal flow between two moments. It is worth noting that the original date line that served as the artist's inspiration is itself a fiction whose layout has often changed depending on a fluctuating geopolitical situation. Thus, to accommodate competing territorial claims, the line has several twists and turns. It is these odd curves – indices of the indeterminate nature of the line's immaterial border – that seem to have triggered Oppenheim's imagination, and which he set out to materialise by taking advantage of the topography of the site with the island in the middle.[25] The result is a complex entity that can be viewed either as a fiction made real or a real space converted into a fictional one, and which cannot be localised precisely either in space nor time.

Commenting on Oppenheim's cartographic works, Smithson described them as 'transforming a terrestrial site into a map'.[26] What he apppears to have had in mind is the fantastic map in Lewis Carroll's *Sylvie and Bruno* (1889/1893), which he refers to in the 'mapscapes' section of his important article 'A museum of language in the vicinity of art' (1968).[27] In Carroll's tale, a German professor recounts how, in his country, cartographers perfected their art to the point of producing a map with a scale of a mile to a mile. Nevertheless, this map was never spread out: 'The farmers objected: they said it would cover the whole country, and shut out the sunlight! So now [they] use the country itself, as its own map, and … it does nearly as well.'[28] Yet, this paradigm of the fusion of the map and the territory seems to resonate more accurately with Smithson's own process of converting reality into a map, as in his essay 'A tour of the monuments of Passaic, New Jersey' (1967), where his vision converts the dull, suburbanite town of Passaic into its own maplike simulacrum: 'I had been on a planet that had a map of Passaic drawn over it … At any moment my feet were apt to fall through the cardboard ground.'[29]

Rather than this vampirising of the site by the map,[30] a more relevant model for Oppenheim's *Time Pocket*, I want to suggest, is Jorge Luis Borges's famous parable on 'Exactitude in Science', which Smithson mentions as well. Pretending to quote from a seventeenth-century travel account, Borges, perhaps inspired by Carroll, depicts an imaginary empire in which cartographers

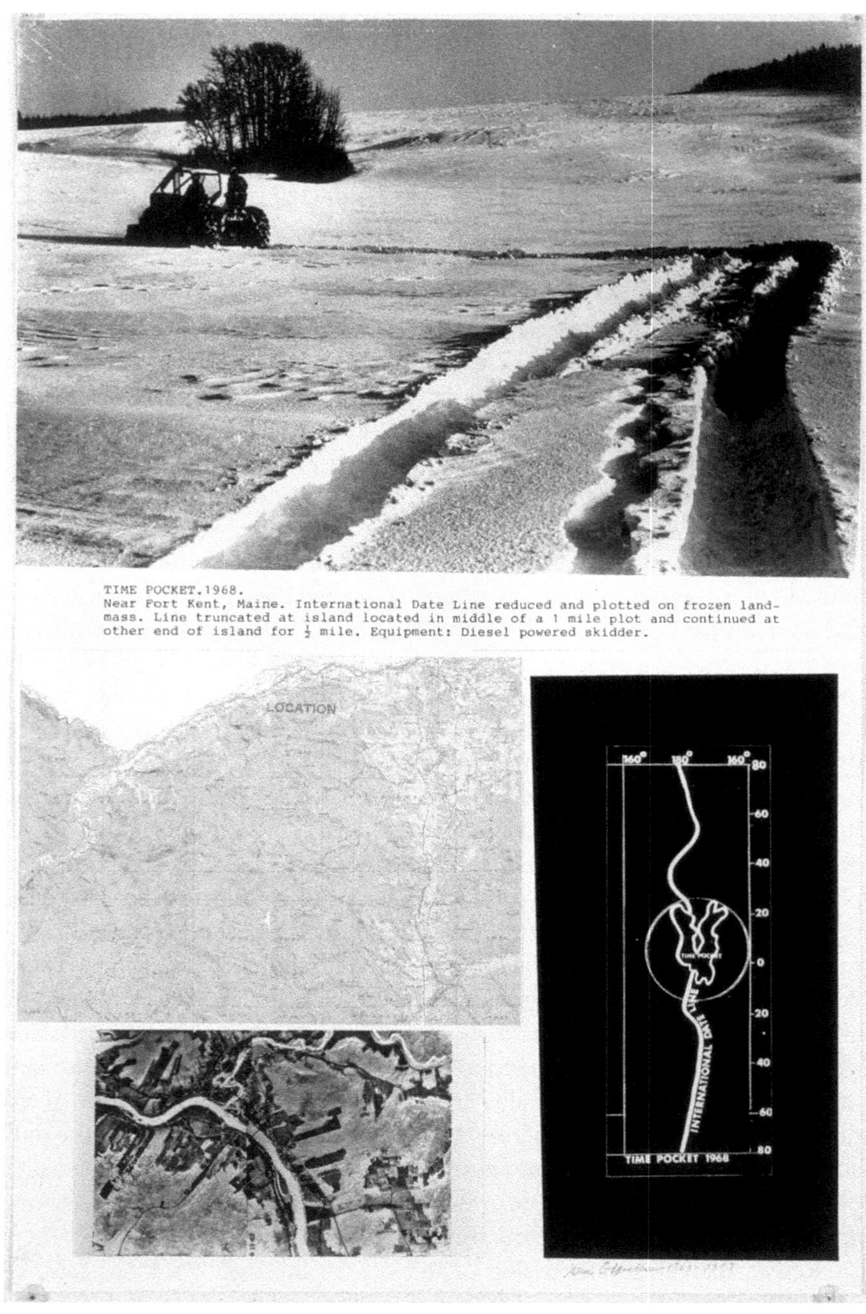

7.1 Dennis Oppenheim, *Time Pocket*, 1968–89. Near Fort Kent, Maine. International Date Line reduced (1 mile) and plotted on frozen land mass. Line truncated at island located in middle of a 1-mile plot and continued at the other end of the island for ½ mile. Equipment: diesel-powered skidder. Black and white, hand-stamped topographic map, aerial map text on rag board.

produced ever more gigantic maps until they finally drew a map of the entire land at a one-to-one scale. Representing the acme of cartographic skill, this accomplishment also signalled its demise. Finding the map useless, the next generations gave it up to the sun and the wind: 'In the deserts of the West some mangled Ruins of the Map lasted on, inhabited by Animals and Beggars; in the whole Country there are no other relics of the Disciplines of Geography.'[31] In a manner different from Carroll, what Borges's text calls attention to is the slight discrepancy between the map and the land. Indeed, according to Marin, this parable designates the utopic nature of cartography in that the Map of the Empire both perfectly coincides with the empire and yet remains fundamentally 'other' than the terrain that it maps – as demonstrated by the fact that, while it crumbles, the land remains. The map is thus not an analogon of the territory but its double: it is the same yet different, albeit the space of this difference is properly impossible to pinpoint. At the same time, this interstice, or 'play', opens up the possibility of a critique of the ideology of representation embodied by the cartographic tradition itself.[32]

Unlike the Map of the Empire, *Time Pocket*'s cartographic inscription is not tautological. Yet the piece thematises cartography's dream of literalness at the same time that it calls attention to its impossibility and to the essentially non-locatable nature of the map itself. And, like the Map of the Empire again, *Time Pocket*'s map, as with all Oppenheim's cartographic works, was destined to vanish under the combined effects of the weather and time. But not, however, without having produced, if momentarily, a disturbance in the ideological order of things.

Waging wars

The process at work in *Time Pocket* still relies on the resemblance between the topography of the site near Fort Kent and the contour of the International Date Line. In subsequent pieces, Oppenheim adopted a more radical approach, bringing into contact sites that are not only geographically distant but whose characteristics are antithetical. Echoing Marin's definition of utopic spaces as those where antagonist positions are held together in their very opposition, Oppenheim did not seek a harmonious synthesis between the places thus juxtaposed but, on the contrary, expressed in these works a polemical attitude towards a certain number of issues in the art world and beyond. A case in point is *Contour Lines Scribed in Swamp Grass* (1968) executed in New Haven, Connecticut, in a wasteland located near a factory and a dump. For this piece, Oppenheim inscribed contour lines from a nearby mountain on the flat terrain of a swamp using a sickle mower, thus 'oppos[ing] the reality of the existing land'.[33] In so doing, the artist metaphorically brought down the mountain, manifesting at the same time his desire, following Carl Andre, to topple sculpture's monumental tradition. The effect in this case was enhanced by the fact that the swamp, being below sea level and situated near a bay, was regularly flooded at high tide. To ensure that the contour lines remained visible under water, Oppenheim filled them with residue from a machine boring aluminium filings.[34] In this way, the artist also manifested his indifference, if not his actual hostility, towards environmental concerns.

Indeed, several of Oppenheim's *Transplants* express his scepticism regarding the idea of nature as a virgin space, situated outside the realm of culture, and appealing to artists for this very reason. In 1969, for the *Earth Art* exhibition at the Andrew Dickson White Museum of Cornell University, a key event in the history of the Earthworks movement, Oppenheim presented a *Gallery Transplant*, which problematised the idea of taking art out of its institutional setting and into the environment (see Figure 7.2). In this case, Oppenheim chose as the site of his cartographic transplant a bird sanctuary near the museum. On the snowy ground of this protected area he used a shovel to trace the floorplan of one of the museum's galleries at a one-to-one scale. Without actually disrupting the birds' habitat, Oppenheim here figured the return of nature within the confines of the museum, thus operating against land art's movement of expansion beyond the walls of artistic institutions. It is true, however, that Oppenheim's move can also be understood on the contrary as a means to create a utopic 'place outside of place' from which, in fact, it would be possible to question the museum as an institution.[35] Seen in this way, the white ground of the bird sanctuary on which the transplant was carried out becomes the site for a *détour*-ing of the sterile spaces of the 'white cube', whose ideology Brian O'Doherty decoded so well a few years later, comparing them to, among other structures, churches.[36]

This view is substantiated by another gallery transplant, which Oppenheim created for the *Op Losse Schroeven* (*Square Pegs in Round Holes*) exhibition of conceptual art organised in 1969 by the Stedelijk Museum in Amsterdam. Following a practice prevalent among many conceptual artists, Oppenheim contributed to the event not with an actual piece in the museum, but from a distance. To this end he virtually transplanted one of the Stedelijk's galleries to Jersey City by inscribing its floor specifications on the ground of an empty lot near or in what, judging from the documentation, looks like an industrial zone. Not only did the transplant to a place several thousand miles away and on another continent imply a 'dislocation' of the museum,[37] but the site chosen for this operation was this time as different as possible from the pristine spaces of the art institution. In this manner, Oppenheim represented the literal degradation of the high cultural ideals embodied by museums, suggesting their obsolescence.

Seen in this light, Oppenheim's position appears more radical than Smithson's. With his Nonsites, Smithson in effect brought the entropic reality

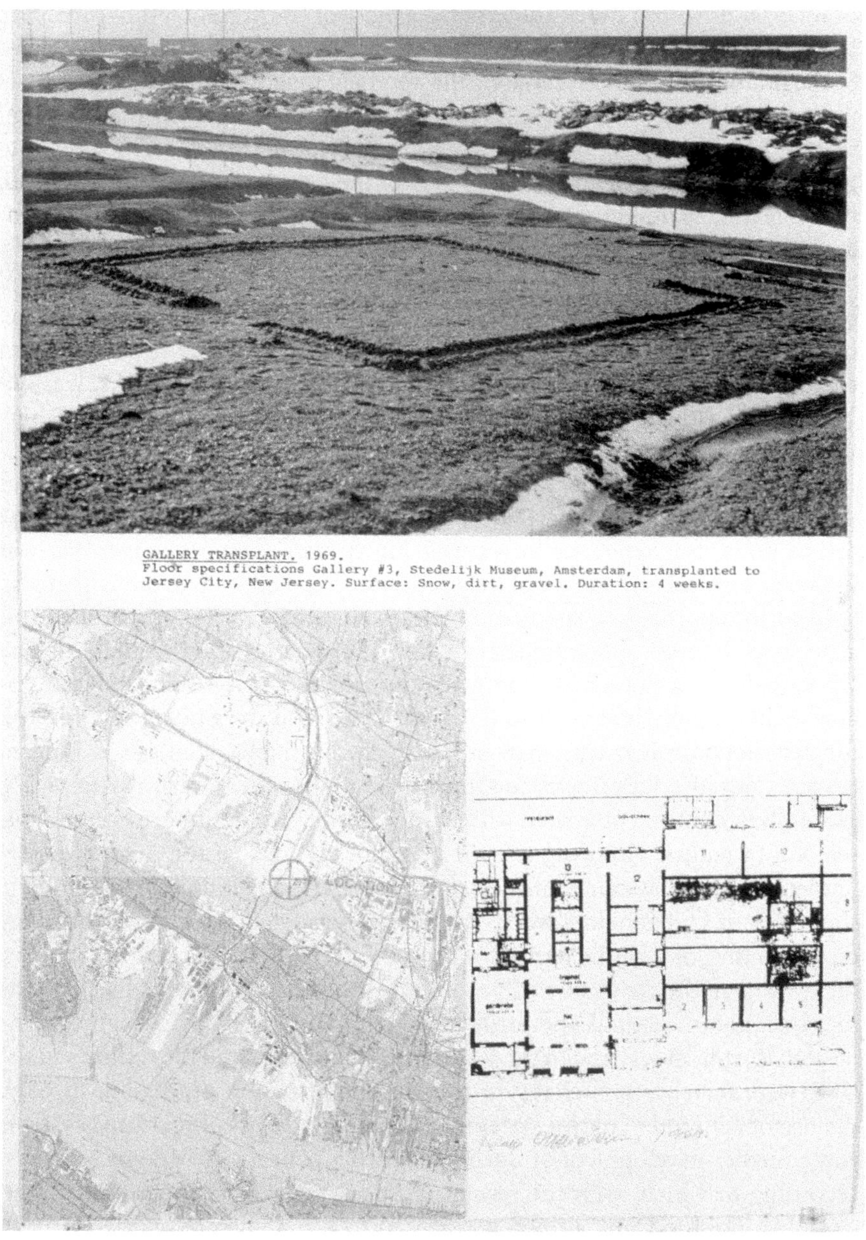

Dennis Oppenheim, *Gallery Transplant*, 1969. Floor specifications of Gallery #3, Stedelijk Museum, Amsterdam, transplanted to Jersey City, New Jersey. Surface: snow, dirt, gravel. Duration: 4 weeks. Black-and-white and colour photography, hand-stamped topographic map, enlarged, marked floor plan, text on rag board. **7.2**

of wastelands within the confines of the gallery or the museum, thus providing it with a frame. 'Why do you bother with non-site at all?', Oppenheim asked Smithson in a series of discussions the two held together with Michael Heizer in 1968 and 1969.[38] Of course, Oppenheim also depended on the presentation in a gallery space of documentation pertaining to his earthworks. But he did not consider this aspect as a part of the process, as did Smithson with his Nonsites. More importantly, Smithson's frame of reference remained profoundly dualistic: site and nonsite being tied to each other as in an infinite play of mirror reflections. Oppenheim, on the other hand, chose to stay focused on the site, not because of any idea of site-specificity, but with the intention of converting that very same site into an *other* through the active confrontation of differing and even opposing realities. Site, in these works, was not 'abolished' as it was with the nonsite,[39] but was envisaged as a space in which productive conflicts could be played out.[40]

Looking back on his earthworks, Oppenheim once explained: 'I was waging wars, combating certain beliefs in contemporary thinking.'[41] In the artist's mind, this reference to war was much more than an image. War was in fact a fundamental source of inspiration for Oppenheim, and one that also defined his approach to space and cartography. Stephen Bann identified this aspect well, mentioning in particular how the square within a circle used by Oppenheim as a pointer on the maps documenting his works 'looks suspiciously like a gun-sight, as if some airborne weapon were targeting the work for destruction.'[42] It is true that, for Bann, such military similes were meant to cast a negative judgement on Oppenheim and American land artists more generally, whom he contrasted with British artists and their more harmonious relation to nature. However, it is worth pointing out that the military environment was also a source of ideas for the art critic Jack Burnham, an early supporter of Oppenheim's work. Burnham considered the artist to be a key representative of what he termed in 1969 the art of 'real time systems': that is, the art that in the 1960s moved beyond the production of finite objects to the manipulation of natural and artificial systems in real time. To explicate this notion, Burnham referred to the way that both business and the military in the USA were increasingly reliant on real-time information processing through the use of computer control systems.[43] The idea of an art of real-time systems was a further development of Burnham's earlier concept of 'systems esthetics', according to which, with the advent of the age of information, humankind was transitioning from 'an object-oriented to a systems-oriented culture'. In defining this notion, Burnham drew on a variety of sources, including the new 'systems analysis' method used by the Pentagon to adapt military decision-making to the context of modern warfare.[44]

There are no traces of such sophisticated military models in Oppenheim's work. Nor are there any explicit references to the conflicts of the times, such as the Vietnam War. However, the theme of war is quite present in several of Oppenheim's pieces, and more specifically in the pieces involving cartography, for which the artist was greatly inspired by diagrams that he found in military manuals and military history books.[45] An example is *Ground Mutations* (1969), a piece based on marching diagrams (see Figure 7.3). During three months in the course of the winter of 1969, Oppenheim wore shoes with grooves etched into their soles and heels. As he walked about, he created a network of patterns on the ground that reminded him of the marching diagrams that 'filled' his thoughts at the time.[46] However, rather than signifying the occupation of land by an actual army, these patterns evoke the covert operations of a guerrilla always on the move.[47]

This approach also informed *Infected Zone* (1969), a complex piece created in Milan on the model of the *Transplants*. In this case, Oppenheim inscribed on a hill near the city, the location of which was kept secret, the outline of three areas arbitrarily selected on a map. Each of the areas thus transplanted

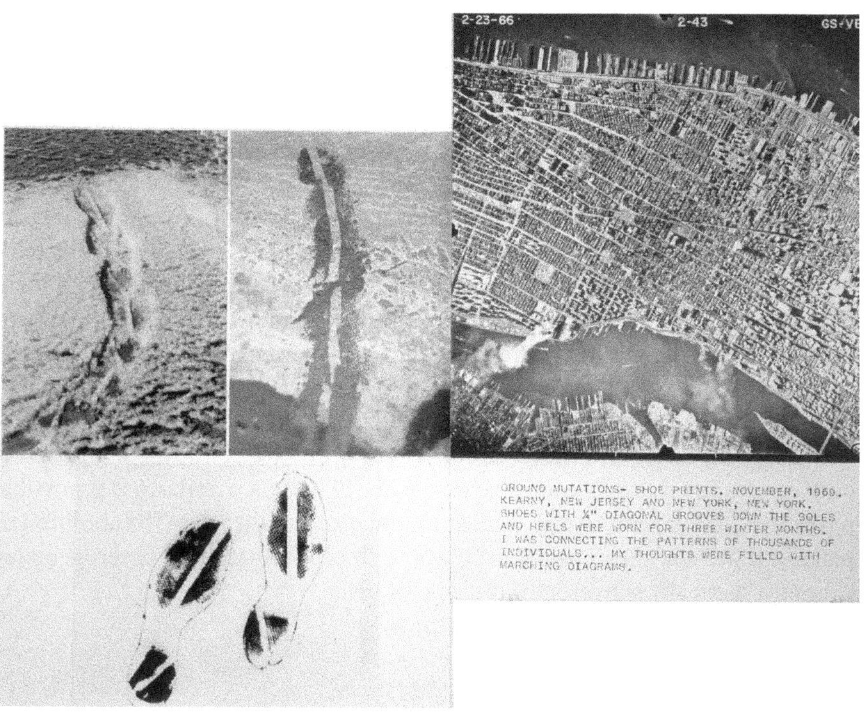

Dennis Oppenheim, *Ground Mutations – Shoe Prints*, November 1969. Kearney, New Jersey and New York, New York. Shoes with ¼″ diagonal grooves down the soles and heels were worn for three winter months. 'I was connecting the patterns of thousands of indivuduals … My thoughts were filled with marching diagrams.' Black-and-white and colour photography, hand-stamped aerial map, text on rag board.   **7.3**

was turned into a fictional war zone: trenches were dug into the ground, parts of the land scorched with a flame-thrower, and one zone covered with traps and rat poison. The secrecy attached to the site again brings to mind irregular warfare. As it is, Oppenheim carried out most of his earthworks in secret, often under cover of night.[48] Indeed, the ephemeral nature of these works is reminiscent of the swiftness of tactical manoeuvres, a model designated by the book appearing in the photographic documentation of one of Oppenheim's most well-known pieces, *Reading Position for Second-Degree Burn* (1970). In this performance, the artist lay on the beach and under the sun for several hours with no protection, his naked torso partially covered by an open book. Here Oppenheim was using his body as a blank canvas, with the sunburn as pigment. The book, whose contour was 'imprinted' on the artist's skin, seems at first to be an odd choice. It is a military manual written by a German colonel following the Russo-Japanese war. No doubt, however, what appealed most to Oppenheim was the book's title, *Tactics*, spread out across his chest as a kind of statement.[49]

Reading Position for Second-Degree Burn does not directly address space or cartography. But tactics do involve a specific way of relating to space. According to Michel de Certeau this is in fact what differentiates a tactic from a strategy. A *modus operandi* of power, strategy 'postulates a *place* that can be delimited as its *own* and serve as the base from which relations with an *exteriority* composed of targets or threats ... can be managed'.[50] A tactic, by contrast, is 'a calculated action determined by the absence of a proper locus'.[51] The fact that a tactic does not have its own proper place is what explains both its weakness and its strength. Operating by trickery and surprise, it is 'a form of legerdemain ... boldly juxtapos[ing] diverse elements in order suddenly to produce a flash shedding a different light on the language of a place'.[52] On the other hand, 'place' – that is, the 'proper' to which strategy is attached – specifically 'excludes the possibility of two things being in the same location'.[53] Certeau was close to Marin, and much could probably be said about the connections between tactic's non-place and the non-place of Utopia. Similarly, it is possible to see in Oppenheim's cartographic manipulations, rather than the abolition of place, a more complex operation in which the combination of heterogeneous elements tactically subverts the 'proper' of place.[54]

Utopics versus utopianism

In the period in which Oppenheim and other conceptual artists began to appropriate cartography for their art, place had in fact become a very uncertain notion. The spread of telecommunications, as Marshall McLuhan famously remarked in the opening pages of *Understanding Media* (1964), was in the process of abolishing both space and time.[55] This 'global village' utopianism transpires in the work of several conceptual artists. The Canadians Iain and Ingrid Baxter, for instance, cited McLuhan as a direct source of inspiration. Operating as an officially incorporated business under the name NETCO (short for N. E. Thing Co.), the couple combined the use of new corporate communication media, such as telex and telecopier machines, with cartographic documentation – in order to produce artworks spanning distant locations that questioned both the notions of authorship and political boundaries. Using a telex machine, NETCO, with *Telexed Triangle* (1969), transmitted a message from Inuvik to Vancouver and Halifax with instructions to inscribe electronically a triangle originally delineated on a map. In this way, the Baxters electronically realised a dematerialised sculpture that ignored physical geographical constraints. Another example is *North American Time Zone Photo-VSI-Simultaneity, October 19, 1970*, for which the couple called on six photographers located in different time zones of the United States, asking them to take simultaneous photographs of the same subject matter. The purpose was to produce an awareness of the simultaneous coexistence of the different time zones.

Although based on procedures that are similar to Oppenheim's, such work, nevertheless, differs profoundly from his. Far from creating a sense of unity, Oppenheim's playing with time zones, as seen above, emphasised rather than narrowed the unbridgeable gap between them. Similarly, Oppenheim's carto-graphic transplantations were meant not smoothly and quasi-instantaneously to transfer a sculpture from one place to another, but rather to bring into friction antithetical, if not antagonistic, realities. It is important to point out that, contrary to the work of the Baxters and of other artists inspired by McLuhan, such as Douglas Huebler, Oppenheim's *Transplants* and related pieces always relied on physical labour and involved generally slow or extended material processes. A good example of this approach is *Removal Transplant – New York Stock Exchange* (February 1969), a work that actually integrated long-distance communication networks as one of its ingredients. For this piece, Oppenheim had four tons of paper data removed from the floor of the New York Stock Exchange and transplanted to the roof of a building in another part of Manhattan. One of the reasons for this action appears to have been the artist's musings on the circulation of financial data from one distant location to another:

> Transactions involving a span of three thousand miles take place on the stock exchange floor. The residue at the end of the day carries vestiges of the distance between two points; the point at which a buy order, and the point at which a sell order, is issued ... A spatial transaction is implicitly contained in the material; a web of components interact within a continental grid.[56]

As Sophie Cras has convincingly demonstrated, Oppenheim in effect offered a subtle critique of the rhetoric of speed and instantaneity associated with modern financial transactions. Although relying on a process of displacement – one that almost literally lifted a bulk of matter up into the air[57] – what this piece brings to light with its accumulation of paper detritus is the inevitable lag, both material and temporal, that always accompanies the accelerating speed of stock exchange operations.[58]

Interestingly, telecommunications appear to have been a source of inspiration for Oppenheim before. In fact, they are to be found as a model alongside cartography at the very moment of Oppenheim's turn to earthworks. In the summer of 1968, the artist executed what is generally considered to be his first earthwork, *Landslide* (see Figure 7.4).[59] He realised the piece on the site of an abandoned gravel pit along the Long Island Expressway. On the slope of the pit, he arranged a series of wooden planks, which he had painted silver. The boards were distributed in expanding arcs along the sloping face of the pit in

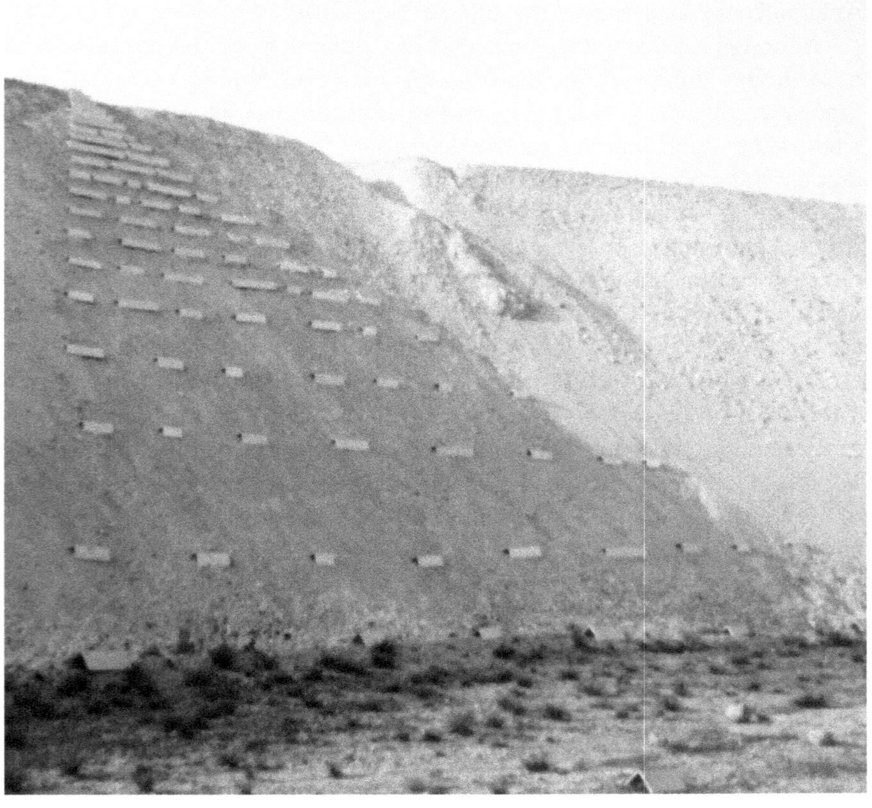

7.4   Dennis Oppenehim, *Landslide*, 1968. Location: Long Island Expressway, Exit 52. Materials: right-angled boards/earth. Dimensions: 1,000 feet long.

such a way as to evoke latitude lines – a 'typical' cartographic reference for earthworks, one might want to say.[60] But, as a statement by Oppenheim in the 1970–71 issue of the magazine *Aspen* reveals, what he also had in mind was another more technological simile, that of 'radar bands' extending across the globe.[61] The association of cartography and radar technology is of course perfectly logical, in that radars are mapping instruments. One is also reminded here of the famous RKO movie studio logo, which, although not referring to radar bands, shows radio waves spreading out above a spinning globe. What is more unexpected, however, is how the image of expanding radar bands fed into Oppenheim's realisation that distance was something to be made 'tangible'. As he explained:

> As for my land pieces: the negative particle slide in Long Island, which continues with expanding arcs for 1,000 feet, could conceptually (in a manner similar to radar bands) travel the extent of the globe. This factor of articulating land area in terms of prescribed distance markers led me to some interesting ideas, in that distance (footage, yardage, etc.) is tangible when applied to specific land surface, it must be regarded as sculpturally significant.[62]

This statement, it would seem, contains a paradox: the ubiquity of electromagnetic energy is precisely used to overcome distance, not to heighten its perception. It would be wrong, however, to try and explain away this apparent contradiction. Rather, it points to the way in which Oppenheim's earthworks and related pieces attempt to articulate the near and the far without abolishing the tension between them.

Writing in the same period that McLuhan proclaimed the utopian collapsing of space and time, Marin described very differently 'utopic practice' as 'introducing the sudden distance by which contiguities and continuities of time and space are broken in historical narrative and the contemplation of geographic space', adding '[i]t is by this fracture that we catch a glimpse – as if illuminated by a flash of lightning – of the free force of unlimited contradiction'.[63] In a comparable way, Oppenheim manipulated cartography – not in order to create new proximities, but rather to precipitate a kind of clash or short-circuit between opposing realities. This produced utopic 'map[s] that are not on the map' but whose subversive power is no less real for their relating to a fictional space.[64]

Acknowledgement

I would like to express my gratitude to Amy Plumb Oppenheim for her generosity over the years and for sharing with me some of her precious knowledge of Dennis Oppenheim's work.

Notes

1 Louis Marin, 'Frontières, limites, *limes*: Les récits de voyage dans *L'Utopie* de Thomas More', in Christian Descamps (ed.), *Frontières et limites: Géopolitiques, littérature, philosophie* (Paris: Editions du Centre Georges Pompidou, 1991), p. 124.

2 Rosalind Krauss, 'Echelle/monumentalité. Modernisme/postmodernisme. La ruse de Brancusi', in Margit Rowell (ed.), *Qu'est-ce que la sculpture moderne?* (Paris: Centre Georges Pompidou, 1986), p. 248.

3 *Ibid.*, p. 250.

4 *Ibid.* Krauss drew this information from Sidney Geist's study of Târgu-Jiu. Sidney Geist, 'Brancusi: The centrality of the gate', *Artforum* 12:2 (October 1973), 70–8.

5 Rosalind Krauss, 'Sculpture in the expanded field', *October* 8 (Spring 1979), 30–44 (p. 41).

6 M. Kwon, *One Place after Another: Site-Specific Art and Locational Identity* (Cambridge, MA: MIT Press, 2004), p. 24.

7 *Ibid.*, p. 13.

8 *Ibid.*, p. 24.

9 Alanna Heiss, 'Another point of entry: An interview with Dennis Oppenheim', in Alanna Heiss (ed.), *Dennis Oppenheim: And the Mind Grew Fingers. Selected Works 1967–90* (exh. cat.) (New York: Abrams, 1992), p. 154.

10 Jean-Marc Poinsot, *Quand l'œuvre a lieu: L'art exposé et ses récits autorisés* (Dijon: Presses du réel, 2008), p. 102.

11 The relevance of Marin's study of utopia for American art of the 1960s and 1970s has also been well explored by Louis Cummins in relation to Robert Smithson, and by Eric De Bruyn in relation to Mel Bochner. Louis Cummins, 'La dialectique site/non-site: Une utopie cartographique', *Parachute* 68 (October–December 1992), 42–6. Eric De Bruyn, 'Alfaville, or the utopics of Mel Bochner', *Grey Room* 10 (Winter 2003), 76–111. As I mention in what follows, Xavier Vert also offers illuminating comments on the 'utopic' nature of Oppenheim's work. Xavier Vert, 'Louis Marin en Utopie: Fiction, idéologie et représentation', in Giovanni Careri and Xavier Vert (eds), *Louis Marin: Le pouvoir dans ses représentations* (Paris: INHA, 2008), pp. 53–75.

12 Marin, 'Frontières, limites, *limes*', p. 109.

13 Louis Marin, *Utopics: Spatial Play*, trans. Robert A. Vollrath (Atlantic Highlands, NJ: Humanities Press, 1984), p. 196.

14 *Ibid.*

15 Algirdas Julien Greimas's semiotic square was an important source of inspiration for both Krauss and Marin. See Krauss, 'Sculpture in the expanded field', p. 37.

16 Patricia Norvell, *Recording Conceptual Art: Early Interviews with Barry, Huebler, Kaltenbach, LeWitt, Morris, Oppenheim, Siegelaub, Smithson, Weiner*, ed. Alexander Alberro and Patricia Norvell (Berkeley: University of California Press, 2001), p. 127.

17 Dennis Oppenheim, interview with the author, 17 June 2010.

18 Marin, *Utopics*, p. 16.

19 The French word for 'play' (*jeu*) also relates to the idea of space, as in the expression *il y a du jeu*, which means that there is enough space for a movement to unfold smoothly. It can also signify that the parts of a mechanism are too loosely held together.

20 Oppenheim, *Rétrospective de l'œuvre 1967–77* (Montreal: Musée d'art contemporain de Montréal, 1978), 34.

21 Louis Marin, 'La fiction poétique de l'Utopie', in *Utopies*, special issue of *Cinéma et littérature* 7 (1989): 15.

22 James Nisbet, *Ecologies, Environments, and Energy Systems in Art of the 1960s and 1970s* (Cambridge, MA: MIT Press, 2014), 106.

23 Marin, 'Frontières, limites, *limes*', pp. 109–10.

24 Vert, 'Louis Marin en Utopie', p. 69.

25 See, for instance, a note in Oppenheim's sketch book from the same period: 'broken dateline (international dateline discontinued at 0 equator)'. Dennis Oppenheim, 'Catalyst 1967–1974', in Germano Celant (ed.), *Dennis Oppenheim: Explorations* (Milan: Charta, 2001), p. 91.

26 Liza Bear and Willoughby Sharp, 'Discussions with Heizer, Oppenheim, Smithson (1970)', in Robert Smithson, *Robert Smithson: The Collected Writings*, ed. Jack Flam (Berkeley: University of California Press, 1996), p. 244.

27 Robert Smithson, 'A museum of language in the vicinity of art (1968)', in Smithson, *The Collected Writings*, p. 93.

28 Lewis Carroll, quoted in Smithson, 'A museum of language', p. 93.

29 Robert Smithson, 'A tour of the monuments of Passaic, New Jersey (1967)', in Smithson, *The Collected Writings*, p. 74.

30 Drawing partly on Marin, Louis Cummins, for his part, describes Smithson's process as 'utopic'. However, as I try to show in what follows, Marin's conception of the utopic nature of the map does not cancel out the reality of the territory. Cummins, 'La dialectique site/non-site'.

31 Jorge Luis Borges, quoted in Smithson, 'A museum of language', p. 91.

32 Marin, *Utopics*, pp. 234–5.

33 Celant, *Dennis Oppenheim*, p. 52.

34 Norvell, *Recording Conceptual Art*, pp. 25–6.

35 Marin, *Utopics*, p. 7.

36 Brian O'Doherty, *Inside the White Cube: The Ideology of the Gallery Space* (Santa Monica: Lapis Press, 1986), p. 14.

37 Bear and Sharp, 'Discussions with Heizer, Oppenheim, Smithson (1970)', p. 244.

38 *Ibid.*, p. 250.

39 Norvell, *Recording Conceptual Art*, p. 130.

40 This difference between Smithson and Oppenheim was well summarised by Jonathan Crary, 'Dennis Oppenheim's delirious operations', *Artforum* 17:3 (November 1978), 38.

41 Allan Schwartzman, 'Interview with Dennis Oppenheim', in Marcia Tucker (ed.), *Early Work by Five Contemporary Artists: Ron Gorchov, Elizabeth Murray, Dennis Oppenheim, Dorothea Rockburne, Joel Shapiro* (exh. cat.) (New York: The New Museum, 1977).

42 Stephen Bann, 'The map as index of the real: Land art and the authentication of travel', *Imago mundi* 46 (1994), 14–15.

43 Jack Burnham, *Great Western Salt Works: Essays on the Meaning of Post-Formalist Art* (New York: George Braziller, 1974), pp. 29–30.

44 *Ibid.*, p. 16. Similar references appear to have already been on the mind of the art critic and curator Lawrence Alloway when he organised the exhibition *Systemic Painting* at the Guggenheim Museum in 1966. As Alloway later explained, his use of the word 'systemic' owed much to game theory. Lawrence Alloway, 'Systemic painting', in Gregory Battcock (ed.), *Minimal Art: A Critical Anthology* (Berkeley: University of California Press, 1995), p. 37.

45 Dennis Oppenheim, 'Catalyst 1967–1974', in Alan Sondheim (ed.), *Individuals: Post-Movement Art in America* (New York: E. P. Dutton, 1977), pp. 246–66. This article lists projects, both realised and unrealised, that Oppenheim was working on during the period from 1967 to 1974. The list contains several war-related projects, such as one for a system of trenches based on the plan of the Pearl Harbor attack, and another inspired by anti-aircraft protection exercises.

46 As per the work's caption.

47 Although there is no room to do this here, it would be worthwhile to explore the possible resonances with Germano Celant's definition of *arte povera* as a form of 'guerrilla'. Germano Celant, 'Arte povera: Appunti per una guerriglia', *Flash Art* 5 (November–December 1967). 3.

48 Oppenheim, interview with the author.

49 Robert Slifkin also comments on the presence of this book, relating it to the context of the Vietnam War. Robert Slifkin, 'Methodological position for second-degree art history', in Sabine T. Kriebel and Andrés Mario Zervigon (eds), *Photography and Doubt* (London: Routledge, Taylor & Francis, 2017), p. 252.

50 Michel de Certeau, *The Practice of Everyday Life*, trans. Steven Rendall (Berkeley: University of California Press, 1984), p. 36.

51 *Ibid.*, pp. 36–7.

52 *Ibid.*, pp. 37–8.

53 *Ibid.*, p. 117.

54 This contrast between tactic and strategy may also be compared within the art world of the period with Alloway's borrowing of the game theorist Anatol Rapoport's opposition between 'systemic' and 'strategic' conflict in order to clarify his own use of the term 'systemic' in relation to recent painting. Alloway, 'Systemic painting', pp. 37–8.

55 Marshall McLuhan, *Understanding Media: The Extensions of Man* (London: Routledge, 2001 [1964]), p. 3.

56 Dennis Oppenheim, 'Statement for *Removal Transplant – New York Stock Exchange* (1969)', in Heiss, *Dennis Oppenheim*, p. 36.

57 The piece is also a good illustration of Oppenheim's particular way of engaging with matter. As he explained at the time, 'I liked the idea of just loose matter, just residue from solid form, as being part of the piece … There's a lot which artists haven't done with that distributional kind of form, form that you can scatter or toss up in the air, just toss up in the air.' Norvell, *Recording Conceptual Art*, p. 26.

58 Sophie Cras, 'Dennis Oppenheim und das Ende des ticker tapes', *Archiv für Mediengeschichte* 17 (2017), 125–39.

59 The year before, Oppenheim had already made a piece in the landscape, *Oakland Wedge* (1967). He cut a wedge along the side of a mountain in the Oakland hills and lined it with Plexiglas. The effect, as recounted by Oppenheim, was that of a 'floating plate of light'. In this sense, the piece appears to have been closer in spirit to the quasi-ethereal art of West Coast minimalism than to the rugged aesthetics of earthworks. Dennis Oppenheim, quoted in Suzaan Boettger, *Earthworks: Art and the Landscape of the Sixties* (Berkeley: University of California Press, 2002), p. 122.

60 Oppenheim, interview with the author. For a particularly detailed and well-informed description of this piece see Christopher Ketcham, 'Dennis Oppenheim and the cartographic expansion of American sculpture', *European Journal of American Culture* 39:1 (2020), 53–4.

61 Dennis Oppenheim, 'Notes on ecologic projects', *Aspen* 8 (Fall–Winter 1970–71), www.ubu.com/aspen/aspen8/ecologic.html (accessed 23 May 2020). The radar reference also probably explains the choice of silver paint: the planks painted in this way must have appeared to 'radiate' in the sunshine.

62 *Ibid.*

63 Marin, *Utopics*, p. xxii.

64 Marin, 'Frontières, limites, limes', p. 124.

Psychophysiology Research Institute, 1969–70: Envisioning an 'invisible museum'

Reiko Tomii

Seishin Seirigaku Kenkyūjo (Psychophysiology Research Institute, PRI) was a short-lived collective (1969–70) in Japan that aspired to create a network of experimentalism using mail art and reproductive technology. Its initial statement clearly articulated its scope and ambition:

> We have founded Psychophysiology Research Institute, as an invisible museum, in which [each participant] in Tokyo, Nagano, Morocco, Hiroshima, Kyoto, Ibaraki and Gunma will contribute through an act [*kōi*] or non-act he undertakes simultaneously with others at a location where he can position himself at a specified time-space.

> The goal of Psychophysiology Research Institute is to accumulate and disperse the record of the acts or non-acts undertaken by individuals who refuse to have direct connections.[1]

With this declaration, sent at precisely 10:22'49" a.m. on 19 November 1969, the group launched a project to orchestrate what may be called a 'museum of performance art' with the organisers in Tokyo, collating the 'records' (*kiroku*) of the acts (or non-acts) undertaken by participating members and sending a duplicated set back to each of them. Over a period of six months, from December 1969 to May 1970, there were six such monthly undertakings and mailings. In August 1970, the group published an artists' book, with their group name as its title, to document the activities (including an unofficial extra undertaking, completed after the sixth), in the format of a portfolio of cards (see Figure 8.1).[2] Their project can be situated at an intersection of local narratives of performance art, conceptualism and collectivism, while many of their individual practices resonated with those by their counterparts in other parts of the world in the 1960s. The group was included in a summer exhibition at the Amsterdam-based Art & Project Gallery between July and August 1970, recommended by the art critic Nakahara Yūsuke,[3] who organised the legendary Tokyo Biennale 1970 in May of that year.[4]

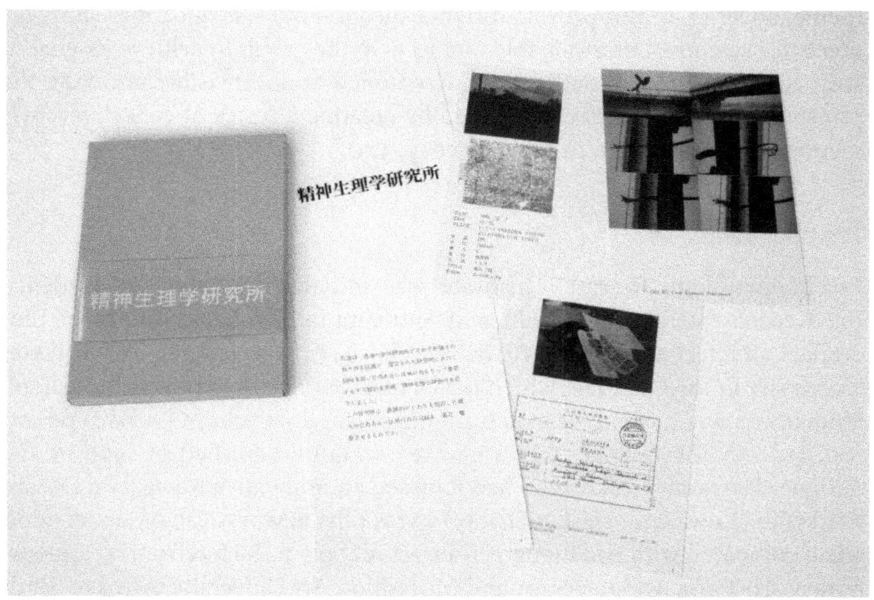

Psychophysiology Research Institute artist's book and portfolio of cards (facsimile   **8.1**
edition, 2009 [1970]). From left, clockwise: portfolio, title page, Ina Ken'ichirō's card (first
undertaking), Shimamura Kiyoharu's card (first undertaking), Horikawa Michio's card
(first undertaking), Matsuzawa Yutaka's card (third undertaking).

Until recently, however, PRI has been a less studied topic of 1960s
Japan, especially in comparison with Mono-ha (School of Things).[5] This is
partly because their works are doubly ephemeral, involving performative
components and the works on paper. Psychophysiology Research Institute
was thus eclipsed by the dominant trend of the materially conscious Mono-
ha, and has been less visible to the eyes of historians. Furthermore, PRI was a
complex project that has nonetheless primarily been known through its final
book form; the project's theoretical, conceptual and technological foundations
and its multipart process are far less talked about, save for what is tersely
stated in the book's preface (which reads almost verbatim from the statement
quoted above).[6]

Notably, PRI was a project initiated by students who aspired to interrogate
what art is by focusing on the fundamental issue of Benjaminian 'aura'. They
formulated and successfully executed a concept- and procedure-driven plan.
Psychophysiology Research Institute constituted an exercise of radicalism in
what I have defined the 'wilderness' – as they sited their out-of-the-box practice outside Tokyo and its mainstream world of contemporary art.[7] The group's
attempt at expanding operational sites beyond Tokyo fits the present volume's

theme; however, in this project, distance (geography) was not a mere impediment to overcome but a valuable tool to help the group to achieve its goal to strip art of the aura. What is more, envisioned as an 'invisible museum', the project was conceived to chart an era by creating a series of collective 'cross sections' (*setsudan-men*) of time-space (p. 323).[8]

The beginning

Psychophysiology Research Institute was initiated by three art students, Ina Ken'ichirō, Takeda Kiyoshi and Shimamura Kiyoharu. The chief theoretical architect of the project was Ina (b. 1947), who entered Tokyo Zōkei University in 1968 and met with Takeda, one year ahead of him at the school; Shimamura was a friend of Ina's from his preparatory school (*yobikō*) period (pp. 321–2).[9] Tokyo Zōkei was a new art school established in 1966 by the designer Kuwazawa Yōko, who had founded an innovative Kuwazawa Dezain Kenkyūjo (Kuwazawa Design School) in 1954. Its newness can be understood when compared with two major private art schools at the forefront of contemporary art: Tama Art University and Musashino Art University in Tokyo. Both dating back to the prewar decades (respectively 1935 and 1929), their university status was reinstated under postwar education reforms (in 1953 and 1962, respectively).[10]

When nationwide campus conflicts broke out in the late 1960s, many schools had their share of problems against which their students initially revolted, and these movements would expand into and conflate with a broader anti-war and anti-establishment movement. Tama and Musashino were no exception any more than other, older art schools. Among the art school activist groups, the most theoretically driven was Bikyōtō (Artists Joint-Struggle Council), a collective founded in July 1969 and headquartered at the barricaded campus of Tama Art University. Their protests against the status quo in the art world continued through the autumn of that year, until the State Government deployed armed police forces to quell the rebelling students and liberated the occupied campuses.[11]

In contrast, as Ina recalls, at Tokyo Zōkei, students were far less organised and there was very little rebellion (p. 322). However, the school could not remain indifferent to reform: in 1969, it introduced a new system of faculty-led seminars. Ina found no teacher appealing enough but, feeling a need to find a new strategy of his own amid the pervasively anti-establishment atmosphere, he decided instead to organise a student-led seminar with four other students, functioning as an independent study group for contemporary art (p. 321). At a school where the student body apparently lacked a taste for activist commotion, such a move for independence stunned the faculty (p. 322). Around October that year, Ina organised a symposium to discuss the issue surrounding the subject and object of expression. After the proceedings, Ina broached the idea of PRI to Takeda, who was attending the symposium. By then, Ina had formulated 80 per cent of the project's concept, including its name. Takeda immediately proposed to put the plan in motion, and Shimamura joined them, too (pp. 323–4, 326).

The project was informed by Ina's analytical temperament, which can be gleaned from the exact date and time that he typed into the first participation request letter. More directly, we can see his methodical aesthetics in the first three contributions to the project. For these, he took meteorological measurements of his location at a specified time. Under the series title *Fūka* (*Weathering*), these acts were translated into the record consisting of a photograph, a map to show the location and the detailed data that he recorded (see Figure 8.2). Not that he was completely prosaic: the title *Fūka* corresponds to the English word 'weathering', while its Chinese characters (風化) rather poetically refer to weathering by the wind (風). Ina encompassed two levels to the word's signification in his data gathering: 'weather' and the 'wind' that causes weathering. For the next three acts the records were simplified, with more emphasis placed on photography than data. The extra undertaking after the final one is represented by a photograph of pocket watch, probably referring to the time he had spent on the project and evoking the time that would continue beyond it.

The group's name, PRI, is also imbued with his penchant for analytics and subtle poetry. At first glance, we may assume that Ina borrowed the name of an established branch of biology. However, the history of psychophysiology as a recognised discipline was relatively new, dating back only to the mid-1950s in the West, while in Japanese academic contexts the term does not seem to have existed before 1949.[12] In fact, at the time, Ina made up the term by combining 'psycho-' and 'physiology' (pp. 325–6). As a result, Ina was criticised, but it didn't matter to him, as the coinage was intended to signal his awareness of the elusive relationship of subjectivity (*shukan*) and objectivity (*kyakkan*), as have long been deliberated in philosophy, including in Husserl's phenomenology. After thinking about the title for almost a year, he decided to combine two incongruous words: 'psyche' (*seishin*), which pertains to the mind, and 'physiological' (*seiri*), which pertains to the functions of the body. The suffix *-gaku* creates a 'branch of study', and this scientific sense is augmented when followed by 'research institute' (*kenkyūjo*). Thus, Seishin Seirigaku Kenkyūjo (精神生理学研究所) was born.

Ina's theoretical concern aside, the group name embodies the spirit of serious and methodical experiment that Ina aspired to conduct. He admits his idea was based on the broader sense of 'anti-' at the time against the status quo in general, but the whole project amounted to 'a dismantling act', in retrospect, 'not unlike when you dismantled an engine and reassemble it again. You may

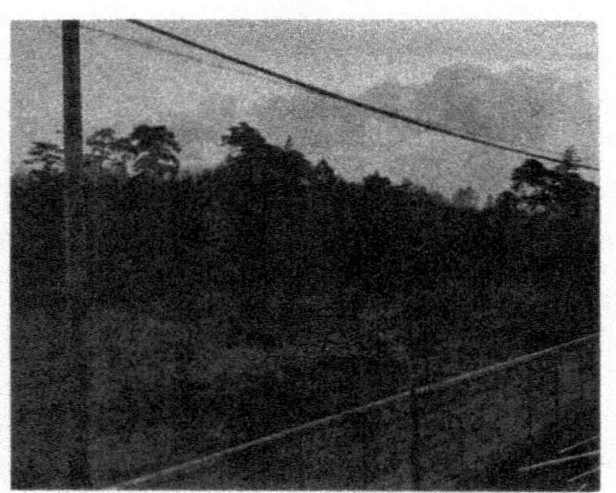

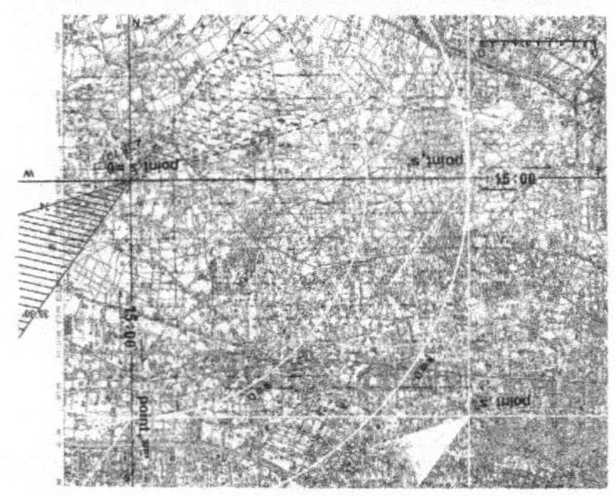

DATE   1969, 12, 7
TIME   15 : 00
PLACE   1—1—7 TAKEOKA KIYOSE
          KITATAMA-GUN TOKYO
気　温   18℃
気　圧   1010 mb
風　力   4
風　向   南南西
天　気   くもり
TITLE   風化（時）
NAME   Kenichiro Ina

8.2 Ina Ken'ichirō, *Weathering (Time)*, 1969. Contribution on 7 December 1969 (first undertaking) to Psychophysiology Research Institute. Reproduced in *Psychophysiology Research Institute* (1970), p. 10.

not get an exact same engine again. There may be unnecessary [parts] and the reassembled engine may differ from the original. Like that kind of process' (p. 330). With PRI, Ina in effect endeavoured to dismantle art itself, the goal he shared with his contemporaries worldwide.

The period when PRI was active was the heyday of Non-Art (*Hi-geijutsu*) – the Japanese terminology for the tendency of dematerialised practices that had numerous global parallels. Where Anti-Art (*Han-geijutsu*), which preceded Non-Art from the late 1950s to the mid-1960s, constituted the fervent assault on the modern construct of 'Art' (*geijutsu*) with a capital 'A', Non-Art was more sober and sombre, focusing on the critique of the institutions of *bijutsu*, or 'art' with a small 'a'. If Anti-Art ultimately embraced the idea of 'making something' in its sometimes chaotic manner, Non-Art decidedly pursued the ideology of 'not making' (*tsukuranai koto*) in three different directions: Mono-ha, conceptualism and performance art. Although it was Mono-ha that articulated the specific ideology of 'not making' predicated on *mono*, or things, Non-Art questioned the conventions of art-making.[13]

It should be noted that Non-Art was in a good part propelled by a number of art school graduates and, sometimes, students who inserted themselves in the forefront of new practices. The most prominent were Sekine Nobuo (b. 1942) and his fellow graduates of Tama Art University, who together formed a loose group of what would later be called 'Mono-ha' in 1968–73, with the theoretical support of the Korean theorist-artist Lee Ufan.[14] The more conceptual directions were represented by Matsuzawa Yutaka (1922–2006), a senior artist who had arrived at a unique version of immaterial conceptualism in the mid-1960s, and a few young individuals who devised their practices out of experiments in the late 1960s.[15] They included Nomura Hitoshi (b. 1945),[16] who developed a photo-based practice out of the sculptural experiment he undertook for his master's thesis in 1968–69, and Horikawa Michio (b. 1946),[17] who launched his series *Mail Art by Sending Stones* in July 1969. The works by these new artists were quickly recognised and presented at such mainstream events as the *Trends in Contemporary Japanese Art* exhibition series at the National Museum of Modern Art, Kyoto, as well as the twin biennials organised by the Mainichi newspaper companies – *Contemporary Art Exhibition of Japan* (so-called *Mainichi Contemporary*) and *International Art Exhibition, Japan* (aka *Tokyo Biennale*, also *Mainichi International*). Particularly noteworthy was an accelerated development during the period between *Mainichi Contemporary* in May 1969 and *Mainichi International* in May 1970 (known as *Tokyo Biennale 1970*), where Nomura, Horikawa, and a few Mono-ha artists were duly included. Such immediate recognitions were possible due to the growing institutionalisation of *gendai bijutsu* (literally 'contemporary art') within the art establishment.

In an accelerated state of development, a few months' difference mattered. Among Non-Art practitioners, Mono-ha artists, as exemplified by Sekine's meteoric rise, had become visible by mid-1969. This period coincided with the time Ina began and continued to develop his idea for PRI. He not only questioned the conventions of art, he was sceptical of Mono-ha's emphasis on materiality, which was intimately tied to the presence of *mono*, be they industrial materials (iron, paper etc.) or natural objects (stones, woods etc.). Ina also questioned the avid theorisation by Lee and Sekine of seeing the world anew, noting that some of their works appeared to rely on the meaning hidden behind the ingredients in their work.[18] This was part of what Ina considered the problematics of art.

The goal: to strip art of the aura

In his effort to dismantle what art is, Ina wanted to 'circumvent various meanings that art engenders', among which the 'aura' of a work of art stood as the most significant. In Ina's interpretation, the aura was associated with 'the "author" [*sakusha*] who looms behind the "work" [*sakuhin*] and its "contents" [*naiyō*] the author summons' (p. 323).

The source of Ina's reference to the aura was Walter Benjamin's *The Work of Art in the Age of Mechanical Reproduction* (1935), which was translated into Japanese in 1965 and readily available for the young artist.[19] The idea of reproduction also entered Ina's thinking via André Malraux's plan for *Le musée imaginaire* (1947), also available in a Japanese translation from 1957.[20] The two works proved influential in postwar Japan.[21] In particular, Benjamin's argument formed the background to a growing interest in the graphic arts towards 1970 and beyond, together with the progress of various reproduction technologies introduced to Japan during the 1960s.

Between two theories, Ina adopted two different possibilities deriving from reproduction. From Benjamin, he developed the idea of stripping the aura through reproduction, via Xeroxing, which he clearly understood as 'helping to minimise the aura as much as possible' (p. 323). From Malraux's 'imaginary museum' Ina envisioned the potential for a 'compilation of reproductions that transcends the limitation of time-space, grouped together in a historically unthinkable manner. '[When these works are] viewed side by side in this way, such a book will engender a new kind of interpretation. I thought that kind of book would be very interesting' (p. 323).

Ina found an ideal tool for his goal to strip art of the aura in the new technology of xerography. He recalls, 'all I wanted was to reproduce the data [sent from the participants] on paper by Xeroxing', because, he then thought, 'Xeroxing can eliminate the depth behind the work, flatten its physical depth', thereby minimising the aura (p. 323). Besides, he was fascinated by Xerox machines. He had previously acquired a secondhand mimeograph device to print documents himself; it was a laborious and untidy process consisting of preparing a stencil, setting it on an inking mechanism and manually printing – sheet by sheet. In contrast, the Xerox machine was so simple: he was happy just to put an original on the platen and have the machine make duplicates automatically (p. 326).

The commercial photocopying machine was introduced to Japan when Fuji Xerox was established in Japan in 1962.[22] By the late 1960s, it was not too difficult to find Xerox machines outside offices. In his neighbourhood, Ina found a store in front of the Ekoda station of the Seibu Railway that had installed a Xerox machine to cater for students at a number of colleges located nearby. Otherwise, he recalls, there were machines at Kunitachi and Kokubunji, neither being as convenient for him (p. 326). In terms of cost, photocopying was still expensive. The initial participation fees, 500 yen, collected from the members, were nowhere near enough to cover the actual expenditure, and later had to be raised to 700 yen.

Two less expensive means were readily available for reproduction. As students, Ina and two organisers could use a darkroom at school: all they needed to prepare was paper, as they could take advantage of the chemicals left by others (p. 326). *Aoyaki* (literally 'blueprint'), a type of diazo reproduction, was still widely used to reproduce office documents, and Ina could easily find blueprinting shops (p. 326). The process was also known as 'Ricopy', taken from the brand name of diazo machines manufactured by Ricoh, which was founded in 1936 as a camera company and began producing diazo machines in 1955.[23] The popularity of blueprinting was characteristic of the reproduction market in postwar Japan. In comparison, the thermal copying process was dominant in the USA prior to xerography. The chemical diazo process was cumbersome and limited, as an original document must be prepared on a translucent sheet necessary for the light-sensitive process. In comparison, the immediacy and versatility of Xeroxing was far superior. Although PRI selectively used blueprinting and the printing of photos, Xeroxing remained the principal means of reproduction – despite its high costs – indicating the technological efficacy of photocopying for Ina's vision.

Importantly, PRI was one of the earliest Japanese works to use the Xeroxing process. By far the best-known examples are Takamatsu Jirō's 1970 conceptualist works, *These Three Words* and この七つの文字 (literally, 'these seven characters'). For these works, reminiscent of Joseph Kosuth's *Five Words in Green Neon* (1965), Takamatsu, a former Hi-Red Center member and arguably the most visible practitioner of contemporary art at the time, deployed a Xerox machine as a printmaking tool.[24] He began with a single original bearing either of these two phrases. He photocopied it, then photocopied the first photocopy, then photocopied the second photocopy, repeating the procedure 100 times. In this operation, various noises (such as blemishes and dust on the platen) were accentuated, becoming an increasingly noticeable part of each print, pointing to the imperfection of technology. For Ina, the merit far outweighed the demerit: he took advantage of what this technology could do – creating a not-so-perfect reproduction – to minimise the aura of a work.

The procedure: plotting art as data in time-space

For Ina, reproduction technology was no more than a tool. While his idea for a Malraux-esque reproduction-based museum served as an organising framework, his organising principle was the reinterpretation of art as 'data' (*dēta*). An important precedence was set by Kashihara Etsutomu, six years senior to Ina. Known for his analytically minded conceptualism, Kashihara led a three-person collaboration to produce an epic project, *What Is Mr X?* (1968–69), in which they attempted to construct a person called Mr X as a composite of the three by accumulating drawings and collages they made under certain rules.[25] Having heard of this project through Shimamura, Ina had been indirectly influenced by Kashihara's strategy in his earlier work (p. 321). Subsequently, Ina had a chance to confirm with Kashihara their shared idea of the 'work as data' and the use of another word, *shiryō* ('document', as in 'archival document'). Ina recalls that both of them wanted to circumvent this meaning as such (p. 323). With these conceptual foundations, he went on to devise a concrete procedure to achieve an invisible museum. To do so, Ina applied his critique to two basic components of art: the artist as author (*sakka*) and the work he makes (*sakuhin*).

At the time, the notion of 'anonymity' (*tokumei-sei*) was contested, because it was generally considered that the artist's name as a signature inscribed onto a painting underscores its aura as a work of art; anonymising it by withholding the artist's name would thus minimise the aura (p. 329). However, Ina thought differently: he felt it necessary to have the artist's name to guarantee the 'certitude' (p. 329) of data provided to the project, just as scientific data comes with the names of researchers to demonstrate 'objectivity as information' (p. 323). Yet, it was certainly not ideal to use a person's name.

Ina solved this problem by assigning a tag to participants in the form of '[blank] Research Institute', wherein the blank was filled with residential locations (prefecture names), as in Tokyo Research Institute, for himself. It at once helped to standardise the name format and signalled the kind of scientific rigour he aspired to emulate. In effect, he turned the artist's name into data and reduced the aura of the artist without jeopardising their agency as a data provider.

The scheme was already hinted at in the initial participation request letter reproduced in blueprint (quoted at the beginning of this essay). Here, the three confirmed participants are identified with their location as part of the form letter: Tokyo, Nagano and Morocco. Four prospective participants are filled in with black marker: Hiroshima, Kyoto, Ibaraki and Gunma. Even as a form letter, it is rather unorthodox to find the addressee mentioned two-thirds of the way through the document, following the statement and the participation guidelines for the inaugural undertaking on 7 December 1969. Under the line 'We cordially request your participation and collaboration' in blueprint, the location of the recipient, Niigata, was parenthetically added in black marker, with his name, Horikawa Michio, nowhere to be found. The only personal information given is the address of PRI: c/o Ina Ken'ichirō (with his home address). This was a necessity, to ensure the delivery of member mails in light of the institute's decisively unofficial existence.

The inaugural roster fully embodies the scheme of artist-as-data. The six inaugural participants indicated parenthetically are:

Niigata Research Institute (Horikawa Michio)
Ibaraki Research Institute (Ezura Takeshi)
Gunma Research Institute (Shimamura Kiyoharu)
Morocco Research Institute (Wada Hideo)
Nagano Research Institute (Takeda Kiyoshi)
Tokyo Research Institute (Ina Ken'ichirō)

For the inaugural undertaking, Ina's desire to capture an expansive geographical cross-section for an invisible museum was so strong that he and his two collaborating students, all of them Tokyo residents, manipulated their locations. Ina took Tokyo as his tag to provide the central address. Takeda took Nagano as his tag, as he was then dividing his time between Tokyo and Nagano (where his parents' home was located), while Shimamura adopted Gunma in reference to his father's hometown in that prefecture.

The students knew the other three participants in person. Ezura Takeshi was Ina's friend from the preparatory school, and they exhibited in a three-person exhibition in June 1969. Wada Hideo was a friend of Takeda's and not an artist, but was enticed to participate on the promise that all he would have to do was to send a letter, because Ina wanted to transcend the boundary of art and life and engage 'expression' (*hyōgen*, a key word that frequently replaced 'art' in the cultural discourse of the late 1960s) outside the art world. Horikawa Michio was recommended to Takeda by Maeda Jōsaku, a painter and a Tokyo Zōkei professor who had known Horikawa since the mid-1960s. Having graduated from a local teachers' college in 1968, Horikawa was active in GUN, a contemporary art collective in Niigata that focused on more localised practices after an intensive exhibition series in Tokyo and Niigata in 1967–68. Most importantly, he began his signature project, *Mail Art by Sending Stones*, in July 1969, and experimented with a wide range of mailings.

Still, because of their desire to expand the membership roster, their scheme of using prefecture names was quickly ended in the second undertaking on 4 January 1970. To accommodate multiple participants from the same prefecture, except for the 'Hiroshima Research Institute' (Saitō Toshinori, who joined from the third undertaking of 8 February 1970), those who subsequently joined received name-based tags. Thus, Maeyama Tadashi, Horikawa's friend and a member of GUN, who joined from the undertaking of 3 March 1970, became Maeyama Research Institute, and Matsuzawa Yutaka, a pioneer conceptualist residing in Nagano prefecture who contributed to the third and sixth undertakings, assumed the title of Matsuzawa Research Institute. Along with Maeda Jōsaku, two other recognisable names are Itoi Kanji (aka Dada Kan), a die-hard Anti-Art practitioner known for his streaking and other outlier happenings, and Tōno Yoshiaki, an influential critic of contemporary art. Over the period from December 1969 to May 1970, a total of sixteen individuals joined the collective, but only the original six contributed to all of the undertakings.[26]

A work or an act does not transform itself into data automatically. For that to happen, some kind of intervention is necessary, either by the artist or by a third party. Ina constructed the participation guidelines so that the first step would be deliberately taken by the artist himself. The guidelines included in the first participation request letter read:

> Date and time: 7 December, at 15:00.[27]

> Place: a location where each participant can position himself at the specified time.

> Work: any form and method will do. However, please post by mail the work or its record [*kiroku*] to Tokyo Research Institute, which will make reproductions of the works or their records assembled from the research institutes and mail [the reproduction set] back.[28]

Although the last instruction on the work (that is, 'an act or non-act', as described in the prefacing statement) gives permission to use 'any form and method', the proviso that follows specifies that participation would be made through something mailable and reproducible. Accordingly, most of the contributions delivered to Ina (Tokyo Research Institute) were already one layer removed from the original acts by the use of reproductive technologies, especially Xeroxing. For example, for the inaugural undertaking, Horikawa mailed a stone to President Richard Nixon as an alleged Christmas gift, incorporating the tacit political gesture of throwing a stone at him. To document this act, he laid out a photo of the stone and a post office receipt for international mailing on an A3 sheet, and photocopied the whole thing on a high-quality Xerox machine.[29] Ina himself prepared three separate items related to his meteorological measurement: a photograph of the site of measurement, an annotated map of the site and a data sheet bearing the measurements (see Figure 8.3).

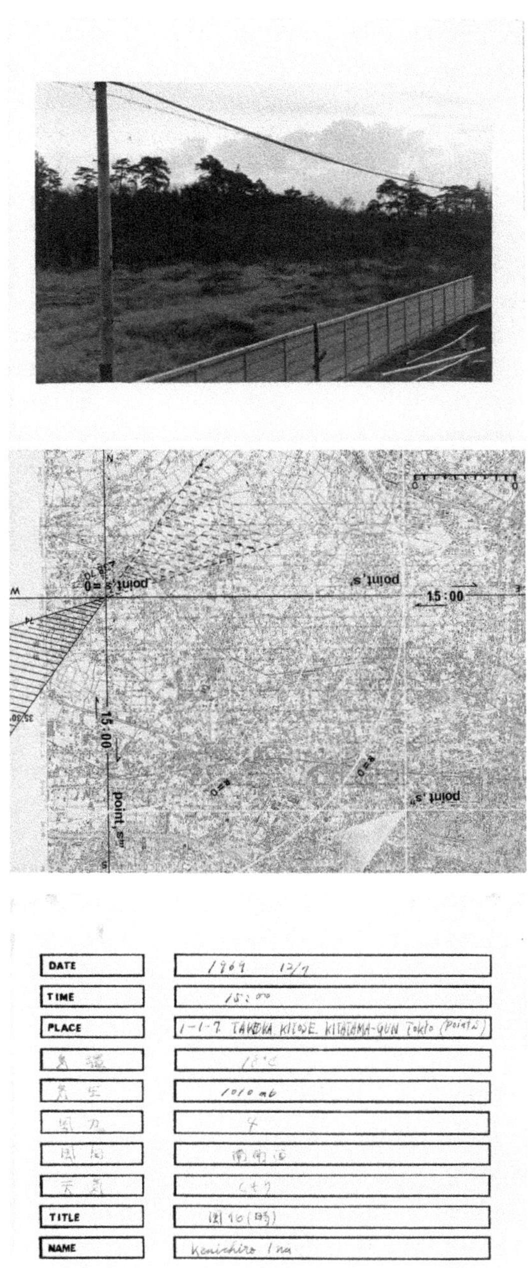

Ina Ken'ichirō, *Weathering (Time)*, 1969. Contribution on 7 December 1969 (first undertaking) to Psychophysiology Research Institute. Three elements (photograph, map and data sheet), as digitised in the CD edition of *Psychophysiology Research Institute* (1970/2009).

8.3

These sundry reproductions were again put through appropriate reproduction processes. For example, Xeroxes were made from Horikawa's already photocopied sheet, while Wada's contribution, which was a message to Ina regarding his forthcoming departure in early January, was turned into a blueprint communiqué. The duplicates were collated by author, each held together by a thin band of paper bearing the institute name in roman characters, stylised as 'TOKYO SEISHINSEIRIGAKUKENKYUJO'. The whole set was enclosed in an envelope that fitted A4 documents, made of tracing paper and bearing the group name in Chinese characters (精神生理学研究所; see Figure 8.4). For the first undertaking, a total of thirty sets were made and sent to the participants, as well as to a number of art world figures, including art critics, who the organisers hoped would disseminate the information on their project in their writings.

It should be noted that, in this project, mail art was deployed not so much as a delivery mechanism but more as a circulation mechanism. It is instructive to compare PRI with On Kawara's *I Got Up* postcards, which were shown at the 1969 Mainichi Contemporary in May. (This, together with Matsuzawa Yutaka's one-year *Postcard Painting* series of 1967–68 and Horikawa's stone-mailing, constituted the examples of mail art that Ina is most likely to have been aware of.) Like Ina's project, in his own series Kawara posted the record of an act as data: the act of getting up at a certain time on a certain date (typed) in a certain city (indicated by a tourist site on the picture side). However, Kawara's mailing was a one-directional monologue, as were many other works of mail art. Ina made a conscious use of mail art as a networking tool to circulate data about acts by a group of individuals. Mail art enabled 'individuals who refuse to have direct connections' (as characterised in the statement) to connect indirectly, while prompting them to explore the idea of a 'record' inventively. The network orchestrated by PRI was not one-to-many but many-to-many – spreading across a considerable geographical range – with Tokyo as their communication hub.

An 'invisible museum'

After the PRI project was completed in a more or less precisely planned way, Ina moved on with his own practice, without looking back. However, PRI is a superb example of an institutional critique whose implications deserve to be re-examined, as they raise fundamental questions for art history and critical theory.

Taking advantage of his international perspective, which he had gained first-hand as the commissioner of *Tokyo Biennale 1970*, the art critic Nakahara Yūsuke left us an important comparative observation of Ina's work. In the September 1970 issue of the art magazine *Sansai* (*Tricolour*), Nakahara

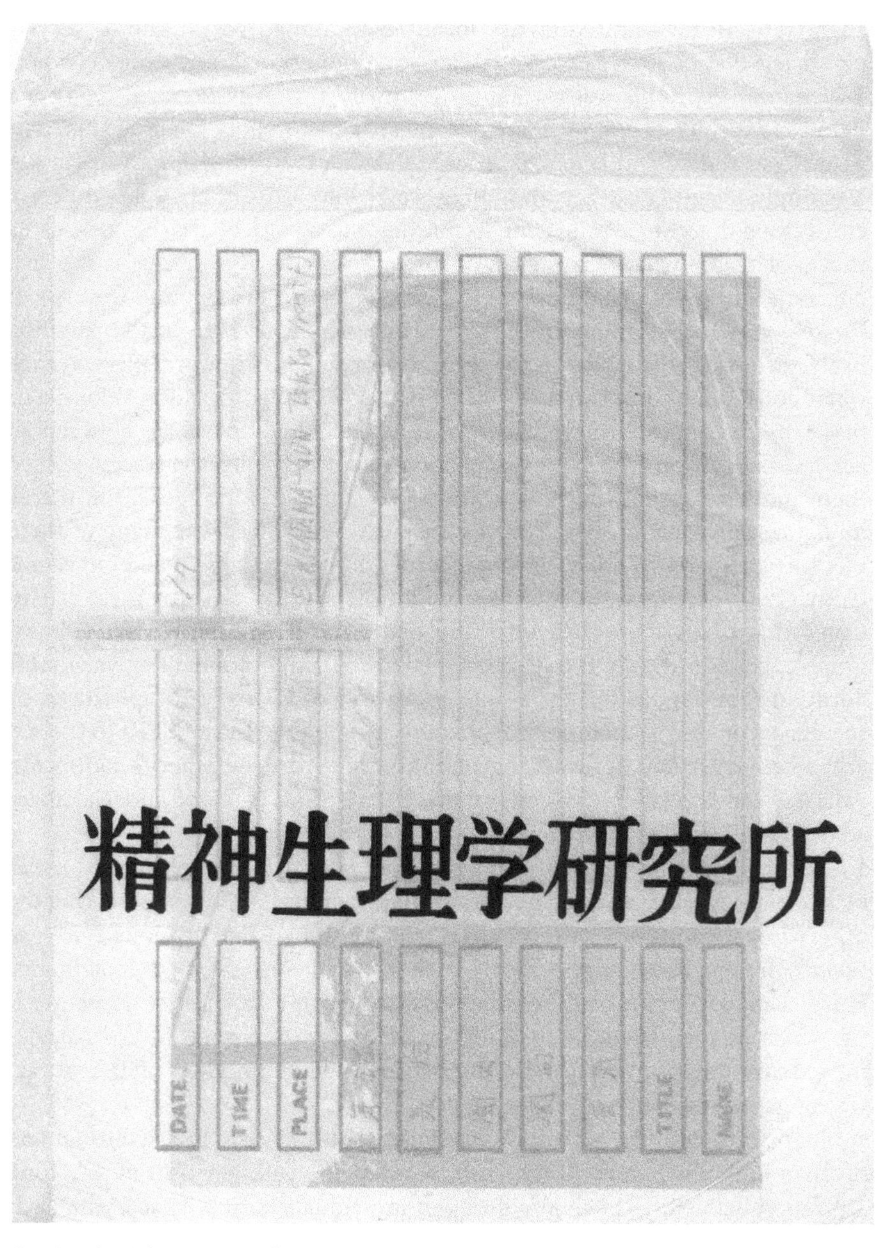

Psychophysiology Research Institute, original copy envelope, 7 December 1969.   **8.4**

characterised Ina's thinking as 'location thinking', which, he observed, paralleled that of such Euro-American practitioners as Klaus Rinke (*Ladling Water from the Rhine*, 1969), Stanley Brouwn (*This Way Brouwn*, 1969) and Douglas Huebler (*Location Piece No. 11*, 1969), as well as On Kawara's 'date paintings' (*Today*) and *I Got Up* series.[30] Nakahara's starting point was Rinke's seemingly meaningless acts of ladling water into a drum at twelve different cities along the Rhine. Pondering its relevance as a work of art, the critic came to a conclusion: what makes each of these repeatable acts unique is the specific date and place that defines it. Put differently, the critic found the crux of Rinke's work not so much in the artist's acts *per se*, or even in the resulting twelve drums, as the labels on the drums recording the time and place of each water collection – 'information'.[31] What Nakahara called 'location thinking' is more than a geographical indicator; it is a conceptual link made between an act, its information (time and space) and its evidence (physical traces) to turn them into an integral whole as a work.[32] For him, it is too facile, too literal, to call certain location-based works 'map art' simply because many of them incorporate maps.[33] Rather, what concerned him was a new type of epistemology predicated upon the information of time-space charted by these artists. Consisting of an act, a data set (information) and a physical trace (photograph), Ina's contributions to PRI satisfied the basic requirement of Nakahara's 'location thinking', as did the whole endeavour of PRI, as conceptualised by Ina. Based on this evaluation, Nakahara recommended Ina and PRI to the Art & Project Gallery for its summer group show in 1970. (The gallery's codirector, Adriaan van Ravesteijn, visited Japan in the spring of 1970, and Nakahara advised him about local art scenes.)

It is notable that Nakahara thought Ina's *Fūka* far simpler than Kawara's or Huebler's work. Nakahara gave a positive appraisal of Kawara's making the otherwise meaningless date or place irreplaceable, even precious (*kakegae nonai*), in his *Today* and *I Got Up* series, while he deemed imaginative Huebler's incorporation of the rotation of the earth into *Location Piece No. 11* (in which he calculated the total distance that a certain point in Los Angeles moved over ninety-two days). In contrast, Nakahara found Ina's matter-of-fact way of gathering data rather lacking.[34]

It appears, with the benefit of hindsight, that Nakahara focused too much on Ina's individual work to take into account the young artist's overarching aspiration with PRI – to chart a group of individuals in time-space, with each acting as an independent agent, undertaking an act and making its record. In fact, in the beginning, Ina was not so concerned with the quality of individual contributions, thinking that 'anybody would do [as a participant], so long as they send in data, if I may use extreme language' (p. 323). Still, Ina gathered a broad range of acts under the banner of PRI. That was what he meant by creating a series of collective 'cross sections' (*setsudan-men*) of time-space. In this

sense, Ina's collectivism was a somewhat reluctant strain in the modern tradition of Japanese collectivism.[35]

In his conception, PRI was a horizontal organisation with no central
committee or organisers as such – he insists in his later recollections that
each local research institute *was* PRI and thus an 'invisible museum' in its
own right (p. 329). If we follow his logic, we may call the first iteration of PRI,
both collectively and individually, an invisible (immaterial) museum. The data
sets PRI duplicated and collated, which he called 'original copies' (*genpon*),
constitute the second visible (material) iteration of these invisible museums.
Looking at them now, we cannot help recognise diverse materiality in these
duplicates: Xeroxed documents obviously feel different from blueprinted
materials. Above all, in order to 'see' them, we need to handle one undertaking
at a time, taking out the data from a brittle tracing-paper envelope, removing
the band from each institute's contribution to view its components and eventually returning them to their packaged state. Put simply, we need to perform
the task of art handler to see PRI in this iteration. It is a strangely aesthetic,
aura-inducing experience.

From the start, Ina planned to turn the whole project into a book, probably
inspired by Malraux's museum without walls, and realised it as a portfolio of
seventy-nine A4 cards. In total, sixty-five acts and non-acts by fifteen artists
are included.[36] The intention was to 'further dilute the aura' (p. 328) and 'see
[the project] from a different perspective', as Ina recalls.[37] Some data elements
were replaced to improve quality (for example, some Xeroxed images were
substituted with their original documents), and handwritten and typed texts
were typeset to conform to a neutral look. The data elements of each act were
arranged to fit a single sheet for equal representation among contributions.
This is the third iteration of PRI as a visible museum. The most portable,
easiest to handle and view, this iteration proved to be a brilliant output,
because, as he hoped, the offset printing process (commercial printing) further stripped each act of its remaining aura while preserving the detachment
among the participating research institutes, because the book is unbound. Ina
himself acknowledges the inversion from the second to the third iteration as
'paradoxical': what was intended as reproduction became the *original* copies,
and what was intended as the final *work* was a product of pure mechanical
reproduction.[38]

Towards a space of information

Psychophysiology Research Institute has a dual significance in world art
history – as a local phenomenon *and* as a global episode. This last section
will examine it by placing it in a broader perspective, both domestically and
internationally.

In the history of performance art, the word *kōi* (acts) is a local term that dates back to Shiraga Kazuo, a member of the legendary experimental collective Gutai in Osaka, who used the term to explain his foot-painted gestural abstraction.[39] Since then, a few imported terms are used for body- and time-based performative practices, such as 'events' and 'happenings'. However, before 'performance art' (*pafōmansu āto*) became dominant in the early 1980s, *kōi* was consistently used in Japanese literature.[40] From today's definition, Ina's meteorological measurements may not be considered performance art, and may be more likely to be understood as task-based conceptualism. It was nonetheless deemed part of act-based practice, as exemplified by his inclusion in *Artists who Undertake Acts*, a special feature in the December 1970 issue of the leading contemporary art magazine *Bijutsu techō* (*Art Notebook*).[41] In this local sense, PRI can be characterised as a museum of performance art.

By envisioning an invisible museum and then, more significantly, also producing physical museums in the forms of works on paper and as a book, PRI unintentionally codified the data of an act as a work (*sakuhin*) authored by an artist and collected by a museum. Compared with the USA and western Europe, presenting 'data as work' was a new development in Japan that began to emerge in the late 1960s. Prior to that, performative acts were documented but primarily circulated in Japan to gain publicity in the mass media, whether by artists themselves or through journalistic photographers. Gutai exemplifies the use of documentary photographs for publicity purposes,[42] followed by such Anti-Art practitioners as Shinohara Ushio, known for his *Boxing Painting*, and Zero Dimension, a group notorious for their naked street rituals.[43]

Ina's formulation of 'data as work' was, as Nakahara berated it, simple. But by laying out the basic procedural principle of turning data into work, it allowed for an individual deviation or expansion from the formula and enabled Ina to gather a wide range of participants. Among the roster of PRI, Itoi Kanji, introduced to them by Horikawa, belonged to the generation of Anti-Art practitioners. Ina was fully aware of the bodily nature of Itoi's performances, but expected to see a different facet of his work under the guidelines he devised (p. 327). Two contributions Itoi made, for the fourth and sixth undertakings, pose a crucial question: how effective were Ina's idea of data and his strategy of using Xerox machines to strip art of its aura? Itoi's contributions are unmistakably marked by his aesthetic personality. The earlier one, ostensibly referencing his act from 1964 at the time of the Tokyo Olympics, is combined with graphic and photo images exuding a sense of erotic subversion; in the later one, reporting on *1970.4.27. 11:45, Dada Kan's Successful Streaking under the Tower of the Sun*, the image of the tower, despite its photocopied fuzziness, remains iconic, juxtaposed with a forceful photograph of his naked running leg (see Figure 8.5). Itoi's body-based act at the site of *Expo '70* is no doubt one of the most memorable protests staged

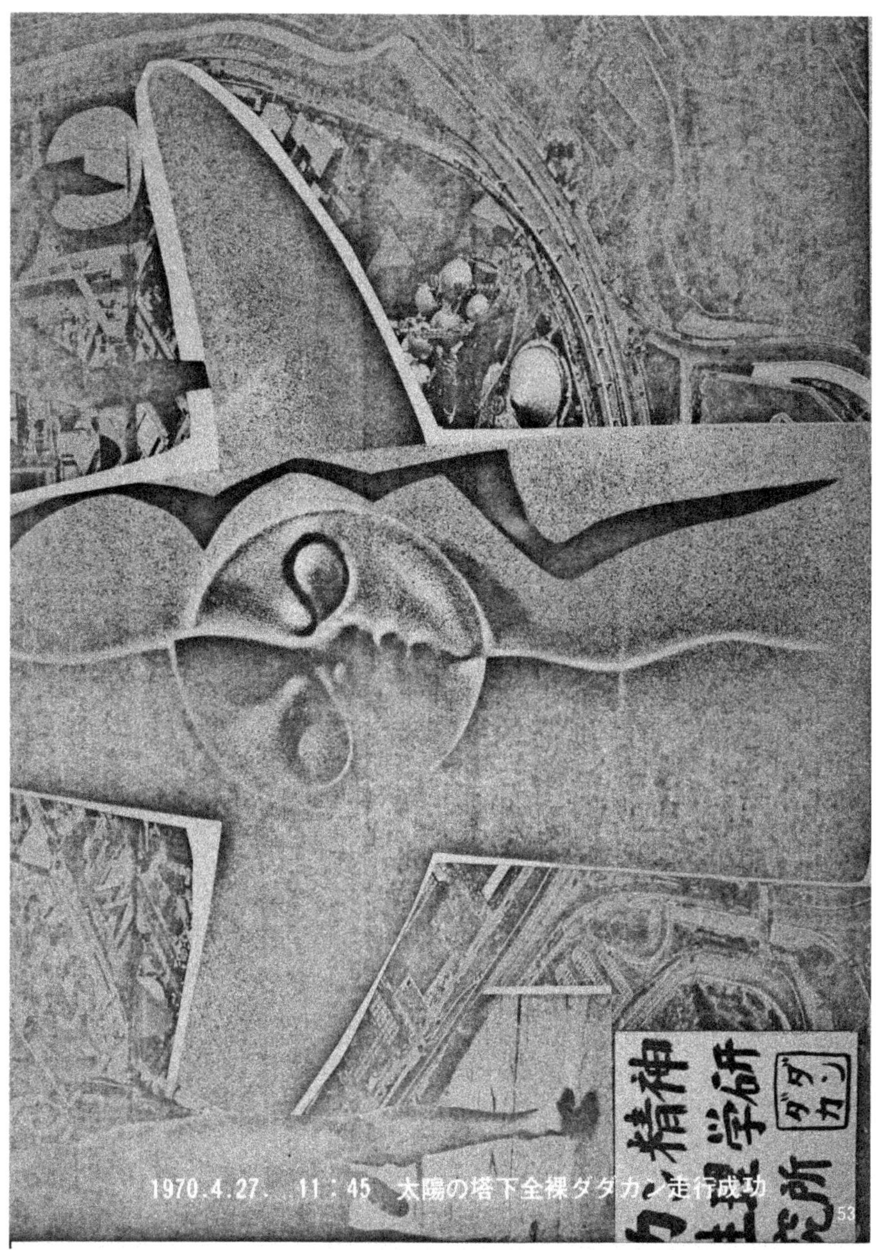

Itoi Kanji, *1970.4.27. 11:45, Dada Kan's Successful Streaking under the Tower of the Sun*. Contribution on 10 May 1970 (sixth undertaking) to Psychophysiology Research Institute. Reproduced in *Psychophysiology Research Institute* (1970), p. 53.

8.5

by a performance-minded artist against a State- and corporate-sponsored technology art extravaganza. The aura emanating from this fact – and the presence of a singular artist – was inerasable.

Neutrality of data is also challenged by Matsuzawa Yutaka, a die-hard conceptualist and an old friend of Professor Maeda's. Ina and Takeda personally paid their respects by visiting him in his home at Shimo Suwa in central Japan and presenting their project plan before he agreed to join the project. Unlike Itoi, who falsified the dates of his acts, Matsuzawa followed the guidelines to the letter, except on his own terms of immaterialism. For the third undertaking, his act was as follows:

> Now, as it silently and steadily snows, while standing at latitude 36° 4' 15" north, longitude 138° 5' 20" east, and altitude 788 m, I am showing this white sheet of paper to Lake Suwa at altitude 759 m, which usually would be visible but is not so today, at time-space void of 12:00 hours, 8 February 1970.

Probably mimicking Ina's scientifically detailed style (by noting exact latitude, longitude and heights), Matsuzawa went for a scientifically implausible act (showing a sheet of paper to the lake), a practice that he had begun as part of his *Non-Sensory Painting* series, which he had formulated in 1964 as an exercise to see the invisible with the mind's eye. In particular, the idea of showing a *Non-Sensory Painting* to inanimate things (including the lake) was a major ingredient of his monthly *Postcard Painting* series in 1967–68.

Ina made a crucial oversight with his reductionism: not all kinds of information can be flattened by a photocopier. Like Matsuzawa's immaterial information or Itoi's personal aesthetics, many types of information fall outside the realm of 'scientific data', or data that can be treated as such. To begin with, these two artists operated precisely in resistance to objective and everyday frameworks. At the same time, Matsuzawa quickly learned the efficacy of making a record of a past act. This was new to the artist, who had previously orchestrated his imaginary acts and exhibitions mostly in the present and future tenses, in the form of announcements and instructions. For his contribution to the sixth undertaking, on 10 May 1970, he happened to be attending the *Tokyo Biennale 1970* on its opening day. He executed a performance titled *My Own Death* in a museum room assigned to him, which he kept empty except for two panels, also titled *My Own Death*, hanging at either entrance to the space. Not included in the exhibition checklist, the performance was a guerrilla act intended solely for PRI. Furthermore, as 'recorded' in his text, his physical performance at the museum had an imaginary counterpart act executed by his imaginary self in a landscape near his hometown in central Japan, which the viewer was required to see with their mind's eye to overcome the constraints of physical space. He went on to launch the second monthly *Postcard Painting* series in October 1970, in which he recorded and reported his often implausible activities, practising 'data as work', probably inspired by his experience with PRI.

Reductionist as it may be, Ina's conception of data had the potential to open up new horizons, as demonstrated by the contributions by Itoi and Matsuzawa. One was to reframe 'data' as 'information', which has a broader application, as seen in *Information*, an exhibition of dematerialised practices organised by the Museum of Modern Art in New York in July–September 1970. It appears that Horikawa Michio struggled with Ina's objective understanding of 'data', as Ina recalls, because of his focus on mail art (p. 323).[44] It should be remembered that Ina and Horikawa had different expectations of mail art. Based in Tokyo, Ina used the form as an impersonalised circulation tool; based in Niigata, away from Tokyo, Horikawa relied on it for personal networking with targeted individuals, such as senior artists (e.g. Sekine Nobuo and Matsuzawa Yutaka), art critics (e.g. Takiguchi Shūzō and Tōno Yoshiaki) and gallerists (e.g. the owners of Tokyo Gallery and Minami Gallery). Furthermore, inspired by the Apollo 11 mission, his *Mail Art by Sending Stones* referenced the moon rocks gathered by the astronauts, thereby not only reaching out to outer space but also redirecting attention back to earth. Taken together, these elements, including the artist's tacit political intention, constitute the 'meanings' that Ina endeavoured to purge – even though Horikawa's stone was certainly not an aura-inducing object. On the contrary, it was intended to demystify space travel and illuminate a conflict-ridden social reality.

Given the one-directional nature of mail art – with no tangible object remaining in the hands of the sender – Horikawa devised an extensive system to record his stone-mailing series. Before he joined PRI, he had already completed two mailings. For the mailing completed in conjunction with Apollo 11 in July 1969, he created a single data card bearing photos, a mailing list, his statement and other information. For the Apollo 12 mission in November 1969 he developed a scheme to have face-to-face interactions with the twelve addressees at later dates, which involved confirming with them the reception of his stones and asking them to countersign documents he had prepared in advance. Through this activity, his mailings engendered a space of dialogue prompted by the information shared by the artist and the recipients. Still, he was yet to understand that these cards could amount to works in their own right – not just evidence of his mailings. That is, until he learned of PRI's work, and was invited to participate.[45]

Horikawa's first act for PRI was part of the Apollo-inspired mailings: with no mission happening until May 1970, he decided to address a stone to the person he thought was the commander-in-chief of the missions, President Nixon, driven by a desire to make a meaningful gift to the student-led project. He went on to contribute to all of PRI's undertakings. Along with Matsuzawa, Horikawa was also invited to exhibit at *Tokyo Biennale 1970*, for which he sent thirteen stones in conjunction with the Apollo 13 mission that April. He decided to conclude his PRI membership, memorably again, with a stone sent to Prime Minister Satō Eisaku, Nixon's Japanese counterpart. Finding it difficult to mail a stone by post in Tokyo on the specified date and time, he sent it on 3 May at 12.00 p.m., with a hope that it would, or could, reach the addressee on 10 May at 12.00 p.m., as stated in the note accompanying a photo of the stone in his contribution.

Ina's conception of data was limited, probably because he deemed a work of art a self-sufficient entity. An assumption of autonomy of art is another issue to be questioned, especially when *kōi*, or performative acts, were introduced to the artist's work, because more often than not acts engender social and participatory dimensions, as examined in the cases of the artists here. Even in the object-based example of Horikawa's stone-mailings, the project was generative of a space of information that cannot be restricted by the notion of data. Ina's conception of PRI thus points to the possibility of creating what I call a 'space for information', not just objective data, which is derived from an act. In this space, information – whether objective or subjective, real or imaginary, actual or speculative, intrinsic or extrinsic – is the second life, as it were, of an act that vanished in time. And with each of these works generating a space of information, PRI, as a museum that consists of these spaces, itself functions as a larger space of information in which each work resides as a subspace.

In his insightful essay on 'location thinking', the critic Nakahara kept asking 'what constitutes a *sakuhin*' – that is, a 'work' that has a coherent presence as art. For example, looking at Rinke's water-ladling project, he could not see a *sakuhin* in either the artist's act, the water-filled drums or the information about the act (especially because it's formless).[46] Thus, he thought of 'location thinking' as something to connect these non-work elements to give some semblance of a *sakuhin*.[47] Ina's analytics result in a space of information that may be simpler, but surely more versatile in encompassing different phases of an act or an ephemeral occurrence within its matrix.

Thus understood, the notion of a 'space of information' is applicable to those artists Nakahara discussed along with Ina – Rinke, Kawara, Huebler and Brouwn – as well as other performative practitioners. The conundrum of performance art – which is the work: the act or the document of it? – will then be moot, as its space of information would integrate these two different phases, corporeal and incorporeal, with its information spatialised and physicalised. Ina's insight was to apply this methodology not just to one act or one artist's acts, but to multiple artists' multiple acts through collaboration with other artists under the premise of a hypothetical museum, to demonstrate a broader significance of such spatialising. We art historians can learn much from Ina and the PRI. One lesson is: in order to chart space, we have first to spatialise information.

Notes

1 PRI, initial request letter to the 'Niigata Research Institute' (Horikawa Michio), 19 November 1969, collection of Horikawa Michio. In this chapter, all translations from Japanese materials are by the author.

2 In 2009, PRI was reissued as facsimile in these two versions: the 'original copies' (*genpon*) or the duplicated material sent to the members, and the final portfolio. In addition, these two versions were digitised and separately issued as a CD.

3 All East Asian names in the text of the chapter are given in the traditional order, surname first.

4 Imura Yasuko, 'Seishim Seirigaku Kenkyūjo: Media-ron to shiteno sakka hyōgen' ['Psychophysiology Research Institute (Seishin Seirigaku Kenkyūjo): Artistic expression as media theory'], *Kokuritsu Shin-Bijutsukan kenkyū kiyō/NACT Review: Bulletin of the National Art Center, Tokyo* 4 (2017), 108–19.

5 Prior to Imura's study (*ibid.*), PRI was included in the exhibition by Charles Merewether and Rika Iezumi Hiro (eds), *Art, Anti-Art, Non-Art: Experimentations in the Public Sphere in Postwar Japan, 1950–1970* (exh. cat.) (Los Angeles: Getty Research Institute, 2007), p. 110. Also see Reiko Tomii, 'After the "descent to the everyday": Japanese collectivism from Hi Red Center to The Play, 1964–1973', in Blake Stimson and Gregory Sholette (eds), *Collectivism after Modernism* (Minneapolis: University of Minnesota Press, 2007), pp. 44–75.

6 The major difference is the replacement of '[each participant] in Tokyo, Nagano, Morocco, Hiroshima, Kyoto, Ibaraki and Gunma' with 'each participating research institute'.

7 See Reiko Tomii, *Radicalism in the Wilderness: International Contemporaneity and 1960s Art in Japan* (Cambridge, MA: MIT Press, 2016).

8 In this chapter, Ina's quotes and his biographical details are taken from the following oral history interview on PRI with page number(s) parenthetically within the text: Imura Yasuko and Suzuki Katsuo, 'Bijutsu shiryō o meguru kaisō: Ina Ken'ichirō-shi ni kiku' ['Recollections on art document: Speaking with Ina Ken'ichirō'], *Kokuritsu Shin-Bijutsukan kenkyū kiyō/NACT Review: Bulletin of the National Art Center, Tokyo* 4 (2017), 318–32.

9 *Yobikō* is a school that high-school graduates (and sometimes high-school students) attend to prepare successfully for university exams.

10 For the history of these schools see 'History', Tokyo Zokei University, www.zokei.ac.jp/university/history; 'History', Tama Art University, www.tamabi.ac.jp/prof/history; and 'History', Musashino Art University, www.musabi.ac.jp/outline/about/history (all accessed 12 December 2019).

11 For Bikyōtō see Reiko Tomii, 'Revolution in Bikyōtō's photography: Naoyoshi Hikosaka and the Group of Five', in Yasufumi Nakamori (ed.), *For a New World to Come: Experiments in Japanese Art and Photography, 1968–1979* (exh. cat.) (Houston: Museum of Fine Arts, 2015), pp. 148–53; Reiko Tomii, 'The impossibility of anti: A theoretical consideration of Bikyōtō', in Mathieu Copeland and

Balthazar Lovay (eds), *Anti-Museum* (exh. cat.) (Fribourg: Fri Art; Cologne: Verlag der Buchhandlung Walther, 2016), pp. 467–79.

12 The date for the West is taken from Robert M. Stern, William J. Ray and Karen S. Quigley, 'Psychophysiology', in Robert M. Stern, William J. Ray and Karen S. Quigley (eds), *Psychophysiological Recording*, 2nd edn (Oxford: Oxford University Press, 2021), p. 3. The oldest volume found via a keyword search for 'seishi seiri' or 'seishin seirigaku' on https://ci.nii.ac.jp/ (the Japanese equivalent of WorldCat) for books and journals is M. Taiei, *Seishin seirigaku: Seishin shintai igaku no kiso* [*Psychophysiology: The Foundation of Medicine on Psyche and Body*] (Tokyo: Hōmeidō, 1949).

13 For various historical details in this section see Tomii, *Radicalism in the Wilderness*, especially 'An overview of history: The rise of "contemporary art"', pp. 26–38.

14 For Mono-ha see Mika Yoshitake (ed.), *Requiem for the Sun: The Art of Monoha* (exh. cat.) (Los Angeles: Blum & Poe, 2012). For Mono-ha's relationship to the mainstreaming of contemporary art in 1960s Japan see Reiko Tomii, 'Six contradictions of Mono-ha', *Review of Japanese Culture and Society* 25 (December 2013), 214–22.

15 For Matsuzawa Yutaka see Tomii, *Radicalism in the Wilderness*.

16 For Nomura Hitoshi see Martha Buskirk and Reiko Tomii, *Hitoshi Nomura: Early Works* (exh. cat.) (New York: McCaffrey Fine Art, 2010).

17 For Horikawa Michio and his activity within GUN, a contemporary art collective, see Tomii, *Radicalism in the Wilderness*.

18 Ina Ken'ichirō, email to the author, 3 October 2019.

19 Walter Benjamin, *Fukusei geijutsu jidai no geijutsu* [*The Work of Art in the Age of Mechanical Reproduction*], trans. Kawamura Jirō *et al.* (Tokyo: Kinokuniya Shoten, 1965 [1935]).

20 André Malraux, *Kūsō no bijutsukan* [*Le musée imaginaire*], trans. Komatsu Kiyoshi (Tokyo: Shinchō-sha, 1957 [1947]). An informative study can be found in Walter Grasskamp, *The Book on the Floor: André Malraux and the Imaginary Museum* (Los Angeles: Getty Research Institute, 2016).

21 See Imura, 'Seishi Seirigaku Kenkyūjo', pp. 114–17.

22 '1960-nendai no Nihon no fukushaki shijō' ['The market of copying machines in 1960s Japan'], Fujifilm, www.fujixerox.co.jp/company/technical/column/sixties.html (accessed 22 December 2019).

23 'Rikō no ayumi' ['History of Ricoh'], Ricoh, www.jp.ricoh.com/company/history (accessed 22 December 2019).

24 For example see *Fukusei gijutsu to bijutsuka-tachi – Pikaso kara Wohōru made: Fuji Zerox hanga korekushon x Yokohama Bijutsukan/Artists in the Age of Mechanical Reproduction – From Picasso to Warhol: Fuji Xerox Print Collection, Yokohama Museum of Art* (exh. cat.) (Yokohama: Yokohama Museum of Art, 2016).

25 For Kashihara Etsutomu see Kashihara Etsutomu, *'Watshi' no kaitai e: Kashihara Etsutomu no baai/The Deconstruction of the 'I': An Experiment by Kashihara Etsutomu* (exh. cat.) (Osaka: National Museum of Art, 2012).

26 Of these sixteen individuals, fifteen are included in the final portfolio.

27 From the second undertaking onwards, the time was changed to 12.00 p.m.

28 PRI, initial request letter to the 'Niigata Research Institute' (Horikawa Michio).

29 Horikawa Michio, 'Seishin Seirigaku Kenkyūjo no koto 2' ['On Psychophysiology Research Institute'], blog, 24 April 2009, https://niigata-art226.hatenablog.com/entry/20090424/1240506705 (accessed 3 October 2019).

30 Nakahara Yūsuke, 'Ningen to busshitsu no aida: Rokēshon no shisō' ['Between man and matter: Location thinking'], *Sansai* (September 1970), 65.

31 *Ibid.*, 61.

32 *Ibid.*, 62.

33 *Ibid.*, 63.

34 *Ibid.*, 62, 64–5.

35 For collectivism in Japan see Reiko Tomii, 'Introduction: Collectivism in twentieth-century Japanese art with a focus on operational aspects of Dantai', *positions* 21:2 (Spring 2013), 225–67. Ina's PRI project fits my definition of collectivism as 'strategic alliances (primarily) of artists motivated to seek and create alternatives to the existing options, be they artistic/expressive or social/operational or both' (p. 232). See also Reiko Tomii, 'Collectivism in Japan reconsidered: Exploring its operational DNA in the spirit of DIY in the prewar and postwar periods', in Maria Brewińska (curator), *Between Collectivism and Individualism: Japanese Avant-Garde in the 1950s and 1960s* (exh. cat.) (Warsaw: Zachęta – National Gallery of Art, 2021), pp. 111–35. However, in reality, Ina was the conceptual ringleader of the project, which offered an alternative platform, with the participants following the protocols he devised, despite Ina's horizontal vision of the project.

36 One participant not included in the final book is Saitō Yoshiaki.

37 Ina, email to the author.

38 Ina, email to the author.

39 For Shiraga Kazuo and *kōi* see Reiko Tomii, with Fergus McCaffrey, *Kazuo Shiraga: Six Decades* (exh. cat.) (New York: McCaffrey Fine Art, 2009).

40 For terminology related to performance art see Tomii, *Radicalism in the Wilderness*, p. 160.

41 'Ina Ken'ichirō: Mizukara no hen'yō no katei o seikan' ['Ina Ken'ichirō: Quietly gazing at my own transformation'], *Bijutsu techō* 335 (December 1970), 84–7.

42 For Gutai's publicity see Reiko Tomii, 'An experiment in collectivism: Gutai's prewar origin and postwar evolution', in Ming Tiampo and Alexandra Munroe (eds), *Gutai: Splendid Playground* (exh. cat.) (New York: Guggenheim Museum, 2013), pp. 248–53.

43 For Shinohara Ushio see Reiko Tomii and Hiroko Ikegami, *Shinohara Pops! The Avant-Garde Road* (exh. cat.) (Albany, NY: SUNY Press, 2012).

44 Ina recalls that Horikawa sent him a stone for the project (p. 323), but this must be his mistake. According to Horikawa's stone-mailing chronology, he did send a stone outside the project in 1969, with no date recorded. For Horikawa's stone-mailing chronology see Horikawa Michio and Reiko Tomii, *Ishi o okuru mēru āto = Mail Art by Sending Stones* (Tokyo: Genda Kikakushitsu, 2022).

45 Horikawa Michio, email to the author, 22 March 2019.

46 Nakahara, 'Ningen to busshitsu no aida' p. 61.

47 *Ibid.*, p. 62.

9 Mapping a dialogue between some possible origins of IBMR and Art & Language

Ann Stephen

> Being Australian, I have come from what is more or less a state of nothingness.
>
> Ian Burn (1965)[1]

Why did antipodean origins condemn an artist to the prospect of annihilation in the 1960s? How was migration crucial to the formation of some early conceptual art, and how could such work articulate distance and map its possibilities? The following account examines these very real questions through the collaboration of Ian Burn and Mel Ramsden (under the acronym IBMR), beginning in 1965.[2] I will argue that Burn's act of relocating from the regional obscurity of Melbourne to London, and then on to New York, intensified a dialogue about space in his work with Ramsden. It brought to a head Burn's critique of centre–periphery relations and, in his collaboration with Ramsden, fuelled their critique of the objects of late modernism. The proto-conceptual work *Soft-Tape* (1966) and the installations *Comparative Models No. 1* and *Comparative Models No. 2* (1971–72) bookend IBMR's early collaborations, which will be examined alongside some of their writing through these years. Comparison will also be made with several contemporary works of their future collaborators in Art & Language to identify how they mapped a distinct trajectory concerned with displacement, estrangement and difference onto that group's early work.

Burn and Ramsden briefly crossed paths at the National Gallery School in Melbourne in the early 1960s. The school offered conventional training in the skills of painting and life drawing that had remained largely unchanged for over a century. Burn, an older student who had already trained as a carpenter, stayed the course. Ramsden's encounter was, by contrast, fleeting. Burn left Australia in 1964 for Britain, a rite of passage for young, ambitious antipodeans. Ramsden had returned to the UK about a month or so earlier. Though five years younger than Burn, he had travelled around as a child migrant, and at the age of fourteen had returned to his birthplace in Ilkeston, Derbyshire, with his mother, after the death of his father in 1958, before attending Nottingham College of Art.

Though profoundly different in origin and outlook, in London in 1965 they found some common ground. At the margins of an art scene that held little interest for either of them, they both sought out the late modernist American paintings of Frank Stella and Ad Reinhardt. It was while in London that Burn became acutely conscious that his origins outside Euro-American modernism meant next to nothing. Writing home, he distinguished his position from Ramsden's: 'this friend of mine seems to have this problem of working from an extremely negative position towards the positive … being Australian I have come from what is more or less a state of nothingness'.[3] At the time, Ramsden was painting blank monochromes that, Burn later recalled, 'were closely related to Reinhardt – for example, in the works titled *Three black rectangles* he painted three concentric rectangles with the same black paint, but separately, so only the residue of the act of separately painting the rectangles allowed them to be visible'.[4] Such painting required the viewer to move about 'until painted edges catch the light'.[5] His observation on how Ramsden's early paintings mobilised the spectator implied, rather than depicted, a spatial dimension.

Burn would confront the dilemmas of translation over his two-and-a-half years in London. His flatly painted abstractions became increasingly reductive, and in 1966, when he sent home five identical minimal painted grids, they were met with disbelief. He came to realise that there was simply no context for understanding minimal art in Australia, and began to theorise the situation. It became the subject of intense conversation, as Ramsden recalls:

> The dislocations were never a matter of simply being far from home. The problems Ian was talking to me about when his work was shown in Sydney – that it was greeted with blank incomprehension – I was very interested in. That's where the emphasis on context and removal of objects originated. It was looking at the dislocation of 'work', 'object' and 'exhibition'.[6]

Ramsden, alongside painting hermetic monochromes of blank, black reflective surfaces, was planning a series of proto-installation works using diagrams that specified the duration of a sound and plotted the movement of a spectator. It was then that he began to draft a script for *Soft-Tape*, which was a call to dematerialise art:

> Some time ago it occurred to Ian Burn and myself that it was not enough to simply have one's objects hanging about the walls but that some way should be found to put the ideas up there too … Art, by disposing of its material nature may widen its possibilities by expanding our own actions and responses.[7]

Soft-Tape: 'Look with thine ears'

Soft-Tape (see Figure 9.1) is a minimal-looking installation consisting of a tape recorder set on a four-foot-high pedestal, playing in the centre of an otherwise empty room, accompanied by a wall statement. As its title suggests, the recording, on a continuous loop, is almost inaudible – but the desire to

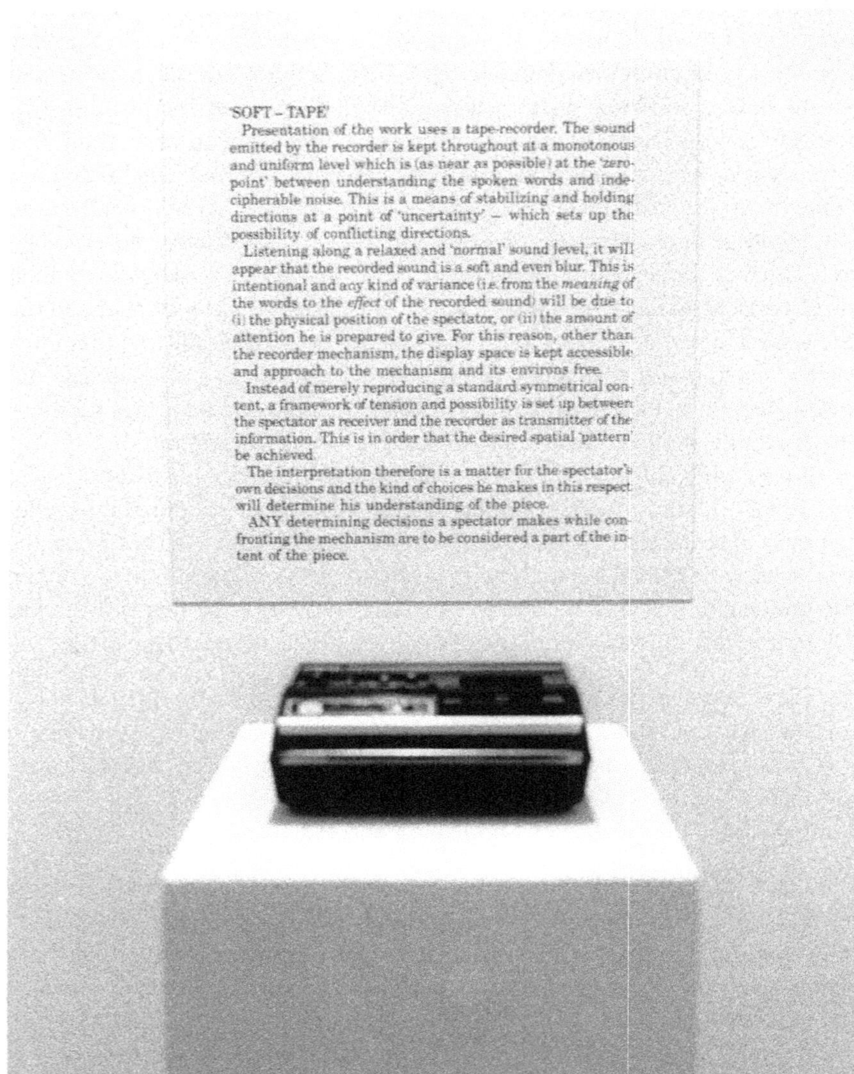

9.1   IBMR, *Soft-Tape*, 1966. Installation for the Biennale of Sydney, 1989.

communicate can be deciphered by close listening. The wall text makes explicit that the sound is deliberately set at 'a monotonous and uniform level … at the "zero-point" between the meaning of the spoken words and mere sound'.[8] Ramsden had speculated on the implications of such a set-up: 'A space could be created entirely by the time it takes somebody to observe the work. Space could be determined only by the length and amount of the observer's involvement. There would be no aesthetic qualities existing outside or independently from this involvement which measures space.'[9]

Soft-Tape proposed to eliminate both conventional art material and aesthetic contemplation, which was dismissed as 'merely reproducing a standard symmetrical content'.[10] Burn and Ramsden imagined a person entering and then straining to discern meaning from the barely audible sound emitted from the tape-machine on the pedestal. The tape spoke of what, in the mid-1960s, were novel conditions for artworks: 'It seems that we are conscious of our art-works no longer "speaking for themselves", they are no longer … self-sufficient. We consider words, either spoken or written, to be a necessary part of our objects.'[11] The introduction of language created the circumstances for a new kind of space. *Soft-Tape* went on to speculate that 'there does seem the possibility of an object which will possess little internal or external determination until perceived … Such a work requires, as possibly its major ingredient, the active participation of a spectator.'[12] The incorporation of the audience suggests the impact of John Cage's avant-garde experiments. From the early 1960s, Cage composed texts that were written to be heard as lectures 'in the course of which, by various means, meaning is not easy to come by'.[13] By having the spectator overstep the normal, invisible distance observed between audience and art object to listen to speech at an almost imperceptible level, *Soft-Tape* creates a Cagean space, precariously balanced between noise and the possibility of meaning.

Burn and Ramsden had also been reading the work of the philosopher Ludwig Wittgenstein, and *Soft-Tape* can be seen to enact his dictum that the limits of language are the limits of the world. In his *Notebooks of 1914–16*, Wittgenstein uses the analogy of a geometric grid to map how particular systems determine what can be seen and described:

> Let us imagine a white surface with irregular black spots on it. We now say: Whatever sort of picture arises in this way I shall always be able to approximate as close as I like to its description by covering the surface with a suitable fine square network and saying of each square that it is white or is black. In this way I shall have brought the description of this surface into a unitary form.[14]

Curiously, for a minimal installation, *Soft-Tape*'s references to art are all to painting. Just as Wittgenstein had used a grid to demonstrate how propositions simultaneously limit *and* articulate space, Ramsden's script for *Soft-Tape* describes the perceptual limits and possibilities confronting abstraction by tracing a line from cubism, through Mondrian to Reinhardt:

> Cubism undermined the normal (standard) level of recognition … When Mondrian spoke of the limiting factor of particular form he meant those natural forms which we could name and which in his eyes prevented the experience

of the universal abstract form. For a wholly abstract art these barriers had to be undermined; and today the barrier which has to be undermined is abstract images themselves … to our minds one must try for an art which is more 'abstract' than abstract art. Ad Reinhardt may have some answers here.[15]

In 1966 Burn and Ramsden would have described themselves as painters, yet both were fascinated by the literal three-dimensional works of minimalism, though their enthusiasm did not extend to fabricating such objects. As the voice on *Soft-Tape* insists: 'It seems to us that light, space, time, materials, motion all exist as a tremendous fabric. Nothing of this "fabric" should be "twisted" or "cut", the world should be left just as it is.'[16] While such a declaration could be read as Duchampian, as the material is ready-made, their refusal to signify – to 'twist' or 'cut' – returned them to Wittgenstein's remarks – that the practice of analytical philosophy necessarily 'leaves everything as it is'.[17] *Soft-Tape* ends with a call to dematerialise art, for 'the streets of our cities are full of objects[;] this may be called the kingdom of the object, oppressive and meaningless. Increasing this ornamentation is not expanding our space-sense but limiting it.'[18]

Its title and material – a tape recorder, at the time an item at the cutting edge of technology – also owed something to Marshall McLuhan's book *Understanding Media: The Extensions of Man*, published two years earlier. *Soft-Tape* draws in part from McLuhan's first section of *Understanding Media* by making an analogy between speech and radio on 'the power of the voice to shape air and space into verbal patterns'.[19] Its components are also described in terms derived from McLuhan's 'electric technology' in specifying the respective roles as that of 'receivers' and 'transmitters'. For instance, the wall text of *Soft-Tape* proposes that 'the desired spatial "pattern" be achieved' once 'an area of tension and possibility is set up between the spectator as receiver and the recorder as transmitter of the information'.[20] McLuhan's utopian optimism envisaged some final condition of enlightened speechlessness in which 'the next logical step would seem to be, not to translate, but to by-pass languages in favour of a general cosmic consciousness'.[21] While *Soft-Tape* is not immune to metaphysics (citing Peter D. Ouspensky on 'a developing space sense' being 'the beginnings of a higher consciousness'), it shifts emphasis to displacement by stressing 'uncertainty' and 'the possibility of conflicting directions'.[22] Much later, in reflecting on the collaborative basis of the work, Ramsden described how, while it was he who had written the script for *Soft-Tape*, the work had been a collaboration, fusing the pair's respective speculations on cultural context:

> We spoke a lot about how things were misunderstood according to the context they were in … None of it would have been about speaking were it not for Ian and he was involved from the very conception of the work even though the writing was done by me … Ian wasn't *interested* in *Soft-Tape,* he was almost its subject matter, he made it what it was about – distance, misunderstanding, contextualisation.[23]

Soft-Tape remained a prototype giving form to a particular kind of 'spacing', filled with conversation, registering the dialogical character of their collaboration. To quote Ramsden, 'It's a migrant object not just an antipodean one and not just in terms of borders and countries but also in terms of the new possibilities of work and exhibition and new problems with these. Nothing could be taken for granted.'[24] *Soft-Tape* implies that displacement creates more than mere misunderstandings – it could be an agency for disrupting the norms and conventions of art.

Back in 1966, when issues of context and locality were foreign to late modernism, Burn and Ramsden's future collaborators in Art & Language were also focused on considerations of space in artworks of virtually no presence. Their proto-conceptual installations, such as the *Air-Conditioning Show* (1966–67) by young English artists Terry Atkinson and Michael Baldwin, speculated on the minimal conditions of exhibition, by exhibiting an empty room fitted with air-conditioning equipment. In the accompanying 'Remarks on air-conditioning', Baldwin wrote that 'neutrality' in New York (in relation to air-conditioned air) 'might indicate an absence of the feeling that what was occurring was technologically miraculous (such feelings are engendered by air-conditioning, in, say, London, whereas people are used to it in New York)', though he later conceded that, even in New York at the time, which he had visited in 1967, 'a certain gleam of technological modernity issued from it'.[25] Another project, *Loop* (1966) by Dave Bainbridge and Harold Hurrell, consisted of a concealed electrified wire under a gallery carpet that, when triggered by spectators, emitted a barely audible signal. Like *Soft-Tape*, these minimal installations shifted attention from object to almost imperceptible elements in a spatial experience.

The following year Atkinson and Baldwin took their reductive tendency to extremes in an absurdist mapping series bearing such titles as *Map of Thirty-Six Square Mile Surface Area of the Pacific Ocean West of Oahu* (1967). The usual conventions indicating scale, longitude and latitude were noted on an otherwise empty square. Another print, *Map to Not Indicate* (1967) names, in the full title, all the US states excluded from the map. The outlines of two states float in an otherwise blank sheet (see Figure 1.2). These representations of the world, 'overlooked by Lewis Carroll', demonstrate with deadpan humour that 'the map is by no means neutral'.[26] It was from these emptied-out spaces that Art & Language's texts and conversations were launched.

Into the centre

The following year, the idea of working in New York – the then indisputable centre of the art world – became a reality for Burn and Ramsden. In July 1967 Burn travelled to North America, arriving via Montreal, where he visited the utopian dream worlds of Expo 67, in particular Buckminster Fuller's vast geodesic dome representing the USA as a futuristic pavilion. It was there that, a month earlier, Canadian media guru McLuhan had launched *Our World*, the first live global satellite broadcast. Interviewed on air just prior to the live cross, McLuhan described both the broadcast and Expo 67 as 'an X-ray mosaic of world cultures'.[27] The televisual link-up cut from the 'super-power' summit in New Jersey, between US President Johnson and USSR President Kosygin, to various quotidian scenes in Canada, Tokyo and finally Melbourne, where in a dark tram-shed two startled workers were interviewed clocking in for their morning shift. Their world appeared remote from the 'electronic age' that McLuhan prophesied. *Soft-Tape* also implied a difference from such instantaneous transmission, because it measured rather than collapsed space, using such unlikely tools as a sound recording and participants moving in space. Arriving in New York City ahead of Ramsden, Burn wrote back describing all the work he was finally able to see, beginning with the *Black Paintings* of Ad Reinhardt, which were of particular significance to his friend:

> You seem to slip into his work, from the 'seeing tactile' *in* the 'seeing illusion', and there is virtually no slip out. Whereas with yours, you have extended the gap between 'tactile' and 'illusion' … so, if you like, your paintings could be called very 'slippery' since there is the effect of instantly slipping out of them. Anyway I like the idea of a wide gap.[28]

Burn's account draws attention to the idea of a space opening up between seeing the tactile/literal and the virtual/illusory. Burn himself began to cast the viewer as the slippery, self-reflexive 'content' of his work in a series of auto-sprayed and polished paintings in *Blue Reflex* (1966–67; see Figure 9.2). When several of these highly reflective panels were hung in his New York loft, the immediate environment became part of their dense blue surface, allowing the viewer to see themselves and their surroundings. Later in 1967 he dispensed with paint in favour of virtually 'invisible' materials such as glass, acetate and mirrors. One such work, *Mirror-Line* (1967–68) consisted of two small mirrors placed at either end of a room and adjusted to reflect each other (and providing partial views of anyone who stepped in between), measuring movement across the space.

For the 1970 New York exhibition *Conceptual Art and Conceptual Aspects*, which Burn cocurated with Kosuth, *Soft-Tape* was not included – although it was listed in the catalogue with the words 'for Australia' added to its title in parenthesis.[29] It was unclear whether the dedication, by stating another destination outside New York, registered a distancing from metropolitan modernism or implied a possible future location. In fact, in early 1972 the Swiss dealer Bruno Bischofberger visited Burn and Ramsden and acquired a version of *Soft-Tape*, including notes; however, it was lost in a fire and never exhibited in Europe. For a quarter of a century *Soft-Tape* was barely seen or heard, though its implications filtered through the works of Burn and Ramsden over the following years as their daily conversations became the basis of a wider collaboration.

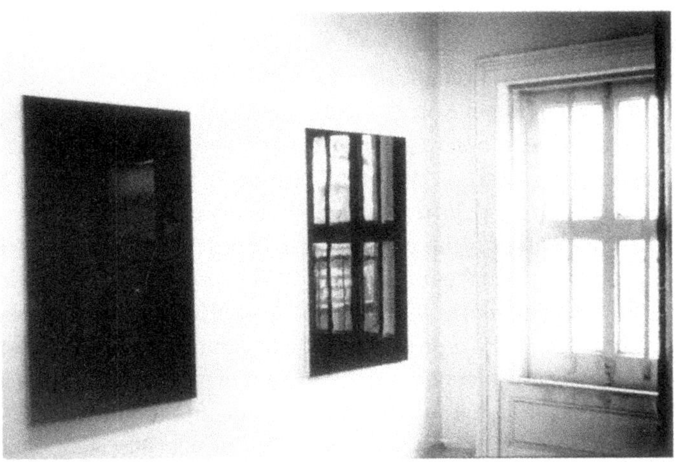

Ian Burn, *Blue Reflex* series, 1967. Installation view, New York.   **9.2**

In 1971, when Burn and Ramsden were invited to exhibit in Melbourne, instead of artwork they sent documentation of their conceptual work in the form of a photocopied book. It was entitled *IBMR: Collected Work 1964–71*, consisting of some forty-five works; the latter half, from 1968 on, were texts. The earliest work included was Ramsden's *Locations* (1964), a spare timber frame photographed standing upright in a Melbourne landscape, made just prior to his return to Europe. As a minimal spatial marker it prefigured the concerns of *Soft-Tape*, also represented in the collection by a floor plan, wall panel and transcription of the tape. Several copies of their unlimited edition were to be placed on chairs in the warehouse gallery.

The Melbourne exhibition that published IBMR's back-list did not mention their new involvement in the transatlantic partnership of Art & Language. By 1971, five of their texts had already been published in the British-based conceptual art journal *Art-Language*.[30] In August 1971, when there was a brief attempt to bureaucratise Art & Language and its journal, Burn and Ramsden would formally join the collective.[31]

INDEX 01 and *Comparative Models*: An alternative mapping

It was the major Kassel-based exhibition, Documenta V, that proved to be a decisive moment, when their writings were incorporated with those of the five other participants of Art & Language into the grand scheme of *Index 01*.[32] This project has been variously described as 'a discursive map', 'a manual hypertext system that allows for the interactive associative linking of ideas' and 'a vast mulch-box of Conceptual Art's internal history'.[33] *Index 01* took the physical form of eight metal filing cabinets and wall charts when it was installed in Kassel, West Germany, in 1972. The initial idea for the Art & Language *Index* had sprung from conversations with Joseph Kosuth during Baldwin's visit to New York in late 1971, in response to the invitation to participate in the project. The indexing system was accompanied by an *Alternate Map for Documenta*, produced by Art & Language in the UK (see Figure 9.3). Its text began: 'Indexing problems are quite interesting. They are coincident with the difficulties encountered in mapping the space in which our conversation takes place.'[34] The IBMR texts were tabulated into its complex internal relations along with the other published and unpublished writings of Art & Language. It was a project riven with doubt, as William Wood has since observed: 'the space it "mapped" was a territory of pitfalls, refusals and resistances that points to the difficulties of mounting critique in the form of art'.[35]

The deserved attention that the *Indexing* project has generated in recent years has obscured alternative strategies intended to reorientate the work of Art & Language in New York. While, earlier, priority had been given to a syntactical approach to describing the meaning of a sentence in isolation, Burn and Ramsden now opted for its capacity to interpret 'the manner in which contexts and public settings determine how a sentence is understood'.[36] They argued that to redefine the function of the artist, 'the "institutionalized" network which surrounds and supports the production of art-works ... the gallery, critical theory, books, art magazines, etc' must all be seen 'as constitutive rather than incidental features of an art-world'.[37] Their approach considered matters of context and ideology, premised upon 'the objectivity of sense ... to erase the opinion of the artist as irrational and as a social liability'.[38] Like the *Indexing* under way in England, their direction had been clarified by a controversy in the philosophy of science, instigated by Thomas Kuhn's book *The Structure of Scientific Revolutions*. Kuhn's 'paradigm of normal science' – of a community with a shared material practice – provided them with a convincing description of how 'the prevailing mechanistic art-world' maintains 'intrinsic value properties'.[39] Moreover, Kuhn's investigation of paradigm shifts, of how change occurs in ways of seeing, was close to their own sense of crisis. They could identify with his account of revolution as 'a special sort of change involving a certain sort of reconstruction of group commitments. But it need not be a large change, nor need it seem revolutionary to those outside a single community'.[40]

Prompted by an invitation to exhibit from Ileana Sonnabend in New York, Burn and Ramsden proceeded to make annotations on *Artforum*, in a work titled *Comparative Models* (1971–72). However, the new requirements of the Art & Language 'formalisation' led to Burn and Ramsden abandoning the show with Sonnabend. They continued nonetheless, making a large public

ALTERNATE MAP FOR DOCUMENTA
(BASED ON CITATION A)

KEY TO MAP

'+' AT THE ORIGIN OF A VERTICAL/HORIZONTAL AXIS INDICATES A COMPATIBILITY BETWEEN THE RELEVANT DOCUMENTS CITED IN THE LEFT-HAND COLUMN AND ON THE TOP ROW OF THE MATRIX:

'—' INDICATES AN INCOMPATIBILITY:

'T' INDICATES THAT THE RELEVANT DOCUMENTS DO NOT SHARE THE SAME LOGICAL/ETHICAL SPACE.

TERRY ATKINSON/DAVID BAINBRIDGE
IAN BURN/MICHAEL BALDWIN
CHARLES HARRISON/HAROLD HURRELL
JOSEPH KOSUTH/MEL RAMSDEN

THE ART & LANGUAGE INSTITUTE
PAUL MAENZ/KÖLN/JUNI 15

Art & Language, *Alternate Map for Documenta (Based on Citation A)*, 1972.
Poster, lithograph on newsprint, 72.5 cm × 50.6 cm.

wall display 'interrupting' the New York art journal with same-sized sheets of pinned pages of their annotations. The art journal's pre-eminent position at that time reflected and reinforced the hegemonic role of New York in the international art market as the capital of late modernism. *Comparative Models No. 1* laid out all the pages of the December 1971 issue of *Artforum* edge-to-edge with their coloured insertions in a continuous band around the walls of a gallery (see Figure 9.4). The display gave dramatic physical expression to the proportional relations between the intellectual content and the commercial infrastructure, with their 'modelling' highlighting points of conflict between the two discourses. Their typewritten pages break up the seamless narrative of relations within the art world constituted by *Artforum*, but in the process their own coherence is fragmented, making it impossible to read their annotations as an essay, an effect enhanced by each sheet bearing a headline, such as 'PARADIGM SHIFTS' and 'PERFORMANCE'. When it was exhibited in Paris, Burn and Ramsden sent the following instructions to the dealer, Daniel Templon, to distinguish the two elements clearly:

> The yellow is meant as a 'code' colour (as is used in filing systems). When people look at the work on the wall, they must be able to pick out easily our introduction and annotations. The work is a concept for an exhibition (or display)[;] it is not a concept for 'a work of art'.[41]

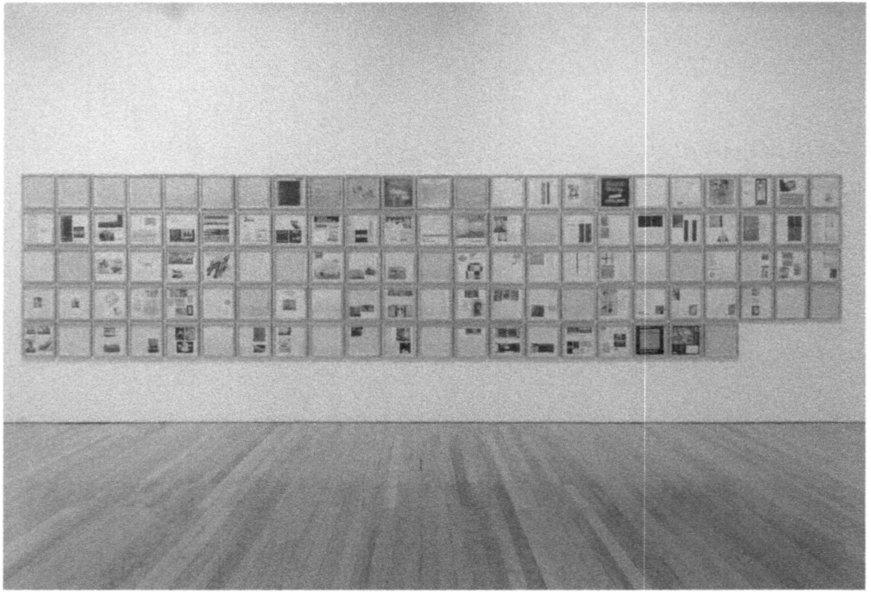

9.4   IBMR, *Comparative Models No. 1*, 1971. Annotated pages of *Artforum* (November 1971). 98 pages, 27 cm × 27 cm; 14 pages, 26.4 cm × 26.4 cm, dimensions variable.

The disclaimer reveals the contradictory ambitions of such a work. When the artists declared *Comparative Models* as not a work of art, its status as something like a wall installation and an exhibition required the viewer to use the gallery as if it were a reading room or library. Their notes were proposed as a model of a possible art world to exhibit a 'knowledge of the framework or rules', a distinction they derived from Noam Chomsky, who argued that 'in learning a foreign language we learn the "rules" (the grammar) of that language, that which any natural speaker tacitly knows. We are not credited with an understanding of the language if we can only repeat sentences whose meaning and composition we have previously been taught.'[42] Certain 'rules' are shown to operate in writing by 'works of art dealing in quality not meaning'.[43] Their alternative was conceived as 'a set of questions to be asked (meaning) and not a certain property to be looked for (quality).'[44] This first set of annotations remained quite schematic, listing the weaknesses of the 'body' they had invaded – it would be another six months before *Artforum* received further interrogation.

In the meantime, Burn and Ramsden separately visited Australia in 1972 after an absence of eight years. While both had maintained contact through writing and exhibiting, their visits to the far-flung periphery not only provoked considerable debate about Art & Language in Melbourne and Sydney, it convinced them to map the unequal character of international exchange. Ramsden spoke at the Preston Institute of Technology – a Melbourne art school – in March 1972, and their jointly written text, titled 'The artist as victim', was subsequently published in the Contemporary Art Society of Australia's *Broadsheet*. Ramsden acknowledged that a 'local artist was far more likely to be a victim of entrenched cultural convention than his counterpart overseas' because of 'relative isolation and lack of any comparative models'.[45] He clearly had in mind their ongoing project on *Artforum* when he called for artists 'to reflexively scrutinize their origins'.[46]

Ramsden would return to New York via Europe, where he briefly worked on the installation of the *Indexing* project at Documenta V with others in Art & Language. His return coincided with the tenth anniversary edition of *Artforum* in September 1972. He and Burn seized upon it as the ideal host for *Comparative Models No. 2* (1972; see Figure 9.5). The front cover of *Artforum*, a black-and-white photograph of the complete, framed set of all the preceding covers mounted on the wall of the New York editorial office, was their opening panel. It introduced their multicoloured sheets of annotations, inserted between the contents and advertising pages. The anniversary had come at an inauspicious moment, during a period of deepening crisis in contemporary art marked by a depressed market with no new vanguard visible on the horizon. Four prominent New York art critics – Lawrence Alloway, Max Kozloff, Rosalind Krauss and Francis O'Connor – were commissioned to present 'a synoptic overview of the art ambience during the last decade'.[47] These commissioned essays provide a defence

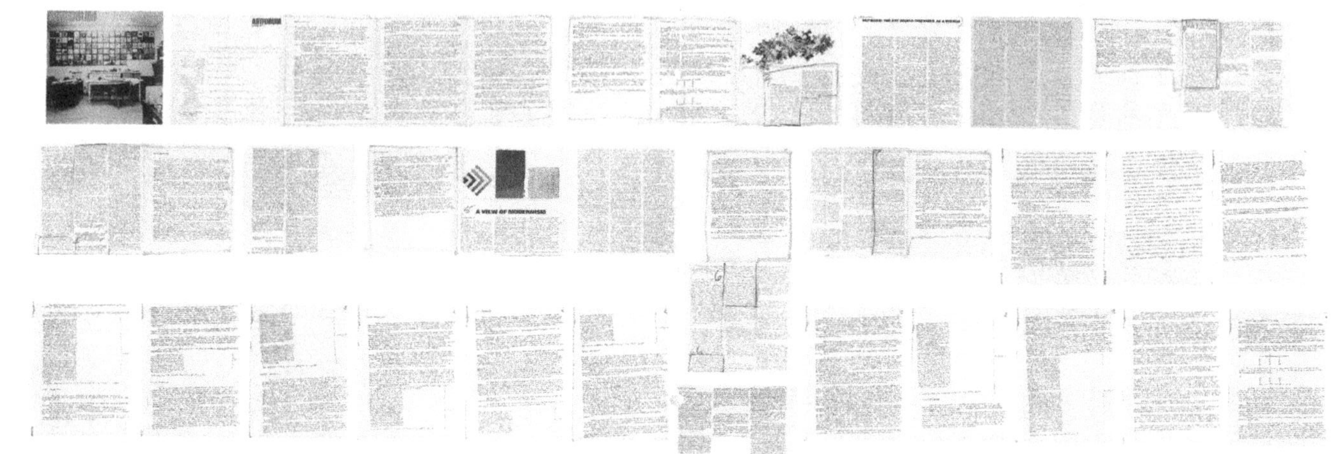

Comparative Models (Version 2), Study, 1972
Felt-tip pen and pencil on *Artforum* magazine pages, reprographics, collage and mixed media
26 elements of various dimensions

9.5   IBMR, *Comparative Models No. 2,* 1972. Annotated pages of *Artforum* (September 1972). Dimensions variable.

for late modernism and its institutions while reluctantly singling out conceptual art as the only contemporary art movement, although most of the work referred to was, by then, five years old. The IBMR annotations addressed the audience as collaborators: 'Remember that in constructing alternatives the aim is to get standpoints to compete, not to replace one monolith with another … Arguing in order to "correct" the *Artforum* model is silly. To show that there may be alternate ways of interpretation is not.'[48] They listed the paradigms of modernism – of the artist as a special individual, of art as an expression of special perceptions and of experience as a fact of nature – to arm their readers for combat, arguing that 'making trouble is a good start: both internally to our own theories and externally by using these theories to criticise other points of view'.[49]

Their first annotation reduced Lawrence Alloway's essay, 'Network: The art world described as a system', to an equation, which they dubbed a 'Heuristic Simplification (H.S.1) of the individualist model (M1)', and countered with an 'alternative equation of a historical materialist model (M2)'.[50] They acknowledged that the abbreviation was 'necessarily over-robust' to 'make different *facts* known'.[51] They argued, to follow the individualistic logic of *Artforum*, that given 'our knowledge of Manet and the origins of modern art, Art & Language work is really a surrogate genre scene'.[52]

Max Kozloff's *Artforum* essay, 'The trouble with art-as-idea', was a litany of complaints that singled out for particular attention 'the inability of the various media – process, conceptual, etc – to come to terms with what can be said of experience'.[53] Their annotations applied a Kuhnian analogy, likening his account of conceptual art to 'someone looking over Einsteinian mechanics using the postulates of Euclid'.[54]

Rosalind Krauss's essay, 'A view of modernism', opened on a hagiographic anecdote featuring Michael Fried's defence of Frank Stella during his show *Three American Painters*, which ends on a grand riposte. 'What he would like more than anything else is to paint like Velasquez. But what he knows is that that is an option not open to him. So he paints stripes. He wants to be Velasquez so he paints stripes.'[55] IBMR refused such transcendence by demonstrating that formalism excluded many practices, such that 'alternatives look like crimes against nature … all you can do is refine and adjust'.[56] They warned the viewer to beware of 'the monolithic Modernist ontology, with its pious appeals to "experience" etc. [that] exerts a psychological grip and should be combated maliciously'.[57]

The annotations were not confined to writers associated with the formalist canon. The final essay was by Francis O'Connor, a social historian of art, whose recent book, *Art for the Millions*, had documented the Federal Government's art programmes of the New Deal era in the 1930s.[58] They accused his essay of being riddled with the ideology of possessive individualism. The popular notion that 'art evolves from the primordial experience of seeing' they declared 'a version of social Darwinism … with its platitudes about genius. The danger in education of such 'no-rules' genetic/psychological expressionism just renders the student harmless.'[59] They warned that anyone 'reluctant to form any widespread and workable concept of community' would become 'increasingly ignorant of the dynamics of the very community within which he or she is enmeshed'.[60]

When Burn returned from visiting Australia in late 1972 he made metropolitan–provincial relations a pressing subject matter for Art & Language New York, struck by how dependency had a stranglehold on Australian artists. There were small cells of followers, as the *Art-Language* journal had developed a readership among a few young artists there, such as John Nixon and George Collin, both recent graduates of the National Gallery School (where Burn and Ramsden had met a decade earlier). Collin and Nixon positioned their work within the journal's framework as 'an *Invisible College* network of research … as an experimental annex to other A-L investigations'.[61] They maintained an intense correspondence with Burn and Ramsden in New York, writing about their individual and collaborative projects. However, Burn was troubled by the positions he confronted in conversations with several other artists who saw themselves as avant-garde, either calling for a complete withdrawal or an uncritical embrace of the global flow of cultural information.

Back in New York, they set out to map the spaces between different contexts. Their first effort was an essay written in early 1973 that posed several provocative questions about how contemporary art, when shown in different contexts, was misunderstood, and the problems attendant upon translating cultures across different contexts.

> In what ways is a travelling exhibition of contemporary American art useful or destructive? From where does the information come for an earthwork to make sense in Australia? Can we presuppose that the viewer of a work by Donald Judd in Paris gets the same information as a viewer in New York? Why do European collectors prefer Art & Language texts in English over translated versions? Why is it that the political concerns of many South American artists have the effect of relegating them to minor artist status in New York?[62]

In each instance, the encounter is underpinned by issues of displacement and loss for those on the periphery. Such a questioning of the 'hierarchical' traffic in contemporary art prefigures by several decades the global turn in late-twentieth-century cultures. This early attempt to critique New York internationalism employs blunt political rhetoric: 'a cultural impotence for artists of provincial contexts … sustains a cultural imperialist policy on the part of those in the dominant context'.[63] Their framework was derived from certain theoretical implications about the limits of intercultural translation raised in the philosophical work of Wittgenstein and Willard Van Orman Quine. For instance, they adapted Quine's dilemma concerning the indeterminacy of meaning to the problems of translating late modernism.

It is not possible to predict (create) what are likely to be significant innovations in a context other than one's own. It means that predictions – such as those 'innovated' by say (say) Jasper Johns, Frank Stella and Donald Judd – about what was problematic, generative and thus significant in a particular context were essentially and necessarily internal predictions and in no sense could have been made externally.[64]

In *Word and Object*, Quine had posited a provincialism at the heart of the dilemma of the indeterminacy of meaning when he asked about the possibility of translating theoretical questions.

Who would undertake to translate 'Neutrinos lack mass' into the jungle language? … We may expect him [the physicist] to plead in extenuation that the natives lack the requisite concepts … It is of such sentences above that Wittgenstein's dictum holds true. 'Understanding a sentence means understanding a language.' … We may alternatively wonder at the inscrutability of the native mind and wonder at how very much like us the native is, where in the one case we have done a more thorough job of reading our own provincial modes into the native's speech.[65]

While the Eurocentricity of Quine's terms was uncontroversial at the time, another crucial source from anthropology was premised upon issues of race. The essay ends on a call for 'better anthropology, of acknowledging what is actually involved in each case'.[66] It echoed the words of the renowned Africanist anthropologist Melville Herskovits, who had documented the retention of traditional African beliefs and practices among the diasporas in North America. He had refuted assumptions underpinning the racist myth of one-sided acculturation. Herskovits described provincialism as a situation in which 'significant judgments are being made according to the rules governing behavior in an ideologically different context'[67] – a call the essay repeated word for word. Such cultural relativism was inconclusive about the pluralist scenario entailed, hopeful that it might 'generate insights presently not available in critical writing … to allow for more dialectical and more equitable relations between contexts'.[68] Up to this point, such issues had not entered into the equations of Art & Language, as conflict rather than equilibrium was envisaged as the product of their negative dialectics. Significantly, the essay was published in Australia, in the first issue of George Collin's Melbourne journal *Art Dialogue*, under the title 'Provincialism'.[69]

The implications envisaged in such texts and installations towards developing a community practice were already taking place within their immediate circle in Art & Language, New York. As Kosuth, Ramsden and Burn were joined by others – first by Michael Corris in 1972, then Preston Heller, Andrew Menard and Terry Smith in 1973 – their internal debates became the subject of a major mapping project for the New York group.[70] The expanded sociality, albeit entirely young and male, with Burn the oldest at thirty-one, would prove an explosive brew.

It was in Sydney, the original destination for the exhibition back in 1966, that *Soft-Tape* was finally reconstructed as part of the 1990 Biennale of Sydney curated by René Block. In the Biennale, the work shared a floor in a warehouse space with *33 1/3*, John Cage's 1969 installation for 100 records and twelve record players, and both were precursors to many subsequent installations and sound environments. In this context, and with the hindsight of history, *Soft-Tape* appears to have anticipated a discursive mode that adopted a different strategy from that of Cage's libertarian anarchism. Looking back, Burn wrote: 'Communication, we argued, isn't just a semantic or conceptual problem of translation … but is also importantly a spatial problem. *Soft-Tape* proposes there is no simple (transparent) "window" between contexts.'[71] Burn now articulated how meaning was contingent upon the spectator's position within a complexity of geopolitical and temporal conditions. In the mid-1960s the work had no presence, and in retrospect it seemed to Burn to have been 'conceived as having more of a future than a past'.[72] After encountering *Soft-Tape* in the Sydney Biennale, Lawrence Weiner, one of the other artists in the early *Conceptual Art and Conceptual Aspects* exhibition, commented that 'it was like your conscience whispering to you'.[73] When exhibited in New York in *Global Conceptualism* in 1999, the regional accent sounded distinctly foreign.[74] After *Soft-Tape* was shown in the Biennale of Sydney, Ramsden concluded that 'in retrospect, the fact that it concerned itself with an antipodean distancing is critical for Ian', adding that 'the content of the taped text was also something that counted'.[75]

A new spatial awareness arose in the conceptual art of Burn and Ramsden from dilemmas about context and displacement. Their act of shifting across hemispheres through the 1960s and relocating for a decade to the cosmopolitan centre of New York prompted an intense dialogue about space and culminated in their critique of late modernism. Their predicament recalls the fact that 'historically, in the European mind Terra Australia (south land) was always defined by position rather than knowledge. It was always the "other" side, the antipodes, already an imaginary displacement'.[76] Such alienation was experienced by those who moved to and from metropolitan centres, not only antipodeans but also migrants. Among their achievements was the mapping of a discursive space that recognised dislocation and decentralising impulses, something not generally analysed in the 1960s and 1970s.

Notes

1 The acronym 'IBMR' was adopted by Ian Burn and Mel Ramsden when they published *IBMR: Collected Works* in 1971, signalling the collaborative nature of their practice. The quotation is from Ian Burn, letter to the artist Paul Partos, September 1965, Burn Archive, estate of the artist.

2 Elsewhere I have focused on how their conceptual work sought the limits of perception: Ann Stephen 'Soft-talk/soft-tape: The early collaborations of Ian Burn and Mel Ramsden', in Michael Corris (ed.), *Conceptual Art: Theory, Myth and Practice* (Cambridge: Cambridge University Press, 2004); and chapters in my monograph, Ann Stephen, *On Looking at Looking: The Art and Politics of Ian Burn* (Melbourne: Miegunyah Press, Melbourne University Publishing, 2006).

3 Burn, letter to Partos.

4 Ian Burn, 'Ian Burn and Imants Tillers in conversation', *Art Monthly Australia* 59 (May 2003), 17.

5 Ian Burn, *Looking at Seeing and Reading, July 1–31, 1993* (Sydney: Ivan Dougherty Gallery, 1993), paragraph 17.

6 Mel Ramsden, email to the author, 12 June 2021.

7 IBMR, *Soft-Tape*, sound-recorded text (London, 1966).

8 IBMR, *Soft-Tape* wall statement. The original work was sold to Bruno Bischofberger in 1972 and subsequently destroyed in a fire. The spoken text was reprinted in the Art & Language Eindhoven catalogue in 1980 and the wall statement was republished in Charles Harrison, *Essays on Art & Language* (Oxford: Blackwell, 1991), Plate 15.

9 Mel Ramsden, 'Unpublished notes', *Spectators* (September 1966), amongst the documents relating to *Soft-Tape*.

10 IBMR, *Soft-Tape* wall statement.

11 IBMR, *Soft-Tape*, transcript.

12 *Ibid.*

13 John Cage, *Silence: Lectures and Writings* (London: Marion Boyars Publishers Ltd, 1987), p. 195.

14 Ludwig Wittgenstein, *Notebooks of 1914–16*, extract made by Mel Ramsden in London, 1966, amongst the documents associated with *Soft-Tape*.

15 *Soft-Tape*, transcript, 1966.

16 *Ibid.*

17 Ludwig Wittgenstein, *Philosophical Investigations*, Vol. I (Oxford: Blackwell, 1958), p. 124; commentary by Ray Monk, *Ludwig Wittgenstein: The Duty of Genius* (New York: Vintage, 1991), p. 533.

18 Monk, *Ludwig Wittgenstein*, p. 533.

19 Marshall McLuhan, *Understanding Media: The Extensions of Man* (London: Routledge and Kegan Paul, 1964), p. 90.

20 IBMR, *Soft-Tape* wall statement.

21 McLuhan, *Understanding Media*. In Part II of *Understanding Media*, McLuhan presents a survey of communication modes beginning with 'The spoken word' and ending on 'Automation or cybernation' (p. 90). Some years later Art & Language published a rebuttal of McLuhan's thinking: Bernard Bihari 'Marshal [*sic*] McLuhan and the behavioral sciences', *Art-Language* 1:3 (June 1970), 11–28.

22 IBMR, *Soft-Tape* wall statement.

23 Mel Ramsden, letter to the author, 1998.

24 Mel Ramsden, email to the author, 12 June 2021.

25 Michael Baldwin, 'Remarks on air-conditioning, 1967': *Art & Language in Practice*, Vol. I (Barcelona: Fundacio Antoni Tapies, 1999), p. 212. Documentation for the *Air Conditioning Show*, with the support of Robert Smithson, was published in *Arts Magazine* in November 1967. The work was first realised as an exhibition arranged by Joseph Kosuth at the School of Visual Arts in New York in 1972. See documentation in *Art & Language Uncompleted: The Philippe Méaille Collection* (Barcelona: Museu d'art Contemporani de Barcelona, 2015), pp. 76–9.

26 Art & Language and Carles Guerra, 'Selection of works, from 1 to 11', in *Art & Language Uncompleted*, p. 112.

27 '*Our World*: Five continents linked by satelite' (1967), CBC Archives, www.cbc.ca/player/play/1834829313 (accessed 15 September 2020).

28 Ian Burn, letter to Mel Ramsden, August 1967, Burn Archive, estate of the artist.

29 Ian Burn and Mel Ramsden, *The Grammarian* (New York: 1970), Section 9.

30 The early IBMR texts published in *Art-Language* were Ian Burn, 'Dialogue', and Mel Ramsden, 'Notes on geneologies', *Art-Language* 1:2 (1970), 22 and 84 respectively; and Society of Art and Analyses, 'Proceedings' #1 and #2, and Mel Ramsden, 'Art-Enquiry (2)', *Art-Language*, 1:3 (1970), pp. 1–3 and pp. 4–6 respectively.

31 As Ramsden recalls: 'Art & Language was turned into a company in the UK, with resolutions, treasurer, managing director. Ian and I were present during these "negotiations" and we were invited to "join" at that time. This all lasted about 3 weeks but it did eventually turn into Joseph Kosuth's fantasy, "The Art & Language Institute" and this was how it was exhibited at Documenta V.' Email to author, 12 June 2021.

32 By 1972 the names of Charles Harrison, Philip Pilkington and David Rushton had been added to those of Michael Baldwin, Terry Atkinson, Dave Bainbridge, Harold Hurrell, Ramsden and Burn.

33 Michael Corris, 'An invisible college in an Anglo-American world', in Corris, *Conceptual Art*, p. 7; Edward A. Shanken, 'Art in the information age', in Corris, *Conceptual Art*, p. 147; and John Roberts, 'Conceptual art and imageless Truth', in Corris, *Conceptual Art*, p. 322.

34 A lithographic poster by Art & Language, titled *Documenta Memorandum (Indexing)* (Broadsheet), 1972.

35 William Wood, 'We are a cell aren't we? Art & Language and the *Documenta Index*' (Ph.D. dissertation, University of British Columbia, 1992), p. 14.

36 Ian Burn and Mel Ramsden, 'Some questions on the characterization of questions', *Art-Language* 2:2 (1972), 1–15 (p. 3).

37 Ian Burn and Mel Ramsden, 'The artist as victim', *Contemporary Art Society of Australia NSW Broadsheet* (May 1972), 108.

38 Ian Burn and Mel Ramsden, 'Four wages of sense', *Art-Language* 2:2 (1972), 36.

39 Burn and Ramsden, 'Some questions on the characterization of questions', p. 8.

40 Thomas S. Kuhn, *The Structure of Scientific Revolutions*, 2nd edn (Chicago: University of Chicago Press, 1970), p. 181. Caroline A. Jones examines the connections between Kuhn's concept of a paradigm and Michael Fried's formalist criticism, making a convincing case for the paradigm as 'a tool of modernism and a modernist tool'. Michael Fried had confessed to 'significant affinities' with Kuhn as part of his teleological claims for late modernist painting, without 'theorising the paradigm's

replacement'. Caroline A. Jones, 'The modernist paradigm: The art world and Thomas Kuhn', *Critical Inquiry* (Spring 2000), 502, 527.

41 Ian Burn, letter to Daniel Templon (1972), Burn Archive, Estate of the artist. Templon exhibited *Comparative Models No. 1* in Milan in April 1972, and at 'Studio D'Arte' in Naples and Paris in September 1972. *Comparative Models No. 1* annotated in the magazine *Artforum*, December 1971; its subjects were Robert Pincus-Witten, 'Bochner at MOMA: Three ideas and seven procedures'; Lawrence Alloway, 'Color, culture, the stations: Notes on the Barnett Newman Memorial Exhibition'; Rosalind Krauss, 'Stella's new work and the problem of series'; John Elderfield, 'Mondrian, Newman, Noland: Two notes on changes of style'; and Willis Domingo, 'Meaning in the art of Duchamp'. There is a second version of *Comparative Models* in yellow and another in many different colours. Daniel Templon even photocopied one, which was shown (version 1) at Lia Rumma in Naples in 1971.

42 *Comparative Models No. 1*, 'Competence and performance', 4, which cites Noam Chomsky, *Aspects of the Theory of Syntax* (Cambridge, MA: MIT Press, 1965).

43 *Comparative Models No. 1*, Annotation No. 2, 8; Annotation No. 3, 9.

44 *Comparative Models No. 1*, Annotation No. 8, 14.

45 Burn and Ramsden, 'The artist as victim', described as an amended version of a talk presented on 28 March 1972 at the Art Department, Preston Institute of Technology, Melbourne.

46 *Ibid.*, p. 129.

47 Editorial statement, *Artforum* 11:1 (September 1972), 3.

48 *Comparative Models No. 2*, p. 1, first exhibited at the Galerie Daniel Templon, Paris, 1973, republished in *Art & Language: Van Abbemuseum, Eindoven, 1980* (Eindoven: Van Abbemuseum, 1980), 51–62; this pagination is used in subsequent citing. Kuhn's structure of incommensurability was supplemented by other philosophers of science: Karl Popper, Paul Feyeraband, Wilfrid Sellars and Norwood Russell Hanson, as well as Chomsky on linguistics, Maurice Mandelbaum on historical materialism and C. B. Macpherson on the political theory of possessive individualism.

49 *Comparative Models No. 2*, 'Heuristic Simplification (H.S.1)', 53–4.

50 *Comparative Models No. 2*, annotation on 'H.S.1'; Lawrence Alloway, 'Network: The art world described as a system', *Artforum* 11:1 (1972), 54–5.

51 Alloway, 'Network', p. 56.

52 *Ibid.*

53 *Comparative Models No. 2*, annotation on 'H.S.2', 32–6; Max Kozloff, 'The trouble with art-as-idea', *Artforum* 11:1 (September 1972), 57–8. The following year a rebuttal by Andrew Menard and Preston Heller was published in *Artforum*, entitled 'Kozloff: Criticism in absentia', *Artforum* 11:6 (February 1973). Heller and Menard subsequently came to work with Art & Language, New York.

54 Kozloff, 'The trouble with art-as-idea', p. 58.

55 Rosalind Krauss, 'A view of modernism', *Artforum* 11:1 (September 1971), pp. 48–51.

56 *Comparative Models No. 2*, annotation on 'H.S.4'; Rosalind Krauss, 'A view of modernism', p. 59.

57 *Ibid.*, p. 59.

58 *Art for the Millions*, ed., Francis V. O'Connor (Boston: New York Graphic Society, 1973).

59 Francis V. O'Connor, 'Notes on patronage: The 1960s', *Artforum* 11:1 (1972), 60–2.

60 *Comparative Models No. 2*, annotation H.S.6 and annotation H.S.7; Francis V. O'Connor, 'Notes on patronage: The 1960s', p. 62.

61 John Nixon, letter to Ian Burn and Mel Ramsden, Melbourne, 20 November 1973.

62 The essay bore the names of both Ian Burn and Mel Ramsden when published in the Belgium catalogue *Deurle 11.7.73*, though only Burn's name was used in 'Art is what we do, culture is what we do to other arists', *Art Dialogue* 1:1 (1973), 131–39. Burn later explained, when republished in *Dialogue: Writings in Art History* (North Sydney: Allen & Unwin, 1991), p. 131, that the essay was developed in part 'through conversations with Mel Ramsden and Terry Smith'.

63 *Ibid.*, p. 136.

64 *Ibid.*, p. 137.

65 W. V. O. Quine, *Word and Object* (Cambridge, MA: MIT Press, 1960), pp. 73–9.

66 Burn [and Ramsden], 'Art is what we do', p. 139.

67 M. J. Herskovits, *Cultural Relativism: Perspective on Cultural Pluralism* (New York: Random House, 1973), p. 136.

68 *Ibid.*, p. 139.

69 For a European audience it was retitled, in a parody of Carl Andre's words, 'Art is what we do, culture is what is done to us', to read, 'Art is what we do, culture is what we do to other artists' – and Ramsden was added as its coauthor.

70 Christopher Gilbert, 'Art & Language, New York, discusses its social relations in "The Lumpen Headache"', in Michael Corris (ed.), *Conceptual Art: Theory, Myth, and Practice* (Cambridge: Cambridge University Press), 2004, Chapter 15.

71 Ian Burn, *Soft-Tape*, ed. René Block, in *The Readymade Boomerang: Certain Relations in 20th Century Art* (Sydney: Art Gallery of New South Wales, 1990), p. 282. Burn had proposed the reconstruction to René Block, director of the 1990 Biennale of Sydney, whose selection emphasised the 'Duchamp effect' in performance and experimental music.

72 Art & Language, 'Moti memoria', in John Roberts (ed.), *The Impossible Document: Photography and Conceptual Art in Britain 1966–1976* (London: Camerawork/Camerawords, 1997), pp. 59–60.

73 Ian Burn, letter to Mel Ramsden (1990), Burn Archive, Estate of the artist.

74 I owe this insight to Geoff Batchen, who visited *Global Conceptualism* in New York in 1999. For those who knew Ian, the work is haunted by the sound of his voice.

75 Art & Language, 'Making art from a different place', in *Ian Burn: Minimal-Conceptual work 1965–1970* (Perth: Art Gallery of Western Australia, 1992), p. 12.

76 Ian Burn, 'The metropolis is only half the horizon', in Anthony Bond (ed.), *The Boundary Rider: 9th Biennale of Sydney* (Sydney: Biennale of Sydney, 1992), p. 33.

Part IV
Itineraries

Alena J. Williams

One of the lasting impacts on the public imagination in the prelude of the United States National Space and Aeronautics Agency's Apollo missions was the imaging of the 'whole earth' in 1967 – a spectacular, singular view of the planet from the vantage point of space.[1] As many scholars and curators have pointed out, in this new visual representation, the planet was no longer a staccato patchwork of disparate histories, cultures, landscapes and experiences, but a unified whole nestled within an infinitely large cosmological context.[2] To this day, humanity continues to understand the earth primarily by way of two-dimensional visual representations – cartography, mapping and digital imaging techniques; as scholar Laura Kurgan intones, by returning the gaze back towards earth, remote sensing and orbital satellites have only intensified the highly militarised, networked nature of global politics.[3] Yet, what is often neglected about these historical developments is the vast range of optical instrumentation that NASA, and corporations such as Eastman Kodak, deployed not only in their media production of space exploration, but also in the scientific experimentation taking place on board these missions and in the celestial milieu itself.[4]

Once the moon became more accessible to human observation, NASA immediately documented, charted and carved it up for study – into what scholar Lisa Parks has identified as a 'televisual' spectacle.[5] It was ultimately the audiovisual transmission of the Apollo moon landing in 1969 that seized American artist Nancy Holt's imagination as a renewed recognition of the *relation between* planetary and celestial milieus; these recordings conscripted extraterrestrial space into a new understanding of 'the real'. As I argue, Holt mobilised this new understanding of space by way of conceptualist practice, which took shape in her early concrete poetry, and in the patterns of signification found in the paper- and lens-based documentation of her major outdoor sculpture *Sun Tunnels* (1973–76) in the Great Basin Desert, Utah. Much like NASA's photographic mapping of the moon through the US Geological Survey, Holt's cameras have served to produce a continuous flow of testimonials and documents, becoming what urban planner Kevin Lynch has called 'a basis for the ordering of knowledge'.[6] Holt's interest in the earth's relationship to its cosmological context engaged the epistemic nature of celestial phenomena in her projects, by coordinating her work with their paths across the sky, among other interventions.[7] In this chapter, I examine Holt's conceptual strategies of the late-1960s and the 1970s, which not only centred embodied experience, but also deviated from normative forms of cartographic representation and signification.

Concrete poetry: Conceptual constellations

Nancy Holt first began composing concrete poems in 1966, shortly before the publication of American Fluxus artist Emmett Williams's 1967 *An Anthology of Concrete Poetry*.[8] Williams's publication featured German poet Eugen Gomringer's compositions among the work of scores of international poets who began working with language in both visual and semantic terms. Much like conceptualist art practices, which took shape in the wake of modernism's global abstractions in the 1960s, concrete poetry centres language within a visual schema of signification. The modernist imperative of leaving behind definitive marks and traces – culminating in the work of American artist Jackson Pollock – was renounced by conceptualists in favour of systems of dialogic exchange, and hypothetical objects brought into being through the imagination of the participant or viewer. In 1969, American artist Sol LeWitt wrote in his landmark text 'Sentences on conceptual art' that 'Ideas alone can be works of art … All ideas need not be made physical.[9] Art historian Benjamin H. D. Buchloh has also pointed out that the work of conceptual artists such as LeWitt resulted in a more pervasive 'redistribution of author/artist functions' across the entire visual field, decoupling artistic practice from any conventional understanding of visuality altogether.[10] While concrete poetry was by no means the strictest example of how language and authorship operated under a conceptualist paradigm, it did reflect a common sensibility about aesthetic reception. Focusing on the transmutability of words, the genre's direct engagement with the reader indicates that the defining and completion of the work of art might be carried out by anyone but the author.

Holt's early poems emerged directly out of these sensibilities, but her approach – in contrast to many of the existing examples of concrete poetry at that time – engaged with place and context as critical construct. For example, deciphering Holt's early concrete poem *Hometown* (1969) involves setting the work's title out in relation to a cluster of proper nouns – Nutley, Hackensack, Bloomfield, Totowa, Paterson, Garfield, Lodi, Montclair, Clifton, Rutherford and Passaic. Hovering loosely at the centre of a white page, the names of these municipalities take shape as a constellation, which, as Gomringer writes, 'is the simplest possible kind of configuration in poetry which has for its basic unit the word; it encloses a group of words as if it were drawing stars together to form a cluster'.[11] Of course, in the absence of any kind of clear topographical grid, the mere inscription of the names stands in for geographical features, or lines denoting roads, or dots signifying that they are, indeed, recognised sites. The configuration was hardly useful as a standard roadmap but was very much in keeping with what one might call a mental picture of northeastern New Jersey. Written using a manual typewriter, these words would appear to be organised at random if they did not include the word 'CLIFTON' rendered in capital letters. Although Holt was born in Worcester, Massachusetts, she relocated with her family to New Jersey, before she ultimately started high school in Clifton, where her parents lived until 1959.

In another poem, *Hammond* (1969) – named after the prolific New Jersey-based map-making firm C. S. Hammond & Company – a unique series of numbers accompanies each occurrence of the word 'Hammond' as it appears on eleven consecutive lines. The recurring word is listed as one might find it in the index at the back of an atlas, where lists of coordinates serve to direct the user to specific geographical sites. As in *Hometown*, ideas migrate from one conceptual realm to the next, establishing connections that can be traced from numerical notation, to map, to topographical grid, and ultimately to the landscape itself. However, in an atlas, the indexing initially moves to the preceding pages of maps, and then from a specific map to a physical location on the earth. By contrast, the intermediary map is absent in *Hammond*, meaning one moves directly from the atlas's index to a physical location. This approach hints at two dominant tendencies in her concrete poems – the first, following Gomringer, being Holt's crucial moment of 'finding, selecting and putting down these words' to create ' "thought-objects" ', and the second her desire to leave 'the task of association to the reader, who becomes a collaborator and, in a sense, the completer of the poem'.[12] By privileging viewer interaction, Holt's poetic 'constellations' (a visual metaphor that also recurs in the materiality of her outdoor sculptural work) represented a subversion of aesthetic reception.

That Holt would first cultivate her interest in geographical locations and sites through the placement of textual elements on paper was telling. Influenced by the conversation-based work of American artist Ian Wilson, whose exhibitions offered the viewer a purely mental 'object' for contemplation, she resisted embracing the full materiality and permanence of the work of art. To be sure, Holt was finding her own voice through critical reflection – reading the works of such European writers and thinkers as T. S. Eliot, Gaston Bachelard and Carl Jung, and discussing them with her peers, such as American minimalist sculptor Carl Andre. In a sentence jotted on a wine list during one of their frequent talks in the art bar at Max's Kansas City in New York, he wrote: 'Poetry is composed by those who believe they can accomplish nothing else in language.'

In the late 1960s, what could or could not be accomplished in language, and by whom, must have meant very different things to Holt and to a poet and artist such as Andre. Andre's investment in the material possibilities of the written word – from his exploitation of the manual typewriter's graphic register in the alignment of letters to the use of different coloured inks – demonstrated the semiotic arbitrariness of the sign as well as its optical nature. In turn, Holt's epistolary exchanges with him – including drawings, poems and postcards – reveal not only the significance of two-way communication to her working process (a process she sought to capture through new technologies, such as the magnetic tape of audio and video recording), but also the possible relation of language to material form.[13]

Indeed, quite a bit can be accomplished in language, but what of the poet's own relationship to that process? Throughout much of Holt's career language is decidedly referential, whereas for writers and poets such as Andre and Robert Smithson words were 'material' and could be freely organised and combined, or they were metaphorical – at times entirely detached from reality. A comparison could be drawn here to Smithson's 'site'/'nonsite' dialectic, as in the discontinuity between the postindustrial landscape and its representation within institutions via the slide lecture of *Hotel Palenque* (1969), for example, or the systems of distribution through art journalism in *Monuments of Passaic* (1967), which represents a similar interplay between textual and photographic documents.[14] However, those texts were resolutely monologic: the 'I' of the *Monuments'* first-person narrative – which suggests a definitive and primary point of view – was exactly what the implied 'you' of Holt's communication of directions or gestures in the landscape emphasised, breaking asunder the author's hold on the work of art and the text.

In another poem, *The World through a Circle* (c. 1970), the words 'sun', 'moon', 'water', 'sky', 'earth' and 'star' typographically render the outer contours of a circle; the very process of reading organises one's gaze around an aperture that is '[c]oncentrated, encompassed', encapsulating a view.[15] The spatial organisation of these words on paper, and the movement between them, signify the reader's active role in their completion.[16] The invitation to complete the work was more overt in works such as *Detach Here* (1967) and *Crossword Work* (1966), which make use of the modernist grid while departing from its rubric. The former – a poem with the instructions 'DETACH HERE' emblazoned in capital letters around a square rendered with dotted lines – proposes a gap or void in the perceptual field; to complete the work would bring about its absence, leaving behind the mere trace of an action. The latter – an actual crossword puzzle, based on art critic and curator Lucy Lippard's 1966 *Eccentric Abstraction* exhibition at the Fischbach Gallery in New York – introduces connections between artists and Holt's own social field through linguistic channels of identification and naming.

By the following year, Holt had shifted her language-based approach from the metropolitan context of the New York art world to rural and unincorporated territories in the United States. This began with her series of tours, one of which – *Stone Ruin Tour* – took place in June 1967, in the Little Falls area of Cedar Grove, New Jersey, far from the institutions of New York City. She guided a group of friends through a wooded landscape and the remains of a stone mansion. What survives of the outing are a series of black-and-white photographs and an unfinished transcription of her monologue, which highlights various sites. Her words have the rhythm of basic walking directions:

> As you walk on the paved road you will see a sign that says West Mount and you will see another sign in the distance – a white sign with blue letters and then on your left there is a sign Great Notch – Cedar Grove. Keep Right. Just keep walking[;] on your right will be trees, on your left Route 3 with a lot of cars going up and down. Also a Sunoco station and West's diner to the left across the highway.

Although the remaining tour instructions capture only a fraction of the experience of being on-site, their syntax gives us an indication of the tour's choreography and how the artist's voice was constitutional to the work. *Stone Ruin Tour*, thus, underscored an interrelation between author and reader beyond the printed page, which took shape as linguistic interventions in nature. Assembled alongside Instamatic photographs depicting sights, and the walking party as they explore the stone ruin, these material traces reorganise Holt's 'author/artist functions' as a series of snapshots and typewritten notes, which have a much more proximal relation to the problems of the archive than to a traditional work of art.[17] Leaving the participants free to develop their own perceptions and associations, pragmatic acts of denotation, disclosure and indication undercut Holt's authorial trace as some totalising construct. At the same time, they underscored that cartography is, factually, a mere system of signs.

In those early years, Holt made active recourse to cartographic systems, albeit in subversive form. In her *Buried Poems* series (1969–71), for example, she prepared different poems for individual receipts, which she buried in remote locations across the United States – national parks, deserts, islands. When they opened a booklet of clues that she made for them, the recipient would encounter a series of maps unfolding across multiple pages, the first starting with an overall Mercator view of the world, and gradually, with each turn of the page, the maps zeroed in on a burial site, shuttling down to a specific location for its recipient, creating a perceptual vortex. Perhaps, as I have observed elsewhere, in Holt's mind she was turning over that concept – plumbed in Dutch educator Kees Boeke's book *Cosmic View* and American designers and filmmakers Charles and Ray Eames's film *Powers of Ten* – of how, in a single granule of matter, one might see the universe.[18] The 'work' of the *Buried Poem* consisted not just of words, but of an entire complex of correspondences among the artist, the viewer/reader, and the material object or site – epitomising philosopher Ludwig Wittgenstein's understanding of semantic meaning emerging not purely from intention but from its use.[19] If its recipient chose to accept the invitation, thinking, planning, reading, travelling, looking, digging, reading again and reflecting all became activities that constituted the work. Through something as simple as directing attention to elements in a landscape, the reader of the poem was transformed into a viewer in space.

Sun Tunnels: Celestial constellations

Located in the open desert over 9.94 miles (16 km) east of the Utah–Nevada state line, *Sun Tunnels* – a large-scale outdoor sculpture that Holt completed in 1976 – consists of four reinforced concrete pipes that sit oppositional to one another. With a cement core embedded in the earth between them, the entire configuration radiates outwards as if positioned along the intersecting lines of a crossed rectangle. In April 1977, in *Artforum*, Holt wrote:

> I wanted to bring the vast space of the desert back to human scale. I had no desire to make a megalithic monument. The panoramic view of the landscape is too overwhelming to take in without visual reference points … Through the tunnels, parts of the landscape are framed and come into focus … [They] extend the viewer visually into the landscape, opening up the perceived space. But once inside the tunnels, the work encloses – surrounds – and there is a framing of the landscape through the ends of the tunnels and through the holes.[20]

Approximately 9 feet (2.74 m) in diameter and nearly twice in length, each of the tunnels invites site visitors to approach, circumnavigate and spend time within them. The work's strong connection to the very environment it frames exemplified the privileging of context found in site-specific work of this period, which, according to art historian Miwon Kwon, 'focused on establishing an inextricable, indivisible relationship between the work and its site, and demanded the physical presence of the viewer for the work's completion'.[21]

At the same time that Holt was developing and laying the groundwork for *Sun Tunnels*, French philosopher Henri Lefebvre opened up a Marxist reading of space in his groundbreaking 1974 publication *The Production of Space*.[22] As art historians Emily Eliza Scott and Kirsten Swenson have noted, the centrality of Lefebvre's spatial theory, and its later reception, continue to catalyse thinking about 'critical landscapes' and the environmental humanities at large.[23] Lefebvre unfolds an expansive reading of three overriding categories for understanding social organisation and action, as he argues '[s]ocial relations, which are concrete abstractions, have no real existence save in and through space'.[24] *Representations of space* encompass 'relations of production' and 'signs' and 'codes'.[25] *Representational space* is 'space as directly lived through its associated images and symbols' and 'systems of non-verbal symbols and signs'.[26] Finally, *spatial practice* 'embraces production and reproduction',[27] and stands in 'dialectical interaction' between society and space.[28] Lefebvre's recognition of the mutual imbrications of his spatial triad is of particular relevance for understanding *Sun Tunnels*.

Sun Tunnels was *produced* in a Lefebvrian sense. First, creating *Sun Tunnels* necessitated intervening in a region chequerboarded with governmental, private and indigenous land claims. Situated within the vicinity of the ancestral territories of the Goshute Nation – and south of the former village of Lucin, which has since become a ghost town – the work exemplifies the contentious layering of cultural and political signification.[29] Subject to US settler-colonial occupation since the nineteenth century, these 40 acres that Holt purchased and occupied were hardly a '*tabula rasa*' of the American West.[30] As Lefebvre's work reminds us, even an environment such as the expansive desert biome only 'appears homogeneous', when it is, in fact, 'a product of violence and war', 'political' and 'instituted by a state'.[31] Subsequent to the encroachment of European colonists, religious missionaries, slave traders, trappers and the US Government in the Great Basin Desert – which only intensified in the 1850s with the incorporation of the Territory of Utah and its subsequent admission to United States statehood in 1896 – this region exemplifies the outcome of the structural violence of the nation-state's *terra nullius* ideology.[32] Such epistemological claims reflect the ongoing dispossession of land by way of capitalist accumulation,[33] and, following Lefebvre, emerge from the conceit that 'the space of nature remains open on every side', in which 'thanks to technology we can "construct" whatever and wherever we wish, at the bottom of the ocean, in deserts or on mountaintops – even, if need be, in interplanetary space'.[34]

Second, much like the 'abstract space' of the natural sciences, Holt conceptualised *Sun Tunnels* by way of scientific-mathematical rationalisation. She worked with astrophysicist Les Fishbone from the University of Utah, and surveyor and engineer Harold Stiles, to set *Sun Tunnels* down on a site west of the Great Salt Lake.[35] Delineating the work along two 32° axes that were 'north and south from east and west',[36] they aligned it so that the sun would rise and set through the two pairs of tunnels during summer and winter solstices (the longest and the shortest days of the year respectively). Holt expands: 'The positioning of the work is also based on star study: the surveyor and I were only able to find True North by taking our bearings on the North Star – Polaris – as it ovals around the North Pole because of the Earth's movements.'[37] One can see the outcome of this preparatory work in a drawing of the *Sun Tunnels* site that Holt mapped out on a 14" × 20" piece of paper. An assemblage of graphical inscription and photographic analogues of nature, the overall drawing captures the tension of staring towards the horizon into infinity from a fixed point in space. Twelve black-and-white Instamatic photographs radiate from the centre, and orthogonal and diagonal lines cut the page like lines of sight piercing the desolate terrain. Two of them – labelled 32° northwest, southwest, northeast and southeast, respectively – refer to the work's ultimate relation to its cosmological context.

In these images we see the sparse scrub of the desert floor; the surface reflecting light like sand; and, off in the distance, the silhouettes of low-profile mountain ridges captured in the silver grain of the prints. It is a fragmented world, unified paradoxically under the rubric of a working collage, illustrating how the constitution of landscape emerges not only from the physicality of the earth, but also from the subjectivity of the person framing its view. As the cultural geographer Denis E. Cosgrove suggests in *Social Formation and Symbolic Landscape*, representations of and discourses on landscape play a key role even in the most seemingly routine characterisations of the outside world; he identified two approaches to understanding landscape: one emphasising the centrality of the eye and ocular sensation in the epistemic understanding of the external world, the other emphasising the empirical, topographical aspects of the analysis of 'a delimited portion of the earth's surface'.[38] This twofold observation circumscribes a useful discursive space for the consideration of the main conceptual foundation of Holt's practice.[39] Of course, part of understanding a site involves mapping its contours, assessing its parameters, ruminating on the shape and constitution of the physical world. Her notes on the drawing identify a handful of geographical landmarks of Utah's Box Elder County: Lucin Hill and the summit of Bald Eagle Mountain, Lemay Island, and Lion Mountain serve to orient the viewer in that vast open desert – parcelling out these existing geological forms as 'view', much like the sites of interest in a nineteenth-century panorama.

After having the four tunnels of *Sun Tunnels* cast in concrete, Holt instructed the industrial company to drill four different stellar constellations – Perseus, Draco, Capricorn and Columba – into the tops of them. The instantiation of these ancient symbolic, mytho-religious schemas within the sculpture inversely mirrors the way the materiality of the earth gives way to immaterial meanderings in the night sky invented in constellation forms, illustrating the way human cognition seeks to make them concrete. The language Holt uses in her '*Sun Tunnels*' text to describe the constellations reflects the practical concerns of the astronomer or sea traveller, who seeks to maximise visibility by deploying observational tools in orbit beyond the earth's atmosphere, or by activating their research within vast international collaborative scientific networks. It seems hardly incidental that Holt positioned the work in the hydrographic enclosure of North America's Great Basin, a complex terrain comprising 'a series of more than ninety basins', 'separated from each other by some 160 mountain ranges'.[40] As American designer and architect Buckminster Fuller has pointed out, sailors also historically identified their location on the surface of the earth by tracing the movement of stars such as Polaris back to 'sectional charts and comprehensive maps' in celestial navigation.[41]

The finalised *Sun Tunnels* work mobilises these cartographies as an active schema in and around the site visitor. As Holt writes, 'The changing pattern of light from our "sun-star" marks the days and hours as it passes through the tunnel's "star-holes".'[42] Theorist Walter Benjamin worked through similar ideas productively: his so-called 'thinking in constellations', which scholars Nassima Sahraoui and Caroline Sauter describe as privileging 'the deferral, disfigurement, and disruption of any linear thinking'.[43] Although humanity conscribes loose configurations of stars into entire and totalising systems of representation, in Benjamin's thought, these inventions of the human imagination become metaphysical: 'Where thinking suddenly comes to a stop in a constellation saturated with tensions, it gives that constellation a shock, by which thinking is crystallized as a monad.'[44] Holt, too, shared Benjamin's captivation with stellar constellations for their associative meanings – pinpoints of light, which figure upon the celestial sphere, become paradoxically material, discursive and metaphysical in her practice. Constellations, thus, stand in for the nature of thought, the infinite points in time and space from which an infinite number of perceptions is possible.

Holt writes that she chose these four constellations because 'Together, they encompass the globe.'[45] I would argue, however, that it is their fugitivity *away from* perception – one that reflects the relativity of their visualisation – that resonates most profoundly in the work. In actuality, the disparate stars that make up constellations only *appear* to be related to one another from a vantage point on earth. For Holt, the cyclical alignment of stellar objects was both fleeting and aberrant: after poring through '12 astronomical charts' in order to site the work, she realised that 'the number and positions of the stars in the constellations varied' across every star chart.[46] Tracking Polaris, as she adds, is difficult because of the wobble of the earth's axis, even though 'the pole star alone seems to float motionless as the world's mooring buoy in the sky'.[47] Moreover, the constellations of Perseus and Draco – located in the work's northern quadrants on the desert floor – are *only visible from the earth's Northern Hemisphere* year-round.[48] And the constellation of Capricorn, to the southeast, is *only seasonally visible* from the Northern Hemisphere in autumn and early winter, while Columba, a primarily Southern Hemisphere constellation to the southwest, '*slips over the edge of the horizon* for a short time each year', as Holt writes, '*but can't be seen* because of the dense atmosphere near the Earth'.[49]

Here, movement renders celestial vision sensible, while simultaneously setting scientific aspirations out of reach.

As I have noted elsewhere, this type of paradoxical interrelation between blindness and sight – particularly as it relates to systems of signification – also resonates within Holt's *Locators* series (1972–2012).[50] These works are static viewing devices made of steel. Much as with *Sun Tunnels*, viewers become conscious of their body's relationship to the object of observation when interacting with them. They must peer through a short horizontal pipe at eye level, comparing this framed view of the world with an unencumbered one. Her first Locator, from 1972, for example, directed one's gaze towards a black irregular shape she had painted at the intersection of two walls. When viewed through the Locator, the shape's overall contours cohered into a perfect circle. As Holt later described it, the Locator 'deadends on the wall', as if to literalise philosopher C. S. Peirce's assertion that indices 'direct the attention to their objects by blind compulsion'.[51] It is an act that works against the eye's visual engagement with space, which, as Lefebvre observes, 'tends to relegate objects to the distance, to render them passive', underscoring the tendency that 'that which is merely seen is reduced to an image'.[52] However, a visit to *Sun Tunnels* gestures towards a consummate awareness of space and time, shifting engagement with the work from one of perception to one of apperception – onto the act of perception itself, reflecting an intertwining of systems of signification found in site-specific work with cartographic ideas.

Recent scholars have pointed out that rather than merely capturing the celestial sphere within a built architectural dome, *Sun Tunnels* operates like an *open-air* planetarium.[53] This comparison hinges upon the field of astronomy's desire for systems of identification and naming in order to develop nomenclatures for particularities of space, within which constellations become infinitesimal vignettes of a larger whole. In the decades before Holt created *Sun Tunnels*, the Hayden Planetarium in New York City and its collateral exhibition spaces created a sensation in popular culture, but met critique within the late-1960s conceptualist art world. First developed by the Carl Zeiss optics company in Jena in 1923, and widely popularised throughout the remainder of the century, the modern projection planetarium afforded viewers highly illusionistic representations of the night sky upon the dome's inner surface, while a live speaker would guide them through often scripted tours of the cosmos.[54] However, Smithson and American artist Mel Bochner vilified the planetarium as a faulty multimedia assemblage in their 1966 article-cum-artwork 'The domain of the Great Bear', arguing that its representational schemas fell far too short of the universe's immensity of time and space.[55] While the title of their essay – and the planetarium show to which they responded – takes its name from the

Ursa Major constellation (also known as 'the Great Bear', the third largest constellation in the Northern Hemisphere), their use of the term 'domain' in the title underscores the way in which our understanding of constellations reflects hegemonic ways of seeing and knowing.

However, in lieu of the planetarium show's narrator, *Sun Tunnels* physically and mentally orients visitors to the *nesting* of the terrestrial and celestial milieus, extending strategies of denotation and indication that Holt engaged in her concrete poetry to a broader cosmological context. Art historian Anne Wagner sagely recognised the pro-filmic, pro-photographic nature of *Sun Tunnels*, arguing that the tunnels 'form a cumbersome camera, an enormous viewing device to record nothing less than the passage of celestial time'.[56] Unlike American artist Walter De Maria's *Lightning Field* (1977) in rural New Mexico – which in practice, as Lefebvre might suggest, operates like 'an object offered up to the gaze yet barred from any possible use, whether this occurs in a museum or in a shop window'[57] – *Sun Tunnels* was conceived as a public work with no visitation appointments necessary. After completing the work, Holt printed an announcement card, charting a visual trajectory to the work from Salt Lake City (marked in red ink) on a black-and-white roadmap, recto, with abbreviated discursive instructions, verso. Although this map fails to capture the region's relationship to 'deep time' – including the paleolake Lake Bonneville's physical transformation over geological epochs – site visitors, animals and the elements enact all sorts of activities around, upon and within the tunnels each year. Passive aesthetic reception cedes to more experiential modes of existence, and human activity assumes a new significance in its arid, remote location; ambulation, rest, subsistence, sweating and breathing all move to the foreground of one's thinking. As Lefebvre argues, 'real social time is forever re-emerging complete with its own characteristics and determinants: repetitions, rhythms, cycles, activities'.[58] Concretisation thus has a double meaning in *Sun Tunnels*; it reflects both the sculpture's materiality and the centrality of sociability in space – subverting cartographic representation in both her creation and her promotion of the work.

Experimental cinema: Producing space

In 1978, Holt assembled factual data, photographic slides and 16 mm footage of the *Sun Tunnels* site before, during and after the work's construction. This creative activity resulted in a film, which for many would stand in for any personal visit to the site. In the opening sequence, the camera focuses on a partial view of a map of the world. If this image depicts a three-dimensional globe, the cinematic frame renders it as a simple conical projection of space. The film's title appears in superimposition over the North American continent at the centre of the frame, as if to concretise *Sun Tunnels'* physical location with respect to cartographic systems of understanding. In the following shot, the camera pans left across a more detailed map from the states of the northeastern seaboard region of the continental USA to the state of Utah, as if to chart the artist's own trajectory from the New York region to the American West.

After the intervening passages capture the processual construction of *Sun Tunnels*, a tracking shot surveys the completed sculpture from a distance. As the camera heads east on Little Pigeon Road from a moving vehicle, the tunnels appear at times to sit like four objects lined up in a horizontal row as the camera circles around them. Hauntingly, the entire formation fluctuates within perception and through the lens; the thickness of the two tunnels in the centre diminishes into thin air as we view them, like gazing through a telescope at a galaxy 'edge-on', or staring at objects on the horizon that appear to shift and shimmer because of the particulates in the atmosphere. As Holt writes, 'Closer in, a mile or so away, the relational balance changes and is hard to read.'[59] She continues, 'When the sun beats down on the site, the heat waves seem to make the earth dissolve, and the tunnels appear to lose their substance – they float like mirages in the distance.'[60] The film then cuts to eight different shots of the drilled constellation holes from varying distances. At times, the camera peers from one set of holes to another. The next two shots rove along the constellation holes, capturing shadow effects with a handheld camera as they scatter across a tunnel's interior surface, and then the screen goes black.

In his essay 'The third meaning', literary theorist Roland Barthes proposes that cinema is discursive; that is, it is not only a system of signs, but it also lends itself to 'digressive' meanderings – which he calls the 'filmic'.[61] He asserts that cinema's 'filmic' characteristics lie somewhere 'where language and meta-language end' – between the frames.[62] As he argues, once the still image has been disassociated from the cinematic flux, it gives rise to extra-diegetic content. As art historian George Baker argues in 'The cinema model' – an essay on Smithson's film *Spiral Jetty* (1970) and its relationship to its eponymous artwork, a massive sculpture on the east side of the Great Salt Lake in Utah – for Smithson, the cinematic still is all about the archive, 'the anomic ordering principles of the archive as a form.'[63] However, in the *Sun Tunnels* film, the freeze-frame enforces stasis upon the cinematic flux, instead of issuing from the film's ontological form, like an isolated film still.[64] Its spatio-temporal nature radically changes when a sequence of 35 mm colour slides of a solitary figure at the completed *Sun Tunnels* site appears as a series of still frames. These photographic images, ontologically dissociated from the film's diegesis – yet tied indexically to the site – are introduced into its fabric like a simulated slideshow. Then, live-action views through each of the four tunnels flash briefly on the screen with the names of their respective constellations as subtitles in the lower register of the frame.

For Holt, filmic digression emerges in the apparent stoppage of time, and, in the final four minutes of the *Sun Tunnels* film, its dilation. A series of short live-action shots captures the movement of light across one of the tunnels on a mid-July day, and the 1977 summer solstice as the sun rises and sets through the Perseus and Capricorn tunnels, respectively. Each of these sequences consists of extremely short takes running at twenty-four frames per second crossfading into one another at regular intervals. Instead of the recording speed being slower than the playback or projection speed – which is what gives true time-lapse photography its uncanny rhythm – the movement within each shot appears to run in a naturalistic manner. Over the entire segment these 'time lapse images' blend into one another, building a dynamic chrono-portrait of work. A small group of birds cuts into the frame. A truck enters from the right, travelling south on Creek Road, and then spontaneously and inexplicably disappears before reaching the edge of the frame. As a result, the gestures of the solar phenomena of sunrise and sunset remain truncated during the solstice, echoing Holt's observation that at the *Sun Tunnels* site the 'feeling of timelessness is overwhelming'.[65]

Indeed, it is Holt's movement away from the evidentiary status of recording techniques towards more conceptualist engagements with space and time that has been of most interest to me in this chapter. As I have outlined here, Holt grounds her implicit critique of cartography in its deferral *away* from embodied experience. Recent research in cognitive science has explored the relationship between representational systems, such as language, and 'tangible and concrete' and 'experience-based domains', within which humans, as cognitive scientist Lera Boroditsky has argued, 'automatically instantiate spatial representations of time that are consistent with the set of spatiotemporal metaphors in their linguistic environment'.[66] This relation between representation and being in the world is very much at work in these projects. Although Holt's production and collection of photographic slides represented a central activity for the artist and her formation of an artistic identity in and through collaboration,[67] these photographs are fragmentary; they emerge from a storehouse of 'memory traces',[68] unified by *Sun Tunnels*' own material persistence – or by way of the *dispositif* of cinema.[69] And yet, these *dispositifs*, too, prove illusory. It is as if Holt's work seeks to address Lefebvre's enquiry, 'what escape can there be from a space thus shattered into images, into signs, into connected-yet-disconnected data directed at a "subject" itself doomed to abstraction?'[70] Of course, during her lifetime, Holt generated thousands of images of *Sun Tunnels*, a sculpture whose very nature is constantly changing over time. In other words, the *Sun Tunnels* film *itself* becomes a spatial practice, recording the incidental light of nearly infinite possibilities and sources; and to this day, the photographic and filmic representation of the work continues to proliferate in the public sphere – photographs, magnetic tape and film – each documenting a unique moment in time and reproduction of the production of space.

Acknowledgement

This chapter is drawn from my previous publication with permission: Alena J. Williams, 'Introduction', and 'Concrete traces: Nancy Holt's speaking media', in Alena J. Williams (ed.), *Nancy Holt: Sightlines* (Berkeley, CA: University of California Press, 2011), pp. 18–38, 183–202, respectively. This version includes assimilation of the copy to Manchester University Press style, as well as modifications and substantial additions by the author based on a lecture originally presented for the Nancy Holt Symposium, Dia:Chelsea, New York, on February 9 2019 and part of a forthcoming monograph on astronomy and experimental film.

Notes

1 On 10 November 1967, NASA's Applications Technology Satellite-3 (ATP-3) captured the first colour image of the whole earth from space; previous images by the Department of Defense Gravitational Experiment satellite were composites of three different black-and-white images shot with filters. See Verner E. Suomi and Robert J. Parent, 'A color view of Planet Earth', *Bulletin of the American Meteorological Society* 49:2 (1968), 74–5; and Guenter Warnecke and Wendell S. Sunderlin, 'The first color picture of the earth taken from the ATS-3 satellite', *Bulletin of the American Meteorological Society* 49:2 (1968), 75–83. Shortly thereafter in the same year, Stewart Brand founded *The Whole Earth Catalog*, a predominantly quarterly publication, which was part and parcel of Brand's campaign to push for NASA to release a view of the entire planet from space. *The Whole Earth Catalog* – a compendium of materials from American counterculture, advancing ideas at the intersection of art, technology and society – exemplified the epistemic, social and political implications of astronomical research, and actively sought both to radicalise and to popularise it. See Caroline Maniaque (ed.), *Whole Earth Field Guide* (Cambridge, MA: MIT Press, 2016).

2 Diedrich Diederichsen and Anselm Franke (eds), *The Whole Earth: California and the Disappearance of the Outside* (Berlin: Sternberg Press, 2013); F. D. Scott, *Outlaw Territories: Environments of Insecurity/Architectures of Counterinsurgency* (New York: Zone Books, 2016); Galeries nationales du Grand Palais, *La lune: Du voyage réel aux voyages imaginaires*, ed. Véronique Leleu (Paris: Editions de la Réunion des musées nationaux–Grand Palais, 2019).

3 Laura Kurgan, *Close Up at a Distance: Mapping, Technology, and Politics* (New York: Zone Books, 2013).

4 See Donald A. Beattie, *Taking Science to the Moon: Lunar Experiments and the Apollo Program* (Baltimore, MD: Johns Hopkins University Press, 2001), pp. 189–93.

5 Lisa Parks, *Cultures in Orbit: Satellites and the Televisual* (Durham, NC: Duke University Press, 2005), p. 12.

6 Kevin Lynch, *The Image of the City* (Cambridge, MA: MIT Press, 1960), p. 126.

7 Holt often invokes the moon in her work, either in a metaphorical way or by tracking its path across the sky through its reflection in the pools of her sculptures, such as *Star Crossed* (1979–80), *O Moon* (1990) and *Sky Mound* (unfinished). In an illuminating, eponymous text that Holt published shortly after completing the construction of *Sun Tunnels*, she writes: 'Crescents of light form inside the rims of the tunnels', and in the original publication she characterises the crescents as 'moonlike'. Nancy Holt, '*Sun Tunnels*', in Alena J. Williams (ed.), *Nancy Holt: Sightlines* (Berkeley: University of California Press, 2011), p. 84; further citations are to this edition. It was originally published as Nancy Holt, '*Sun Tunnels*', *Artforum* 15:1 (April 1977), 36.

8 Emmett Williams (ed.), *An Anthology of Concrete Poetry* (New York: Something Else Press, 1967).

9 Sol LeWitt, 'Sentences on conceptual art', in Alexander Alberro and Blake Stimson (eds), *Conceptual Art: A Critical Anthology* (Cambridge, MA: MIT Press, 1999), p. 107.

10 Benjamin H. D. Buchloh, 'Conceptual art 1962–1969: From the aesthetic of administration to the critique of institutions', *October* 55 (Winter 1990), 140.

11 Eugen Gomringer, 'From line to constellation', in Mary Ellen Solt (ed.), *Concrete Poetry: A World View*, trans. Mike Weaver (Bloomington: Indiana University Press, 1968), p. 67.

12 Eugen Gomringer, as quoted in Williams, *An Anthology of Concrete Poetry* (unpaginated).

13 During her lifetime, copies of Holt's concrete poems and the text collages sent to Andre were located in her personal archive and studio, along with Andre's whimsical notes, drawings and poems on tourist and announcement postcards to both Holt and her partner, Robert Smithson. This collection contained serial photographic narratives, such as an eleven-part work by Andre entitled *The Lily-Tulip Cup Case*, which he sent to Holt on eleven nearly consecutive days in 1974.

14 See also Robert Smithson, 'A tour of the monuments of Passaic, New Jersey', *Artforum* 6:4 (December 1967), 52–7.

15 This poem was later exhibited in the *Language III* show at the Virginia Dwan Gallery in New York in 1969, and was eventually submitted as a contribution to a catalogue for a Sol LeWitt exhibition at the Wadsworth Atheneum Museum of Art in Hartford, Connecticut; however, this section of the publication, for which responses from numerous artists were solicited, was never published by the Wadsworth Atheneum.

16 Empty holes and voids were fraught terms in the late 1960s and early 1970s – think of Mary Miss's sequence of disappearing concentric circles cut out of wood bulwarks

in *Battery Park Landfill* (1973), or even Smithson's discussion of Lewis Carroll's void map in *The Hunting of the Snark* and Jo Baer's 'empty' paintings in the essay 'A museum of language in the vicinity of art' (1968), or Smithson's consideration of 'false windows (frames)' in the text 'Some void thoughts on museums' (1967). Both of Smithson's texts are reprinted in Jack Flam (ed.), *Robert Smithson: The Collected Writings* (Berkeley: University of California Press, 1996), pp. 41–2, 78–94.

17 Ines Schaber elegantly discusses this problematic in 'The claims she stakes: A reading of Nancy Holt's archive', in Williams, *Nancy Holt*, pp. 162–81.

18 Alena J. Williams, 'Passages: Nancy Holt (1938–2014)', *Artforum* (May 2014), www. artforum.com/passages/id=46803 (accessed 23 March 2023).

19 Ludwig Wittgenstein, *Philosophical Investigations*, trans. and ed. P. M. S. Hacker and J. Schulte, 4th edn (Oxford: Wiley-Blackwell, 2009), p. 43. See also Joseph Kosuth's discussion of Wittgenstein in relation to conceptual art: 'Art after philosophy', in Joseph Kosuth, *Art after Philosophy and After: Collected Writings, 1966–1990*, ed. Gabriele Guercio (Cambridge, MA: MIT Press, 1991), pp. 13–32.

20 Holt, '*Sun Tunnels*', p. 84.

21 Kwon traces the genealogy of site-specificity as a critique of Cartesianism and capitalism, and as an 'epistemological challenge to relocate meaning from within the art object to the contingencies of its context'. See Miwon Kwon, *One Place after Another: Site-Specific Art and Locational Identity* (Cambridge, MA: MIT Press, 2004), pp. 11–12.

22 Henri Lefebvre, *The Production of Space*, trans. Donald Nicholson-Smith (Oxford: Blackwell, 1991).

23 See Scott and Swenson's introduction in their recent edited volume, as well as contributions by Julian Myers-Szupinska and Trevor Paglen. Emily Eliza Scott and Kirsten Swenson (eds), *Critical Landscapes: Art, Space, Politics* (Oakland: University of California Press, 2015), available at https://hdl.handle.net/2027/heb33029.0001.001 (accessed 23 March 2023).

24 Lefebvre, *The Production of Space*, p. 404.

25 *Ibid.*, p. 33.

26 *Ibid.*, p. 39.

27 *Ibid.*, p. 33.

28 *Ibid.*, p. 39.

29 Research on indigenous dispossession on the North American continent is ongoing. The Goshute Nation (which has been a maintained official reservation since the early twentieth century) is now located at the Confederated Tribes of the Goshute Reservation and the Skull Valley Indian Reservation (of the Skull Valley Band of Goshute Tribe); the Goshute Nation has long been in close contact with the Northwestern Band of the Shoshone Nation of northern Utah and southern Idaho. See Dennis R. Defa, 'The Goshute Indians of Utah', in Forrest S. Cuch (ed.), *History of Utah's American Indians* (Boulder: University Press of Colorado, 2000); and William C. Sturtevant (ed.), *Handbook of North American Indians*, Vol. XI, *Great Basin* (Washington, DC: Smithsonian Institution, 1978). See also 'Goshute: Demography', Utah American Indian Digital Archive, https://utahindians.

org/archives/goshute.html (accessed 23 March 2023); Native Land Digital, https://native-land.ca/ (accessed 23 March 2023); and Sean J. Patrick Carney, 'Ground control: Land art and American entropy', *Artforum* (July 2021), www.artforum.com/slant/sean-j-patrick-carney-on-land-art-and-american-entropy-86221 (accessed 23 March 2023).

30 Lefebvre, *The Production of Space*, p. 285.

31 *Ibid.*

32 See Defa, 'The Goshute Indians of Utah'; and Sturtevant, *Handbook of North American Indians*, Vol. XI.

33 David Harvey's conception of 'accumulation by dispossession' addresses the relationship among Marx's 'accumulation of capital' and 'primitive accumulation', Lefevbrian analyses of late capitalism, and the United States' neo-imperialistic foreign policy since the 1970s. David Harvey, 'The "new" imperialism: Accumulation by dispossession', in *The New Imperial Challenge*, special issue of *Socialist Register* 40 (2004), 63–85; and David Harvey, *The New Imperialism* (New York: Oxford University Press, 2005). See also Part VII, 'The accumulation of capital', and Part VIII, 'Primitive accumulation', in Karl Marx, *Capital: A Critique of Political Economy*, Vol. I, trans. B. Fowkes (London: Penguin, 1990). For an examination of this idea in ecocritical filmmaking see Ashley Dawson, 'Documenting accumulation by dispossession', in Scott and Swenson, *Critical Landscapes*, pp. 161–78.

34 Lefebvre, *The Production of Space*, p. 330.

35 Holt, 'Sun Tunnels', p. 89n5.

36 The angle was precisely 31° 0' 98"; Holt, 'Sun Tunnels', p. 89n7.

37 *Ibid.*, pp. 81, 84.

38 Denis E. Cosgrove, *Social Formation and Symbolic Landscape* (Madison: University of Wisconsin Press, 1998), p. 9.

39 In fact, Cosgrove's work sets out the nature of the debates at play in the disciplines of architecture and geography during the 1970s and 1980s, when Holt carried out many of her major works of outdoor sculpture.

40 Defa, 'The Goshute Indians of Utah', p. 74.

41 Buckminster Fuller, 'Fluid geographies', *American Neptune* 4:2 (April 1944), 132.

42 Holt, 'Sun Tunnels', p. 84.

43 Nassima Sahraoui and Caroline Sauter, 'Introduction', in Nassima Sahraoui and Caroline Sauter (eds), *Thinking in Constellations: Walter Benjamin in the Humanities* (Newcastle upon Tyne: Cambridge Scholars Publishing, 2018), p. xi.

44 Walter Benjamin, 'On the concept of history', trans. Harry Zohn, in Howard Eiland and Michael W. Jennings (eds), *Walter Benjamin: Selected Writings*, Vol. IV, *1938–1940* (Cambridge, MA; London: Belknap/Harvard University Press, 2006), p. 396.

45 Holt, 'Sun Tunnels', p. 88.

46 *Ibid.*

47 Fuller, 'Fluid geographies', p. 120.

48 I thank scholar Hikmet Sidney Loe for helping me determine the location of each tunnel with respect to the cardinal coordinates on the site of *Sun Tunnels*.

49 Holt, 'Sun Tunnels', p. 88 (emphasis mine).

50 Alena J. Williams, 'Productive estrangements: Remembering Nancy Holt (1938–2014)', *Texte zur Kunst* 94 (May 2014), 255–9.

51 Charles Sanders Peirce, 'Logic as semiotic: The theory of signs', in Charles Sanders Peirce, *Philosophical Writings of Peirce*, ed. Justus Buchler (New York: Dover Publications, 1955), p. 108.

52 Lefebvre, *The Production of Space*, p. 286.

53 Serge Paul, for example, situates this cosmologically oriented work among those of other contemporaries: Robert Morris, Charles Ross and James Turrell. Serge Paul, 'Sensorium dei: Observatories of the American West', in Beate Reifenscheid (ed.), *The Last Freedom: From the Pioneers of Land Art in the 1960s to Nature in Cyberspace* (Milan: Silvana Editoriale, 2011), pp. 38–58. Holt also stated that visiting the planetarium in Salt Lake City was part of her research for *Sun Tunnels*. See Hikmet Sidney Loe, 'Construction and significance of *Sun Tunnels*: Interview with Nancy Holt', in J. Wallace Gwynn (ed.), *Great Salt Lake: An Overview of Change* (Salt Lake City: Utah Division of Natural Resources/Utah Geological Survey, 2002), p. 564.

54 For recent discussions on the planetarium see Joachim Krausse, 'Das Wunder von Jena: Das Zeiss-Planetarium von Walter Bauersfeld', in *Gebaute Weltbilder von Boullée bis Buckminster Fuller*, special issue of *Arch+: Zeitschrift für Architektur und Städtebau* 116 (March 1993), 40–9; J. D. Marché, *Theaters of Time and Space: American Planetaria, 1930–1960* (New Brunswick, NJ: Rutgers University Press, 2005); Alison Griffiths, ' "A moving picture of the heavens": The planetarium space show as useful cinema', in Charles R. Acland and Haidee Wasson (eds), *Useful Cinema* (Durham, NC: Duke University Press, 2011); Alison Griffiths, *Shivers down Your Spine: Cinemas, Museums and the Immersive View* (New York: Columbia University Press, 2013); Charlotte Bigg, 'The view from here, there and nowhere? Situating the observer in the planetarium and in the solar system', *Early Popular Visual Culture* 15:2 (2017), 204–26; and Boris Goesl, Hans-Christian von Herrmann and Kohei Suzuki (eds), *Zum Planetarium: Wissensgeschichtliche Studien* (Paderborn: Wilhelm Fink, 2018). For historic attention see Henry C. King, *Geared to the Stars: The Evolution of Planetariums, Orreries and Astronomical Clocks* (Bristol: Adam Hilger, 1978).

55 Robert Smithson and Mel Bochner, 'The domain of the Great Bear', *Art Voices* 5:4 (Fall 1966), 44–51. See also Tim Griffin, 'Secrets of the domes: Mel Bochner on "The domain of the Great Bear" ', *Artforum* 45:1 (September 2006), 340–5.

56 Anne M. Wagner, 'Being there: Art and politics of place', *Artforum* 43:10 (Summer 2005), 267.

57 Lefebvre, *The Production of Space*, p. 319.

58 *Ibid.*, p. 339.

59 Holt, '*Sun Tunnels*', p. 84.

60 *Ibid.*, p. 88.

61 Roland Barthes, 'The third meaning', in *Image-Music-Text*, trans. Stephen Heath (New York: Hill and Wang, 1977), p. 64.

62 *Ibid.*

63 George Baker, 'The cinema model', in Lynne Cooke and Karen Kelly (eds), *Robert Smithson: Spiral Jetty. True Fictions, False Realities* (Berkeley: University of California Press/Dia Art Foundation, 2005), p. 105.

64 See Stanley Cavell, *The World Viewed: Reflections on the Ontology of Film* (New York: Viking Press, 1971).

65 Holt, '*Sun Tunnels*', p. 78.

66 Lera Boroditsky, 'How languages construct time', in Stanislas Dehaene and Elizabeth M. Brannon (eds), *Space, Time and Number in the Brain: Searching for the Foundations of Mathematical Thought* (Amsterdam: Elsevier Academic Press, 2011), pp. 334–5.

67 See Schaber, 'The claims she stakes', pp. 163–81.

68 Holt, '*Sun Tunnels*', p. 89.

69 See Gilles Deleuze, 'What is a *dispositif?*', in Timothy J. Armstrong (ed.), *Michel Foucault, Philosopher: International Conference, Paris, 9, 10, 11 January 1988* (New York: Routledge, 1992), pp. 159–68.

70 Lefebvre, *The Production of Space*, p. 313.

11 André Cadere's peripatetic art

Inesa Brašiškė

My art is the situation of my work in the art world.

André Cadere (1976)[1]

'WHO HAS SEEN … this strange guy who walks with a colourful baton on his shoulder? We are looking for him', read a brief note published in an issue of the Genovese quotidian periodical *Corriere Mercantile* of 14 May 1975.[2] Alongside this statement, the newspaper printed a black-and-white photograph showing a man with his back to the camera and a distinctive pole on his shoulder, ready to cross a busy street. The image, which must have puzzled readers of the Italian daily, announced the presence of André Cadere in the city. Cadere arrived in Genoa from Paris for his exhibition at Samangallery, a local art gallery run by Italian art dealer Ida Gianelli, who mainly exhibited conceptual and postminimal art.[3] However, the exhibition was not exactly *at* the gallery. As indicated on a map on the invitation card (see Figure 11.1) and confirmed by the photographs published in the gallery's newsletter soon after, the artist showed his bar – among other places – in a bar and at another art gallery. On the last day of his exhibition, after spending a few days wandering around the city, the artist mounted a round bar of wood on one of Samangallery's walls for a day. Two days later, the same bar was on view in Milan for a one-night exhibition at Toselli Gallery.

Showing his works in multiple places and forgoing the usual procedures regulating their exhibition was undoubtedly an effective and efficient strategy (as he was always around, Cadere may well have been the most seen artist in Europe in the 1970s), earning him as much sympathy as hostility. The artist's ability to move – and the bar's potential to be moved – between different sites allowed him to enter museums and galleries without being invited, circumventing such professional protocols as invitations, and organising exhibitions outside conventional venues, thus shuffling institutional hierarchies and expanding his audience.[4] As one critic put it, 'Like a creature that survives by some extra capacity for adaptation, he has found a way of slipping through the mesh of any institution.'[5]

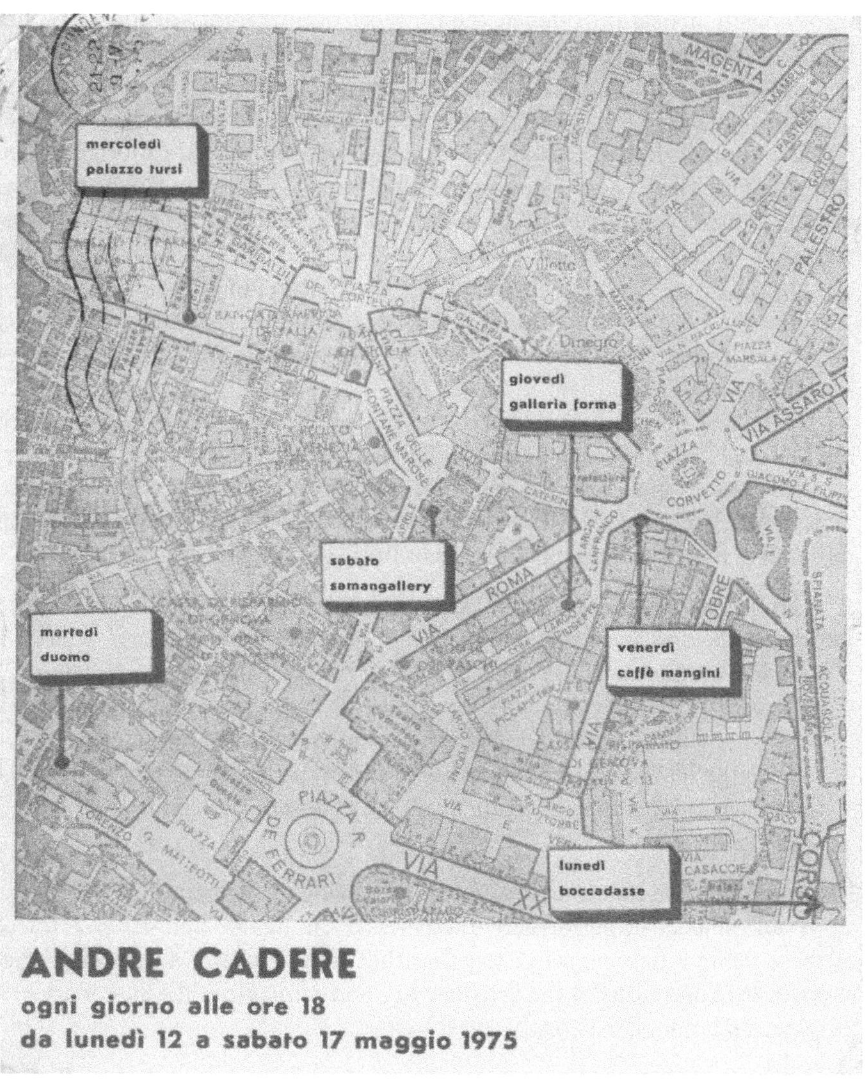

Invitation to André Cadere's exhibition at Samangallery, Genoa, 1975.   **11.1**

As these actions and the communication surrounding them demonstrate – from navigating the city's different venues to taking transnational journeys from Paris to Genoa (and Milan soon after) – Cadere's artistic practice had a particular relation to space. His moving from one place to another with a round bar of wood as a portable object was contemporaneous with the emergence of a generation of poststudio artists who turned to the literal space of art as a conditioning agent in their work. In the wake of minimalism, artists introduced the physical inseparability of the work and its site, extending aesthetic experience beyond the object's boundaries to its contextual surrounding. Other artists, grouped under the umbrella term 'institutional critique', regarded space not as a neutral architectural container but as a charged framework, and, working in museums and galleries, aimed at laying bare their social, economic and political conditions.[6] If, as Douglas Crimp argued, a site-specific work opposed the idealism of the modernist tradition of the autonomous object 'and unveiled the material system it obscured – by its refusal of circulatory mobility, its belongingness to a *specific* site',[7] then Cadere's embrace of mobility and placelesness suggests a diversion of this critical enterprise with further ramifications for the understanding of the space of art itself.

Describing the site-oriented practices emerging in the 1990s as an expanded institutional critique going beyond the literal site explored by the first generation of institutional critics, James Meyer proposed a new kind of site he called 'functional'. According to Meyer, a functional site relies not on a fixed place but rather on a discursive aggregation of multiple sites, manifesting as:

> a process, an operation occurring between sites, a mapping of institutional and textual filiations and the bodies that move between them (the artist's above all). It is an informational site, a palimpsest of text, photographs and video recordings, physical places, and things … It is no longer an obdurate steel wall, attached to the plaza for eternity. On the contrary, the functional work refuses the intransigence of literal site-specificity. It is a temporary thing, a movement, a chain of meanings and imbricated histories: a place marked and swiftly abandoned.[8]

It is my contention that Cadere's project, by relying on the painting rendered as a portable object, the performative activities of circulation and material traces of these perambulations, wove together this kind of 'chain of meanings' that exposes the conditions of the artistic work and reimagines the site of art as a passage, a relation, a network.

The round bar of wood

The round bars of wood that Cadere first realised sometime in late 1971 or early 1972 were colourful poles put together by joining individual wooden cylinders – each covered in a bright, viscous house paint. A quick look at the bars confirms their rather quirky appearance: the irregularly stringed individual units, bruises, cracks, stains, uneven coating and sometimes even signs of repair on the surface. The bars were unmistakably handmade and used. Though they were far from sleek, industrially fabricated objects, in arranging them Cadere relied on a cool, preconceived order explored by minimal and conceptual artists. Not immediately recognisable as such when encountered in real life by an uninitiated spectator, the bars were strictly determined pieces.

The artist used a limited colour selection: black, white, yellow, orange, red, violet, blue and green. Colour in Cadere's paintings – deprived of symbolic or expressive content – served as a building unit in the quasi-mathematical formal syntax. Indeed, every single bar was translated into a code featuring a letter, a number of eight digits marking the use of colours in a given bar, a diameter in milimetres and a placement of an error.[9] The coloured units were arranged following two kinds of permutational systems addressed simply as 'A' and 'B'. The variation of the permutational system 'A' involved five modes of arrangement with no fewer than three and no more than seven colours, with a minimum of twelve and maximum of fifty-six segments, while the order 'B' enjoyed only two variations, three colours and twenty-one segments, or four colours and fifty-two segments.[10] Though invested in a serial attitude, Cadere nevertheless made efforts to disrupt this well-tempered system, introducing a glitch in a bar's otherwise precise arrangement by inverting two adjacent segments, thus complicating the reading of the initial order.

It was of course Sol LeWitt who stipulated in 1967 in his 'Paragraphs on conceptual art' that '[t]he idea becomes a machine that makes the art'.[11] Indeed, by the early 1970s, Cadere was well informed about LeWitt's work. He was able not only to see it in Paris in person but also to familiarise himself first-hand with the artistic principles driving the American artist's work. In June 1970, at the time when in his own work Cadere was still preoccupied with what one can call his proto-bars, freely composing colourful pieces of wood into three-dimensional arrangements with no apparent mathematical logic or compositional schema, the artist served as one of the draftsmen responsible for the execution of LeWitt's wall drawings for the artist's first exhibition at Yvon Lambert Gallery.[12] The show at the Lambert featured three wall drawings in black pencil, one made by LeWitt himself (dedicated to Eva Hesse, *Wall Drawing #46*) and two by a group of local assistants following the artist's elaborate instructions (*Wall Drawing #44* and *Wall Drawing #45*).[13] In his round bars of wood, however – not unlike LeWitt – Cadere embraced a rigid methodical programme. He communicated the latter on multiple occasions, including as verbal statements in magazine inserts and announcements, or as explanatory schemas on invitation cards. Locked by three interdependent parameters – namely colour, permutational system and a mandatory error – Cadere's working method suggested a closed system of a finite number of possible combinations that the artist never exhausted.[14] If LeWitt may indeed have been instrumental in Cadere's gradual decision to empty his work of arbitrary decision-making in favour of preset plans and to engage his audience in an active decoding of the rationale behind the artwork, their treatments of space were significantly different.[15] Where the American artist's wall drawings responded to the physical properties of a particular site, taking it as yet another variable in his system, Cadere was determined to abandon the wall as a structural support for his own work.[16]

The bars were made not only by hand, but specifically *for* hand (see Figure 11.2) The smallest bars were compact enough to be squeezed into the inner pocket of a jacket, but for the most part they were designed to be comfortably and visibly carried while holding them in a hand.[17] In a letter to Yvon Lambert, Cadere pointed out that 'The biggest size [of a bar] is one that I can carry (there is maybe a certain relation to Ad Reinhardt, who limited the dimensions of his canvases – the length of the square – to the maximum stretch of his arms).'[18] The bar's size, shape and weight were largely determined by the artist's body and his ability to handle the object while moving. Glancing through photographs featuring a bar in public and private spaces, one cannot shake the feeling that it is there only for a moment, ready to be somewhere else. But also, when inspecting the object itself, one immediately notices bruises and cracks that are the material traces recorded on its surface upon its daily displacements. These were the paintings designed for travelling. Their formal features – including haptic impulse and morphological versatility – suggest itinerancy as their central conceptual premise. Seth Siegelaub once noticed the velocity with which conceptual art traverses space: 'One becomes very much

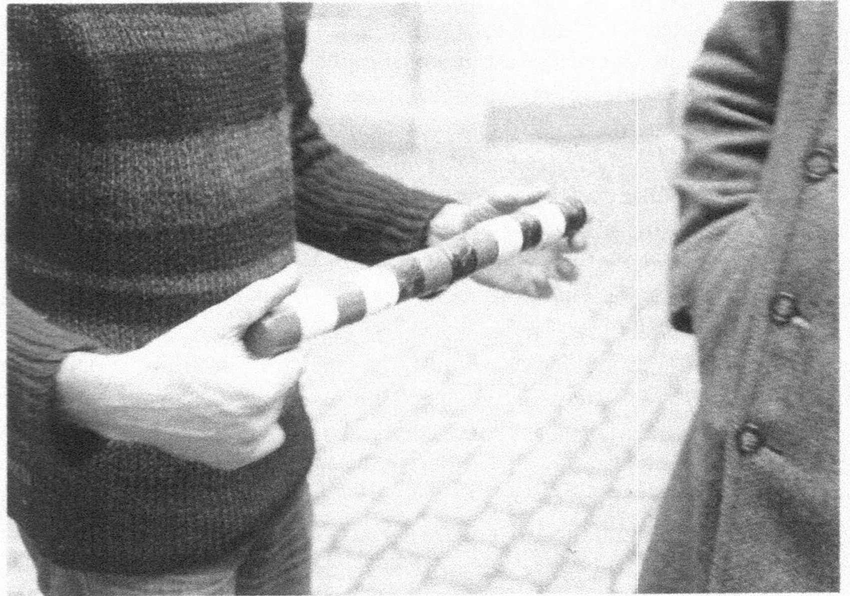

11.2   André Cadere holding one of his bars, ICC Antwerp, 1975.

aware of the speed with which this art travels, of the way it is rapidly trans-ferred from continent to continent or city to city, by virtue of its portability, more quickly than other art.'[19] Though Siegelaub had in mind art that had minimal material residue, including textual works, photographs, books and magazines that the cohort of conceptual artists he represented were engaged with, Cadere's bars were arguably much bulkier than any dematerialised art-work, but nonetheless enjoyed this very principle of mobility and spatial dis-persion. It is indeed this stubborn materiality of the bars, their particular weight and length, and the indexical registers of their being in a perpetual displacement that communicate itinerancy, transition and dispersion as their central concern. To paraphrase Jennifer L. Roberts, the space does not simply surround the bar, it *inhabits* it.[20]

Bouncing between bodies and sites, Cadere's bar stands as an early example of what David Joselit conceptualised as a transitive painting. According to Joselit, painting is capable of variously manifesting its belongingness to a net-work.[21] This capacity shows up in at least two manners in Cadere's work. First, each bar belongs to a 'closed', relatively small, family of bars – for example one sharing the same permutational system, colours and dimensions, but differing in the placement of an error; at the same time, each bar, translated into a code following its formal arrangement, stands as a single unique element in a vast but nonetheless exhaustible set determined by the preconceived restrictions discussed above.

Moreover, as the bar was, by design, conceived to be exhibited under various conditions and circumstances, through its passing apparitions in public and private spaces it accumulated social relationships and institutional networks. This otherwise virtual experience of the past, present and future passages of the round bars of wood is mediated in Cadere's communiqués, one of the genre of copious paperwork that the artist produced and distributed alongside his perambulations throughout the 1970s. Sent out to a selected number of addressees, the communiqué dated June 1975, for example, listed the 'geographical situation' of eight bars belonging to the group following the same permutational system in blue, yellow and red (the only difference among them being the location of an error in a sequence). The receiver of the paper learned that four bars were in France (three in Dijon and one in Paris), one in Brussels, one in Bari, and one in possession of the artist and thus presented in different places, while the last one was not yet made.[22] In another communiqué, issued on 8 December the same year, he made known the whereabouts of four of his bars: two could be found in galleries in Berlin and Naples, one could be seen placed in a private balcony in Paris visible from the street, and the premises of the last were unknown as it had disappeared from the exhibition after the artist had placed it there illegitimately two years before. Later, while preparing his book *Histoire d'un travail* (1977–78), the artist noted, apropos of the latter communiqué: 'One needs to point out that upon the day this book is printed at least two out of four pieces in question have changed their place or an owner.'[23] The self-distributed papers undoubtedly served as a means for publicity, as they indicated contacts at the galleries or persons in possession of the bars, and were sent to gallerists, dealers, critics and other artists. At the same time, these texts registered a history of the situated positions of a bar (or halts in a bar's passing) beyond the sites of its production and reception, and thus pointed out the work's characteristic quality of incessant dispersion, both actual and virtual.

'L'espace et la politique'

The bar's key feature was its autonomous structure, and therefore its adaptability to a wide range of situations: it rested on a floor, on a table, in a baker's vitrine, against or on a wall (interior as well as exterior), or was subjected to a perpetual dislocation by the travelling artist. In an interview with Lynda Morris in London in March 1976, where he came for his show at the Institute of Contemporary Art, the artist argued:

> Because my work has a degree of independence from the white space it is possible from the boundaries of my work to critically reflect the situation of the gallery. So it means that my work does not have anything to do with the architecture, with the style, with the aesthetics of the gallery, but it does have something to do with 'what is a gallery'. A gallery is a structure of power. My work has a critical attitude against that power. So it is possible to look at what is the power of galleries from the position of my work.[24]

This rumination originated in a period marked by Cadere's sustained enquiry into the problem of the bar's relation to space and its conceptual (critical) implications, alongside his attention to site-specificity as an artistic practice in particular.

'The history still to be made will take into consideration the place (the architecture) in which the work comes to rest (develops) as an integral part of the work in question and all the consequences such a link implies', stated Daniel Buren, arguably one of the most outspoken progenitors of site-specificity.[25] This statement appeared in his essay titled 'Function of architecture: Notes on work in connection with the places where it is installed', first published in a special issue of *Studio International* dedicated to examination of the interaction between art and architecture. The issue featured on its cover a photograph of Sol LeWitt's *Wall Drawing #257*, installed on Samangallery's vaulted ceilings less than a week after Cadere's exhibition at the same gallery.[26] Arguing against the idealism of an autonomous work, Buren advocated for a dialectical conflation of art object and the site of its appearance, framing his own work as a visual tool (*util visuel*). The pieces of striped canvas that the French artist placed in various artistic and non-artistic venues acquired their critical potential on the condition of their physical situatedness in a particular site, thus laying bare a presupposed neutrality of the institutional confinement and the artwork's presumed autonomy.[27] 'As for those who wish to ignore the architectural context in which they exhibit', continued Buren, 'they are the ones who still believe that a work is self-sufficient, no matter what surrounds it and no matter what the conditions in which it is perceived'.[28]

Shortly after Buren's essay was published, and a few months after his own exhibition at Samangallery, Cadere sent a text to Gianelli asking her to publish it.[29] In this short piece, soon printed in the gallery's bimonthly newsletter *Saman*, the artist aimed at conceptualising his exhibition at the gallery, framing the latter, for the first time, in a double bind of 'l'espace' and 'la politique':

> The exhibition focuses on two themes: space and politics. The themes are interdependent and share a basic common reality: the reality of the piece being exhibited.
>
> (1) Space: a round bar of wood, being cylindrical (without a right or wrong side) and being based on a systemic structure, has no relation with the wall …
> (2) Politics: in the art world, power belongs to those who select – these are the galleries and the museums. The exhibition described here illustrates the reversal of this situation.
>
> Through its ability to choose, and to be independent of institutions, this work raises questions about the absolute power wielded by these institutions. This is therefore a work which thanks to its specific relationship with space, inscribes itself in the field of politics.[30]

Not unlike Buren's conceptualisation of his striped canvas, Cadere understood his multicoloured bar as a tool – albeit one that enjoyed its aesthetic-cum-functional capabilities on the premise of its dislocation, its site-aspecificity. The political (critical) potential of the work of art lay for him, contra Buren, in the work's structural autonomy, affording it a possibility to promptly enter and exit different sites. The power of the institutional apparatus, in Cadere's case, is detected in a diffuse set of techniques and operations determining the possibility of appearance of a work of art in any institution (and the art world at large) in the first place.[31]

This question of the relation between artwork and space preoccupied Cadere for some time, and his references to the poststudio artistic context while positioning his own work became more explicit in the following months. In December 1975 the artist began a series of exhibitions that he framed under the rubric of space and politics. The first out of four exhibitions took place in

Belgium, at Elsa von Honolulu Loringhoven Gallery in Ghent, before continuing in Milan, London and Paris.[32] Sandwiched between a week during which Cadere showed his work in private venues in Ghent (coordinated by the gallery's owner, Belgian artist Jan Vercruysse) and the subsequent installation of a series of bars spread across the gallery's space, was a debate that Cadere organised titled 'Space and Politics: Interdependence'. A transcript of the debate (Cadere apparently wished to publish it as an essay) informs one that the key question the artist hoped to discuss was art's relation to architecture.[33] Though other names surfaced in the discussion, including Buren, Robert Ryman and Blinky Palermo, Cadere afforded a central focus to, in his view, 'the most powerful' work in this regard, Carl Andre's *39th Copper Cardinal*. The floor piece in Andre's exhibition at the Gallery Gian Enzo Sperone in Rome in October that year was installed under the *trompe-l'œil* fresco ceiling in one of the rooms of Palazzo del Drago occupied by the gallery, and was present at Cadere's debate as a postcard glued to the gallery's wall. This piece, consisting of a modular arrangement of copper plates, responded to the Palazzo's site, and thus, ruminated Cadere, would lose its meaning outside it; it depended on the gallery:

> There is the gallery, there is the museum; the thing is designed exactly to fit the gallery, it's total submission. There's nothing more to be said about the work, it's all about the gallery, the ceiling and all that … [D]uring recent times in different ways and by different routes everyone seems to be beginning to toe the line, to be coming back into museums and galleries. This can be observed at different levels, but the most recent level is the most alarming … it's a kind of total submission, they are thinking of nothing, they just measure up the gallery and make the thing the right length to fit the gallery and that's it.[34]

Pressed by the somehow anxious audience to speak about his own work instead, he argued that his bars, though also appearing in galleries and museums, work in a totally different manner.

Cadere had an occasion to prove his point while exhibiting at the Gian Enzo Sperone Gallery's original outpost in Turin in October that year – a show that ran simultaneously with Andre's in Rome.[35] Showing his bar in the gallery on the last day of the exhibition, the artist primarily treated the gallery not as a site providing a physical frame for his work, but as what he himself described as 'une fiche' (an index file). For his exhibition, Cadere asked an Italian dealer to provide him with the business cards of people living in Turin whom he would visit and show his bar to. He ended up with about thirty names and addresses. Thus, Cadere approached a gallery not as a physical entity, but as a dematerialised site of infrastructural support. In Sperone, as much as in the Elsa von Honolulu Loringhoven

Gallery, Cadere's engagement with the space was as a discursive site generating communication and contact.[36] Neither inducing a phenomenological experience nor performing a situated dialectical juxtaposition, his peripatetic work fashioned performative, relational situations.

Circulation

Cadere was a busy traveller.[37] His book *Histoire d'un travail*, the chronicle of his work from 1972 to 1977 that he himself compiled, outlines his busy transnational itinerary.[38] But it only partially covers the scope of his actual movement. For example, between 22 November 1973 – the date of his intervention into Adami's exhibition at the Parisian gallery Maeght, organised by the itinerant gallery run by Ida Biard, Galerie des Locataires – and 25 June 1974, the next inscription in the book marking his self-organised perambulations in Paris, the artist travelled to Milan, Rome and Naples, among other places.[39]

Though Siegelaub invoked the increased velocity with which the artworks traversed space, the artists themselves started to travel with or in their place. Lucy Lippard noted that 'much art now is transported by the artist, or *in* the artist himself … The artist is travelling a lot more, not to sightsee, but to get his work out.'[40] Formal innovations such as relatively affordable air and ground transportation; institutional transformations such as the emergence of a close-knit transnational network of dealers, collectors and museum curators; and the arrival of the global art events (biennales, art fairs) boosted and facilitated this artistic migration.[41] The Belgian collector Anton Herbert, also an early supporter of Cadere, pointed out the increasing presence of the travelling artists, remembering how in the 1960s and 1970s, together with his wife Annick, he:

> became part of a small family: Konrad Fischer, Jack Wendler, Art & Project, Harald Szeemann, Rudi Fuchs and – especially – Fernand Spillemaeckers. Through them we gained direct contact with artists such as Carl Andre, Daniel Buren, Robert Barry, Joseph Kosuth. These artists did not work in ateliers, but were nomads, going from one city to another, mostly in Europe, as there was little interest for them in America at the time.[42]

In his pursuit to conceptualise the increased mobility of artists as a paradigmatic shift, Michael Sanchez, taking as his case study one of the major actors in this process, the influential German art dealer Konrad Fischer, has recently described a 'logistical inversion' of the art world where 'a supply chain for artists themselves' developed as they worked *in situ* and established tête-à-tête connections as a challenge to the typical circulation of art objects.[43] As Sanchez put it, by the time Buren advocated against the circulation of portable objects, it had already been updated to a new system relying on the circulation of persons.[44] Navigating (largely European) terrain, Cadere was crossing paths with this new type of artists as nomads, whose work was not necessarily mobile in a performative way, but was no less so in its realisation and functioning.

Contact and communication played a central role in Cadere's conceptual project, as is further attested in his activity reports (*comptes-rendus d'activité*). These were documents registering the whereabouts of a single bar (B 02403010) that the artist issued twice, in February and March 1978. The first communicated his daily whereabouts in Paris and Brussels, whereas the second was sent by the artist to a number of people as he visited New York City, where he had travelled for his exhibition with Françoise Lambert at Julian Pretto Gallery. While in New York, he listed days and names of multiple artists (Carl Andre, Charlemagne Palestine, Sol LeWitt, Robert Ryman, Rosemarie Castoro), collectors (Herbert and Dorothy Vogel, Martin Visser), curators (Jean Hubert-Martin), dealers (Ileana Sonnabend, John Weber) and critics (Benjamin Buchloh) to whom he showed his bar during his visit (see Figure 11.3). The communiqué did not announce Cadere's upcoming exhibitions or the whereabouts of the bars, but simply reported the rendez-vous that had already taken place. As such, it brings to mind David Lamelas's *Antwerp-Brussels (People + Time)* (1969; see Figure 11.4), the work the artist produced a year after moving to Europe from Argentina. This is a collection of photographs featuring a number of art dealers, collectors and artists as they were crossing the streets of the two Belgian cities on their way to meet him. A caption in each photo provided the name of the person and the exact time and place that the artist encountered them.[45] As Kristina Newhouse notes, the series indicates social and professional relationships as a 'structural support' for the work: '*networking* is presented as a way of working'.[46] Similarly, Cadere's report, registering direct encounters, and his very use of mail, which the artist often employed throughout his career as a means of reaching out to a number of individuals, including collectors, critics and fellow artists, suggest this idea of the space of art as a social network.

Cadere's peripatetic work appears less as an anathema to site-specific practices (after all, as we have seen, poststudio artists were no less peripatetic; just think of LeWitt's and Buren's extensive travels). Rather, the round bar of wood in its material and performative capacity points out the shared conditions of the art world as a primarily networked space sustained by the circulation of artworks and artists, as well as direct social contact. In his interview with Sylvère Lotringer during the artist's visit to New York in 1978, when asked if his work was done once the bar was produced, Cadere replied: 'There must first of all be the reality of work. I sell this work; I make my living from it. Therefore, with respect to the reality of art, I have no exterior point of view. I am completely inside of it. I move throughout the circuit.'[47] Cadere's work not only belonged to conceptual art's networks of distribution and exhibition deux

compte-rendu d'activite adresse a:

- code de la piece:

    B 0 2 4 0 3 0 I 0 =35= =44x45=

- j'ai montre cette piece a:

        4.3.1978: charlemagne palestine, mario bartolini, marcel just,
                  michael sonnabend, angela westwater, carl andre, pat
                  steir, martine rapin, peter downsbrough, david bourdon.
        5.3.1978: connie beckley, ara arslanian.
        6.3.1978: jack lisveld.
        7.3.1978: jeanne claude + christo, yvon lambert, diego cortez,
                  heiner friedrich.
        8.3.1978: sylvere lotringer, antonio, gilbert + george, amy baker,
                  leo castelli, edda renouf.
        9.3.1978: tony shafrazy, hal bromm, benjamin buchloh, rosemarie
                  castoro.
       10.3.1978: robin white.
       11.3.1978: kosuth, sarah charlesworth, jean + santiago boutan,
                  sol lewitt, joe neil, ileana sonnabend, alain middleton,
                  holly solomon.
       12.3.1978: saska.
       13.3.1978: robert ryman, david ebony, peter zabelius, duncan
                  smith.
       14.3.1978: marina urbach, francoise lambert.
       15.3.1978: dorothy + herbert vogel.
       17.3.1978: julian pretto, john weber, robert barry.
       18.3.1978: jean-hubert martin, mac adams, speyer.
       19.3.1978: jean-marie haessle, maria broodthaers, distel, lawrence
                  weiner, richard nonas, martin visser, kennedy, brenda
                  miller.
       20.3.1978: brice marden, robert indiana, litvinov, ronald feldman.

andre cadere
new york, 27.3.1978

André Cadere's activity report, 1978.

11.3

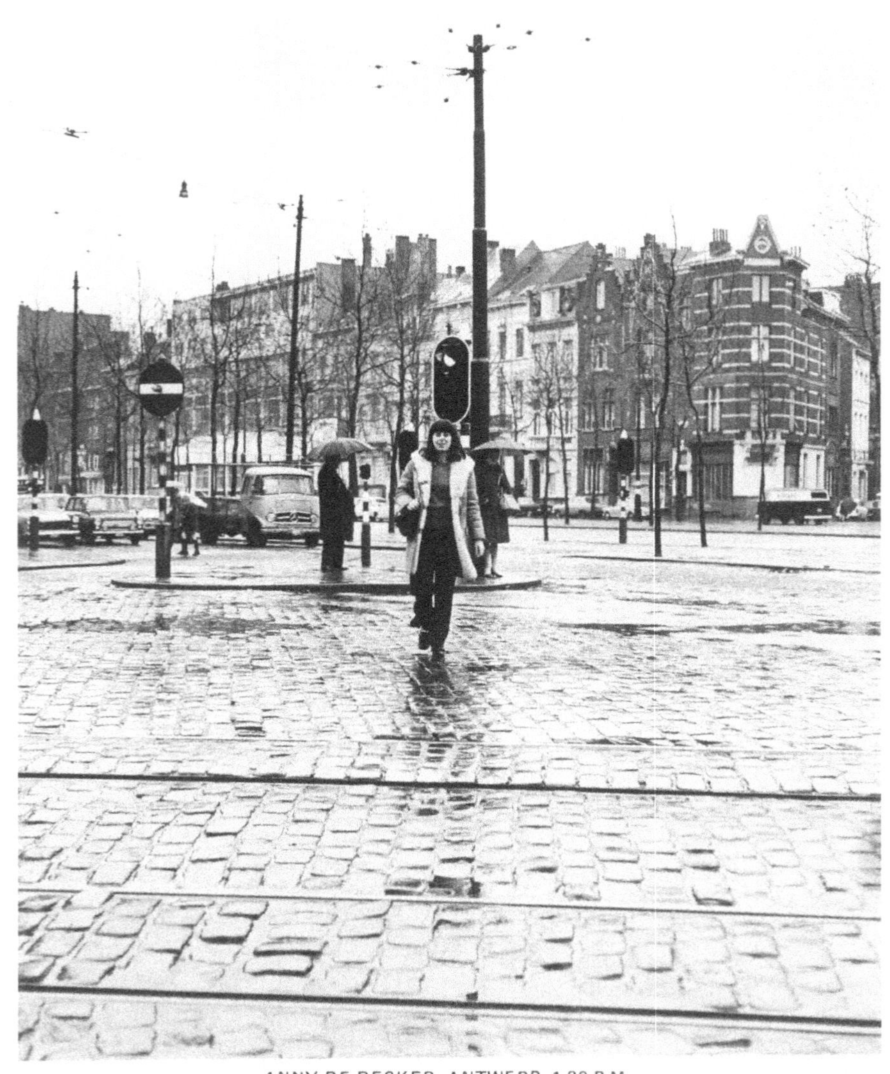

11.4 David Lamelas, *Antwerp-Brussels (People + Time)*, 1969. Black-and-white photograph, 29.5 cm × 23.5 cm.

(either legitimately or in an illicit manner) but, by being inside the circuit, captured this new dynamic of the art system transforming seemingly invisible conditions of art's production and reception – namely the artist's nomadic presence – into an observable – and traceable – reality. What might well have begun as a strategy motivated by a pure necessity to invent new models of showing one's work bereft of institutional support grew into a practice that both tested and illuminated the functioning of the art world and explored the artists' place – and their *work* – within it.[48]

Notes

1 André Cadere, 'Talking with Lynda Morris', in Karola Grässlin, Fabrice Hergott and Alexander van Grevenstein (eds), *André Cadere: Peinture sans fin* (Cologne: Walther König, 2007), p. 17.

2 *Corriere mercantile*, 14 May 1975; translation mine.

3 Among the international roster of artists featured in the gallery's programme were Niele Toroni, Daniel Buren, Giulio Paolini, Giuseppe Penone, Michelangelo Pistoletto, Charles Simonds, Sol LeWitt, Dan Graham, Lawrence Weiner and Joseph Kosuth.

4 See Lily Woodruff, 'André Cadere's disorderly conduct', in Catherine Dossin (ed.), *France and the Visual Arts since 1945* (New York: Bloomsbury, 2019), pp. 227–36; and Lily Woodruff, *Disordering the Establishment: Participatory Art and Institutional Critique in France, 1958–1981* (Durham, NC: Duke University Press, 2020).

5 Andrew Forge, 'Letter from Paris', *Studio International* 953 (March 1973), 116.

6 For a genealogy of site-specific art see Miwon Kwon, *One Place after Another: Site-Specific Art and Locational Identity* (Cambridge, MA: MIT Press, 2002).

7 As quoted in *ibid.*, p. 169n1. Originally in Douglas Crimp, *On the Museum's Ruins* (Cambridge, MA: MIT Press, 1993), p. 17.

8 James Meyer, 'The functional site; or, The transformation of site specificity', in Erika Suderburg (ed.), *Space, Site, Intervention: Situating Installation Art* (Minneapolis: University of Minnesota Press, 2000), p. 27.

9 Cadere kept records of the bars produced, noting their codes in his personal notebook. These codes also appear on the certificates issued to the owners of the bars.

10 For a detailed description of the permutational systems and formal features of the round bar of wood see Bernard Marcelis, 'How to look at a round bar of wood', in Karola Grässlin, Astrid Ihle and Fabrice Hergott (eds), *André Cadere: Catalogue raisonné* (Cologne: Walther König, 2008). The most recent retrospective, *André Cadere: Step by Step*, curated by Frédéric Paul at the Centre Pompidou in Paris in 2018, presented a great variety of round bars of wood from private and public collections dispersed throughout the permanent display of the museum's collection.

11 Sol LeWitt, 'Paragraphs on conceptual art', *Artforum* (Summer 1967), 79–84, reprinted in Alexander Alberro and Blake Stimson (eds), *Conceptual Art: A Critical Anthology* (Cambridge, MA: MIT Press, 1999), pp. 12–16.

12 Sol LeWitt, *Wall Drawings* (4–27 June 1970). Other art workers were Maurice-Frédérick Calatchi, Andrei Doicescu, Mikolt Kemény, Yvon Lambert and Alfred Pacquement. Sol LeWitt, *Wall Drawings*, ed. Lindsay Aveilhé (online *catalogue raisonné*) (New York: Artifex, 2018). Three years later, Cadere helped Lambert to realise yet another piece by LeWitt, *Wall Drawing #186*, this time in the gallerist's apartment in Saint-Germain-des-Prés. 'Interview: Stéphane Ibars with Yvon Lambert', in Stéphane Ibars (ed.), *Sol LeWitt* (Arles: Actes Sud, 2019), p. 29.

13 Alfred Pacquement, 'Sol LeWitt et les systèmes de combinaison', *Opus International* 22 (1970), 30–1. The idea of error was made explicit in these works by LeWitt: 'if there are errors in execution, they have been left and not erased, they are part of the work also'. Quoted in Pacquement, 'Sol LeWitt', p. 30. The errors, though not excluded, were for LeWitt accidental and involuntary, whereas for Cadere the error became an obligatory principle purposefully deranging the order.

14 During his lifetime, the artist made around 200 pieces. See Grässlin *et al.*, *André Cadere: Catalogue raisonné*.

15 Cadere would use a wall as a support for the spray paintings he made in 1972. Consider, for example, his entry for Expo+500. With the goal of presenting the largest panorama of contemporary art, the exhibition in question was organised by Relais Culturel d'Aix-en-Provence in 1972 as an itinerant project exhibiting artists' responses to three questions mailed to the organisers: 'What do you do?', 'Why?' and 'How?'. Instead of answering those questions, Cadere submitted the proposal 'take three colors: RED (R), YELLOW (Y), BLUE (B). Execute the following work on a fence somewhere in the city or in the exhibition space: R/Y/B/Y/B/R etc. … (following schema and dimensions).' Maurice Allemand, *Dossier France – Expositions, manifestations, programmation*, Archives de la critique d'art, Rennes.

16 'The physical properties of the wall: height, length, color, material, and architectural conditions and intrusions, are a necessary part of the wall drawings.' Sol LeWitt, 'Wall Drawings', *Arts Magazine* (April 1970), reprinted in Alicia Legg (ed.), *Sol LeWitt: The Museum of Modern Art, New York* (New York: The Museum, 1978), p. 169. For informed analysis of LeWitt's wall pieces see Anna Lovatt, 'Ideas in transmission: LeWitt's Wall Drawings and the question of medium', *Tate Papers* 14 (Autumn 2010), www.tate.org.uk/research/tate-papers/14/ideas-in-transmission-lewitt-wall-drawings-and-the-question-of-medium (accessed 24 March 2023); and Erica DiBenedetto, 'LeWitt's locations, to a point', in David S. Areford (ed.), *Locating Sol LeWitt* (New Haven, CT: Yale University Press, 2021), pp. 147–75.

17 The bars were of varying length and diameter – some as short and lean as to fit easily in a handbag, whereas the biggest ones could hardly be lifted. The longest bar, which was probably made as a gift for the French artist Jean Le Gac and his wife Jacqueline sometime in 1971–72, measures 285 cm in length and 3 cm in diameter. Cadere determined the length of the bar, also somewhat unusually, by following the length of a wall of a corridor at Le Gac's house. However, these kinds of extremities were quite rare and appear largely in the early years of the bars' production.

18 André Cadere, letter to Yvon Lambert, 27 November 1977, Herbert Archive. All translations from unpublished materials, unless otherwise noted, are my own.

19 Seth Siegelaub at the symposium 'Art without Space'. Radio transcript quoted in Lucy Lippard (ed.), *Six Years: The Dematerialization of the Art Object from 1966 to 1972* (Berkeley: University of California Press, 1997), p. 132.

20 Jennifer L. Roberts, *Transporting Visions: The Movement of Images in Early America* (Berkeley: University of California Press, 2014). In her book, Roberts argues that real and illusionary transport and mobility were concerns expressed in the paintings and prints of artists of the eighteenth and nineteenth centuries, such as John Singleton Copley, John James Audubon and Asher B. Durand.

21 David Joselit, 'Painting beside itself', *October* 130 (Fall 2009), 125–34.

22 André Cadere, *Histoire d'un travail* (Ghent: Herbert-Gewad, 1982), p. 21.

23 *Ibid.*, p. 28.

24 Cadere, 'Talking with Lynda Morris', p. 31.

25 Daniel Buren, 'Function of architecture: Notes on work in connection with the places where it is installed. Taken between 1967 and 1975, some of which are specially summarized here for the September/October 1975 edition of *Studio International*', *Studio International* 977 (September/October 1975), 124.

26 For the exhibition *Sol LeWitt: Disegni su parete e disegni* at Samangallery (23 May–22 June 1975), LeWitt made two wall drawings: *Wall Drawing #257* in red, and *Wall Drawing #258* in blue. They are the first wall drawings conceived by LeWitt to be installed entirely on a ceiling. Cadere's exhibition at the gallery ran on 12–17 May 1975. The artists probably crossed paths, as LeWitt arrived in Genoa on 13 May. Email exchange between the author and Janet Passehl, Curator at the LeWitt Collection, 14 April 2021.

27 See Benjamin H. D. Buchloh, *Formalism and Historicity: Models and Methods in Twentieth-Century Art* (Cambridge, MA: MIT Press, 2015), pp. 1–79; Alexander Alberro, 'The turn of the screw: Daniel Buren, Dan Flavin, and the Sixth Guggenheim International Exhibition', *October* 80 (Spring 1997), 57–84.

28 Buren, 'Function of architecture', 125.

29 'Here you will find my text about my show in [G]enova[;] for me this text is important because it is here [I] mention about the relationship [of] space and politics … that I never did before … I ask you, if possible, to publish this text in [I]talian but also in [F]rench.' André Cadere, letter to Ida Gianelli, 9 September 1975 (original in English), Archive of Bibliothèque Kandinsky, Ida Gianelli papers.

30 Originally published in *Saman* 3, October/November 1975. Translated into English in Lynda Morris, *André Cadere: Documenting Cadere 1972–1978* (London: Koenig, 2013), p. 84, with my corrections following the French version of the text, Caderé, *Histoire d'un travail*, p. 18.

31 Shortly before Cadere began articulating his ideas about space and politics, he started exhibiting his bars more often in what he called a 'classical' manner, sometimes installed as a series. Apart from his perambulations outside the galleries, these exhibitions featured a series of bars arranged in a gallery's space in such a manner as to elucidate their formal qualities (the principle of error, for example). In April 1975, the first of such series was exhibited at Galerie MTL in Brussels.

32 After the exhibition at Elsa Von Honolulu Loringhoven Gallery, which closed on 8 January 1976, the series continued the following month at the Françoise Lambert Gallery in Milan, followed by his exhibition at the Institute of Contemporary Art in London in March, and finally a solo wrapping-up presentation in the bus shelter at Saint-Germain-des-Prés in Paris in May.

33 Jan Vercruysse Archive, Brussels, 'Espace et politique: Interdépendance' ['Space and Politics: Interdependence'], transcript of the debate, p. 13.

34 *Ibid.*

35 Carl Andre at Gian Enzo Sperone in Rome, 20 September–18 October 1975; André Cadere at Gian Enzo Sperone in Turin, 6–14 October 1975.

36 Cadere would also often use a gallery as a place for discussions and debates.

37 The Paris-based gallerist Anka Ptaszkowska recalled that 'Cadere had a quality of being everywhere at the same time. If you were at the documenta, he would be there; at the same time he would be at the fair in Düsseldorf; and at the vernissage in Paris, etc.' 'Portrait of a wooden bar', in Magda Radu (ed.), *André Cadere = Andrei Cădere* (Bucharest: Muzeul Național de Artă Contemporană, 2011), p. 409.

38 The draft of the book was handed by the artist to Anton Herbert and published posthumously in 1982.

39 Cadere's handwritten CV, reproduced in Morris, *André Cadere*, pp. 146–9. See also Bernard Marcelis, 'André Cadere: The strategy of displacement', in Carole Kismaric *et al.* (eds), *André Cadere: All Walks of Life* (New York: Institute for Contemporary Art, P.S. 1 Museum, in association with Musée d'Art Moderne de la Ville de Paris: Chambre, 1992), pp. 41–74.

40 Lucy Lippard, 'Preface', in Lippard, *Six Years*, p. 8.

41 Sophie Richard, *Unconcealed: The International Network of Conceptual Artists 1967–77. Dealers, Exhibitions and Public Collections* (London: Ridinghouse, 2010). See also Christoph Cherix (ed.), *In & out of Amsterdam: Travels in Conceptual Art, 1960–1976* (New York: Museum of Modern Art, 2009).

42 Anton Herbert, Hans-Joachim Müller, Peter Pakesch and Manuel J. Borja-Villel, 'On collecting: Private and public. A round table', in *Public Space/Two Audiences: Inventaire* (Barcelona: Museu d'Art Contemporani di Barcelona; Kunsthaus Graz, 2006), p. 37.

43 Michael Sanchez, 'A logistical inversion: From Konrad Lueg to Konrad Fischer', *Grey Room* 63 (2016), 6–41.

44 *Ibid.*, 18.

45 The documentary nature of the piece is indicated by the fact that it was misclassified as a 'document' rather than an artwork. The folio was originally acquired by the Archives of Contemporary Art in Brussels as a record of art-world figures. It was later reclassified as a conceptual artwork and transferred to the Musée Modern Museum, Brussels. María José Herrera and Kristina Newhouse (eds), *David Lamelas: A Life of Their Own* (Los Angeles: Getty Publications, 2017), p. 222.

46 Kristina Newhouse, 'Time + situation + people: An introduction', in Herrera and Newhouse, *David Lamelas*, p. 26 (original emphasis).

47 Sylvère Lotringer, 'Andre Cadere: Boy with stick', *Semiotext(e)* 2 (1978), 141.

48 In the interview with Sylvère Lotringer, Cadere commented on his initial motiv-
ation of 'operating from the margins': 'Perhaps it's because I came from Roumania
[*sic*], a country which is outside the Western cultural system, a totally marginal
country. I came to France without money, without relations. With respect to the
social order, I was nothing at all. I had no means of support. The sole possibility
that was left for me was to do my work all alone, independently of the existing
social system.' *Ibid.*, 140.

Delirium ambulatorium – city walks as conceptual mapping: From Hélio Oiticica to Rasheed Araeen and Lee Wen

Eva Bentcheva and María José Martínez Sanchez

> I love that city and it is the only place in the world that interests me …
> This trip and now the prospect of coming back have cheered me up so much
> that it seems I'm alive again … I felt such an 'ambulatory delirium' that
> I couldn't stop walking day and night around the city.
>
> Hélio Oiticica (October 1970)[1]

Writing during a brief stay in New York in October 1970, Brazil-born artist Hélio Oiticica (1937–80) first used the term 'ambulatory delirium' to describe his feelings of intense elation when walking through the city. The year marked a number of successes for the young artist. Having departed from Brazil in 1968, Oiticica held his first solo exhibition at the Whitechapel Gallery in London in 1969, followed by an invitation to participate in the influential exhibition *Information* at the Museum of Modern Art in New York in 1970. Concurrently, he was awarded a prestigious Guggenheim Foundation fellowship to develop further work between 1971 and 1973. 'Ambulatory delirium' thus not only captured the artist's immense joy and sense of personal success, it also conveyed one of the central premises of his artistic practice since his time in Brazil: namely, how the simple act of wandering served as a means for the city's space to be imprinted upon, and conceptually 'charted' by, the artistic imagination.

With the start of his new residence in New York in December 1970, Oiticica's previous practice became permeated by a budding fascination with the metropolis's cosmopolitan vibrancy. Within this context, his incessant drive to walk mirrored a desire conceptually to 'map' the city onto the self and, in turn, allow the self to become imbued with its energy, identity and topography. Over the course of the decade, Oiticica would pursue this idea in a number of conceptual, sculptural, multimedia and textual projects. The most notable of these included *Subterranea tropicália*, an unrealised participatory structure to be installed under Central Park; as well as *Penetrables*, installation-like spaces in which viewers could enter and embody an architectural space of their own; and finally *Newyorkaise*, an expansive and unfinished collection of poetic and propositional writings centred on a conceptual engagement with New York. Despite the richness of these works, however, Oiticica's celebration of New York gave way to feelings marked by pessimism, discrimination and exile by the end of the decade. In 1978, he departed from New York and returned to his native Brazil, where he reactivated the notion of 'ambulatory delirium'.

In November 1978, he wrote *delirium ambulatorium*, a short poetic proposition for an interactive performance conceived for an arts festival in São Paulo.[2] Calling upon audiences to traverse the outskirts of the city, observe its inhabitants, and collect natural materials and elements from the city's structures, Oiticica divorced *delirium ambulatorium* from its original elated reflection of New York. Instead, he invoked an act of 'mapping' rooted in 'non-linear movement', and collective resilience against political dictatorship and worsening socio-economic divisions in Brazil. Returning to his earlier explorations of dance and walking in the favelas of Rio de Janeiro in participatory works such as *Tropicália* (1967) and *Parangolés* (1964) – and further echoing discourses around anthropophagy and postcolonial community theatre in Brazil – *delirium ambulatorium* tapped into issues of race, visibility and cultural resilience.

While much scholarship has been devoted to Oiticica's installations and sculptural works, this chapter highlights *delirium ambulatorium* as an oft-overlooked 'textual extension' of his practices.[3] It revisits its iteration as a performative text from 1978, arguing for its importance in connection to two of Oiticica's central ideas. The first was Oiticica's search for forms to convey what Guy Debord termed the 'psychogeographies', or playful and personal explorations of a city.[4] In Oiticica's practice, this manifested itself in terms such as 'supra-sensorial' to describe his wandering around Rio de Janeiro, and 'environmental artworks', for which he developed installation-like structures to convey the conceptual and sensorial encounters between bodies and the urban realm. The second importance of *delirium ambulatorium* relates to Oiticica's interest in conceptually 'mapping' social, racial and economic divisions within city spaces. Within this framework, walking emerged as an artistic methodology both to divest the self and to witness divisions along the lines of socio-economic status, race and class while allowing the self to be conceptually imprinted by these experiences.

This latter understanding resonates beyond Oiticica's own work and reflects a shared philosophy of urban movement, particularly in the works of artists exploring biography at the junction of racial and political divisions in city spaces. In its final section, this chapter examines how this was manifested in two performance-based artworks by artists of diasporic backgrounds: Pakistan-born Rasheed Araeen's one-off photo-documented walk *Paki Bastard (Portrait of the Artist as a Black Person)*, staged in London in 1977, and Singapore-born artist Lee Wen's performance series *Journey of a*

Yellow Man, also first staged in London in 1992, and subsequently performed internationally until 2001. This chapter aims to show not a direct historical influence, but rather a conceptual 'resonance' between the works of Oiticica, Araeen and Lee. Through this, it highlights a common ethos and commitment to walking as a charting of personal imagination and the self within urban spaces, as well as a gesture of decolonial 'ingestion' or 'digestion' of the metropolis's unwelcoming structures.

Towards a methodology of non-linear movement

Soon after returning from an eight-year residence in New York, Hélio Oiticica wrote *delirium ambulatorium* in Brazil on 24 October 1978 (see Figure 12.1). The piece took the form of a poetic and instructional 'proposition' for an interactive performance to be staged as part of the festival *Mitos vadios* (November 1978), organised by the artist Ivald Granato in São Paulo.[5] In the original, handwritten text, Oiticica deployed his characteristic fragmented statements interspersed with lines and arrows, suggestive of the movement of bodies and thoughts. Here, the artist announced his intention to 'walk to and fro without linearity' around the boundaries (or what he termed the 'wasteland') of São Paulo. Inventing a number of actions along the way, the artist would guide participants to wear self-made capes (a reference to his longstanding participatory performance *Parangolés*), as well as to collect 'token fragments' of the city such as sand, pieces of pavement and river water. Echoing his original reference of 'ambulatory delirium' in the aforementioned letter to fellow artist Lygia Clark from 1970, Oiticica once again invoked Clark's presence through an enigmatic quote on the process of mystification and demystification involved in the act of walking: 'They do and undo themselves like walking in the streets of the nocturnal delirium ambulatorium.'

As one of Oiticica's late propositions before the artist's untimely passing away in 1980, this text may be considered as a retrospective reflection upon his own practice.[6] It demonstrates Oiticica's return to a number of his earlier explorations. Here, the simple act of walking served as a conceptual 'mapping' of the self within the city, and vice versa. This interpretation emerges when *delirium ambulatorium* is contextualised alongside Oiticica's experiments with space and spatiality in Brazil during the 1960s, before departing for Europe and the USA.

While Oiticica's early career was marked by explorations of colour and geometry as part of the neo-concrete movement in Brazil (1959–61),[7] his conceptually oriented works during the mid-to-late 1960s engaged directly with the lived realities of Brazil's cities. During this period, he developed the practice of walking or drifting through the city's poor neighbourhoods without a fixed objective – a practice that he related back to his teenage years. Drawn to

ho
rio
ATAULFO ———➤   24 out. 78

                        texto-release para a minha participação em
MITOS VADIOS de IVALD GRANATO a ser realizado como performance de
participação vária a 5 de NOV. de 1978 em SÃO PAULO

DELIRIUM AMBULATORIUM

                H. OITICICA
                LFER

                        a dupla
                        a minha participação

                                        Ⓐ caminhar pela
periferia da área-baldia demarcada durante a duração da performance:
caminhar to and fro sem linearidade

                        ambulatoriar:
                                inventar "coisas para
fazer" durante a caminhada

                        Ⓑ levar do RIO capa-faixa de murim
plastificado com cola vinílica para ser enrolada em corpos
diversos:
                'procurar' a pele preta ideal para o toque da
faixa-murim:
                essa capa está ainda por ser feita

                                Ⓒ levar em sacos
ou talvez solucionado de outro modo: talvez nos containers de vinil de
fotografia apanhados em SÃO CRISTOVÃO ———➤   fragmentos-tokens do
RIO

        samples de asfalto da AV. PRES. VARGAS ———➤   terra do MORRO DA
MANGUEIRA ———➤   água da PRAIA DE IPANEMA ———➤   pequenos objetos de
bazares da RUA LARGA

Hélio Oiticica, *Delirium ambulatorium*, 24 October 1978.

exploring the areas of Rio de Janeiro where bodies had a prominent presence, such as the bohemian zone of Lapa and Mangué, which had the highest concentrations of sex workers, Oiticica went on to incorporate his impressions into a number of installations and performances in which the act of walking became synonymous with mapping.[8] In one of his most well-known works from this period, *Tropicália* (see Figure 12.2), Oiticica went as far as describing the installation as 'a map of Rio … and a map of my imagination'.[9]

Tropicália comprised a geometric maze containing materials such as sand, plants, gravel, a living parrot and even a television set that visitors could watch at the end of their experience.[10] For Oiticica, *Tropicália* was to be encountered as a sensory 'environment', or what he termed a 'supra-sensorial' experience.[11] As one of Oiticica's *Penetrables*, or works with labyrinthine

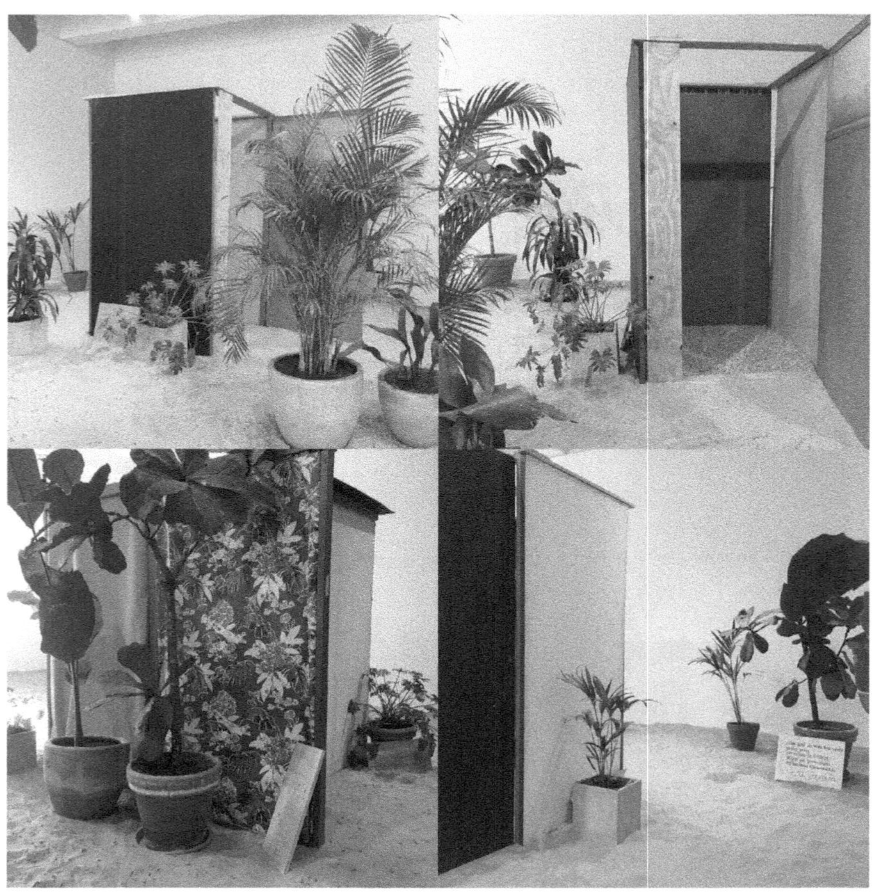

12.2 Hélio Oiticica, *Tropicália*, 1967.

structures, *Troplicália* was also built in such a way that the viewers could walk around in a non-linear manner and decipher the structure on their own terms. By actively encouraging individual perambulation, *Tropicália* thus mirrored Oiticica's wandering of Rio's favelas. And yet, it was not intended to serve as a literal map. Rather, it embodied Oiticica's imaginative charting of his observations and sensations of this urban reality, as well as his conceptual projection of himself onto the space. Here, the urban environment, whether performative or architectural, could become assimilated into the artist's body via movement or choreography (*corpocidade*) as it came into contact with the non-tangible elements of the city.[12] Simultaneously, space could imprint itself or cause transformations in the viewer (*corpografia*) when it acquired a social dimension.[13] As Luciano Figuereido has poignantly described this relationship: 'no favelas in Rio have spaces and environments that we could figuratively associate with the environment of *Tropicália*. We should focus rather on the existential meaning the favelas gave to his life, his art.'[14] This understanding of walking as an imaginative mapping of the self onto space, and vice versa, would later feature in *delirium ambulatorium* as a site-specific methodology.

In addition to its emphasis on sensory experiences and impressions, Oiticica's understanding of walking from the 1960s also echoed what Guy Debord and the situationists described as 'psychogeography'.[15] This referred to playful, drifting encounters with urban environments aimed at breaking down the barriers between art and life. In a similar vein, Oiticica's early wanderings embraced playfulness and dynamic interactions with others.[16] Particularly influential for this was the artist's participation in carnival as a *passista*, or samba dancer, in the favela of Morro da Mangueira in Rio de Janeiro. For Oiticica, samba represented an opposition to the intellectualisation of the repetitive movement in classical dance forms such as ballet.[17] Instead, it reflected a dynamic means of expression in which the body could absorb the spirit of the favela and mirror its physical and topographical, as well as cultural, political and social, stimuli.[18] Oiticica notably elaborated upon this fascination with irregular and socially produced movements in his renowned participatory dance capes, *Parangolés*. However, this also appeared in *delirium ambulatorium*'s encouragement to enter into dream-like states and conduct poetic gestures in the urban realm: 'the streets and nonsense of our daily daydreams are enriched'.[19]

Speaking of Oiticica's interest in generating erratic and open-ended encounters, art critic Guy Brett has described a number of the artist's works as striving towards 'a non-repressive collectivism'.[20] This description situates *delirium ambulatorium* beyond the notion of 'psychogeography'. It draws attention to how Oiticica's call for a non-linearity and dream-like poetic encounters not only celebrated the dilapidated peripheries of São Paulo (as

Oiticica had once developed in relation to Rio de Janeiro's favelas and, later, towards New York). Instead, walking in *delirium ambulatorium* also stood for an act of 'ingestion' akin to the discourses of anthropophagy in Brazil.[21] As articulated by Brazilian writer Oswald de Andrade in the 'Anthropophagic manifesto' of 1928, anthropophagy evoked the eating of human flesh, including tissues and bones, as a metaphor for cultural appropriation. In a similar vein, *delirium ambulatorium* called for an absorption and conceptual 'digestion' of found materials and fragments of the city during the walk – a gesture that Oiticica further elaborated as aiming to 'mythify/demystify'.

This evocation of mythology was, on the one hand, a direct reference to the title of the arts festival *Mitos vadios*, for which *delirium ambulatorium* was conceived. On the other, it also pertained to the role of 'myths' around identity politics, and movements for democracy and decolonisation as they were being 'mapped' within the urban spaces of Brazil. As already noted by Oiticica in 1965:

> [The social layers] became somehow schematic, artificial for me, as if I was suddenly seeing from a great height their scheme. Marginalisation, which exists naturally for the artist, became suddenly basic for me, a complete 'lack of social place', and at the same time the discovery of my 'individual place' as a whole person in the world, as a social being in a common sense, not belonging to any elite, even an artistic one … social in its most noble sense.[22]

Echoing Brett's characterisation of Oiticica's work as 'non-repressive collectivism', this desire to expose myths and fabrications lent *delirium ambulatorium* a strong affinity with social, participatory and activist practices, particularly as voiced by the Brazilian drama theorist Augusto Boal.[23] In *Theatre of the Oppressed* (1974), Boal called for an activation of theatrical forms to reflect socio-political realities in the wake of postcolonial and authoritarian Brazil. Seen within this intellectual backdrop, *delirium ambulatorium* similarly reflected a wider turn towards performative methodologies that could, in the words of Henri Lefebvre, chart 'the spatial practice of a society [which] secretes that society's space'.[24] This socio-political dimension of *delirium ambulatorium*, in turn, lent Oiticica's works a wider resonance within artistic practices seeking to test the limits of conceptual and abstract art by way of walking in public and city spaces.

Transnational resonance

The contextualisation of Oiticica's *delirium ambulatorium* reveals an understanding of urban walking as rooted in both a personal exploration of space and an imaginative 'mapping' of the artist's body onto the city, and vice versa. However, speaking of this conceptual and performative relationship,

Oiticica did not adopt a homogeneous understanding of city spaces. Instead, he acknowledged the importance of historical developments and social predicaments in shaping what he described as the individual 'scenographic' nature of each city:

> Everything [in New York] is scenographic: even the street, do you understand? If you do something on the street it is not participation any more, people start to rationalise as if it were an 'event' and they call it installation. 'I'm going to do an installation in Washington Square, do you get it?' Then why not do it inside your house, since in New York there is not so much of a difference between the inside of a museum and the street? While in Brazil there is [a difference].[25]

This proposition yields a further insight into *delirium ambulatorium*: namely, its insistence on the historical positionality of artists' own identities as they came into contact with different urban spaces. This lent Oiticica's works a transcultural adaptability that had a particular resonance in the context of London. *The Whitechapel Experiment* (1969) received praise for its novel explorations of participation in works such as *Tropicália* and *Ninhos* (*Nests*, 1969), but Oiticica's ideas had in fact circulated in London among artists working with performance art and kinetic and participatory art since the mid-1960s.[26] Particularly important for his legacy were the networks of the Signals Art Gallery (1964–66) in London and its accompanying publication, the *Signals Newsbulletin*, edited by Philippines-born artist David Medalla. Here, Oiticica's work gained a new following within the framework of 'kinetic art'. In works by Medalla, Jesus Rafael Soto, Lygia Clark, Sergio Camargo and Takis (Panayiotis Vassilakis), the kinetic art of Signals reflected an understanding of sculptural movement as a reflection of the artists' peripatetic lifestyles, as well as allegiances with socialist ideology and anti-dictatorial internationalism, particularly in relation to Asia and Latin America.[27]

While Oiticica was not present in London in person at this point, his inclusion in discussions at Signals on movement served to anchor his ideas around 'non-linearity', 'supra-sensorial' experiences and 'environments' within nascent conversations around identity politics and internationalism, which would later come to flourish in the UK between the 1970s and 1990s. In what follows, this chapter explores the resonance of Oiticica's ideas around urban movement (as they were expressed in *delirium ambulatorium*) within two works initially staged in London by the artists Rasheed Araeen and Lee Wen, both artists whose practices show connections to Signals. While Araeen and Lee's works did not abide by the participatory dimension of Oiticica's practice, they echoed *delirium ambulatorium*'s emphasis on conceptually mapping the self within socio-political, economic and racial terrains at given moments in time.

Rasheed Araeen's *Paki Bastard (Portrait of the Artist as a Black Person)* (1977–78)

Parallel to Oiticica's explorations of dance and space upon returning to Brazil, the practice of walking through the city was investigated in a highly politicised way in the 1970s by UK-based artist Rasheed Araeen. Arriving in the UK from Pakistan in the early 1960s, Araeen engaged early on with minimalist and symmetrical geometric 'structures'. In the period from 1975 to 1982, his works took a decisive turn towards investigating how space, politicisation and identity could be manifested through conceptual art.[28] Deeply aware, via a personal friendship with David Medalla, of the work of Signals and its discourses, Araeen became increasingly preoccupied during the 1970s with performative and sculptural movement as a means of championing the causes of the 'Third World' and making visible the works of artists of diasporic backgrounds working in 'the West'.[29]

In 1978, Araeen voiced the need for the greater artistic and public presence of artists in a text titled 'Preliminary notes for a black manifesto'.[30] This text featured a disclaimer that it was not an objective analysis but a 'personal statement' whose knowledge was derived from Araeen's observations of modern art in Pakistan and his experiences as 'a third world man' with the art institutions in Britain. Here, Araeen stated:

> The experience of living in the West has led him [referring to himself] to *black consciousness* and to the awareness that HIS REAL PLACE IS IN THE THIRD WORLD. This is an attempt now on his part to re-examine his relationship with the West, and redefine his artistic role in the cultural context of his people, whether they live in their own countries or in the West.[31]

Calling on artists of Asian, Latin American and Afro-Caribbean origin to reassess and assert their contribution to contemporary art in Britain and the wider 'West', 'Preliminary notes for a black manifesto' argued for a break with the notion that western culture was superior to that of the Third World. The text concluded by inviting artists living and working in the 'West' to undertake a series of actions through which they demanded equal recognition and fostered greater exchange of information and ideas with their contemporaries in the Third World. By calling for a greater exchange, Araeen's manifesto intended to transcend the realm of academic discourses, and set in motion a series of real actions and exchanges in which artists devoted themselves to overcoming global inequalities.

In 1977, Araeen conceived a three-part series of performances to accompany this text. These were intended to visualise and explore Araeen's growing interest in the themes of cultural imperialism, discrimination, and the dynamics of how racial identities were formed and projected onto others.[32] The works were entitled *Towards the Centre and Back, Paki Bastard (Portrait of*

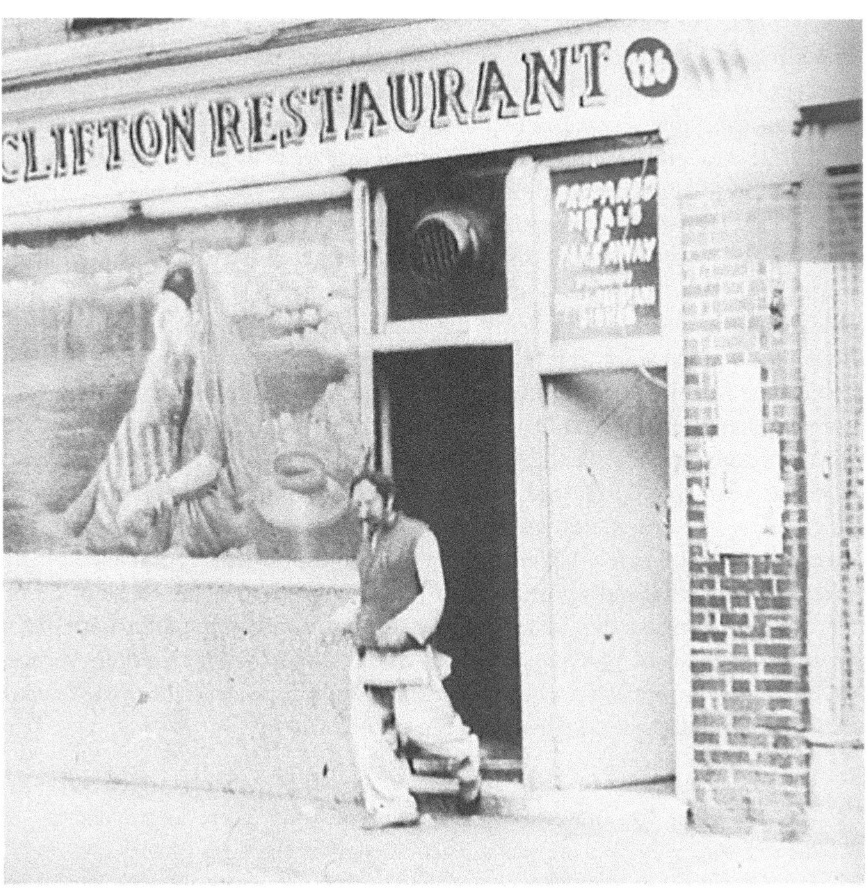

Rasheed Araeen, *Paki Bastard (Portrait of the Artist as a Black Person)*, image of the artist   **12.3**
exiting Clifton Restaurant. Private performance, Brick Lane, London, 1977.

the Artist as a Black Person) (see Figure 12.3) and *I'm a Noble Savage Come and Find Me*, and Araeen planned to stage them in front of a live audiences as part of the manifesto's outreach and call for action. While all three were planned in detail, only *Paki Bastard* was realised. The work comprised two parts: a private, photographically documented walk by Araeen around the area of Brick Lane in east London in June 1977, followed by a live performance enacted in front of an audience at the headquarters of the artistic collective Artists for Democracy on Whitfield Street in central London in July of the same year.[33] In the first part, Araeen set out to deploy walking as a means to explore his 'own body, its relationship to the culture I was living in and the environment and what was happening around'.[34] The performance commenced with a series of private actions that the artist staged on Brick Lane on a Sunday in late June.

He first entered the Clifton Restaurant (regularly visited by the artist) dressed in a kurta and shalwar, which he had brought back from a visit to Pakistan in 1972–73.[35] He subsequently strolled around the area, drank tea and ate food, while his everyday actions were photographed by his wife, Elena Bonzanigo.

While Araeen has contested readings of this work as purely autobiographical, the performance undoubtedly drew on the everyday act of walking as a way of discreetly and conceptually asserting his own biographical trajectory into the wider landscape of discourses around geography, diasporic identity, migration, labour and exploitation.[36] Recounting how he regularly visited Brick Lane in the 1970s to drink tea and shop, Araeen selected this neighbourhood for the work as it represented one of London's urban areas strongly associated with histories of migration. Formerly the site of a thriving Jewish community, after the Second World War the area became a settlement site for the South Asian – particularly Bangladeshi-Sylheti – communities living in council housing.[37] Referred to colloquially as 'Banglatown', the area around Brick Lane became synonymous with ethnic ghettoisation in the popular media during the 1970s. Given the personal and political significance of this site, Araeen capitalised upon the location to convey both the sense of familiarity and the unease that he felt upon visiting the area in the aftermath of the Grunwick strikes of 1976–78, in which South Asian factory workers in northern England protested for better working conditions. Describing the tension between familiarity and unease, Araeen stated:

> what was happening in Brick Lane and what was happening in other areas was that Asian women were on strike against factories. There are two contradictory places: Brick Lane was a place of comfort (because when I used to feel nostalgic, I used to go to Brick Lane in the sixties with my wife and sit in a café and drink tea or eat something; there was no other reason). So, that experience came back; I wanted to politicise that experience. At the end of the sixties, there were the Skinheads. They used to go out and beat up Asian people. This is how the [idea for] *Paki Bastard* came about. I also heard on TV that some Pakistanis and Indians were beaten up by police during the strike and one person was called 'Paki bastard' by the police – these were the things happening at that time. I wanted to put them all together through my own experience and involvement because I *did* used to go to the strikes and join them sometimes.[38]

Carried out in an everyday context without the knowledge of passers-by that they were witnesses to and participants in a work of art, this method of performance-making was not new to Araeen.[39] Already, in 1962, the artist had staged a performance in Karachi in which he had walked down a public street in the name of art, thus expressing a criticism towards the lack of appreciation for modern art in Pakistan.[40] For *Paki Bastard*, Araeen once again looked to render the everyday experience an artistic and political act. In the artist's own words, the act of documenting these journeys and the knowledge that these photographs would be incorporated into a later work of live art rendered his simple actions both artistic and political gestures: 'unlike my previous visits to this restaurant, what I was doing now was a performance of which people around were unaware of [*sic*], but part of.'[41]

Performed shortly prior to Oiticica's writing of *delirium ambulatorium* in 1978, this performance echoes a similar, shared ethos towards self-documentation and urban walking as both an act of introspection, and an exposition or 'mapping' of ongoing socio-political struggles in east London. By carrying out a performative walk in which he mapped the perimeters of racially charged spaces in east London, Araeen also produced a personal cartography, charting his own biography and identity within the city. Alluding to other performances that had employed the black body as a source of antagonism and disruption of the public space – notably Adrian Piper's series *Catalysis* (1970–71) – Araeen's movements (and their documentation) further captured the discord the artist felt while being framed as a foreigner and Asian in Britain. Yet, to reduce Araeen's actions solely to political protest would not capture the true breadth of this work.

Returning to Oiticica's *delirium ambulatorium* as a framework for understanding artists' city walks as both acts of personal exploration and a two-way mapping of the self onto space, Araeen's journey through east London may also be interpreted as a moment symbolically imbuing the body with the histories and rhetoric of that space at that specific moment in time. As further suggested by the presence of the derogatory term 'Paki bastard' in the work's title, Araeen's walk may be seen as a conceptual 'ingestion' (and 'digestion') of racist terms that had been used as acts of both aggression and resistance within the riots of east London.[42] Without producing any active community engagement, as seen in Oiticica's engagement with the favelas, Araeen's private walk instead turned to self-documentation, producing a series of photographs that yield glimpses into the different stages of the work. Functioning as a visual 'map' of the area, these photographs also charted the boundaries of Araeen's freedom to move around, see and be seen, within the heightened racial tensions of 1970s Britain.

Lee Wen's *Journey of a Yellow Man* (1992–2001)

In contrast to the discreet, nonchalant nature of Araeen's walk, the performances of Singaporean artist Lee Wen (1957–2019) delved into mapping socio-political boundaries by making the presence of the walker hyper-visible. Recognised as one of Singapore's foremost performance artists, Lee is best remembered for his iconic series of performances titled *Journey of a Yellow Man*. First enacted in London in 1992, this series saw the artist paint his nearly naked body (wearing only underwear) in acrylic yellow and perform ceremonial gestures with chains in galleries and public spaces. Conceived a total of fifteen times in various galleries, museums, city spaces and rural areas across Asia, the work has most often been analysed with a focus on Lee's yellow-tinted body as a signifier of ethnic and racial discrimination (a visual reference to the legacies of discriminatory systems of racial classification and orientalist discourses around the 'yellow peril').[43] However, *Journey of a Yellow Man* also began a relationship with its surroundings, particularly as it evolved away from a gallery-based act and towards a durational practice of urban walking.

Journey of a Yellow Man No. 1 was first staged in April 1992 at the City of London Polytechnic in London, where Lee was studying. The performance's focus – as emphasised in the artist's statement – was a counteraction to the artist's perception that in London he was constantly being mistaken as Chinese.[44] Also performed in the aftermath of the seminal exhibition of Afro-Asian art curated by Rasheed Araeen at the Hayward Gallery in London, *The Other Story: Afro-Asian Art in Postwar Britain* (1989–90), in which two artists, David Medalla and Li Yuan-chia – of Southeast and East Asian descent respectively – had been featured, *Journey of a Yellow Man* reacted to the notable absence of Southeast Asian artists within 'black British' art history.[45] For this enactment, Lee appeared in the persona of 'yellow man' and proceeded to perform a series of actions using a red chain and solid fuel in front of a small live audience. While this inaugural work took place indoors, subsequent iterations took place in public spaces, where walking emerged as one of his central actions. While always planned, and mediated by the presence of a camera, *Journey of a Yellow Man* also occasioned a setting for Lee to discover and document urban spaces within which the artist presented himself as other. As noted by June Yap:

> the notion of 'journey' is for him less of an actual perambulation during the performance – although the performance does involve some form of traversal – than it is a reference to cultural diaspora and its effects, a condition that may be seen as echoed in the movement of the body from performance artist and its representation, travelling from event to event around the world.[46]

Conceived a further fourteen times (not all of which were realised) between 1992 and 2001 across Singapore, India, Japan, Thailand, Mexico, Australia and China, each of the works' enactments evoked different readings when Lee's alter ego interacted with the specific contexts.[47] The second performance, *Journey of a Yellow Man No. 2: Fire and Sun*, in Gulbarga Karnataka, India, stressed connections to nature and outdoor landscapes. The third instalment, in Singapore in 1993, *Journey of a Yellow Man No. 3: Desire*, focused on the gallery space once again, shortly predating Singapore's 1994 ban on performance art (following Joseph Ng's *Brother Cane*).[48]

With *Journey of a Yellow Man No. 5: Index to Freedom* (1994; see Figure 12.4), staged at the Fukuoka Art Museum in Japan, Lee first extended the performance's remit to walking in an urban context. In a performance 'workshop' spanning five days, the artist performed a series of indoor actions (incorporating floor drawings with rice, and actions with chains), yet also ventured 'out for field study' into the city, as heralded by a sign hung in the gallery. Evoking ethnographic practices of 'traversing' foreign landscapes, as well as 'entering into' native communities, Lee's journey through the city is an ironic play on the scientific 'mapping' of unknown territories and communities. Meanwhile, his documented journeys across Fukuoka capture the encounters and ambience of the city and people's responses to his naked yellow body as he traverses shopping malls, the subway and alleys while holding a birdcage. Here, the relationship between the cartographer and his subjects became blurred – Lee both observed and documented, while simultaneously being observed and becoming a visual marker of otherness on the streets of Fukuoka.

In subsequent iterations, including *Journey of a Yellow Man No. 6: History and Self* at the Setagaya Art Museum, Tokyo in 1995, Lee developed a more close-knit visual conversation or response system between his city encounters and the actions performed inside the gallery. This practice culminated in *Journey of a Yellow Man No. 11: Multiculturalism* (1997), performed at the Substation in Singapore, which marked the first work in which Lee appeared in public wearing a suit painted yellow. With Lee subsequently partaking in a panel discussion, before publicly washing himself in a basin and distributing the yellow water to viewers in jars, this iteration of *Journey of a Yellow Man* marks the explicit ways in which his cartographies of public spaces offered a visual statement on the rhetoric of Singapore's multiculturalism policies, echoing what Kobena Mercer described as a state where cultural diversity was recognised and made visible as a marker of a ' "progressive" disposition'.[49] Describing the nature of policies supporting 'cultural diversity' in the UK, Mercer used the term 'multicultural exhibitionism' to describe funding schemes and exhibition opportunities that promoted the view that art could reflect Britain's cultural and ethnic minorities.[50] This idea of 'multicultural exhibitionism' is, however, also fitting to the form of *Journey of a Yellow Man*. Returning to the work's roots in London in 1992, Lee's walking yellow figure was at once an exploratory persona, producing a subtle conquest of foreign spaces, and at the same time a benign *persona non grata*, or an uninvited and hyper-present intruder and observer of otherness in real time.

Unlike Araeen's familiarity with Brick Lane, Lee's walk was one of embracing estrangement and caution within unfamiliar terrains. While on a visual

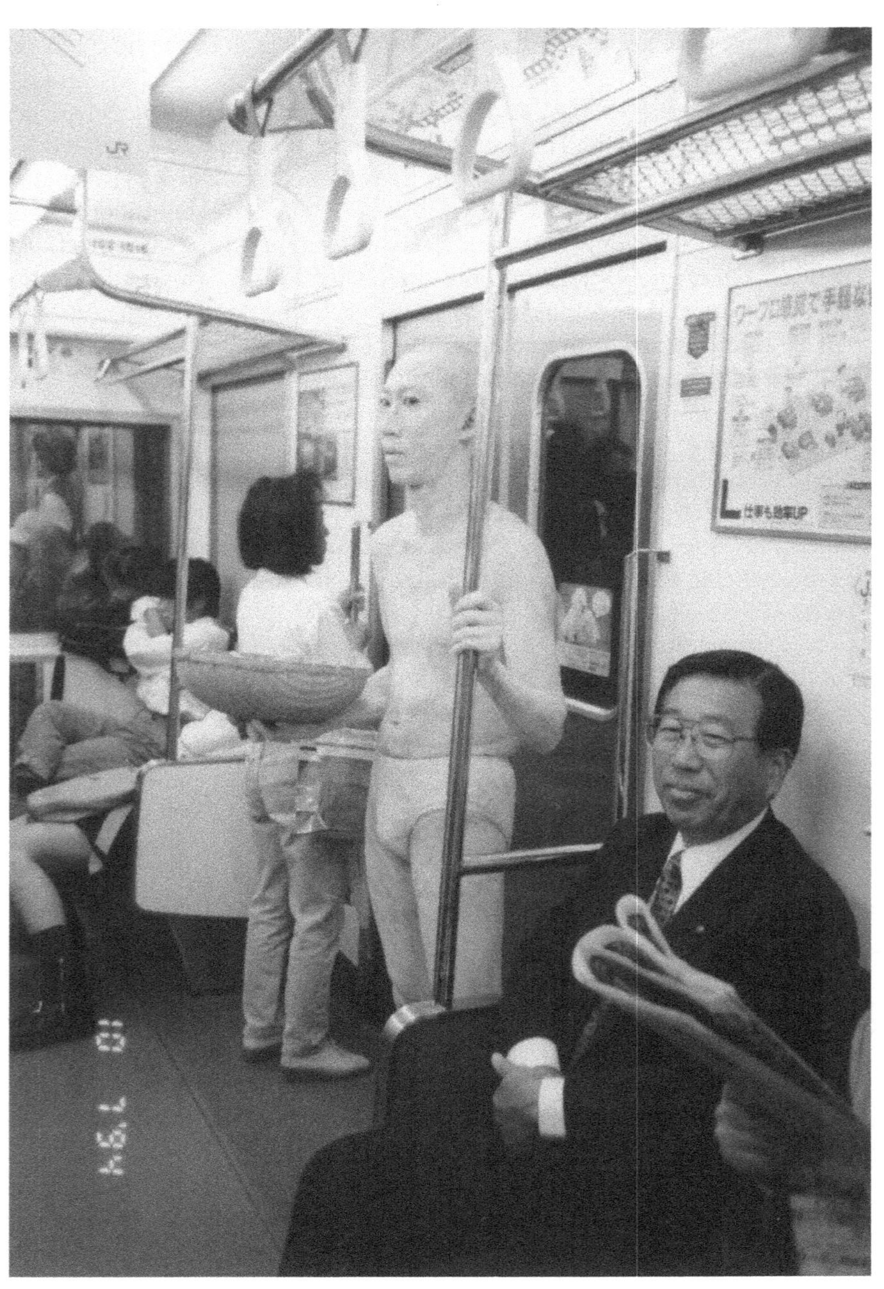

12.4 Lee Wen, video stills from *Journey of a Yellow Man No. 5: Index to Freedom*. Fukuoka, Japan, 1995.

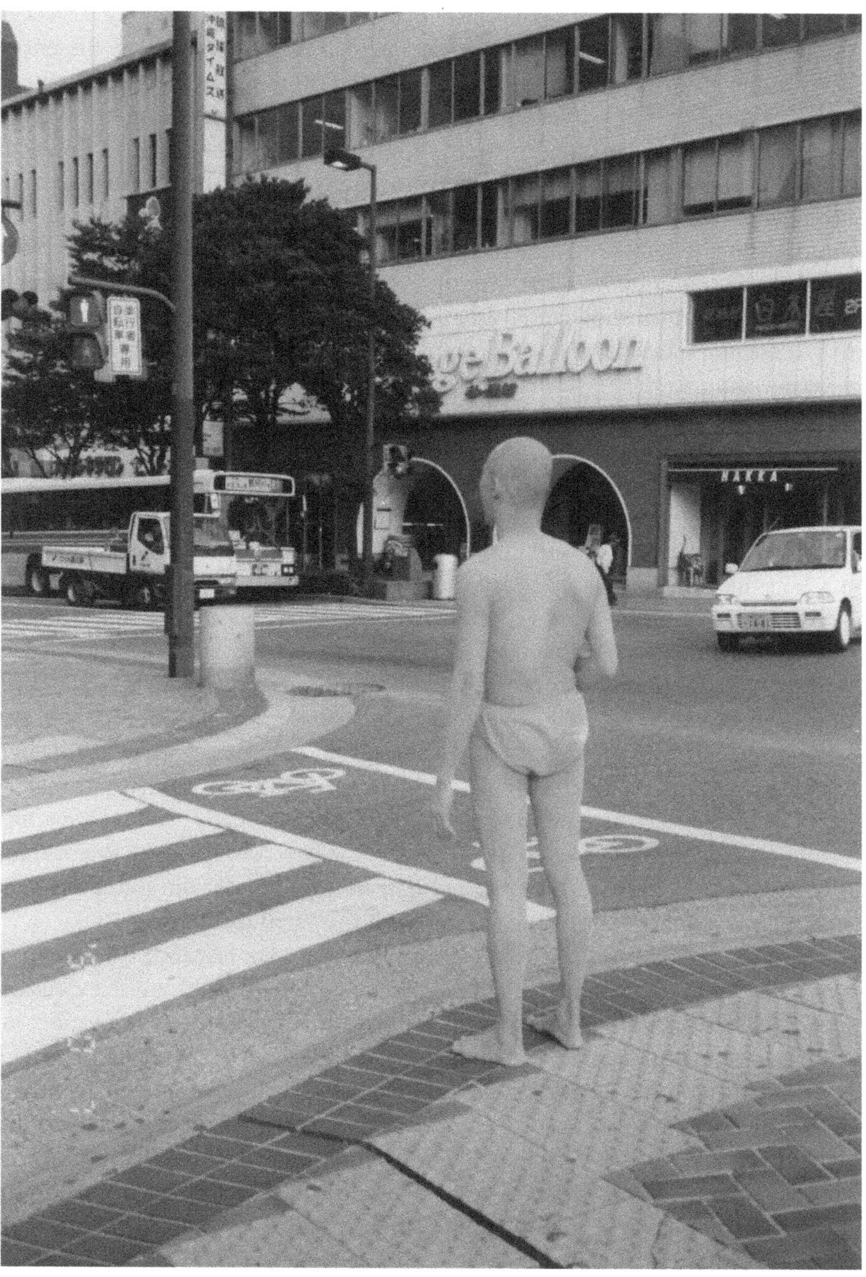

12.4

level echoing works such as Günter Brus's *Vienna Walk* (1965), a series of performances in which the artist wore formal attire and painted his entire body white with the aim of presenting himself in public as a 'living picture',[51] Lee's colouration and public appearance may be read beyond the body as art object. Rather, the work has an affinity to the notion of 'ingestion' in Oiticica's *delirium ambulatorium*. Documented in detail as he walked across various urban environments, Lee emerged as both as an object and the viewing subject, internalising his surroundings and asserting his space within them. The artist's inquisitive stare mirrors what Wenny Teo has described as the 'un/desirable guest' for whom cannibalism presents a metaphor for methodologies seeking to unravel the hidden histories, presences and cultures of Southeast Asia.[52]

Returning to the relationship between conceptualism and mapping, this chapter has singled out Hélio Oiticica's proposition *delirium ambulatorium* as a central premise across a number of the artist's works. Unique to this concept has been its simultaneous emphasis on the personal and imaginative experience of walking through cities. Concurrently, *delirium ambulatorium* also implies a mapping of the self onto the city space, and vice versa – a notion that has lent the concept deeply social, political and activist undertones. Looking beyond the individual work of Oiticica, this chapter has argued that *delirium ambulatorium* as a concept has had resonances in the work of other artists dealing with the themes of diasporic identity and urban lived realities. Honing in on the examples of Rasheed Araeen and Lee Wen, it has emphasised the broader circulation of ideas around 'conceptual mapping' activated through walking, particularly in the context of artists working in a transnational or diasporic milieu in which public presence evokes a politically charged meaning. While neither of these examples invoked Oiticica's commitment to community interaction, they both embodied *delirium ambulatorium*'s emphasis on walking as an act of integrating the self with the surroundings.

In light of these individual examples, the significance of *delirium ambulatorium* may also be considered as a counterproposition, or extension of dominant analyses of conceptual art and identity politics. A number of studies on conceptual and performance-based practices by 'black' artists in the USA and Britain have emphasised expressions of 'radical presence' in public domains. The exhibition *Radical Presence: Black Performance in Contemporary Art* (2012), curated by Valerie Cassel Oliver, is one notable example of this approach focusing on artists' search to undermine racist and exclusionary discourses by 'charting' themselves as other in public spheres.[53] In the British context, Catherine Ugwu's influential publication *Let's Get It On: The Politics of Black Performance* (1995) similarly asserted that the exclusion of black artists from the canon of Euro-American art lay in their works' conceptual concerns and desires for visibility.[54] In contrast to these accounts, however, Oiticica's *delirium ambulatorium* does not emphasise the visibility of the artist. Rather, it spotlights the imaginative and deeply personal intersections through which the self becomes mapped on space, and space asserts an influence on the body. As reflected in Araeen's subtle gestures of drinking tea in Brick Lane, or Lee Wen's inquisitive look, *delirium ambulatorium* does not insist on the representational function of the artist's body. Echoing Darby English's caution that not all works of 'black art' are about identity politics and that there is a need to explore the politics of representation itself, Oiticica's *delirium ambulatorium* spotlights the subtle nuances as well as real and imaginative divisions between the body and the mapping of the self onto space.[55]

Notes

1 Hélio Oiticica, letter to Lygia Clark, 8 August 1970, in Luciano Figueiredo (ed.), *Lygia Clark, Hélio Oiticica: Cartas, 1964–74* (Rio de Janeiro: Editora de UFRJ, 1996), p. 160.

2 On 12 November 1978, Hélio Oiticica participated in the event organised by the artist Ivald Granato in São Paulo entitled *Mitos vadios* (*Vagabond Myths*).

3 Frederico Coelho has used the term 'textual extension' to describe the central role of Oiticica's writings as expanding upon his artistic practice. See Frederico Coelho, '*Subterranean Tropicália Projects → Newyorkaises → Conglomerado*: The infinite book of Hélio Oiticica', in Philomena Mariani and Katie Reilly (eds), *Hélio Oiticica: To Organize Delirium* (New York: Prestel, 2017), p. 200.

4 Debord used the term 'psychogeography' in 1957 to describe the intersection between imagination and real space, a concept inspired by Charles Baudelaire's notion of a 'flâneur' wandering the urban environment in a playful way. Guy Debord, *Psychogeographic Guide of Paris* (Roskilde: Permild & Rosengreen, 1957).

5 *Mitos vadios* took place on 12 November 1978. See Moacir dos Anjos, 'As ruas e as bobagens: Anotações sobre o *delirium ambulatorium* de Hélio Oiticica', *ARS Sao Paulo* 10:20 (2021), 23–45.

6 Irene V. Small, 'Permanent evolution: Hélio Oiticica and the return to Rio, 1978–80', in Mariani and Reilly, *Helio Oiticica*, p. 266.

7 The neo-concrete movement in Brazil (1951–61) was developed by Rio de Janeiro's Grupo Frente, a collective of artists that worked on concrete art. Grupo Frente's members were Oliveira Bastos, Hélio Oiticica, Ferreira Gullar, Teresa Aragão, Bezerra, Mario Pedrosa, Lygia Clark, Vera Pedrosa, Ivan Serpa, and Lea and Abraham Palatnik.

8 Hélio Oiticica, *Materialismos* (Buenos Aires: Ediciones Manantial, SRL, 2013), p. 76. During his walks in the bohemian zones of Rio de Janeiro, Oiticica became friends with the sculptor Jackson Ribeiro, from Morro da Mangueira. Oiticica ended up joining the Mangueira samba school and parading as a *passista* at the Rio de Janeiro carnival between 1965 and 1968. The fact that the samba is considered an art form owes much to the *Parangolés*, since it was due to the popularity of the colourful fabrics that people were wearing when they danced the samba.

9   Hélio Oiticica and Guy Brett, 'Oiticica talks to Guy Brett', *Studio International* (March 1969), 134.

10 The individual elements of *Tropicália* may be contextualised within the tropicalism movement, one of the most influential artistic styles to champion Brazilian identity by embracing forms and aesthetics specific to Brazil's context. While Oiticica distanced himself from tropicalism on the grounds that he perceived it to be a discourse appropriated by the elite classes, *Tropicália* is recognised as one of the earliest formative artworks for this movement. Oiticica, *Materialismos*, p. 97.

11 *Ibid.*, p. 39.

12 *Corpocidade* (corpocity) is a Portuguese term formed by *corpo* (body) and *cidade* (city). This term is used as a name by the research platform of a group of the Federal University of Bahia (Salvador de Bahia, Brazil). Their investigations are based on relations between the body and the city from an artistic point of view. See the website of *Plataforma Corpocidade*, www.corpocidade.dan.ufba.br (accessed 27 November 2019).

13 The term *corpografia* (corpography) was published in Augustin Berque, Alessia de Biase and Philippe Bonnin, *L'habiter dans sa poétique premiére: Actes du colloque de Cerisy-la-salle* (Paris: Editions donner lieu, 2008). The city is also read by the body as a set of interactive conditions, and the body expresses the synthesis of this interaction by describing in its corporeality what we call urban corpography. Corpography is a body cartography, that is, part of the hypothesis that the urban experience is inscribed in various temporal scales, in the very body of the person who experiences it, and thus also defines it, even if involuntarily. F. D. Britto and P. B. Jacques, 'Cenografias e corpografías urbanas: Um diálogo sobre as relações entre corpo e cidade' *Cadernos PPG-AU/UFBA* 7:2 (2008), 79–86. For a discussion of these terms see Maria José Martínez Sanchez, *Dynamic Cartography: Body, Architecture and Performative Space* (Abingdon: Routledge, 2020), pp. 132–3.

14 Guy Brett and Luciano Figueiredo, *Oiticica in London* (London: Tate, 2007), p. 23.

15 Francesco Careri, *Walkscapes: Walking as an Aesthetic Practice* (Barcelona: Editorial Gustavo Gili, 2002).

16 Hélio Oiticica, *O aparecimento do suprassensorial in 'Aspiro ao Grande Labirinto'* (Rio de Janeiro: Rocco, 1986), p. 11.

17 *Ibid.*, p. 130.

18 This point has been argued in Sánchez, *Dynamic Cartography*, p. 140. With these reflections, we approach the environmental policies that Peter Sloterdijk spoke about in his *Spheres* trilogy. Peter Sloterdijk, *Spheres*, 3 vols (Los Angeles: Semiotexte, 2011–16).

19 Hélio Oiticica, *Delirium ambulatorium* (1978).

20 Guy Brett, *Hélio Oiticica: The Experimental Exercise of Liberty*, reprinted in Guy Brett, *Carnival of Perception: Selected Writings on Art* (London: Institute of International Visual Arts, 2004 [1993]), p. 52.

21 The notion of 'ingestion' may be traced back to a preceding movement, anthropophagy (1928). First articulated by Brazilian writer Oswalde Andrade in the 'Anthropophagic manifesto', published in the first issue of the *Revista de antropofagia*

(*Anthropophagy Magazine*), anthropophagy contrasted primitive Brazilian culture with the European models imposed on it that, together with native and national material, were essential in the cultural construction of Brazil. This movement took as its inspiration the cannibalistic rituals of some indigenous cultures, such as the Tupi Indians, with Andrade's motto 'Tupi or not Tupi', referring to Shakespeare's *Hamlet*. In doing so, anthropophagy evoked the eating of human flesh, including tissues and bones, as metaphoric of cultural appropriation. See Aleksandar Dundjerovic and Luiz Fernando Ramos, *Brazilian Performing Arts* (Madrid: Abada Editores, 2019), pp. 81–2.

22 Hélio Oiticica, 'Dance in my experience', in Claire Bishop (ed.), *Participation* (London: Whitechapel Gallery, 2006), p. 106.

23 Augusto Boal, *Theatre of the Oppressed* (New York: Theatre Communications Group, 1979).

24 H. Lefebvre, *The Production of Space*, trans. D. Nicholson-Smith (Oxford: Blackwell, 1991), p. 38.

25 Aracy Amaral, 'Hélio Oiticica: Tentativa a dialogo', in Aracy Amaral (ed.), *Textos do Trópico de Capricórnio: Artigos e ensaios (1980–2005)* (Sao Paolo: Editora 34, 2006), Vol. III, p. 106.

26 See Guy Brett, *Kinetic Art* (London: Studio Vista and Reinhold Book Corp., 1968).

27 For discussion of kinetic sculpture and international allegiances see Chanon Kenji Praepipatmongkol, 'David Medalla: Dreams of sculpture', *Oxford Art Journal* 43:3 (February 2021), 339–59; and Isobel Whitelegg, 'Everything was connected: Kinetic art and internationalism at Signals London, 1964–66', in Catherine Spencer, Amy Tobin and Jo Applin (eds), *London Art Worlds* (Philadelphia: Penn State University Press, 2018), pp. 21–38.

28 In the artist's own words, 'It wasn't that I was defining identity – I had no problem with it. You see, I wanted to explore the idea of identity. I wanted to problematize it because it's not a simple thing like coming from one place in the world, possessing one culture, one country, one race, which are the things on which identity is primarily based. I wanted to caution against all of these things. So, it was a process of questioning identity, not asserting identity.' Eva Bentcheva, unpublished interview with Rasheed Araeen, London, 26 February 2014.

29 See Rasheed Araeen, 'Conversation with David Medalla', *Black Phoenix* (1979), 10–19.

30 'Preliminary notes for a black manifesto' was originally published in the first issue of the art magazine *Black Phoenix* in January 1978 and was reprinted in the journal *Studio International* later that year. The manifesto has been subsequently reproduced in Araeen's monograph: Rasheed Araeen, *Making Myself Visible* (London: Kala Press, 1984). See Rasheed Araeen, 'Preliminary notes for a black manifesto', *Black Phoenix: Third World Perspective on Contemporary Art and Culture* 1 (January 1978), 3–12.

31 Araeen, 'Preliminary notes', 12 (original capitalisation).

32 Araeen's increased interest in the political discourses around the cultural and religious identities of migrants from Asia, Africa and the Caribbean during the 1970s may be attributed to his own experiences of discrimination and racial politics in

Britain. See John Roberts, *Postmodernism, Politics and Art* (Manchester: Manchester University Press, 1990).

33 Writings on *Paki Bastard* have often failed to mention that this work began with a private performance in Brick Lane. Examples of texts that omit to mention the importance of Araeen's performance include Iftikhar Dadi, *Modernism and the Art of Muslim South Asia* (Chapel Hill: University of North Carolina Press, 2010); and Courtney J. Martin, 'Rasheed Araeen, live art, and radical politics in Britain', *Getty Research Journal* 2 (2010), 107–24. In contrast, personal interviews with the artist have highlighted that he considered his actions in Brick Lane to be works of performance art that followed in the tradition of 1950s 'happenings' in New York and the work of Fluxus artists in Germany and the USA, in whose practices everyday acts and objects could be reinterpreted as works of art.

34 Bentcheva, unpublished interview with Araeen.

35 *Ibid.*

36 In a letter to a colleague dated 7 June 1978, Araeen stated 'although you are right about the autobiographical aspect of "Paki Bastard", the work as a whole is not autobiographical. I would rather describe it as "subjective".' Araeen, *Making Myself Visible*, p. 122.

37 For an overview of Bangladeshi settlements in east London see Ali Riaz, *Islam and Identity Politics among British-Bangladeshis: A Leap of Faith* (Manchester: Manchester University Press, 2010), pp. 18–45.

38 Bentcheva, unpublished interview with Araeen.

39 Allan Kaprow has described the staging of 'happenings' as situating art amid everyday life, without viewers necessarily being aware that they are witnessing the making of art. See Allan Kaprow, *Assemblages, Environments and Happenings* (New York: Harry N. Abrams, 1966). While Araeen has not commented upon drawing directly upon the model of happenings, numerous happenings had been staged by international artists in the UK during the 1960s, and by the 1970s performance-making of this kind was well known in the UK. For a discussion of the popularity of happenings in Britain during the 1960s see Deirdre Heddon, 'The politics of live art', in Deirdre Heddon and Jennie Klein (eds), *Histories and Practices of Live Art* (Basingstoke: Palgrave Macmillan, 2012), p. 181.

40 Bentcheva, interview with Araeen.

41 Unpublished email correspondence with Rasheed Araeen, 7 December 2013.

42 Drawing on a quote by fellow artist Dominic Dawes, in which the artist commented: 'In our towns and cities, on our subways and walls, etc., and just as much in our minds, there is racial abuse: Wogs go home, N.F. [National Front] rules, Black Bastards, etc. but who made us the so-called "bastards"?'. Dominic Dawes, artist's statement, in *The Pan-Afrikan Connection* (exh. cat.) (London: Africa Centre, 1982), unpaginated.

43 Wenny Teo, 'The long journey of a "yellow man": Remembering Lee Wen (1957–2019)', *Frieze*, www.frieze.com/magazines/frieze-magazine/issue-206?_ga=2.70414934. 771586231.1600605621–1085142295.1593183476 (accessed 28 September 2020).

44 Alice Ming Wai Jim, 'Lee Wen: Performing yellow', *Afterall*, https://afterall.org/journal/issue.46/lee (accessed 28 August 2020).

45 The development of black art in the 1980s is often seen as culminating in Araeen's *The Other Story: Afro-Asian Artists in Post-War Britain* (29 November 1989–4 February 1990). This is regarded as the first exhibition of 'black British artists' in a major museum. See Rasheed Araeen, *The Other Story: Afro-Asian Artists in Post-War Britain* (London: Hayward Gallery, 1989).

46 June Yap, 'I feel the earth move', in *Lee Wen: Lucid Dreams in Reverie of the Real* (Singapore: Singapore Art Museum, 2012), p. 49.

47 'Lee Wen', *Asia Art Archive*, https://aaa.org.hk/en/collections/search/archive/lee-wen-archive (accessed 27 August 2020).

48 Jim, 'Lee Wen'.

49 Kobena Mercer, 'Ethnicity and internationality: New British art and diaspora-based blackness', *Third Text: Critical Perspectives on Contemporary Art and Culture* 13:49 (1999), 51–4.

50 *Ibid.*, p. 57.

51 For a description of Brus's performance as a 'living picture', see Mechtild Widrich, *Performative Monuments: The Rematerialisation of Public Art* (Manchester: Manchester University Press, 2014), p. 56.

52 Wenny Teo, 'The un/desirable guest: Hospitality, effective history and the (post)colonial archive', in Erika Tan (ed.), *Come Cannibalise Us, Why Don't You?* (Singapore: National University of Singapore Press, 2014), pp. 10–14.

53 *Radical Presence: Black Performance in Contemporary Art*, curated by Valerie Cassel Oliver, was exhibited at the Contemporary Arts Museum Houston (17 November 2012–15 February 2013), the Studio Museum in Harlem (14 November 2013–9 March 2014), and Grey Art Gallery in New York (10 September–7 December 2013), finally showing at the Walker Art Centre, Minneapolis (24 July 2014–4 January 2015).

54 Catherine Ugwu, *Let's Get It On: The Politics of Black Performance* (London: Institute of Contemporary Arts and Bay Press, 1995), p. 57.

55 Darby English, *How to See a Work of Art in Total Darkness* (Cambridge, MA: MIT Press, 2007).

Index

Page numbers for figures are in *italics*; page numbers for notes are in the format 156n.44.

abstraction 47, 53, 57, 109–10, 185–6
Acconci, Vito, *Points, Blanks* 48–50
acts 174, 176, 178
 non-acts 158, 168, 173
agency 64, 83–4, 90, 92
Akerman, James R. 92
Alloway, Lawrence 156n.44, 156n.54,
 193, 195
Anderson, Benedict 109, 110–11
Andre, Carl 207–8, 232, 234
Andrew Dickson White Museum,
 Cornell University, *Earth Art*
 (1969) 146
annotations 190–2, 193–6
anthropophagy 103, 130, 248
Anti-Art 163, 168, 174
Araeen, Rasheed 11, 250–3, 258
 *I'm a Noble Savage Come and
 Find Me* 251
 The Other Story (exhibition,
 1989–90) 254
 *Paki Bastard (Portrait of the Artist as a
 Black Person)* 243–4, 250–3, *251*
 'Preliminary notes for a black manifesto'
 250, 251
 Towards the Centre and Back 250–1
architecture 230–1
Argentina 31, 35–9
Art & Language 25–31, 33, 40, 189–90
 Air-Conditioning Show 187
 Alternate Map for Documenta 190, *191*
 Indexing project 189–90, 193
 Loop 187

Map of an Area of Dimensions 12" × 12"
 24, 25–8, *26*
*Map of Thirty-Six Square Mile Surface
 Area* 187
Map to Not Indicate 24, 28–9, *29*, 187
 New York group members 197
Art & Project Gallery, Amsterdam 158, 172
Art Dialogue (journal) 197
Arte Gráfico Grupo Buenos Aires 35
Artforum (magazine) 190, 192, *192*,
 193–6, *194*
art institutions 81–2, 163, 190
 gallery space 23, 104–5, 146, 230–3
 museums 146, 160, 166, 173
 as networked space 234, 237
 see also institutional critique
artist notebooks 130, 131–2, *131*
artists' books 59, 158, 173
Artists Union, Women's Workshop 64–7
Art-Language (journal) 189
Art without Space (symposium, 1969) 6–7
art world 81–2, 83–4, 208
 as framework 24–5, 28, 34, 190, 192–3
Ascott, Roy 64
Asher, Michael, *Untitled* 5
Atkinson, Terry *see* Art & Language
Attalai, Gábor 77–98
 African Ocean 77
 Amerasia 77
 Big Star Lake 77, 79
 Big Triangle Gulf 77
 Continental Change I–II 77, 89–90, 92
 Kopaszítás (Balding) 80, 87, 89–90, *91*

Negatív csillag (*Negative Star*) 85–7, 86,
        89–90, 92
    Round Lake 77
    Schnee-Arbeiten (*Snow Works*) 80, 85–7,
        86, 89–90, 92
    South-American Ocean 77
    Square Lake 77
    Transfer of Japan 77, 78
    Transfer of Sweden 77
    Transfer Paintings 88–9
aura 159–60, 164–6, 173, 174
Australia 182, 183, 193, 196, 198
authorship 64, 166, 209
autonomy 38, 178, 231

Bainbridge, Dave, *Loop* 187
Bak, Imre 82–3, 87
Baker, George 216
Baldwin, Michael 187, 190
    see also Art & Language
Bann, Stephen 148
Barry, Robert 6, 7
Barthes, Roland 216
Baxter, Ian and Ingrid (N.E. Thing
        Company, NETCO) 151
Beke, László 84–5, 87, 88
Benhabib, Seyla 68
Benjamin, Walter 109, 164
Beuys, Joseph, *Hearth* 102
Biard, Ida 233
Biennale of Sydney, 1990 198
Bijutsu techō (*Art Notebook*, journal) 174
Bikyoto (Artists Joint-Struggle
        Council) 160
Bilbao, Francisco 125–6
Bischofberger, Bruno 188
black art and artists 250–1, 258–9
blankness 102–3, 104–5
blindness 214
Block, René 198
blueprints 165
Boal, Augusto 248
Bochner, Mel 11, 214
bodies
    of artists 53–4, 89, 150
    as artwork 174–6
    collective corporeality 119, 121

organs/viscera 116–19
    size of artworks, relation to 228
    and space 50–1, 121, 246, 247, 253
    space and 120–1
body art 80, 90
Boeke, Kees 209–10
Bonzanigo, Elena 251–3
borders/boundaries 25, 40, 56–7, 68,
        80, 142–3
Borges, Jorge Luis, 'Exactitude in Science'
        143, 145
Boroditsky, Lera 217
Bowles, John 50–1, 55n.16
Brancusi, Constantin, Târgu-Jiu
        ensemble 139
Brazil 116–17, 124, 126–7, 134, 243–8
    Rio de Janeiro 119–21, 246–7
    São Paulo 126, 132, 243, 244, 247–8
Brett, Guy 33, 247–8
Brouwn, Stanley 172, 178
Brus, Günter, *Vienna Walk* 258
Buarque, Chico 127–8
Buchloh, Benjamin 2, 206, 234
Buckminster Fuller, Richard 6, 187, 213
Buenos Aires Museum of Modern Art 39
Bulson, Eric 109–10
Buren, Daniel 230–1, 232
Burn, Ian 182–3, 187–8, 193, 197, 198
    'The artist as victim' (with Mel
        Ramsden) 193
    'Art is what we do' 196
    Blue Reflex 188, 189
    see also IBMR
Burnham, Jack 148

Cadere, André 224–41, 225
    communiqués 229, 234, 235
    exhibitions 231–2, 232–3
    Histoire d'un travail (book) 229–30, 233
    round bars of wood 226–30, 228, 231
Cage, John 6, 185, 198
Camden Arts Centre, London
    Environmental Reversal (1969) 32, 33
    Figuration Art to Systems Art
        (1971) 41
camp spaces 111–12
Carroll, Lewis 30, 143, 145

cartography
  alternative 64, 68, 89
  conceptuality of 9
  cosmic 121–4
  countercartography 77–80, 84, 88–92
  definitions of 1
  as information science 2
  subepidermal 116–19
  symbolic 119–21
censorship 82, 119
centres 119–20, 125, 127
Centro de Arte y Comunicación (CAYC,
    Buenos Aires) 39, 41
Certeau, Michel de 150
Chomsky, Noam 193
cinema *see* film
class 57, 60–1, 68, 126, 127
codes 108, 227–8, 229–30
Cold War 8, 23, 30, 34, 79, 123
collaboration/collective practice 56, 60–4,
    84, 158, 166–8, 172–3, 186–7, 247–8
collage 47, 77–8, 92, 125
Collin, George 196, 197
colonisation 90, 105–6, 107, 108, 125–6, 211
colour 227, 229
communication 2, 3, 127–8, 234
communication technologies 8–9, 35, 188
  telecommunications 39–40, 48–50, 141,
    143–5, 150–1
communities 57, 60–4, 111–12, 128
Conceptual Art and Conceptual Aspects
    (exhibition, 1970) 188, 198
conceptualism
  vs. conceptual art, as term 133–4
  creative processes of 45–6
  definitions of 83
  in eastern Europe 83–4
  exhibitions 33, 133–5
  global 13–14
  histories of 11–13, 23–4
  in Hungary 84–7
  immaterial 163
  maps/mapping, affinity with 1–2
  political engagement in 12–13
  spatial turn of 5–11
  time frame of 12–13
conflict/war 124–5, 127, 141, 143, 148–50
  see also Cold War

Contemporary Art Exhibition of Japan
    (1969) 163
content 56, 65–6
context 23, 25, 47–8, 186–7, 190, 196,
    211–12, 230–1
Cosgrove, Denis 1, 212
Craib, Raymond B. 77–8, 80
Cras, Sophie 1, 143–4
Crimp, Douglas 226
critique 33, 40, 41, 195
  via artwork 35–8, 40, 42
  see also institutional critique
Crossley, N. 69
cubism 185–6
curation 84–5

data 2, 161, 164, 166–70, 176, 217–18
  as artwork 64–7, 151, 172–3, 174, 176–7
  collaborative production of 56, 61–2
  information and 9–10, 177, 178
Debord, Guy 243, 247
De Cauter, Lieven 111
decolonisation 8, 77–9, 92, 102, 110,
    112, 248
Dehaene, Michiel 111
Delmar, Rosalind 65–6
De Maria, Walter, *Lightning
    Field* 215
dematerialisation 6–7, 87, 140, 186, 229
demystification 244, 248
disorientation 109–10, 112
distance 152–4
documenta 5 (Kassel 1972) 87, 189–90, 193
documentation 1–2, 56, 142, 189, 190,
    209, 217
  of performance 174, 176, 178, 251
  of peripatetic art 229–30, 234
Douglas Hyde Gallery (DHG) 106
Draxler, Helmut 47
Dryansky, Larisa 8, 11–12

Eames, Charles and Ray, *Powers of
    Ten* 209–10
earth, image of 205
education 119–21, 131–2, 160–1, 163
Ehrenberg, Felipe 57–60, 68, 69
  La Poubelle 58–9, *58*
  Vanishing Rubbish Pile 59

Eliade, Mircea 119–20
Elsa von Honolulu Loringhoven Gallery,
    Ghent 232
encaustic 132–3
English, Derby 259
engravings 116–19
environments (artworks) 120–1
ephemerality 83, 87, 92, 139–40, 150, 159
exhibition practices 6, 62–4, 65–7, 84–5, 224
exile 110, 127–8
Expo 67, Montreal 187–8

factuality 33–4
familiarity 109–10, 255, 258
Fehér, Dávid 89–90, 96n.49
feminism 67, 68–9
Figueiredo, Luciano 246–7
film 31–5, *31*, 58–9, 85–7, 120–1, 215–18
Fischbach Gallery, New York, *Eccentric
    Abstraction* (1966) 208
Fishbone, Les 211–12
Flavin, Dan, *Untitled (For Sonja)* 5
Fluxus 3, 206
food 130, 248
Forge, Andrew 224
Foucault, Michel 7–8, 27, 69, 111
frameworks and framing 29, 38, 40, 42
    art world as 24–5, 28, 34, 190, 192–3
friezes 130, 132

Galántai, Gyölgy 83, 84
Gallery Gian Enzo Sperone, Rome and
    Turin 232–3
Gallery House, London 64
garbage 57–60
gaze 30, 87, 108, 205, 208, 214–15
Geiger, Anna Bella 11, 116–36
    Am. Latina 128
    Circumambulatio 119, 120–1
    Correntes culturais 129–30, *129*
    Fígados conversando 116
    Fronteiriços 132–3, *133*
    Local da ação engravings 127
    Lunar series 121–2, *122*
    macios 132
    Mapas elementares 127–8
    Mesa, friso e vídeos macios 132

O novo atlas I and *II* 8–9, 125, 128–9, 130
Orbis descriptio 132–3, *133*
O pão nosso de cada dia 130
Polaridades/Lunares 122–4
*Rio de Janeiro como centro cultural do
    mundo* 125
Sem título (Trevas/luz) 123–4, *123*
Sobre a arte 130, 131–2, *131*
gender 64–5, 67, 68
Gianelli, Ida 224, 231
*Global Conceptualism: Points of Origin
    1950s–1980s* (exhibition, 1999) 11, 13,
    88, 133, 198
globalisation 8, 9, 13
Glusberg, Jorge 41
Gomringer, Eugen 206–7
Gottdiener, Mark 10
grids 46–7, 53, 108, 185
Groys, Boris 83
GUN (collective) 167, 168
Gutai (collective) 174

Haacke, Hans, *MoMA Poll* 9
Habermas, Jürgen 57
Halder, Severin 89–90
Harrison, Charles 31, 41
Harrison, Margaret, *Women and Work*
    (exhibition 1973–75) 9–10, 11, 56,
    64–9, *66*, *67*
Hayward Gallery, London, *The Other Story:
    Afro-Asian Art in Postwar Britain*
    (1989–90) 254
Herskovits, Melville 197
Hime, Francis 127–8
Holt, Nancy 205–23
    Buried Poems series 209–10
    Crossword Work 208
    Detach Here 208
    Hammond 207
    Hometown 206–7
    Hotel Palenque 208
    Locators series 214
    Monuments of Passaic 208
    Stone Ruin Tour 209
    Sun Tunnels (film) 215–18
    Sun Tunnels (sculpture) 205, 210–15
    The World through a Circle 208

Horikawa Michio *159*, 168, 177–8
  Mail Art by Sending Stones 163, 167,
    170, 177
Huebler, Douglas 5, 6, 7, 11, 178
  Location Piece series 2, 172
Hungary 81–7
Hunt, Kay Fido, *Women and Work*
  (exhibition 1973–75) 9–10, 11, 56,
    64–9, *66*, *67*
Hurrell, Harold 31, 187

IBMR (Ian Burn and Mel Ramsden)
    182–202
  Comparative Models No. 1 182, 190–2, *192*,
    193, 201n.41
  Comparative Models No. 2 182, 190,
    193–6, *194*, 201n.41
  IBMR: Collected Work 1964–71 189
  Soft-Tape 182, 183–7, *184*, 188, 189, 198
identity 103, 126, 128, 130–1, 249
identity politics 249, 258, 259
immateriality 87, 88–9, 163, 173, 176
imperialism 125–6, 250–1
Ina Ken'ichirō *159*, 160–6, 170–2, 176, 178
  Fūka (*Weathering*) 161, *162*, 172
  Weathering (*Time*) 168, *169*
indexicality 2, 15, 50–1, 207, 216, 229, 232–3
individualism 195–6
information
  artwork constructed by 172
  compilation and analysis 65
  conceptual 9
  cultural, transmission of 196
  data and 9–10, 177, 178
  generation of 47
  mobilisation of 56
  presentation 65
  real-time processing of 148
  social space, productive of 9–10
  transmission 2
ingestion 248, 258
installation 120–1, 130, 183–7, 198, 243
Institute of Contemporary Art (ICA,
    London) 230
  Cybernetic Serendipity (1968) 24, 33
institutional critique 6, 36–8, 89, 140,
    170–3, 226, 230–3, 250

interconnectedness 82–3, 85, 87–9
internationalism 82–3, 87–9, 196, 249
interpretation 23, 30–1, 34
Ireland 99–104
irony 26–7, 30
Italy 224, 230–1, 232–3
Itoi Kanji (Dada Kan) 168, 174–6, *175*

Japan 158, 159–60, 255
Joselit, David 229
Joseph Ng, *Brother Cane* 255
Joyce, James 106–7, 109–10
Julian Pretto Gallery, New York 234
Jung, Carl 119
juxtaposition 34, 35, 141

Kádár, János 81, 82, 90
Kashihara Etsutomu, *What Is Mr X?* 166
Kelly, Mary
  Nightcleaners 64–5
  Post-Partum Document 66
  Women and Work (exhibition, 1973–75)
    9–10, 11, 56, 64–9, *66*, *67*
Kemp-Welch, Klara 84–5, 88
kinetic art 249
Kosuth, Joseph 6, 95n.48, 190, 197
Kotz, Liz 2
Kozloff, Max 193, 195
Krauss, Rosalind 114n.14, 139, 140, 193, 195
Kriesche, Richard 57–60, 68, 71n.20
Kuhn, Thomas S. 190, 195
Kurgan, Laura 205
Kuwazawa Yōko 160
Kwon, Miwon 140, 210

labour 57–60, 64–7, 68, 252
labyrinths 106–7, 246–7
Lambert, Françoise 234
Lamelas, David 31–5, 40
  Antwerp-Brussels (People + Time)
    234, *236*
  Office of Information 24, 35
  A Study of Relationship 31–5, *31*
land art 8, 80, 85–6, 88, 90, 139–40
  earthworks 143–6, 152–3, *152*
landscape 211–12
language 7, 9, 10, 26–7, 185, 206, 207–8

Latin America 125–7, 128
Lee, Pamela 7
Lee Ufan 163, 164
Lee Wen, *Journey of a Yellow Man* 243–4,
    253–8, *256*, *257*
Lefebvre, Henri 7–8, 10, 29, 210–11, 215,
    217, 248
Levinsohn, Tomy 121
LeWitt, Sol 45, 45–6, 48, 206, 227
    Wall Drawing series 227–8, 230–1
Licht, Jennifer 5–6, 17
Lippard, Lucy 19n.43, 20n.49, 87–8, 208, 233
literacy 27
Li Yuan-chia 254
location thinking 172, 178
logic 39, 40, 46–7
London 64–7, 182–3, 249, 251–3, 254
Low, Setha 17
Lynch, Kevin 205–6

Maeda Jōsaku 167, 176
Maeyema Tadashi 168
Magritte, René, *La trahison des images* 27
mail art 80, 158, 163, 166–70, 177–8
Malraux, André, *Le musée imaginaire* 164
map projections 125, 127, 128–9
maps 2, 10, 46–7, 124, 143
    absent 207
    alternative 64, 68
    astronomical 211–14
    blank/empty space in 29–30, 102–3
    conceptualism, affinity with 1–2
    coordinates 53, 107
    definitions of 2–3, 28, 89–90
    of divisions 243
    modified 77–8, 80, 107, 108, 128–30, 131–3
    subversive 79, 209–10
    of the unfamiliar 255, 258
    walking, created by 244, 246–7
    of women's labour 67, *67*
Marin, Louis 139, 140–1, 150, 152–3
Massey, Doreen 1, 11, 54, 57
Mastai, Judith 67
materiality 163, 164, 207–8, 229
Matsuzawa Yutaka *159*, 163, 168, 176
    My Own Death 176
    Non-Sensory Painting series 176
    Postcard Painting series 170, 176–7

Maurer, Dóra 88
McDonough, Thomas F. 10
McDowell, Linda 68
McLuhan, Marshall 8, 24, 150–1, 186, 188
McShine, Kynaston 9, 20n.49, 24
meaning 27, 185, 209–10, 226
Medalla, David 249, 250, 254
Meltzer, Eve 2, 9
Mercator projection 125, 128–9
Mercer, Kobena 255
Meyer, James 226
Michel, Boris 89
minimalism 27, 183, 186
Mitos vadios (festival, São Paulo, 1978) 244
Mix, Miguel Rojas 125–6
mobility
    of artists 82–3, 88, 134–5, 142, 187–8,
        224–6, 233–4
    of artworks 84–5, 88–9, 134–5,
        228–30, 233–4
    migration 31, 101, 109–10, 182, 198
    transportation 233
modernism 12, 23–4, 30, 33, 139, 182–3, 195
modernity 109–10, 187–8
Mono-ha (School of Things) 159, 163, 164
montage 77–8
moon 121–2, *122*, 205
More, Thomas 140–1
movement 53–4, 228–9, 242–4, 254–5
Musashino Art University, Tokyo 160
Museo Nacional Centro de Arte Reina
        Sofía, Madrid, *Heterotopías*
        (2000/2001) 133
Museu de Arte Moderna do Río de Janeiro
        (MAM Rio) 119, 120, 134
Museum of Fine Art, Buenos
        Aires 36–7
Museum of Modern Art (MoMA, NY)
    Information (1970) 9, 24, 177, 242
    *The Machine as Seen at the End of the
        Mechanical Age* (1969) 24
    Spaces (1969) 5–6
museums 146
    'invisible' 160, 166, 173
mythology 104, 106–7, 212, 248

Nakahara Yūsuke 158, 170–1
names/naming 99, 101, 104, 166, 168

NASA (National Space and Aeronautics
Agency) 205
nationalism 110, 124, 131
National Museum of Modern Art, Kyoto,
*Trends in Contemporary Japanese
Art* 163
neo-avant-garde 81, 83–4, 87, 88
N. E. Thing Company (NETCO, Iain and
Ingrid Baxter)
North American Time Zone 151
Telexed Triangle 151
networks 229–30, 234
neutrality 23, 38, 124, 176, 187
Newhouse, Kristina 234
New York 44, *45*, 47, 48–50, *48*, *49*, 242–3
Nixon, John 196
Nomura Hitoshi 163
Non-Art 163–4
Northern Ireland 102–5

objectivity 46–7, 161, 166
O'Connor, Francis 193, 195–6
O'Doherty, Brian (Patrick Ireland)
99–115, 146
Inside the White Cube 104–5
Ireland: A Modest Proposal 99, *100*,
102–5, 110–11, *112*
Patrick Ireland pseudonym, use of 99,
101, 104
Portrait of Marcel Duchamp 99
Studies on O.S. Maps 99, *101*, 105–9,
111, *112*
Oiticica, Hélio 242–9
delirium ambulatorium 242–3, 244, 245,
247–9, 253, 258
Newyorkaise 242–3
Ninhos 249
Parangolés 243, 244, 247
Penetrables 242, 246–7
Subterranea tropicália 242
Tropicália 243, 246–7, *246*, 249
The Whitechapel Experiment 249
Oliver, Valerie Cassel 258
On Kawara 172, 178
I Got Up postcards 170
I Went series 2
Location 2
Oppenheim, Dennis 8, 12, 139–57
Boundary Split 143
*Contour Lines Scribed in Swamp
Grass* 145–6
Gallery Transplants 146, *147*
Ground Mutations 149, *149*
Infected Zone 149–50
Landslide 152–3, *152*
Oakland Wedge 157n.59
*Reading Position for Second-Degree
Burn* 150
Removal Transplant 143–4
Site Markers 141–2
Time Line 142–3
Time Pocket 143, *144*
Transplants 140, 143, 146
Ordnance Survey 105
Osborne, Peter 33

Pàez i Blanch, Roger 30
paintings 88–9, 132, 183, 185–6, 188,
226–8, 229
participation 185, 207, 208, 209–10,
227–8, 244
Patrick Ireland *see* O'Doherty, Brian
Paula Cooper Gallery, New York 48–50
Peirce, C. S. 214
perception, minimisation of 183–5, 187
performance art 44–5, 158, 173–6,
250–3, 253–8
performativity 53–4, 178
photocopying 164–6, 168, 170, 173, 174
photography 53, 57, 165, 174, 209, 234, 251
Piper, Adrian 44–55
Area Relocation #2 48, 50, *51*
Catalysis 44, *45*, 53–4, 253
Hypothesis 50–3
Situation #6 52
Situations 50, 53
'Idea, form, context' 47–8
Mythic Being 44, 53–4
Utah–Manhattan Transfer 47, *48*, *49*
place
'black sites' 112
and bodies 121
consciousness of 64
dislocation 41, 230
displacement 6–7, 144, 186–7, 198
individual experience of 120–1

localisation 139
    manipulation of 166–8
    non-localisation 141–5, 150
    non-places 141–5, 150
    relocation 50
    spatio-temporal 42
    thinking and 172
    Utopia 140–1, 143
    see also sites
placelessness 226
planetariums 214–15
Poéticas visuais (exhibition, 1977) 134–5
poetry, concrete 206–10
politics 12, 23–4, 44, 109–12, 231–2
    authoritarian 31, 80–2, 92, 116–17
    democratic 248
    identity 249, 258, 259
    satire of 103, 105
    socialist 80, 81, 90, 126
Polygonal Workshop, *Garbage Walk* 56,
    57–60, 68
portability 224–6, 228–9, 233–4
portraits 65, 66
poststudio art 225, 231, 234
power
    colonial 104, 107–8, 110–11, 126–7
    inequalities 40, 54
    institutional 230–1
    maps and 128–9, 131
    of naming 25–31
    social 57, 68
    spatial 79–80, 110–12
    tactics vs. strategy and 150
    visualisations of 8–9
PRI *see* Psychophysiology Research
    Institute
printmaking 116–19, 121–3
process art 80
project art 80, 84
propaganda 38–9
Prospectiva (exhibition, 1974) 134–5
provincialism 196–7
psychogeographies 243, 247
Psychophysiology Research Institute (PRI)
    158–81, *171*
    artist's book *159*
    founding of 160–4
    Fuka (Weathering) 162

    goals 164–6
    Weathering (Time) 169
Pulsa (artist group) 5

Quine, Willard Van Orman 196–7

race 68–9, 126, 243–4, 250–3, 257–8
racism 69, 131, 250–1, 253, 254
Radical Presence (exhibition, 2012–15) 257–8
Ramsden, Mel 182–3, 185–6, 187, 188,
    193, 197
    'The artist as victim' (with Ian Burn) 193
    Locations 189
    Three black rectangles 183
    see also IBMR
reality 27–8, 110, 119, 121
regulations/rules 81–2, 83–4, 193, 224
Reich, Steve, *Pendulum Music* 47–8
Reinhardt, Ad 188, 228
relationality
    of artworks 228, 229, 232–3
    spatial 10, 29–35, 53–4, 225–6
    of viewers 25, 38, 41, 209
religion 102–3, 105–6, 130
representation 27–8, 30, 53, 211, 213, 217
reproduction 158, 164–6, 168, 170, 173, 174
Rinke, Klaus, *Ladling Water from the Rhine*
    172, 178
Roberts, J. M. 69
Romero, Juan Carlos 35–40
    4,000,000 m² 24, 36–9, *36*, 41
    Segmento de linea recta 39
    Violencia (exhibition) 39
rope drawings 105–9

Sadler, Simon 10
Samangallery, Genoa 224, 225, 230–1
Sanchez, Michael 233–4
Sansai (*Tricolour*, magazine) 170–2
São Paulo Biennale 132, 134
Sarathy, Jennifer 9–10
satire 33–4, 103, 105
scales 128, 132, 143, 145
Schmuck (journal) 88
Schneemann, Carolee 89
Scott, Emily Eliza 210–11
screenprints 121–4
Sekine Nobuo 163, 164

self, mapping of 247, 249, 253, 258
self-referentiality 27, 30, 39, 65–6
Sharp, Joanne P. 68
Shimamura Kiyoharu *159*, 160, 161, 167
Shinohara Ushio 174
Shiomi Mieko, *Spatial Poems* 3, *4*, *5*
Shiraga Kazuo 174
Siegelaub, Seth 6–7, 56, 228–9
Sigi Krauss Gallery, London, *The 7th Day
    Chicken* (1971) 59–60
Signals Art Gallery, London 249, 250
Singapore 254–5
sites
    as absence 139, 140, 142–3, 146, 148
    artistic, claimed as 141–2
    connection to 141
    functional 226
    multiple 226
    nonsites 208
    physical properties of 227–8
    see also place
site-specific art 5–6, 56, 59, 139–40,
    225–6, 230–1
Situationist International (SI) 1, 10
Smith, Roberta 1
Smith, Terry 12, 197
Smithson, Robert 12, 208, 214
    Asphalt Rundown 47–8
    Nonsites 139, 146, 148
    Spiral Jetty 216
    'A tour of the monuments of Passaic,
        New Jersey' 143
Soja, Edward 7
songs 127–8
Sonnabend, Ileana 190
sound 183–7, 198
South London Gallery, *Women and Work*
    (1973–75) 64–9, *66*, *67*
space 1
    and bodies 50–1, 121, 246, 247, 253
    celestial 122–3, 205, 215
    class and 60–1, 68
    definitions of 2–11, 17
    empty 29–31
    experiential 8, 38–9, 120–1
    extraterrestrial 32, 205
    gallery 23, 104–5, 146, 230–3
    global/local 84

    heterotopic 111–12
    inside/outside 32, 124, 131
    logical systems of 46–7
    metropolitan/provincial 196–7, 198, 242
    modification of 80
    networked 234, 237
    perception of 5–6
    performative 53–4
    physical 10
    power and 110–12
    private/domestic 67, 68
    production of 38
        descriptive 48–50
        social 7–8, 10, 17, 210–11
        by viewers 184–5
    public 56–7, 68–9
    relationality and 10, 29–35, 53–4, 225–6
    representations of 211
    rural 209
    sacred 119–20
    social 10, 24–5, 34, 38–9, 53–4, 68
    terrestrial 215
    urban 8, 10, 108–9, 112, 242, 244–7, 248–9
    Utopia 141
space exploration 6, 8, 32, 34, 122–3,
    177–8, 205
space-time 8, 53, 172–3
spatiality 1, 3–5, 5–11, 8, 77–9, 178, 211
stars 211–14
stasis 54, 92, 216
Stedelijk Museum, Amsterdam, *Op Losse
    Schroeven* (1969) 146
Stella, Frank 195
St Martin's College, London 31
structuralism 2, 9, 10
Studio International (journal) 230–1
subjectivity 34, 53–4, 161, 258
Sutherland, Zöe 83
Swenson, Kirsten 210–11
Swift, Jonathan 103, 107
symbolism 119–21
systems 9, 11, 24–5, 41, 148
    cartographic 46–7, 53, 185, 209–10, 216
    colour codes 227–8, 229–30
    finite 45–6
    of representation 211, 213, 217
Szeemann, Harald 82
    Live in Your Head 87

Takamatsu Jirō 165–6
Takeda Kiyoshi 160, 161, 167, 176
Tama Art University, Tokyo 160, 163
task-based art 174
Tate 28
tautologies 27, 28, 30, 40, 145
technologies 24, 110–11, 148, 183–7
    see also communication technologies
Teo, Wenny 258
textiles 83, 130
texts 120, 185, 189, 190, 242–3, 244
time 7–8, 143, 215, 216–17
    space-time 8, 53, 172–3
    zones 143, 151
time-lapse film 216–17
Tokyo Biennale, 1970 163, 176, 177–8
Tokyo Zokei University i 161, 167
Tōno Yoshiaki 168
Toselli Gallery, Milan 224
transplantation 118–19, 140, 143, 146
Trinity College Dublin (TCD) 105–6, 107,
    108, 110–11, 112

Ugwu, Catherine 258
Ukeles, Mierle Laderman 70n.11
Unconcealed (exhibition, 2009) 88
understanding, lack of 186–7
unfamiliarity 109–10, 255, 258
Union of Soviet Socialist Republics
    (USSR) 81–2
United Kingdom 102, 105–6, 182–3
University of São Paulo Museum of
    Contemporary Art (MAC USP)
    134, 135
Utah 210–15
utopianism 140–1, 143, 150–3

velocity 228–9
Venice Biennale, 1968 35
Vert, Xavier 143
viewers
    artwork completed by 207, 208, 209–10
    connection with 33, 34
    participation 59–60, 184–5, 195,
        227–8, 247
    reflections of 188

relationality of 25, 38, 41, 209
responses of 40, 46–7
transformation of 247
understanding of 26–8
viewing 23, 211–12, 214
    gaze 30, 87, 108, 205, 208, 214–15
Village Voice (newspaper) 50, *51*
violence
    colonial 110–11
    military 99, 103, 108
    political 37, 39
    state 116–17, 119
visibility 160, 166, 173, 253–8

walks/walking 59, 209, 242–63
    'ambulatory delirium' 242, 244,
        258–9
    (de)mystification and 244, 248
    everyday 250–3
    hyper-visible 253–8
    as mapping 244, 258–9
Weiner, Lawrence 6, 198
Whelan, Yvonne 108
Whitechapel Gallery, London
    242–9
Willats, Stephen 69
    Control (magazine) 64, 71n.21
    London Re-Modelling Book 61–2
    West London Social Resource Project 56,
        60–4, *62*, *63*, 68
    West London Wasteland 64
William, Emmett 206
Wilson, Ian 207
Wittgenstein, Ludwig 23, 95n.48, 185,
    186, 196
Wollen, Peter 1–2, 10, 17
Wood, Denis 1
Wood, William 190

xerography *see* photocopying

Yap, June 254
Yoshimoto, Midori 3

Zero Dimension (art group) 174
Zuglói Kör (Zugló Circle) 82

EU authorised representative for GPSR:
Easy Access System Europe, Mustamäe tee 50,
10621 Tallinn, Estonia
gpsr.requests@easproject.com

www.ingramcontent.com/pod-product-compliance
Ingram Content Group UK Ltd.
Pitfield, Milton Keynes, MK11 3LW, UK
UKHW021826150726
7214IPUK00017B/342